Contents at a Glance

Marketing

FOR DUMMIES®

A Wiley Brand

4th Edition

by Alexander Hiam

FOR DUMMIES®
A Wiley Brand

Dummies®, 4th Edition

John Wiley & Sons, Inc., 111 River St., Hoboken, NJ 07030-5774, www.wiley.com

2014 by John Wiley & Sons, Inc., Hoboken, New Jersey

Simultaneously in Canada

For general information on our other products and services, please contact our Customer Care Department within the U.S. at 877-762-2974, outside the U.S. at 317-572-3993, or fax 317-572-4002. For technical support, please visit www.wiley.com/techsupport.

Wiley publishes in a variety of print and electronic formats and by print-on-demand. Some material included with standard print versions of this book may not be included in e-books or in print-on-demand. If this book refers to media such as a CD or DVD that is not included in the version you purchased, you may download this material at http://booksupport.wiley.com. For more information about Wiley products, visit www.wiley.com.

Library of Congress Control Number: 2013957976

ISBN 978-1-118-88080-7 (pbk); ISBN 978-1-118-88090-6 (ebk); ISBN 978-1-118-88065-4 (ebk)

Manufactured in the United States of America

10 9 8 7 6 5 4 3 2 1

Table of Contents

Introduction

Marketing is part science, part art, and it can be challenging to bottle up both parts into a winning campaign. Your business (or nonprofit or service agency) needs to communicate what it does clearly and well; present a positive, compelling brand identity; focus its resources where they'll do the most good; grow its market share by attracting and retaining good customers or clients; and migrate to new media, techniques, and technologies as soon as your customers are ready to move along with you.

Since I researched and wrote the first edition of *Marketing For Dummies,* the field of marketing has fragmented into ever more narrow specialties. Now you can find entire books on how to market on Pinterest or Facebook. The poor marketer gets the impression that he must be incredibly clever, technically skilled, and able to whip up web page designs in the morning, code crafty meta tags over coffee break, attract a frenzy of social media followers before lunch, and then present the marketing plan complete with budget and sales projections to the board of directors in the afternoon.

Marketing is best approached as a more hands-off endeavor, in which the marketing manager or planner thoughtfully selects services and people to implement a sound plan. I challenge you to do a little reading and a little thinking before you allow yourself to get caught up in some complex and wearying new technical challenge.

Every business needs *marketing imagination* — creative thinking from a marketing perspective, such as reviewing strategic options and considering new product ideas, new distribution channels, new pricing or packaging, or interesting ways to communicate the benefits. It's like the trip planner or navigator who considers the road ahead and chooses the best way to go based on the terrain and conditions. You wouldn't head off on a trip without an itinerary and a GPS or map at the very least. Don't leave home without reading up on marketing plans and programs, at least enough to be able to engage your marketing imagination.

This book will help if you really have to roll up your sleeves and do some fundamentals yourself, but it will also help you think more big-picture by identifying smart ways for getting the job done rather than stretching yourself ever more thinly over ever more varied technical details.

About This Book

I wrote this book with a variety of marketers in mind, including small business owners and entrepreneurs who wear the marketing and sales hats and several other hats. I also wrote for managers and staffers of larger organizations who work on plans, programs, product launches, ad campaigns, printed materials, websites, and other elements but who lack a macro-level reference to help them think about and integrate all the varied elements of good marketing. And I didn't forget about political campaign managers, public health educators, directors and board members, museums, nonprofits, and the army of independent consultants, who must not only be experts in their own field but also promote their personal brands to guarantee a steady flow of clients.

Ultimately, *every* marketer can benefit from trying to smarten his approach, embracing new strategies and media, and seeking ways to increase impact while reducing costs. Those are my goals as an author, too.

Before diving into the pages that follow, I want you to be aware of a few specific terms I use throughout this book:

- **Marketing program:** This phrase refers to any organized, coordinated use of sales, advertising, publicity, customer service, the web, direct mail, or any other efforts to contact and influence customers. Creating a marketing program means avoiding random or disconnected activities. It also means thinking about how everything interlinks and contributes to achieving your marketing goals.

- **Customer:** The customer is whoever buys what you sell — whether a person, a household, a business, a government agency, a school, or even a voter — the rules of sound marketing always apply.

- **Product:** This is whatever you sell or offer to customers. Your product can be animate or inanimate, tangible or intangible. Even if you offer a service or a person (such as a political candidate or a celebrity), that's considered a product in marketing jargon.

- **Sales:** I treat person-to-person sales as one of the many possible activities under the marketing umbrella. You need to integrate selling into the broader range of activities designed to bring about sales and satisfy customers. I address ways of managing sales better in my overall efforts to make each of your marketing activities more effective.

Foolish Assumptions

I assume that you're intelligent, which is great because you need to be clever, caring, and persistent to do marketing well. But I don't assume that you have all the technical knowledge you need to do great marketing, so I explain each technique as clearly as I can. I also assume that you're willing to try new ideas to improve sales and grow your organization. After all, marketing requires an open mind and a willingness to experiment.

I assume that you don't mind calling or e-mailing people to ask whether they can help. Marketers often employ outside services, and it's important to build a long list of service providers and get good at selecting, managing, and, if need be, replacing them. To this end, I contribute hundreds of names and websites that may be helpful leads for you.

Of course, I also assume that you're willing and able to switch from being imaginative and creative one moment to being analytical and rigorous the next, because being successful at marketing requires both approaches. Sometimes, I ask you to run the numbers and do sales projections. Other times, I ask you to dream up a clever way to catch a reader's eye and communicate a benefit to that person. These demands pull you in opposite directions. If you can assemble a team of varied people, some of them numbers-oriented and some artistic, you can cover all the marketing bases more easily. But if you have a small business, you may be all you have, so you need to wear each hat in turn. (At least you never get bored tackling marketing's varied challenges!)

I certainly do *not* assume that you have an unlimited budget. Most marketers are eager to find low-cost marketing methods, so I emphasize economical approaches throughout this book.

In fact, I believe that the best marketing is, paradoxically, no marketing. It's not likely that you'll achieve that romanticized goal, but imagine for a moment that your brand is so well respected, your product or service so excellent, and your customers so loyal that all your business comes from repeat sales and word of mouth, and the media, social media, and blog reviewers give you all the public exposure you need, without ever having to buy a single ad. Pretty good, huh? Although you may never drive your budget to zero, you may be able to improve results while reducing costs. More impact, more focus, and more loyalty all add up to better results at lower cost. Think about it: A world with 100 percent efficient marketing is a world virtually without advertising. Ahh. The sound of silence . . .

Icons Used in This Book

Look for these symbols to help you find valuable info throughout the text:

All marketing is real-world marketing, but this icon means you can find an actual example of something that worked (or didn't work) in the real world for another marketer.

When I want to get you up to speed on essential or critical information you need to know to succeed, I mark it with this icon.

This icon flags specific advice you can try out in your marketing program right away. And because sometimes you need the right perspective on a problem to reach success, this icon also points out suggestions on how to handle the task at hand in an easy manner.

You can easily run into trouble in marketing because so many mines are just waiting for you to step on them. I've marked them all with this symbol.

Beyond the Book

In addition to the great content in the book or e-book you're reading right now, you can find more marketing tips and suggestions at `www.dummies.com/cheatsheet/marketing`. And be sure to check out the articles (well, really more like blogs) at `www.dummies.com/extras/marketing`. These, plus the numerous narrow-topic books on marketing in the *For Dummies* line, give you lots of additional options for researching your marketing program.

Where to Go from Here

If you read only one chapter in one business book this year, make it Chapter 1 of this book. I made this chapter stand alone as a powerful way to audit your marketing and upgrade or enhance the things you do to make profitable sales. I packed the rest of the book with good tips and techniques, and it all deserves attention. But whatever else you do or don't get around to, read the first chapter with a pen and action list at hand!

Perhaps you have a pressing need in one of the more specific areas covered in this book. If fixing your website is the top item on your to-do list, go to Chapter 10 first. If you need to increase the effectiveness of your sales force, try Chapter 17. Working on a letter to customers? Then Chapters 6 and 13 on marketing communications and direct mail can really help you out. Whatever you're doing, I have a hunch that this book has a chapter or two to assist you. So don't let me slow you down. Get going! It's never too early (or too late) to do a little marketing.

Part I
Getting Started with Marketing

In this part . . .

- ✔ Discover how to coordinate your sales and marketing activities in an effective marketing program that optimizes your spending and allows you to track results across numerous media formats, including traditional advertising, the web, and hand-held devices.

- ✔ Position your brand, products, services, or self to maximize impact and differentiate from the competition. Select the marketing strategy that fits your scale and current position to generate realistic growth.

- ✔ Create a simple yet sufficiently detailed marketing plan to help you track progress, note areas of success, and eliminate unprofitable activities.

- ✔ Make constructive changes by shifting your effort and spending away from low-growth or shrinking market segments and seeking waves of growth to ride to higher levels of sales.

- ✔ Create clear, simple statements of your strategies and tactics to share with your marketing team, from graphic designers and media buyers to sales representatives, distributors, or other marketing partners.

Chapter 1

Optimizing Your Marketing Program

······································

In This Chapter

▶ Succeeding by understanding your customers — and yourself

▶ Formulating a winning marketing strategy

▶ Leveraging your marketing program with focus and control

▶ Figuring out what to realistically expect from your program

▶ Maximizing the appeal of your product, service, or business

······································

*M*arketing is all the activities that contribute to building ongoing, profitable relationships with customers to grow your business. The traditional goal of marketing is to bring about healthy sales through advertising, brand development, and other activities. A more long-term goal is to become increasingly useful or valuable to a growing number of customers so as to ensure your future success. Watch both short-term sales and long-term development of value to make your organization a growing success.

Your *marketing program* is the right mix of products or services, pricing, promotions, branding, sales, and distribution that will produce immediate sales and also help you grow over time. You'll know when you've found the right mix for you and your organization because it will produce profitable sales and enough demand to allow you to grow at a comfortable rate.

This chapter serves as a jumping-off point into the world of marketing. By reading it, you can begin to design a marketing program that works for you. The rest of this book can help you refine the program that meets your needs.

Know Yourself, Know Your Customer

To make your marketing program more profitable and growth oriented, think about how to reach and persuade more of the right customers. When you understand how your customers think and what they like, you may find better ways to make more sales. The next sections help you get better acquainted with what you have to offer and start communicating those offerings to your customers.

Asking the right question

Traditional marketers ask just one key question:

> What do we need to tell customers to make the sale?

Then they flood the environments (both virtual and actual) with competing claims, trying to outdo each other in their efforts to prove that they have what customers want. This barrage of noisy advertising and one-up salesmanship is inefficient, wasteful, and, to many, an unfortunate source of social pollution.

A better initial question to ask is this:

> What do I/we have uniquely to offer?

When you start right off by examining yourself in the mirror and identifying your genuine, honest-to-yourself strength(s), you're many laps ahead of most marketers, whether you're selling something as simple as your résumé, as complex as a new high-tech product, or anything in between. Your unique strengths form the core of your offering, and you should keep building your strengths in ways that are true to your identity.

Whether you're marketing yourself (perhaps you're a consultant or someone else who offers individualized services) or a business entity of some kind, you can't make consistent and efficient headway by deceiving yourself and trying to deceive others. The more true to your core the marketing message is, the more effective it is. If you can't find any unique qualities to advertise, postpone those media purchases and work on self-improvement or product development. (Perhaps you simply need to listen harder to what your customers say and make sure they're so happy that they recruit new customers!) Then come back to your program with a stronger set of claims that any customer can clearly see are of benefit — that is, unique benefit, not just a run-of-the-mill, everybody-does-it-that-way benefit.

If you draw a large enough circle around your market, you'll probably encompass competitors who are better than you. There are so many people out there, working hard and innovating, just like you! So as you work to improve your offerings and become ever more unique and special, draw that circle appropriately. It's the equivalent of your bar, so don't set it too high. Perhaps you should try to be the best distributor of alternative, organic, and local foods in just one city. After you have that city sewed up, expand to the next closest market. Don't, however, try to advertise and distribute across a ten-state area right out of the starting blocks. Knowing yourself means knowing your limitations as well as your strengths.

Marketing programs communicate *benefits*. Benefits are the qualities that your customers value. For example, your product may offer benefits such as convenience, ease of use, brand appeal, attractive design, local sourcing, healthiness, or a lower price than the competition. A service business, or an individual who provides services like consulting, may list benefits such as expertise, friendliness, and availability. The right mix of benefits can make your product or service particularly appealing to the group of customers who value those benefits. Make your list now: What are your core benefits, things that you can honestly say you're good at and that customers may value?

Even if you're better from a logical or rational perspective, customers may still choose the competition. Say your new cola scores better in blind taste tests or is made of organic ingredients. So what? Who wants to buy an unknown cola rather than the brand they know and love? No, this trust issue isn't rational, but it still affects the purchase — which is why you absolutely must take a look at the emotional reasons people may or may not buy from you. Is your brand appealing? Do you use an attractive design for your packaging? Is your presentation professional and trustworthy? Do people know you or your business and look upon you favorably? Positive image isn't hard to build for free when you market locally or regionally; you just need to show up consistently in ways that demonstrate your concern for the community.

Image isn't everything in marketing, but it *is* just about everything when it comes to the emotional impact you make. So pay close attention to your image when you're looking for ways to boost sales. To truly know your customers, you also need to explore the answers to these two questions:

- ✔ **What do customers think about my product?** Do they understand it? Do they think its features and benefits are superior to the competition and can meet their needs? Do they feel that my product is a good value given its benefits and costs? Is it easy for them to buy the product when and where they need it?

- ✔ **How do customers feel about my product?** Does it make them feel good? Do they like its personality? Do they like how it makes them feel about themselves? Do they trust me?

To answer these questions, find something to write on and draw a big *T* to create two columns. Label the left column "What Customers Know About," and put the name of your brand, company, or product in the blank. Label the right column "How Customers Feel About," and fill in as much as you can from your own knowledge before asking others to give you more ideas. Keep working on this table until you're sure you have an exhaustive list of both the logical thoughts and facts and the emotional feelings and impressions that customers have.

If you have access to a friendly group of customers or prospective customers, tell them you're holding an informal focus group with complimentary drinks and snacks (doing so helps with your recruiting) and ask them to help you understand your marketing needs by reviewing and commenting on your table. The goal is to see whether your lists of what customers know and feel about your product agree with theirs. Do they concur with how you described their emotional viewpoint and/or their factual knowledge base? (Chapter 4 gives more information about researching customer attitudes.)

Filling the awareness gap

Are prospective customers even aware that you exist? If not, then you need to bump up your marketing communications and get in front of them somehow to reduce or eliminate the *awareness gap,* which is the percentage of people in your target market who are unaware of your offerings and their benefits. (How? That's what the rest of this book is about, so keep reading!) If only one in ten prospective customers knows about your brand, then you have a 90 percent awareness gap and need to get the word out to a lot more people.

If you need to communicate with customers more effectively and often, you have some options for bumping up the impact of your marketing communications and reducing the awareness gap:

- ✔ **You can put in more time.** For example, if customers lack knowledge about your product, more sales calls can help fill this awareness gap.

- ✔ **You can spend more money.** More advertisements help fill your awareness gap, but of course, they cost money.

- ✔ **You can communicate better.** A strong, focused marketing program with clear, consistent, and frequent communications helps fill the awareness gap with information and a positive brand image, which then allows interest and purchase levels to rise significantly. See Figure 1-1 for a graphic that illustrates the awareness gap, and consider creating your own graph in the same format to see how big your awareness gap is. (Communicating better is my favorite approach, because it substitutes to some degree for time and money.)

- ✔ **You can become more popular.** Sometimes you can create a buzz of talk about your product. If people think it's really cool or exciting, they may do some of the communicating for you, spreading the news by word of mouth and via social media (this is sometimes referred to as viral marketing). If your customers are active on any social media, then you need to be, too.

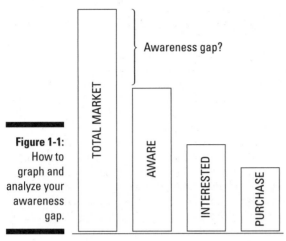

Figure 1-1:
How to graph and analyze your awareness gap.

Focusing on your target customer

Your *target customer* is the person for whom you design your product and marketing program. If you don't already have a clear profile of your target customer, make one now; otherwise, your marketing program will be adrift in a sea of less-than-effective options.

To craft your target customer profile, assemble any and all facts about your target customer on a large piece of poster paper: age, employer, education level, income, family status, hobbies, politics (if relevant), favorite brand of automobile, or anything else that helps you focus on this person. Also list your target customer's motivations: what he or she cares about in life and how you can help him or her achieve those goals. Finally, cut and paste one to three pictures out of magazine ads to represent the face or faces of your target customer. This is the audience you have to focus your marketing program on. Everything from product design or selection to the content, timing, and placement of ads must specifically target these people.

You can further increase your focus on your target customer by deciding whether he or she prefers marketing that takes a rational, information-based approach; an emotional, personality-based approach; or a balanced mix of the two. By simply being clear about whom to target and whether to market to them in an informational or emotional manner, you ensure that your marketing program has a clear focus.

Identifying and playing up your strengths

One of the best steps you can take as a marketer is to find your chief strengths and build on them so you can add an additional degree of focus and momentum to your marketing program. The key is to always think about what you do well for the customer (don't get hung up on shortcomings) and make sure you build on your strengths in everything you do.

For example, imagine that customers say your pricing isn't as good as larger competitors, and you also feel that your brand name isn't very well known. That's the bad news, but the good news is that existing customers are loyal because they like your product and service. The thing to do here is build on this strength by creating a loyalty program for customers, asking for and rewarding referrals, and including testimonials in your marketing materials and on your website. Also, remind customers and prospects that you are the local alternative. "Shop Locally to Support Your Community" may be a good phrase to sneak into every marketing communication, whether on paper, signs, your vehicles, or the web. Building on your strength in this manner can help you overcome the weaknesses of your higher pricing and lesser name recognition.

Focus on your strengths by clearly and succinctly defining what your special strength or advantage is. Grab a piece of paper and a pen and start your sentence like this: "My product (or service) is special because. . . ." Take a minute to think about what makes your firm or product special and why customers have been attracted to you in the past. Then make sure you talk about your strengths or show them visually whenever you communicate with customers. (Some marketers call the resulting statement of what makes you special a *unique selling proposition,* or USP. As its name implies, it ought to be unique to your product, to help differentiate it from your competitors.)

Discovering the best way to find customers

Another aspect of your customer focus is deciding whether you want to emphasize attracting new customers or retaining and growing existing customers. One or the other may need to dominate your marketing program, or perhaps you need to balance the two. Marketing to new prospects is usually a different sort of challenge from working with existing customers, so knowing which goal is most important helps you improve the focus of your marketing.

I periodically survey managers of successful businesses to ask them about their marketing practices. The first and most revealing question I ask is, "What's your best way to attract customers?" Here are some of the most common answers — things that marketers often say are most effective at bringing them customers:

✔ **Referrals:** Your customers may be willing to help you sell your product (see coverage of word of mouth in Chapter 11 for how to stimulate referrals).

✔ **Social media:** Your presence as a provider of helpful or interesting content can't be underestimated in its potential impact on brand development and as a source of customer leads, so try to get ever more comfortable with blogging, Twitter, Facebook, and similar options (see Chapters 10, 11, and 13).

✔ **Trade shows and professional association meetings:** Making contacts and being visible in the right professional venue may be a powerful way to build your business (see Chapter 12).

✔ **Sales calls:** Salespeople sell products, so make more calls yourself, or find a way to put commissioned salespeople or sales representatives to work for you (see Chapter 17).

✔ **Advertising:** Advertising sells the product, but only if you do it consistently and frequently, whether in print, on radio and TV, outdoors, or on the web (see Chapters 7, 8, 9, and 10).

✔ **Product demonstrations, trial coupons, or distribution of free samples:** If your product is impressive, let it sell itself (see Chapters 14 and 15).

✔ **Placement and appearance of buildings/stores:** Location is still one of the simplest and best formulas for marketing success (see Chapter 10 to position yourself for high web traffic and Chapter 16 for prominent placement in the real world).

As the preceding list indicates, every business has a different optimal formula for attracting customers. However, in every case, successful businesses report that one or two methods work best. Their programs are therefore dominated by one or two effective ways of attracting customers. They put between one-third and two-thirds of their marketing resources into their primary way of attracting customers and then use other marketing methods to support their most effective method.

To find your business's most effective way of reaching out to customers, you need to ask yourself this important question: What's my best way to attract customers, and how can I focus my marketing program to take fuller advantage of it? You can't look the answer up in a book, but you can take heart from the fact that, with persistence, you'll eventually work out what your winning formula is, and then you may have to make only minor changes from year to year to keep your program working well.

Embracing sustainability

Sustainable marketing is the thoughtful selection or modification of methods, materials, and technologies to make your marketing, and your organization in general, more sustainable environmentally as well as economically. You may not have heard the term, but it's a good bet that you will in the future, because sustainability is looming as the greatest long-term challenge ahead for society and business in general. Innovators who seek to make marketing more local, more low-impact, more natural, and less wasteful (of time and tangible resources) will be seen as leaders in their field in the future — a fact that makes sustainable marketing an interesting frontier to think about as you design your next marketing program.

When you answer this question, you're taking yet another important step toward a highly focused marketing program that leverages your resources as much as possible. Your marketing program can probably be divided into four tiers of activities:

- ✔ Major impact
- ✔ Helpful; secondary impact
- ✔ Minor impact
- ✔ Money loser; very low impact

If you reorganize last year's budget into these categories, you may find that your spending isn't concentrated near the top of your list. If that's the case, then you can try to move up your focus and spending. Cut the bottom tier, where your marketing effort and spending isn't paying off. Reduce the next level of spending and shift your spending to one or two activities with the biggest impact.

I call this the *marketing pyramid,* and in workshops, I challenge marketers to try to move their spending up the pyramid so their marketing resources are concentrated near the top (which reflects the most effective activities). Ideally, the pyramid gets turned upside down, with most of the spending on the top floor rather than the bottom. What does your marketing pyramid look like? Can you move up it by shifting resources and investments to higher-impact marketing activities? Ideally, your marketing pyramid should have clear distinctions between the primary, secondary, and tertiary activities so you know where to concentrate your resources for best effect.

If you haven't done much marketing yet, go forth and ask nosey questions. Find marketers who sell something at least remotely similar to what you plan to sell, and ask them what activities bring them customers. First, draw out a list of at least six different things they do to find or close customers. Then ask them which are the most and least effective. Combine all this data into a speculative marketing pyramid, and begin to get quotes on and experiment with the methods yourself. Hopefully, the benchmark information you gathered will get you closer to an effective program the first time around, but plan on testing and refining your methods. Each marketer's winning formula is unique. There is no one sure-fire marketing plan that everybody can use.

Finding Your Marketing Formula

A marketing program should be based on a *marketing strategy,* which is the big-picture idea driving your success (if you don't have one yet, check out Chapter 2). The marketing program is all the coordinated activities that together make up the tactics to implement that strategy. To make both strategy and program clear, write them up in a *marketing plan* (see Chapter 3).

For example, a general contractor (builder) may choose the strategy of renovating and building residential homes close to downtown areas in appealing smaller cities and larger suburbs in their region to take advantage of a trend where professional couples are moving out of the suburbs and back to revitalized downtowns. Stating this strategy clearly is a great way to bring focus to the marketing program. You now know what kinds of projects to talk about in blogs and to local media and acquaintances and to show in your website portfolio. And you know who your customers are and will soon be brainstorming ways to find more of them (for example, by networking to local realtors who help relocate them).

You don't have to get fully into the technicalities of strategies and plans right now, because in this chapter, I go over a lot of simpler, quicker actions you can take to leverage your marketing activities into a winning program. The following sections require you to think about and write down some ideas, so get out your pencil and paper or tablet to jot down notes while you're reading.

Analyzing your Five Ps

What really matters in marketing are the points of contact between the customer and your communications, products, and people. These customer interactions (or *influence points*) with you constitute your marketing program. I always take care to list these influence points when designing a marketing program. To make a list of your own influence points, use the following Five *P*s of marketing for your categories.

Product

Determine which aspects of the *product* itself are important and have an influence on customer perception and purchase intentions. List all tangible features plus intangibles, such as personality, look and feel, and packaging — these are the aspects (both rational features and emotional impressions) of your product that influence customer perception.

First impressions are important for initial purchase, but performance of the product over time is more important for repurchase and referrals.

Price

List the aspects of *price* that influence customer perception. What does it cost the customer to get and use your product? The list price is often an important element of the customer's perception of price, but it isn't the only one. Discounts and special offers belong on your list of price-based influence points, too. And don't forget any extra costs the customer may have to incur, like the cost of switching from another product to yours; extra costs can really affect a customer's perception of how attractive your product is. (If you can find ways to make switching from the competitor's product to yours easier or cheaper, you may be able to charge more for your product and still make more sales.)

Placement

List the aspects of *placement* or distribution (in both time and space) that influence the accessibility of your product. When and where is your product available to customers? Place is a big influence, because most of the time, customers aren't actively shopping for your product. Nobody runs around all day every day looking for what you want to sell her. When someone wants something, she's most strongly influenced by what's available to her. Getting the place and timing right is a big part of success in marketing and often very difficult (see Chapter 16 for help with placement).

The web allows you to define your market narrowly and locally, or globally, or (and this is the really exciting idea that many businesses haven't yet picked up on) in local markets other than your physical one. For example, if you have a bookstore specializing in children's and young adult titles, then you would do best to be present in the local areas where there are the most children and young adult readers (see Chapter 4 for how to sleuth out demographic growth waves). The web can narrowly target the top five cities for your product. (See Part IV for lots of low-cost ways to find the best customers in the best markets.)

Promotion

List all the ways you have to *promote* your offering by communicating with customers and prospects. Do you have a website? Do you routinely update your blog, Facebook page, and Pinterest boards? Do you advertise? Send mailings? Hand out brochures? What about the visibility of signs on buildings or vehicles? Do distributors or other marketing partners also communicate with your customer? If so, include their promotional materials and methods in your marketing program, because they help shape the customer's perception, too. And what about other routine elements of customer communication, like bills? They're yet another part of the impression your marketing communications make.

The web hasn't finished revolutionizing promotion, and you can innovate to get messages out creatively and inexpensively in a lot of ways (see Chapter 10 for details).

People

The fifth *P* is perhaps the most important one, because without *people,* you can't have a marketing program. List all the points of human contact that may be important to the success of your program. If you run a small business, this list may just be a handful of people, but even so, include this list in your planning and think about ways each person can help make a positive impression and encourage a sale.

The web has also revolutionized the process of making connections with people. Your professional and business Facebook pages, your blogs (which should be pulled into your Facebook page and your website), your tweets, your Pinterest boards, and so forth are all opportunities to build followers and friendships.

Refining your list of possibilities

You need to find efficient, effective ways to positively influence customer perception. You want to use elements of your marketing program to motivate customers to buy and use your product (service, firm, whatever). The list of your current influence points for each of your Five *P*s (see the previous related sections) is just a starting point on your journey to an optimal marketing program.

Now ask yourself the following questions: What can be subtracted because it isn't working effectively? What can be emphasized or added? Think about each of the Five *P*s and try to add more possible influence points. Look to competitors or successful marketers from outside your product category and industry for some fresh ideas. The longer your list of possibilities, the more likely you are to find really good things to include in your marketing program. But in the end, don't forget to focus on the handful of influence points that give you the biggest effect.

To craft your own winning formula, think of one or more new ways to reach and influence your customers and prospects in each of the Five *P*s and add them to your list as possibilities for your next marketing program.

Avoiding the pricing trap

Don't be tempted to make price the main focus of your marketing program. Many marketers emphasize discounts and low prices to attract customers. But price is a dangerous emphasis for any marketing program because you're buying customers rather than winning them. That's a very, very hard way to make a profit. So unless you actually have a sustainable cost advantage (a rare thing in business), don't allow low prices or coupons and discounts to dominate your marketing program. Price reasonably, use discounts and price-off coupons sparingly, and look for other tactics to focus on in your marketing program.

Controlling Your Marketing Program

Little details can and do make all the difference in closing a sale! Does your marketing program display inconsistencies and miss opportunities to get the message across fully and well? If so, you can increase your program's effectiveness by eliminating these pockets of inconsistency to prevent out-of-control marketing.

Consider the numerous eBay sellers who fail to take and post high-quality photographs of the products they're trying to sell and then wonder why they get few bidders and have to sell for low prices. These sellers can easily upgrade their photography, but they fail to recognize the problem, so they allow this critical part of their marketing mix to remain poorly managed.

Given the reality that some of your influence points may be partially or fully uncontrolled right now, draw up a list of inconsistent and/or uncontrolled elements of your marketing program. I think you'll find some inconsistencies in each of the Five *P*s of your program (don't worry, though, that's common!). If you can make even one of your marketing elements work better and more consistently with your overall program and its focus, you're improving the effectiveness of your marketing. Answer the questions in Table 1-1 to pinpoint elements of your marketing mix that you need to pay more attention to.

Table 1-1	Getting a Grip on Your Marketing Program	
Customer Focus		
Define your customers clearly: Who are they? Where and when do they want to buy?		
Are they new customers, existing customers, or a balanced mix of both?		
Understand what emotional elements make customers buy: What personality should your brand have? How should customers feel about your product?		
Understand what functional elements make customers buy: What features do they want and need? What information do they need to see to make their decision?		
Product Attraction		
What attracts customers to your product?		
What's your special brilliance that sets you apart in the marketplace?		
Do you reflect your brilliance throughout all your marketing efforts?		
Most Effective Methods		
What's the most effective thing you can do to attract customers?		
What's the most effective thing you can do to retain customers?		
Which of the Five *P*s (product, price, placement, promotion, and people) is most important in attracting and retaining customers?		
Controlling Points of Contact		
What are all the ways you can reach and influence customers?		
Are you using the best of these right now?		
Do you need to increase the focus and consistency of some of these points of contact with customers?		
What can you do to improve your control over all the elements that influence customer opinion of your product?		
Action Items		
Draw up a list of things you can do based on this analysis to maximize the effectiveness of your marketing program.		

Refining Your Marketing Expectations

When you make improvements to your marketing program, what kind of results can you expect? As a general rule, the percentage change in your program will at best correspond with the percentage change you see in sales. For example, if you change only 5 percent of your program from one year to the next, you can't expect to see more than a 5 percent increase in sales. Check out the next sections for help refining what to expect from your marketing plan.

Projecting improvements above base sales

Base sales are what you can reasonably count on if you maintain the status quo in your marketing. If, for example, you've seen steady growth in sales of 3 to 6 percent per year (varying a bit with the economic cycle), then you may reasonably project sales growth of 4 percent next year, presuming everything else stays the same. But things rarely do stay the same, so you may want to look for threats from new competitors, changing technology, shifting customer needs, and so on. Also, be careful to adjust your natural base downward if you anticipate any such threats materializing next year. If you don't change your program, your base may even be a negative growth rate, because competitors and customers tend to change even if you don't.

After you have a good handle on what your base may be for a status quo sales projection, you can begin to adjust it upward to reflect any improvements you introduce. Be careful in doing this, however, because some of the improvements are fairly clearly linked to future sales, whereas others aren't. If you've tested or tried something already, then you have some real experience upon which to project its impact. If you're trying something that's quite new to you, be cautious and conservative about your projections until you have your own hard numbers and real-world experience to go on.

Preparing for (ultimately successful) failures

Start small with new ideas and methods in marketing so you can afford to fail and gain knowledge from the experience; then adjust and try again. Effective marketing formulas are developed through a combination of planning and experimentation, not just from planning alone. In marketing, you don't have to feel bad about making mistakes, as long as you recognize the mistakes and take away useful lessons.

When it comes to marketing, I'm a positive pessimist. My philosophy is, "What can go wrong, will go wrong . . . and we'll be fine!" I try to avoid being too heavily committed to any single plan or investment. I keep as much flexibility in my marketing programs as I can. For example, I don't buy ads too far in advance even though that would be cheaper, because if sales drop, I don't want to be stuck with the financial commitment to a big ad campaign. And I favor monthly commissions for salespeople and distributors because then their pay is variable with my sales and goes down if sales fall — so I don't have to be right about my sales projections.

Flexibility, cautious optimism, and contingency planning give you the knowledge that you can survive the worst. That knowledge, in turn, gives you the confidence to be a creative, innovative marketer and the courage to grow your business and optimize your marketing program. And you can afford to profit from your mistakes.

Revealing More Ways to Maximize Your Marketing Impact

You can improve a marketing program and increase your business's sales and profits in an infinite number of ways. Following are just some of the ideas you may be able to put to use; keep searching for more ideas and implement as many good ones as you can.

- ✔ **Talk to some of your best customers.** Do they have any good ideas for you? (Ignore the ideas that are overly expensive, however. You can't count on even a good customer to worry about your bottom line.)

- ✔ **Thank customers for their business.** A friendly "thank you" and a smile, a card or note, or a polite cover letter stuffed into the invoice envelope — all are ways to tell customers that you appreciate their business. People tend to go where they're appreciated.

- ✔ **Change your marketing territory.** Are you spread too thin to be visible and effective? If so, narrow your focus to your core region or customer type. But if you have expansion potential, try broadening your reach bit by bit to grow your territory.

- ✔ **Get more referrals.** Spend time talking to and helping out folks who can send customers your way. And make sure you thank anyone who sends you a lead. Positive reinforcement increases the behavior.

✔ **Make your marketing more attractive (professional, creative, polished, clear, well written, and well produced).** You can often increase the effectiveness of your marketing programs by upgrading the look and feel of all your marketing communications and other components. (Did you know that the best-dressed consultants get paid two to five times as much as the average in their fields?)

✔ **Smile to attract and retain business.** Make sure your people have a positive, caring attitude about customers. If they don't, their negativity is certainly losing you business. Don't let people work against your marketing program. Spend time making sure they understand that they can control the success of the program, and help them through training and good management so they can take a positive, helpful, and productive approach to all customer interactions.

✔ **Offer a memorable experience for your customer or client.** Make sure doing business with you is a pleasant experience. Also, plan to do something that makes it memorable (in a good way, please!).

✔ **Know what you want to be best at and invest in being the best.** Who needs you if you're ordinary or average? Success comes from being clearly, enticingly better at something than any other company or product. Even if it's only a small thing that makes you special, know what it is and make sure you keep polishing that brilliance. It's why you deserve the sale.

✔ **Try to cross-sell additional products (or related services) to your customer base.** Increasing the average size of a purchase or order is a great way to improve the effectiveness of your marketing program. But keep the cross-sell soft and natural. Don't sell junk that isn't clearly within your focus or to your customer's benefit.

✔ **Take advantage of the increasingly local options for advertising on the web.** Don't think of the web as worldwide. Google ads can be tailored to customers in your region who are looking for services or products like yours. Now, that's incredibly local, and often an inexpensive way to get leads. There are lots of ways to localize your reach on the web, and I introduce more of them in Part IV.

✔ **Debrief customers who complain or who desert you.** Why are they unhappy? Can you do something simple to retain them? (But ignore the customers who don't match your target customer profile, because you can't be all things to all people.)

Every time you put your marketing hat on, seek to make at least a small improvement in how marketing is done in your organization and for your customers.

Chapter 2

Strengthening Your Marketing Strategy

*W*hen I teach workshops on marketing, I find that most of my participants don't know what a marketing strategy is. If most people don't
know what marketing strategies are, how important can they be? Very important, actually. A *marketing strategy* is a way to achieve success. There are only
a dozen or so main ways to achieve success in marketing.

In this chapter, I explain what the different marketing strategies are and help
you select the right one for your business or project. I also show you how to
use strategic thinking to make your marketing program more effective and
profitable than most.

Finding and Riding a Growth Wave

The simplest and most reliable marketing strategy you can adapt for your
business or product is to go where the growth is. Find it and ride the *growth
wave* — an opportunity to sell something with increasing demand — for as
long as you can. Doing so is important because growing and prospering when
selling into a growing market is much easier than when facing stagnant or
shrinking demand.

The following sections help you determine what the growth rate of your market is and evaluate other markets to find one that's growing. With this information, you can make sure you're focused on growth opportunities.

Measuring the growth rate of your market

At any point in time, a minority of markets are growing rapidly. However, most markets are growing at a slow pace, and some markets are shrinking. Knowing how quickly or slowly your market is growing is vital because it's a key driver of your sales growth and profits. Take a moment to evaluate the current growth rate and future growth potential of *your* market. If it's not fast enough, then find a new and faster market to target (check out the next section for how to find a growing market). Your market ought to be experiencing at least 5 percent overall annual growth (although my preference is for a 10 percent or better growth rate). Anything slower than 5 percent makes it hard to grow your own business.

To assess your market's growth potential, think of one or several simple indicators of your market's overall growth rate and use them to gauge market growth. These indicators include the year-to-year trend in industry-wide sales, the trend in number of customers, and the trend in type and size of purchases per customer. If you find that the market is shrinking or static, then you need to look for a growth opportunity.

Sometimes, finding a direct measure of your market's size and growth rate is difficult. For example, if you sell office equipment and furniture in the greater Chicago area, your market is the dollar value of all office furniture purchased in that area. Can you find out what that figure is? Not very easily, if at all, so you need to find indirect indicators of your market's growth rate that you can use instead. Statistics on business employment in Chicago are useful because as business employment grows, so does the need for furniture. If corporate headquarters are leaving the downtown area or laying off workers, then you can assume that the overall market for office furniture is shrinking.

Responding to a flat or shrinking market

When faced with a declining market, do the following to adjust to the growth rate:

- ✔ Reduce retail stores and other major investments to avoid losses.
- ✔ Eliminate low-margin products from your line so you can survive in a slow market.
- ✔ Look for other places to sell your product or find another product line to sell that offers more growth potential.

Don't waste your time trying to grow and prosper in an unhealthy market. By keeping a regular eye on market growth rates and focusing on selling into growth markets, you simultaneously ensure that you can grow your sales and increase the ease of operating at a profit. Slow-growth and no-growth markets are brutally competitive. To win sales in either case, you often have to slash prices, ruining your profit margins. That's why smart marketers make a strategic point of focusing on growth markets. They also keep careful track of the growth rate in their market so as to be alert to a slowdown that may indicate a need to move on again.

To identify the best market for your future growth, ask yourself where growth is. Some types of customers may be increasing in number while others are declining (for instance, the United States has a lot of consumers in their 20s, so some marketers are shifting away from older consumers and targeting the newer ones). Furthermore, certain types of businesses are expanding (such as healthcare businesses), so a business-to-business marketer can grow by providing specific products or services to them. Also, geographic areas vary in their economic health and strength, so if you're willing to relocate or expand into new markets, you can target cities or states with relatively strong economies.

Growing with a Market Expansion Strategy

Market expansion is the most common strategy in marketing. The idea is to start selling to new groups of prospective customers. If you find a way to get in front of more prospects than last year, you should be able to make more sales than last year, too (see Chapters 10, 12, 13, and 16 for specific ways).

Two powerful ways to expand your market (and business) involve introducing more products into the market, which can give you access to multiple new customer bases, and taking advantage of a product that's especially popular, which allows you to piggyback sales of other products when customers are drawn in by your bestseller. The sections that follow highlight how you can go about accomplishing both.

Offering more products

Introducing new products is a strong way to expand your share of a particular market — eventually. If you sold only 10 products last year, and you offer 20 this year, you just may find that your sales double, too. Of course, it's quite likely that the new products won't sell as well as your old ones at first, but if you persist, you should be able to ramp up their sales over the course of a few years.

When looking to offer more products, you have two options:

- ✔ Add new products simply by reselling or distributing products that complement your current line and meet some need of your current customer base.
- ✔ Innovate to create one or more new products that nobody else sells.

Either way, you have the two-fold challenge of informing customers that you have something new to offer and convincing them to take a look. That's why being especially visible and persistent in the first few months of your campaign to open a new market is so crucial. A concentrated blast of marketing communications is the key to opening a new market successfully.

Create visibility by showing people your brand or product often and in a consistent, professional manner. You can do this through advertising, direct mail, e-mail blasts, paid placement of your web address for key-term searches, signage (such as billboards and transit ads), sales calls, or presence at conferences and trade shows. Plan to use at least three of these or similar methods in the beginning of your campaign to open a new market (see Parts II and III for details).

Risks and costs increase when you experiment with new products — defined as anything you're not accustomed to making and marketing. Consequently, you should discount your first year's sales projections for a new market by some factor to reflect the degree of risk. A good general rule is to cut back the sales projections by 20 to 50 percent, depending on your judgment of how new and risky the product is to you and your team. It may also cost you double the time and money to make each sale when entering a new market, because your new prospects won't be familiar with your brand, and you likely won't have a well-defined marketing formula at the start. Budget accordingly.

Riding a bestseller to the top

If you have a *bestseller* on your hands — in other words, a product that outsells your other products by a multiple, which means it ought to sell at least three times as much as anything else — why not make the most of it? Some marketing experts look for bestsellers to achieve sales that are at least ten times the norm; outstanding bestsellers can achieve a hundred or more times the normal level of sales for a product in their category. If you have just one bestseller in your line, growing your revenues and profits is a piece of cake.

How do you create a bestselling product? First, look for one. Don't be content with products that sell moderately well. Keep looking for something that has more excitement and potential. Test many alternatives. When you find one that seems to have momentum (you'll know it has momentum when early sales figures surprise you by their rapid growth), quickly refocus your marketing efforts on that product. Make it the heart of sales calls and ads, feature it at the top of your website's home page, talk to the media about it, and offer specials for new customers who try it. Bestsellers are found and made by marketers who believe in them. Be a believer!

When you have a product with bestseller potential, your marketing strategy should be to ride it as hard and far as you can. Write a marketing plan that puts the majority of your budget and efforts behind the bestseller and gives the rest of your product line as minimal a budget as you think you can get away with. The bestseller will tend to lift all sales by attracting customers, so don't worry about the rest of your products.

After you have a bestseller, you should see your profits grow. Use some of these profits to look for the next bestseller. Why? Because eventually your bestseller will lose its momentum. Your best bet is to find another bestseller, which may take a while, so you can have it ready and waiting in the wings. Test ideas and options, and be patient. If you can't find another bestseller, switch to another marketing strategy. You don't have to have a bestseller to succeed, but it sure is nice if you can find a product that fits this strategy.

Specializing with a Market Segmentation Strategy

A *market segmentation strategy* is a strategy in which you target and cater to (or specialize in) just one narrow type or group of customer. The object of this approach is to be so well suited to that specialized customer that you become the top seller in your segment. The main way to develop a segmentation strategy is to look at your current customers and identify one particular type that seems most profitable for you right now. Or if a subset of your customers is growing faster than the rest, consider specializing in those types of customers to gain more of their business. (And you don't have to limit yourself to just one segment. If you see several with potential, adjust your product, pricing, promotion, or distribution for each, and, in essence, operate several parallel marketing programs that have enough synergy, such as through a common core product, to be economical and easy to manage.)

The advantage of a segmentation strategy is that it allows you to tailor your product and your entire marketing effort to a clearly defined group with uniform, specific characteristics. For example, the consulting firm that targets only the healthcare industry knows that prospective clients can be found at a handful of healthcare industry conferences and that they have certain common concerns around which consulting services can be focused. Many smaller consulting firms target a narrowly defined market segment to compete against larger, less specialized consulting firms.

If you're in the consulting business, you can specialize in nonprofits, for example, instead of trying to be a consultant to all businesses. If you sell office furniture, you can decide whether to focus on corporate sales, small businesses, government offices, schools, or home offices. Each segment has different needs and buying patterns, and at any particular time, one of these segments is going to be easier for you to dominate (and it may be growing faster, too). As an added bonus, marketing is usually easier and less expensive when you're highly specialized because you know exactly where to find your customers.

The next sections explain how to determine whether a market segmentation strategy is right for you and how to expand your business by focusing on more than one specific target customer base.

Gauging whether specializing is a good move

Specializing in a specific market segment can give you the momentum you need to power past your competition, but it may not always be the right approach for your operation. The segmentation strategy may work well for you if

- ✔ You think your business can be more profitable by specializing in a more narrowly defined segment than you do now.
- ✔ You face too many competitors in your broader market and can't seem to carve out a stable, profitable customer base of your own.
- ✔ It takes better advantage of things you're good at.
- ✔ You're too small to be one of the leaders in your overall market or industry. Maybe you can be the leader in a specific segment of your market.

Adding a segment to expand your market

If you're running out of customers and market and need to expand (see the earlier "Growing with a Market Expansion Strategy" section), one way to do so is to decide to target a new segment. For example, the consulting firm specializing in coaching healthcare executives can decide to start offering a similar service to nonprofits. A different approach and marketing program may be needed, because the two industries are different in many ways and have only partial overlap (some hospitals are nonprofits, but many nonprofits aren't hospitals). By specializing in two segments rather than just one, the firm may be able to grow its total sales significantly while still maintaining a grasp in niche markets that gives it an edge over the competition.

Developing a Market Share Strategy

The bigger you are in comparison to your competitors, the more profitable you'll be. Scale helps. That's why trying to be relatively big is a good idea. A powerful strategy is to increase your market share through your marketing activities. In essence, that means taking some business from your competitors. *Market share* is, very simply, your sales as a percentage of total sales for your product category in your market (or in your market segment if you use a segmentation strategy). If you sell $2 million worth of shark teeth and the world market totals $20 million per year, then your share of the global shark teeth market is 10 percent. It's that simple. Or is it?

To help you comprehend how increasing your market share can be beneficial for you and your business, the following sections provide some basics on this strategy and how you can implement it.

Choosing a unit

Before you can completely determine your market share, you must know which *unit* (what you're measuring sales in) you're going to reference. Dollars, pesos, containers, or grams are fine — as long as you use the same unit throughout. Just pick whatever seems to make sense for your product and the information you have access to.

Estimating market share

To effectively increase your market share, you must have an accurate picture of how large your market is and what your current share of it is. Take a look at this simple method for estimating market size and share (you can even sketch it out on the back of a napkin if you haven't the time or money for fancier approaches):

1. **Estimate the number of customers in your market.**

   For instance, guess how many people in your country are likely to buy toothpaste or how many businesses in your city buy consulting services.

2. **Estimate how much each customer buys a year, on average.**

   Does each customer buy six tubes of toothpaste? Fifteen hours of consulting services? You can check your sales records or ask some people what they do to make your estimate as accurate as possible.

3. **Multiply the two figures together to get the total size of the annual market and then divide your unit sales into it to get your share.**

For example, if you import fine English teas to the U.S. market and wholesale them to grocery stores, specialty shops, and the growing number of online specialty tea stores (such as www.theteaspot.com), you can look up U.S. tea wholesalers by visiting www.census.gov (where the latest U.S. Census data is posted) and selecting the Economic Census link under the Data drop-down. Doing so brings you to a constantly evolving window into the economic census data, which includes data from 2002, 2007, and 2012. There will be a way to look up your category or industry and find the code number for it; this code number acts as a key to tables of relevance to you. I can't tell you exactly how to find your way through the website because the site has changed every week or two for the last few years and likely will continue to evolve.

If you were to research tea sales, code 4244901, you may find out that there were 98 tea wholesalers with a total of $3.886 million in annual sales. If your sales of tea are $525,000, then your market share is 0.525 ÷ 3.886, or 13.5 percent. (My numbers may be out of date by the time you read this, but the source — the industry series of the U.S. Census — is a great place for all sorts of market statistics. Check it out.)

Alternatively, you may estimate that three-quarters of the wholesalers handle low-cost, inexpensive teas and therefore don't compete directly with you. In that case, you can calculate your market share of the quarter of total sales that are similar specialty teas as 0.525 ÷ (0.25 × 3.886), which gives you 54 percent. That's a much larger share based on a narrower definition of the market. Estimating your market share helps you determine which market share numbers are correct.

Understanding where your product fits in the market

To create a market share strategy, you need to clearly identify and define your product and where it fits into your market. In other words, you need to know your *product category:* the general grouping of competitive products to which your product belongs (be it merchandise or a service). Knowing your product category is extremely important. If you don't know where your product fits into the market, you can't begin to develop a strategy to build on and increase your existing market share. For example, if you sell specialty teas, are you competing with mass-market brands? Should you count their sales in your market calculations and try to win sales from them? Or, if you've noted the rise in specialty tea suppliers who are online and don't have physical stores, do you want to segment by focusing on the faster-growing online category? If so, should you sell as a wholesaler still or leap in as a retailer who does all your own sourcing from overseas?

To get an accurate picture of your product category, you really need to get feedback from your customers. Doing so helps you create goals to drive your planning, as explained in the following sections.

Ask your customers

Your customers can provide you with valuable information and help you determine exactly where your product fits in the market. What matters is *customer perception:* how the customer sees the category. So watch your customers or ask them to find out what their purchase options are (see Chapter 4 if you want to conduct a formal study). Get a feel for how they view their choices. Then include all the likely or close choices in your definition of the market.

To stick with the tea example, are they choosing among all the tea options or just some of them? With specialty teas, you may find that a majority of consumers sometimes drink the cheaper mass-market brands, too. You may also find that you, as a wholesaler, must fight the mass-market brands for shelf space in grocery stores and mentions on restaurant menus. So you probably do need to use total market sales as your base, not just specialty sales.

On the other hand, you compete more closely against other specialty teas, so you may want to track this smaller market share number also and set a secondary goal for it. A wholesale tea importer's strategic goals may therefore look something like this:

- ✔ Increase dollar sales of our products to U.S.-end tea consumers from 13.5 percent to 15 percent.

- ✔ Protect our share of the specialty tea market by keeping it at 54 percent or higher.

- ✔ Differentiate ourselves even more from mass-market tea brands by emphasizing what makes our tea special to avoid having to compete directly against much larger marketers.

Make a plan

To achieve your market share goals, you must plan accordingly and look at what you need to do to get the market share you want. For starters, a wholesaler needs retail shelf space, so you may need to push to win a larger share of shelf space from retailers. And to earn the right to this shelf space, you may need to do some consumer advertising or publicity, provide the stores with good point-of-purchase displays or signs, improve your product packaging, or do other things to help ensure that consumers take a stronger interest in buying your products.

This plan needs to revolve around the goal of increasing share of tea sales by 1.5 percentage points. Each point of share is worth roughly $40,000 in annual sales (one percent of the total sales in the market), so a plan that involves spending, say, an extra $25,000 to win a 1.5 percent share gain can provide an extra $60,000 if it works. But will it work? To be cautious, you, as the marketer, may want to discount this projection of $60,000 in additional sales by a risk factor of, say, 25 percent, which cuts your projected gain back to $45,000.

Then consider timing. Remember that the plan can't achieve the full gain in the first month of the year. A sales projection starting at the current level of sales in the first month and ramping up to the projected increase by, say, the sixth month, may be reasonable. Dividing $45,000 by 12 to find the monthly value of the risk-discounted 1.5 share point increase gives you $3,750 in extra monthly sales for the sixth month and beyond. Lower increases apply to earlier months when the program is just starting to kick in. But the marketing expenses tend to be concentrated in the early months, reflecting the need to invest in advance to grow your market share.

Knowing your competitors

So what if your competitors have more market share than you? Don't fear them; use them instead! Study your closest and/or most successful competitors to figure out how you're going to gain market share. The better you understand your competitors, the more easily you can take customers away from them.

Ask yourself what your competitors do well, how they take business from you now, and what new initiatives they're trying this year. Talk to customers, suppliers, distributors, and anyone else with good knowledge of your competitors' practices and gather any online information about them from their websites. Also, collect their marketing materials and brochures and keep track of any information you come across on how they market. For example, if they're picking up good business by having a booth at a trade show you don't attend, consider getting a booth next time to make sure you're able to compete against them there. Also find out what your competitors do badly. Those things are the chinks in their market share armor where you can easily succeed by being better!

Studying market trends and revising if need be

Market share gives you a simple way of comparing your progress to your competitors from period to period. If your share drops, you're losing; if your share grows, you're winning. It's that simple. Consequently, most marketing programs are based at least partly on a *strategic market share goal,* which is the percentage of sales you want to win during a specific period, such as a year. For example, you can say, "Increase share from 5 percent to 7 percent by introducing a product upgrade and increasing our use of trial-stimulating special offers," which is a clear goal.

You also need to study the market and see how your products compare year to year and against your competition. The postmortem on last year's program should always be based on an examination of what market share change accompanied it. (If you don't already do routine *reviews* — careful analyses of what happened and why it differed positively or negatively from your plans — you should. The planning process in Chapter 3 takes you through an analysis of past results, along with plans for improving your program and results in the future.) If the past period's program doubled your market share, seriously consider replicating it. But if your market share stayed the same or fell, you're ready for something new. *Note:* Whether you make share gain the focus of your marketing program, at least keep it in mind and try not to lose any share.

Designing a Positioning Strategy

A *positioning strategy* takes a psychological approach to marketing. It focuses on getting customers or prospects to see your product in a favorable light and think of it before competitors' offerings. The positioning goal you articulate for this kind of strategy is the position your product holds in the customer's mind. The following sections break down how to find your position and craft your positioning strategy.

Your positioning strategy can be as simple as saying that you want your brand to be the easiest to buy, or as complex as saying your brand is easier to purchase, more affordable, hipper, and more contemporary than the competition. Just make sure your claims are truthful and believable.

Envisioning your position: An exercise in observation and creativity

Good positioning means your product has a prime parking space in customers' minds thanks to its strong, clear image. People recognize your brand and know immediately what it stands for. If you're in a fairly new or uncompetitive market, standing out in customers' minds should be easy. But if a lot of other marketers are involved, as in older, well-established markets, chances are they've already used positioning strategies and secured their places in customers' minds. That's why it's important not to get hung up on what you *want* your positioning to be. Instead, focus on what it *needs* to be to resonate and stick.

To help you figure out your position compared to other brands, start by drawing a simple, two-line graph. The two lines represent the range, from high to low, of the two core dimensions of your positioning strategy. You find these dimensions by asking yourself — and ideally some talkative customers, too — what the main differences between products are. The differences may be price and quality, or any number of other possible variables, depending on the product in question. (See Chapter 4 for help conducting your customer research.) Map all the major competitors and look for a space where you can fit your brand.

For example, if you're marketing soap, your dimensions can be how gentle or harsh the soaps are as well as how natural they are. A brand that claims to be all natural and as gentle as the rain is obviously in the gentle and natural quadrant. Another brand that claims to be tough on dirt and germs is going to score low on the all-natural scale and high on the harsh scale, placing it squarely in the opposite quadrant. If the marketers of these two brands consistently communicate their different positions, the two brands won't compete directly. Consumers who want a gentle, natural soap buy one brand, whereas consumers who want a strong soap that kills germs buy the other. Both marketers can succeed by virtue of their unique positioning strategies.

Writing a positioning strategy: The how-to

After you're clear on what the consumer values most (see the preceding section and Chapter 4), position your product in relation to that. For example, if bank customers say in a survey that they're desperate for better interest rates, then a bank's advertising can focus on a special, high-interest rate introductory offer. To refine your positioning strategy and make sure it gets incorporated into all your marketing communications, you need to write down a positioning statement. Fortunately, writing a positioning statement is pretty easy. Just follow these two simple steps:

1. **Answer the following questions:**
   - What type of customer do you target?
   - What attribute does the customer value most?
   - What do you do for that customer with respect to that attribute?
   - How do you fulfill your customer's wants and needs?
   - Why do you do it better than the competition?

2. **Fill in the following with your own words:**
   - Our product offers the following benefit (which the customer values):
   - To the following customers (describe target segment):
   - Our product is better than competitors in the following manner:
   - We can prove we're the best because of (provide evidence/ differences):

Here are some of the common approaches for a positioning strategy:

- ✔ **You may position against a competitor.** "Our interest rates are lower than XYZ Bank's." (This tactic is a natural in a mature product category, where the competitive strategy applies.)

- ✔ **You may emphasize a distinctive benefit.** "The only peanut butter with no harmful trans fats."

> ✔ **You can affiliate yourself with something the customer values.** "The toothpaste most often recommended by dentists." (Doing so allows some of the virtues of this other thing to rub off on your brand.) A celebrity endorser, an image of a happy family playing on the beach, a richly appointed manor house set in beautiful gardens, a friendly giant: All have been used to position products favorably in consumers' minds.

Write your positioning strategy in big print and post it above your desk to make sure you stay focused on its execution. Handing out copies of it to your ad agency, distributor, publicist, salespeople, and anyone else who works on or in your marketing program also pays off.

Considering Other Core Strategies

Are there other winning marketing strategies? Certainly. In fact, strategy, like everything in marketing, is limited only by your imagination and initiative. If you can think of a better approach to strategy, go for it. The following sections present a few examples of other proven marketing strategies. Perhaps one of them may work for you.

Simplicity marketing

With *simplicity marketing,* you position your business as simpler, easier to understand, and easier to use or work with than the competition. For example, I'm usually in a hurry, so I remember being excited when they first introduced gas pumps that allowed you to swipe your credit card. It's so simple and quick — and a perfect example of a simplicity strategy.

Some customers are willing to pay a premium to avoid complexity and make purchase decisions simply and quickly. Can this approach be useful to customers in your market? Look for technologies or processes that can make your customers' lives simpler and easier. For example, try making it easy to reorder on your website by storing information about what customers last purchased so they don't have to search through many options to find the right item.

Quality strategies

Most marketers grossly underrate quality. All else being anywhere near equal, a majority of customers choose the higher-quality option. But be careful to find out what your customers think the word *quality* means. They may have a different view from you. Also, be careful to integrate your quality-based marketing messages with a genuine commitment to quality in all aspects of your business.

You can't just say you're better than the competition; you really have to deliver. But if customers see you as superior on even one dimension of quality — then by all means emphasize that in your marketing. Quote customer testimonials praising your quality, describe your commitment to quality in your marketing materials, and make trial usage easy for prospective customers so they can experience your quality, too. And make sure your pricing is consistent with a high-quality image. Don't advertise cheap prices or deep discounts, which signal cheapness, not quality.

Reminder strategies

A reminder strategy is good when you expect that people will buy your product if they think of it — but they may not without a reminder. A lot of routine purchases benefit from this strategy (for example, "Got milk?").

Point-of-purchase (POP) marketing is often an effective way to implement the reminder strategy. *Point-of-purchase marketing* simply means doing whatever advertising is necessary to sway the consumer your way at the time and place of his purchase. For retail products, this often means a clever in-store display or sign to remind the consumer about your product. For the rest of us, it may mean a pop-up coupon-like special offer on Facebook (which is easy enough to do and can be targeted at your friends or a certain population).

Wenger NA promotes its Swiss Army knife product line in jewelry and knife stores by offering it in attractive, attention-getting countertop display cases. Although the pocketknife market has been mature for decades, POP displays remind consumers about the option of buying a Swiss Army knife as a gift — for someone else or even for themselves.

Innovative distribution strategies

Sometimes the most important feature of a purchase is when and where people can buy it. With *innovative distribution strategies,* you can capture sales from your competitors by being more convenient or available than other options.

For example, can you recall the brand of gas you purchased the last time you stopped at a highway rest stop? Probably not, because it didn't matter. Whatever brand was offered, you bought it because you needed gas, and highway rest stops offer only one or two options. The gas station owner who manages to secure one of the slots at a rest stop is using a distribution strategy. As the old saying goes, the three secrets of success in retail are location, location, and location. (Funny how this turns out to be true online, too! If you aren't on the first page of the search engine list, you're in trouble, so use Google ads, daily social media activity linked to your site, rich content, and lots of website babysitting to make sure you have a good location when someone searches online.)

The three rules of success actually hold true in all businesses, not just in retail. Always consider what you can do to be more present and convenient for your buyers. The Internet offers opportunities for innovative distribution, and many businesses are building online stores that make it easy to shop at midnight from the comfort of your own bed, or whenever and wherever you please. See Chapters 16 and 21 for details of how to win the marketing game through effective distribution.

Selling Innovative Products

Every product category has a limited life. At least in theory — and usually in all-too-real reality — some new type of product comes along to displace the old one. The result is called *the product life cycle,* a never-ending cycle of birth, growth, and decline, fueled by the endless inventiveness of competing businesses. Product categories arise, spread through the marketplace, and ultimately decline as replacements arise and begin their own life cycles. If you're marketing an innovative product that's just beginning to catch on (in what marketers call the growth phase of the life cycle), you can expect rapid growth in sales and profits. Fast-growing products are every marketer's dream.

As a strategic marketer, you need to keep a sharp eye on your product line and weed out any fading old products before they drag you down with them. Keep looking for adding hot new ones, so your marketing efforts will be supplemented by the natural growth of exciting new options.

Some marketers do hardcore product development and regularly file patents on their inventions. However, if you don't, that's okay. Most marketers source their products from elsewhere and resell them. That's fine, but don't forget to keep looking for new, better options. Make a strategic point of upgrading your product line (or services if you don't sell products) to stay on the growth curve. Don't let innovation pass you by. See Chapter 5 for tips on how to create innovations.

Writing Down and Regularly Reviewing Your Strategy

What's your marketing strategy? Is it a pure version of one of the strategies reviewed in this chapter, or is it a variant (or even a combination) of more than one of them? Whatever it is, take some time to write it down clearly and thoughtfully. Put it in summary form in a single sentence. (If you must, add some bullet points to explain it in more detail.) After you write it down, don't put it away in a drawer and forget about it. Keep it close by and review it on a regular basis.

Write a strategy that's a clear statement of the direction you want your business's or product's marketing to take. This statement needs to be a big-picture game plan. With this strategy on paper, you can work on designing good products and packaging, friendly services, and impressive ads that communicate your quality to consumers. Here's what one company's marketing strategy looks like:

> Our strategy is to maximize the quality of our security alarm products and services through good engineering and to grow our share of a competitive market by communicating our superior quality to high-end customers.

After you develop a marketing strategy, be sure to follow it and make it obvious in all that you do. In fact, I highly recommend that you do some formal planning to figure out exactly how you'll implement your strategy in all aspects of your marketing program. (I show you how to develop a plan as painlessly as possible in Chapter 3.) After you adopt a specific marketing strategy, you must actually read it from time to time and check that you're following it. I'm often amazed at the lack of relationship between marketers' strategies and their actions. Everyone involved in your organization's marketing needs to understand how their work ties to the strategy.

Outside vendors you work with need to be aware of your marketing strategy, too. When you interact with a graphic designer, web designer, ad rep, list broker, or tech support person from any of the big online web environments (Google and Facebook being great examples of where to purchase well-focused web ads), tell them your strategy. "We are trying to . . . " finish the sentence with whatever is appropriate for you, such as "attract serious collectors of antiquarian books," "let people know that they don't have to feed their families grocery store food with low nutritional value and many contaminants," or "bring broadband interfaces to every trade show display."

Your strategic imagination is the only limitation to your growth, but make sure you share your vision with everyone who contributes to your marketing.

Chapter 3

Writing a Marketing Plan

. . . .

In This Chapter

▶ Reviewing planning rules and do's and don'ts

▶ Crafting an executive summary and refining your strategic objectives

▶ Getting the whole perspective with a situation analysis

▶ Defining your marketing program, including the all-important details

▶ Forecasting and controlling your result for beat-the-odds survival and success

. . . .

*I*f you have a very simple business that makes more sales than it needs to and is already growing as fast as it can, then you don't need a marketing plan. However, most businesses are a tad more complex and therefore *do* require a marketing plan. A *marketing plan* is basically just a description, in words and numbers, of how you plan to run your marketing program. This chapter shows you how to draft your own plan or revise your current plan so you can improve your bottom line.

Grasping the Value of the Marketing Plan

Having a marketing plan is important because it helps you identify, execute, and control the marketing activities that will produce a successful year. You should write one if you

✔ **Have a big enough business that organizing, controlling, and budgeting all your marketing activities is too complex to hold all the details in your head:** Most businesses are too complex for the marketer to reliably hold all the variables in his or her head. A plan helps you identify the best practices, eliminate the unprofitable ones, and keep everything on schedule and on budget.

✔ **Face challenges or uncertainties that can affect sales or profits:** The planning process helps you think through what needs to be changed to improve your results.

✔ **Don't already know exactly what the best way is to handle your business's branding, pricing, communications, sales, and other marketing matters:** Planning helps clarify and control all the elements of your marketing plan.

Naturally, planning takes time and energy. But its payback is rapid and large. Unplanned marketing rarely, if ever, pays off.

Another big benefit of planning is that it gets you thinking creatively about your marketing program. As you plan, you find yourself questioning old assumptions and practices and thinking about new and better ways to boost your brand and optimize sales and profits.

Software programs, like JIAN's Marketing Plan Builder (www.jian.com), can simplify and support marketing planning. If you want to make your planning a group effort and/or you're looking for planning templates, consider online options, the best of which offer both of these benefits and can shorten the time it takes to produce a coherent and competent plan. LivePlan (www.liveplan.com) from PaloAlto Software makes it easy for a team to work remotely on the same plan at the same time. SecurePlan (www.secureplan.com), also from PaloAlto Software, offers sales and marketing plans as well as general business plans from the same source. Also check out enloop's online planning tools (slanted more toward financial plans but still of some use) at www.enloop.com. Mplans offers free sample marketing plans and sells the quite sophisticated Sales and Marketing Pro software download (www.mplans.com). Usually free, but less sophisticated, are the marketing forms and templates offered by Entrepreneur (www.entrepreneur.com/formnet/marketingforms.html).

If you want to write a more free-form plan using basic aps like spreadsheets, calendars, and word-processing documents but want to make them accessible to a team of authors and post them interactively on a website, you may spend quite a lot to have a web developer put all these functions on a secure part of your website. Or you could just use the free Google Apps for Business. I like the free option myself, and I love the way you can create a living plan on a web page that's easily accessible by all stakeholders.

Other options include

✔ Smartsheet (www.smartsheet.com), a cloud-based planning platform that carries through to project management by the team. It also offers links for crowdsourcing, which may, to a creative marketer, be a cool new way to do living marketing research during the planning phase and even as the plan is being implemented. I have a hunch that marketing plans will be designed and implemented entirely in online environments such as Smartsheet within the coming decade.

✔ SCORE (`www.score.org`; the nonprofit set up to help U.S. small businesses) offers a suite of free templates for marketing strategy and plans, hidden away beneath the category Business Planning & Financial Statements Template Gallery at the Templates & Tools tab. You may also pursue mentoring and other forms of direct assistance by real live experts from SCORE or the nearest Small Business Administration District Office, Small Business Development Center, Veteran's Business Outreach Center, or Woman's Business Center, mapped on the U.S. SBA's website at `www.sba.gov/tools/local-assistance`.

Reviewing the Contents of a Good Plan

Before you can write a successful marketing plan for your business, you need to know the ins and outs of what a marketing plan includes. Marketing plans vary significantly in format and outline, but all of them have sections about the following:

✔ **Your current position:** This is in terms of your product, customers, competition, and broader trends in your market.

✔ **What results you got in the previous period (if you're an established business, that is):** You need to look at sales, market share, and possibly also profits, customer satisfaction, web visibility, or other measures of customer attitude and perception. You may also want to include measures of customer retention, size and frequency of purchase, or other indicators of customer behavior, because they're often helpful in thinking about where to focus your marketing efforts in the future. Your plan should also itemize the key attributes that customers desire and how your benefits match up with those attributes.

✔ **Lessons learned:** A postmortem on the previous period helps identify any mistakes to avoid, insights to take advantage of, or major changes that may present threats or opportunities. Also include lessons learned from competitors or even dissimilar businesses that have had good (or bad) luck with marketing initiatives you may want to try.

✔ **Your strategy:** This is the big focus of your plan and the way you'll grow your revenues and profits. Keep the strategy statement to a few sentences so that everyone who reads it gets it at once and can remember what the strategy is. Think like a sports coach or field commander: "Where is the opportunity to win, and what resources should we swing into the gap to gain ground?"

✔ **The details of your program:** You want to cover all your company's specific activities in this section. Group them by area or type, with explanations of how these activities fit the company's strategy and reflect the current situation. If the details are overwhelming, do some pruning by using the marketing pyramid so that your resources are more focused (see Chapter 2).

✔ **The numbers:** These definitely include sales projections and costs but may also include market share projections, sales to your biggest customers or distributors, costs and returns from any special offers you plan to use, sales projections and commissions by territory, and any other details that help you quantify your specific marketing opportunities and activities.

✔ **Your experimentation plans:** If you have a new business or product, or if you're experimenting with a new or risky marketing activity, set up a plan (or pilot) for how to test the waters on a small scale first. You need to determine what positive results you want to see before committing to a higher level. After all, wisdom is knowing what you don't know — and planning how to figure it out.

Be careful! You mustn't think of your plan as written in stone. In fact, your plan is just a starting point. As you implement it throughout the coming year, you'll discover that some things work out the way you planned, and others don't. Good marketers revisit their plans and adjust them as they go. The idea is to use a plan to help you be an intelligent, flexible marketer, not a stubborn one who refuses to learn from experience.

Starting with baby steps

The more unfamiliar you are with writing a marketing plan, the more flexibility and caution your plan needs, so make flexibility your first objective if you're creating a marketing plan for the first time. Consider crafting a gradual plan that includes a pilot phase with a timeline and alternatives or options in case of problems. For example, instead of taking advantage of cheaper bulk printing with a vendor you don't know for a marketing piece you've never tested, use short runs of marketing materials at the local copy shop.

Optimizing your plan for flexibility means preserving your freedom of choice, avoiding commitments of resources, and spending in small increments so you can change the plan as you go. Ultimately, you need to decide how much flexibility you require and build it into the schedule and budget. You may want to consider milestones achieved as the mechanism to release additional activities or budget funds.

Maximizing efficiencies

If your business has been around the marketing block before and your plan builds on years of experience, you can more safely favor economies of scale over flexibility. (*Economies of scale* are the cost savings from doing things on a larger scale.) But always leave yourself at least a *little* wiggle room, because reality never reflects your plans and projections 100 percent of the time.

Adjust your marketing plan to favor economies of scale if you feel confident that you can make sound judgments in advance. Advertising is cheaper and more efficient if you do it on a large scale, because you get deeper discounts on the design of ads and purchasing of ad space or air time. If you know a media investment is likely to produce leads or sales, go ahead and buy media in larger chunks to get good rates. And don't be as cautious about testing mailing lists with small-scale mailings of a few hundred pieces. A good in-house list supplemented by 20 percent or fewer newly purchased names probably warrants a major mailing without as much emphasis on advance testing.

Understanding the Do's and Don'ts of Planning

Marketing programs end up like leaky boats very easily. Each activity seems worthy at the time, but too many of them fail to produce a positive return — ending up as holes in the bottom of your business's boat. Get too many of those holes, and the water inside the boat starts rising. The next sections share some of the common ways marketers lose money (so you can try to avoid them), plus two effective strategies for using your cash wisely.

Don't ignore the details

Good marketing plans are built from details such as customer-by-customer, item-by-item, or territory-by-territory sales projections. Generalizing about an entire market is hard and dangerous. Your sales and cost projections are easier to get right if you break them down into their smallest natural units (such as individual territory sales or customer orders), do estimates for each of these small units, and then add up those estimates to get your totals.

Don't imitate the competitors

You may be tempted to just do what your bigger competitors are doing, but don't fall into that trap. You need to have some fresh ideas that make your brand and plan unique.

Imitation isn't a winning strategy in the long run.

Do find your own formulas for success

Start by building on whatever successes you've had in the past. For instance, if you ran an ad this year that got a good response, double or triple the number of ads of this kind in next year's plan.

Don't feel confined by last period's budget and plan

When putting together your marketing plan, don't allow past results to trap you in what you want to do. Repeat or improve the best-performing elements of the past plans and cut back on any elements that didn't produce high returns. Every plan includes some activities and spending that aren't necessary and can be cut out (or reworked) when you do it all over again next year. Be ruthless with any underperforming elements of last year's plan! (If you're starting a new business, at least this is one problem you don't have to worry about. Yet.) Also, monitor your plan over the business cycle and adjust it as you go so you can catch problems early and avoid wasting too much time and money on underperforming activities.

Don't engage in unnecessary spending

Always think through any spending and run the numbers before signing a contract or writing a check. Many of the people you deal with to execute your marketing activities are salespeople themselves. Their goal is to get *you* to buy their ad space, use their design or printing services, or spend money on fancy websites. They want your marketing money — and may care less about whether you get a good return on it. So keep them on a tight financial rein. Google and Facebook both provide excellent support for small business advertisers, for example, so it may pay to do some advertising yourself. See what you can accomplish before you run into a wall and have to hire the experts.

One of the biggest areas of waste is advertising agencies. Sure, sometimes you need a good agency, like when you want to design and run a large ad campaign. But if you're placing fewer than a thousand ads, you probably can't afford the typical agency with its big upfront fees for consultation and design. A local, independent graphic designer who has created successful ads in your industry before is a more affordable alternative. In terms of placing the ads, you may need to be the one who negotiates good rates, so be prepared to roll up your sleeves and do some of the work yourself.

Do break down your plan into simple subplans

If your marketing activities are consistent and clearly of one kind, you can go with a single plan. But what if you sell services (like consulting or repair) and also products? You may find that you need to work up one plan for selling products (perhaps this plan aims at finding new customers) and another plan for convincing product buyers to also use your services. And if you have multiple stores (physical and/or on the web) or multiple products, consider a short plan for each rather than one big, confusing umbrella plan.

If your plan seems too complicated, simply divide and conquer! Then total everything up to get the big picture for your overall projection and budget. For example, if you have 50 products in five different product categories, writing your plan becomes much easier if you come up with 50 sales projections for each product and five separate promotional plans for each category of product. (This method may sound harder, but it really is much simpler, and forecasts that are built up from smaller forecasts are often the most accurate.)

Every type of marketing activity in your plan has a natural and appropriate level of breakdown. Find the right level, and your planning will be simpler and easier to do. Following are some methods to help you break down your planning:

- Analyze, plan, and budget sales activities by sales territory and region (or by major customer if you're a business-to-business marketer with a handful of dominant companies as your clients).

- Project revenues and promotions by individual product and by industry (if you sell into more than one).

- Plan your advertising and other promotions by product line or other broad product category because promotions often have a generalized effect on the products within the category.

- Plan and budget publicity (including social network site presence and blogs) for your company as a whole. Only budget and plan publicity for an individual product if you introduce it or modify it in some way that may attract media attention. (Of course, exceptions exist for every rule. If you have a single bestselling product that carries your company, you need a publicity plan for it. You should also plan product-oriented activities on the web, such as blogs and fun videos that go viral, so as to keep a buzz going about your star product.)

- Plan and budget for brochures, websites, Facebook pages, and other informational materials. Be sure to remain focused in your subject choices: Stick to one brochure, one blog, one page, one bulletin board, and so on per topic. Multipurpose brochures or websites never work well. If a website sells cleaning products to building maintenance professionals, don't also plan for it to broker gardening and lawn-mowing services to suburban homeowners. Different products and customers need separate treatment.

Writing a Powerful Executive Summary

A carefully crafted executive summary is an essential component of every marketing plan. An *executive summary* is a one-page plan that conveys essential information about your company's planned year of programs and activities in a couple hundred well-chosen words or less. If you ever get confused or disoriented in the rough-and-tumble play of sales and marketing, this clear, one-page summary can guide you back to the correct strategic path. A good executive summary actually keeps everyone across the entire team (operations, sales, marketing, and outside contractors) on the same page. It's a powerful advertisement for your program, communicating the purpose and essential activities of your plan in such a compelling manner that everyone who reads it eagerly leaps into action and takes the right steps to make your vision come true.

 Draft a very rough executive summary early in the planning process as a guide to your thinking and planning. Then revise it (or, if necessary, rewrite it completely) after finishing all the other sections of your plan, because the summary (no surprise here) needs to summarize everything. When summarizing the main points of your plan, make it clear whether the plan is

- **Efficiency oriented:** A focus on efficiency means you'll be scaling up known success formulas and aiming to increase the volume of business. For example, your summary may open with high sales goals and then review the various improvements over last year that you think will help achieve the new higher goals. If you have a pretty good marketing formula already, then the plan should help you refine and scale up that formula to achieve higher sales and profits.

- **Effectiveness oriented:** This means a focus on testing and developing one or more new ways of marketing. For example, say your plan identifies a major opportunity or problem and a new strategy to respond to it. If you need to make major changes in your marketing program, then the plan is a tool for finding new, more effective marketing methods. It should include a wider range of marketing activities, along with ways of testing to see which ones work best.

If your plan has to help you overcome a problem, such as shrinking sales due to a large new competitor, state the problem clearly in the summary and also point out any links to other aspects of the business. Will the marketing plan have to be coordinated with a business plan that includes cost controls and layoffs? If so, state this fact upfront in your executive summary and make sure the rest of your business is working on the necessary changes so you aren't stuck with a problem you don't have full control over.

At the end of your executive summary, describe the bottom-line results: what your projected revenues will be (by product or product line, unless you have too many to list on one page) and what the costs are. Also, show how these figures differ from last year's figures. Keep the whole summary under one page if you possibly can.

If you have too many products to keep the summary under one page, you can list them by product line. But a better option is to create more than one plan because you probably haven't clearly thought out any plan that can't be summarized in a page. I've worked with many businesses in which marketing prepares a separate plan for each product. Dividing and conquering is the key.

Preparing a Situation Analysis

A situation analysis is the one tool every marketer needs to ensure her marketing tactics are taking advantage of real opportunities and solving real problems. In other words, it provides the context you need to move forward with your planning. Your *situation analysis* helps you define the context for your marketing plan by looking at trends, customer preferences, competitor strengths and weaknesses, and anything else that may impact sales. The question your situation analysis must answer is, "What's happening?" To answer this question, you should analyze the most important market changes affecting your company. These changes can be the sources of problems or opportunities. (See Chapter 4 for formal research techniques and sources.)

To prepare a situation analysis, you must consider challenges and trends that can affect your marketing program, be prepared for economic cycles, and review your competition's current status. After you identify these threats and opportunities, you need to give some serious thought to how to respond to them. Your marketing strategies are basically your responses to your strengths, weaknesses, opportunities, and threats, so your situation analysis feeds naturally into your strategies and plans.

Knowing what to include in your analysis

One good (and very traditional) way to organize a situation analysis, also known as SWOT analysis, is to write something for each of these four categories:

- ✔ **Strengths:** Identify the strong points of your products, brand image, and marketing programs so you know what to build on in your plan. Your strengths are the keys to your future success. For example, if your website is a strength, then your plan should focus on making it even better, and your objectives should include increased web sales.

- ✔ **Weaknesses:** Pinpoint the areas in which your products, brand image, and marketing programs are relatively weak. For example, perhaps you have several older products that are losing to hot new competitors, or maybe you rely too heavily on newspaper advertising (which is a weakness, because newspaper readership is dropping). Your plan should propose changes that shore up or eliminate weak products and practices.

✔ **Opportunities:** Your situation analysis needs to look for opportunities, such as a hot new growth market you can participate in (see Chapter 2 for help finding growth markets) or an exciting new way to reach prospective customers (see Part IV for a variety of ways).

✔ **Threats:** A *threat* is any external trend or change that can reduce your sales or profits, or make it hard to achieve your growth goals. Common threats include new technologies that create new competitors, large competitors that can outspend you, and economic or demographic shifts that cut into the size or growth rate of your customer base. Your plan needs to respond to threats effectively, so identify the main ones as accurately and honestly as you can.

Table 3-1 shows you some of the typical marketing challenges and opportunities to get you thinking.

Table 3-1   Common Marketing Threats versus Opportunities

Common Threats	Common Opportunities
New, tough competitors	New products
Economic problems or trends	New ways to promote or sell
Aging or loss of a customer base	New types of customers to pursue

You also want to make sure you review trends in your situation analysis, because trends can have a big impact on your business — for better or for worse. Identify the trends that can hurt you and plan how to respond to them; similarly, note the trends that can help you and plan how to take advantage of them. Check on the economic growth rate of the population to which you sell (the cities in which you operate if you're a regional operation, for example). Also check the growth rate of the demographic group you sell to. Are there going to be more or less people in the age range of your typical customer? Then look at technological and social trends. Is the technology you use going out of date, or is it increasing in popularity? What new lifestyle choices or trends in fashion might affect your customers' buying habits?

Being prepared for economic cycles

When preparing your business's situation analysis, you need to be in close contact with the pulse of the economy. Watch the leading published economic indicators and regularly monitor the numbers. If you notice a decline for more than two months in a row, look closely for any signs of sales slowdowns in your own industry and be prepared to take action.

Try to avoid being lulled into a false sense of security. Because the economy in the United States (and many other countries) grew at a fairly steady rate for most of the 1990s, the majority of marketers forgot to keep an eye on the economic weather. When economic growth suddenly began to slow in December 2007, those same marketers faced major problems. Now most markets face slow but steady growth but with important exceptions. The rust belt is still by and large in recession and not a great place to grow your sales, but web-based businesses; green, local, and sustainable businesses; and businesses in any of the Milken Institute's Best Performing Cities annual list (`www.best-cities.org`) may enjoy the economic and social success of their city.

The Conference Board (`www.conference-board.org`), a nonprofit in New York City, compiles an index of leading economic indicators that has successfully predicted the last half dozen recessions. However, it has also predicted five recessions that didn't occur, so if you slavishly cut back every time the economists publish negative forecasts, your marketing plans will be too gunshy and conservative. You have to take some risk to grow, but if you watch the economic weather closely, you can scale back sooner than most marketers when it becomes obvious that economic growth is slowing.

When your own sales are weak *and* economic forecasts are poor, assume the worst and cut back aggressively to weather the coming storm. To do so, I suggest you do the following:

- ✔ **Avoid large marketing commitments.** Expensive and/or long-term contracts for advertising, store rentals, and large inventories are dangerous in down times. For example, don't purchase a full year of expensive advertising. Instead, buy month to month, even though doing so may cost you a bit more. The flexibility is well worth a slightly lower discount.

- ✔ **Keep an eye on your mix of fixed and variable costs.** A *fixed cost* is one that doesn't change with sales. For example, if you have a long-term lease on an office or warehouse, you must pay the costs of that facility no matter if your sales are up or down. *Variable costs* are costs that can fluctuate, such as the cost of goods sold and commissions. A marketing plan with a lot of variable costs is relatively recession-proof because your costs will go down proportionately to sales.

Taking stock with a competitor analysis table

Gathering information about your competitors via an analysis table can help you draft a more complete situation analysis. A *competitor analysis table* summarizes the main similarities and differences between you and your competitors. You can compete more effectively after you have a good understanding of how your competitors operate and what their strengths and weaknesses are.

Use a shared Google spreadsheet document or other online team platform so all your salespeople, distributors, or friends can add competitor analysis data. Or how about going even further and cloud-sourcing input about which products are best on which dimensions?

The kinds of information you can collect about your competitors varies significantly, so I can't give you a pat formula, only suggestions. You can certainly gather and analyze samples of your competitors' marketing communications, and you can probably find some info about how they distribute and sell, where they are (and aren't) located or distributed, who their key decision makers are, who their biggest and/or most loyal customers are, and even (perhaps) how much they sell. To get their customers' perspectives, try pulling customer opinions from surveys or informal chats and group the information into useful lists to help you figure out the three most appealing and least appealing factors about each competitor. Ultimately, you want to gather any available data you can on all-important competitors and organize the data into a table for easy analysis.

A generic competitor analysis table should have entries on the following rows in columns labeled for Competitor #1, Competitor #2, Competitor #3, and so on:

- ✔ **Company:** Describe how the market perceives it and its key product.

- ✔ **Key personnel:** Who are the managers, and how many employees do they have in total?

- ✔ **Financial:** Who owns it, and how strong is its *cash position* (does it have spending power, or is it struggling to pay its bills)? What were its sales in the last two years?

- ✔ **Sales, distribution, and pricing:** Describe its primary sales channel, discount/pricing structure, and market share estimate.

- ✔ **Product/service analysis:** What are the strengths and weaknesses of its product or service?

- ✔ **Scaled assessment of product/service:** Explore relevant subjects, such as market acceptance, quality of packaging, ads, and so on. Assign a score of between 1 and 5 (with 5 being the strongest) for each characteristic you evaluate. Then sum the scores for each competitor's row to see which characteristic seems strongest overall.

- ✔ **A comparison of your ratings to your competitor's ratings:** If you rate yourself on these attributes, too, how do you compare? Are you stronger? If not, you can include increasing your competitive strength as one of your plan's strategic objectives (see the later "Clarifying and Quantifying Your Objectives" section for more on setting your objectives).

JIAN's *Marketing Plan Builder* software (www.jian.com) has a template for writing a competitor analysis table, along with many other planning tools. I helped design the program, and so I may be biased, but to my eye it's the best strategic marketing plan template out there. You may want to pick it up if you have to write a detailed plan in a hurry.

Explaining your marketing strategy

Your situation analysis identifies your weaknesses and threats, but it also identifies your strengths and opportunities. You need to take these findings and further clarify and build your marketing strategy around them to have the best chance for success. (Refer to Chapter 2 for help selecting a marketing strategy.)

If you want to help your business grow and prosper, make sure you know your marketing strategy like the back of your hand. That way you can explain your strategy, which leads to specific marketing objectives that are rolled out into marketing tactics to implement the strategy. So edit and clarify the strategy section of your plan until you're certain it explains your marketing strategy clearly.

Clarifying and Quantifying Your Objectives

After you have a handle on your current situation and also have one or a few marketing strategies in mind to help you succeed, you need to think about what objectives (such as brand building or sales growth) are realistic and appropriate for you at this time. *Marketing objectives* are quantified, measurable goals, such as "grow market share from 5 to 6 percent" and "shift 25 percent or more of our catalog customers over to website ordering."

Your chosen marketing strategies suggest specific objectives. For example, if your strategy involves opening a new territory to grow your sales, you need to set a specific goal for sales in that territory. This number becomes your objective. Unless you specify clear, measurable objectives, you won't have any idea of what the returns from the plan will be, nor will you know how to track your performance as you execute the plan.

Objectives are such a key foundation for the rest of your plan that you can't ever stop thinking about them. Yet for all their importance, they don't need a lot of words. Devote a half-page to two pages to your objectives, at most. Check out the following sections for what you need to do to come up with objectives and then quantify them.

Ecological objectives

Ecologic Brands is a young business dedicated to reducing the environmental harm of disposable bottles by making them out of recycled (and compostable) cardboard, pressed into a thin, smooth bottle shape, with a thin recycled (and recyclable) plastic liner. The innovative design was just that, a design, because packaging companies have to rely on companies that sell stuff needing packaging. So the company's founder, Julie Corbett, and her team looked for a marketing partner that strongly values sustainability and has the visibility to introduce the packaging innovation. A partnership with Seventh Generation features the distinctive Ecologic packaging for natural laundry detergent, bringing helpful sales revenue and lots of visibility and publicity to Ecologic Brands at a critical time in its development.

If you write clear, compelling objectives, you'll never get too confused about what to write in other sections of your marketing plan — when in doubt, you can always look back at these objectives and remind yourself of what you're trying to accomplish and why. These points give the plan its focus. For instance, what objectives do you want your marketing plan to help you accomplish? Will the plan increase sales by 25 percent, reposition a product to make it more appealing to upscale buyers, introduce direct marketing via the web, or launch a new product? Maybe the plan combines several products into a single family brand and builds awareness of this brand through web, print, and radio advertising to cut the costs of marketing.

Think about the limitations in your resources

Don't make your ambitions greater than the resources you have available to pull them off. If you're currently the tenth-largest competitor, don't write a plan to become the number-one largest by the end of the year. Attempting that would likely require more marketing dollars, product inventory, and such than you actually have. For example, Proof Eyewear, an Eagle, Idaho, startup, makes attractive glasses from natural, sustainably grown woods. Quite a unique product, but still, the eyeglass frame market is crowded with larger competitors. The company began by wholesaling sunglasses to hip and alternative stores, many of the small chains or one-off independents, and many of them run by and selling to younger people, just like Proof's founders. This niche market approach has helped the company grow to the point that its prescription frames are beginning to be offered by traditional optometrists, too.

Always make sure your objectives are reasonable. Would the average person agree that your objectives sound attainable with a little hard work? (If you're not sure, find some average people and ask them.) Also, make sure you have enough resources to fulfill the objectives in the available time.

Don't expect to make huge changes in customer behavior

You can move people and businesses only so far with a marketing program. If you plan to get employers to give their employees every other Friday off so those employees can attend special workshops your firm sponsors, well, I hope you have a backup plan. Employers don't give employees a lot of extra time off, no matter how compelling your sales pitch or brochure may be. As the owner of a company that does management training, I discovered that I need to adjust my firm's products and services so they fit into the training time employers are willing to spare. Such adjustments are necessary; without them, your marketing program can't succeed.

The same is true of consumer marketing. You simply can't change strongly held public attitudes without awfully good new evidence and a lot of marketing communications. In your plan, first make sure your strategies are built on strengths and opportunities. Then set realistic objectives that fit your time, money, and talents. **Remember:** You want your plan to be 100 percent achievable.

Sales are, of course, the ultimate objective of any marketing plan, so also include a realistic objective for how much you hope to sell. People usually define sales in terms of dollars of sales revenue, but that's not all that helpful in the strategic part of your plan. Instead, try to find a way to measure how well you're doing at reaching your target customers. For example, if you're launching a new pet treat, you can set an objective of getting at least 100,000 households to buy and try your product. This objective helps keep you focused on the all-important goal of spreading the product throughout your market. If enough households try and like your product, then you should get plenty of repeat business from them, and future sales should be robust, assuming you find ways to remind people to purchase (either by marketing on the web, by sending them direct mail or e-mail about the product, or by placing the product in grocery or pet stores where they'll see it). Check out Figure 3-1 for an example of how a marketing strategy leads first to specific marketing objectives and then marketing tactics.

Sample Strategy

Create a hip new brand of dog treats and sell it to younger, active pet owners.

Sample objectives:

Brand the product to appeal to hip, younger consumers.

Build awareness and interest through the web, advertising, press coverage of events, and word of mouth.

Get at least 10,000 households to try samples of the product.

Build distribution through the web and retail grocery and pet stores.

Sample tactics:

Product: Design a product that makes dogs healthier and more energetic. Brand it to appeal to younger, hip pet owners.

Pricing: Price it slightly above competitors' products to signal that it is a specialty product and to fund an aggressive marketing campaign.

Placement: Make it available both on the web and through pet stores. Expand to grocery stores as soon as volume allows.

Promotion: Create a catchy, hip brand and logo. Use events, social networks, print advertising in magazines with the appropriate demographics, and in-store displays to communicate the product's special image and message.

Figure 3-1:
Seeing how objectives and tactics flow from your marketing strategy.

© John Wiley & Sons, Inc.

Your strategies accomplish your objectives through the tactics (the Five *P*s) of your marketing plan. (See Chapter 1 for an explanation of the Five *P*s.) The plan itself explains how your tactics accomplish your objectives through your marketing program.

Summarizing Your Marketing Program

A *marketing program* (which I fully define in Chapter 1) is the combination of marketing activities you use to influence a targeted group of customers to purchase a specific product, product line, or service. Usually you find it useful to include tactics in all five of the marketing *P*s: product, price, placement, promotions, and people (refer to Figure 3-1 for a helpful example).

I suggest that you prioritize by picking a few primary marketing activities (such as web advertising, direct mail, and trade show displays) that will dominate your program for the upcoming planning period. This approach concentrates your resources for maximum impact. Make the choice carefully, and try to pick no more than three main activities to take the lead in your program. Use the (typically many) other marketing activities in secondary roles to support your primary points.

If you try to use more than three main marketing activities to a high degree, you may find it difficult to fund and support them sufficiently to make a big impact with each one because you're competing for attention with so many other marketers. The Internet, airwaves, and mailboxes are stuffed full of ads and offers, and signs and billboards elbow each other for attention everywhere. To even stand a chance of making an impact in any single marketing medium, you need to concentrate your resources so as to be able to buy plenty of visibility. A plan that spreads cash, salespeople, or other resources across too many activities and products is going to be too thin to make much of an impact. Small to mid-sized businesses must be especially careful to keep their plans focused, because they lack the deep pockets of giant marketers who routinely use many different marketing methods and tactics all at once.

As you think about your plan's tactics, drill down to the specifics of how to execute the plan and do whatever research is needed to work out the details. Perhaps you're considering using print ads in trade magazines to let retail store buyers know about your hot new line of products and the in-store display options you have for them. That's great, but now you need to get specific by picking some magazines. (Call their ad departments for details on their demographics and prices; see Chapter 7 for additional guidance on placing print ads.) You also need to decide how many and what type of ads to run and then price out this advertising program.

Do the same analysis for each of the items on your list of program components. Work your way through the details until you have an initial cost figure for what you want to do with each component. Total these costs and see whether the end result seems realistic. Is the total cost too big a share of your projected sales? Or (if you're in a larger business) is your estimate higher than the boss says the budget can go? If so, adjust and try again. After a while, you get a budget that looks acceptable on the bottom line and also makes sense from a practical perspective.

A spreadsheet greatly helps in this analysis process. Just build formulas that add the costs to reach subtotals and a grand total; then subtract the grand total from the projected sales figure to get a bottom line for your program. Figure 3-2 shows the format for a very simple spreadsheet that gives a quick and accurate marketing program overview for a small business. In this figure, you can see what a program looks like for a company that wholesales products to gift shops throughout the United States. This company uses personal selling, telemarketing, and print advertising as its primary program components. It also budgets some money to finish developing and begin introducing a new line of products.

This company's secondary components don't use much of the marketing budget when compared to the primary components (which use 87 percent of the total budget). But the secondary components are important, too. A new web page is expected to handle a majority of customer inquiries and act as a virtual catalog, permitting the company to cut way back on its catalog printing and mailing costs. Also, the company plans to introduce a new line of floor displays for use by selected retailers at the point of purchase. Marketers expect this display unit, combined with improved see-through packaging, to increase turnover of the company's products in retail stores.

If your marketing plan covers multiple customer groups, you need to include multiple spreadsheets (such as the one in Figure 3-2), because each group may need a different marketing program. For example, the company whose wholesale marketing program you see in Figure 3-2 sells to gift stores — that's the purpose of that program. But the company also does some business with stationery stores. And even though the same salespeople call on both customer groups, each group has different products and promotions. They buy from different catalogs. They don't use the same kinds of displays. They read different trade magazines. Consequently, the company has to develop separate marketing programs for them, allocating any overlapping expenses appropriately (meaning if two-thirds of sales calls are to gift stores, then the sales calls expense for the gift store program should be two-thirds of the total sales budget).

Overview of Program to Target Retail Store Buyers	
Program Components	**Direct Marketing Costs ($)**
Primary influence points:	
– Sales calls	$450,700
– Telemarketing	276,000
– Ads in trade magazines	1,255,000
– New product line development	171,500
	Subtotal: $2,153,200
Secondary influence points:	
– Quantity discounts	$70,000
– Point-of-purchase displays	125,000
– New web page with online catalog	12,600
– Printed catalog	52,000
– Publicity	18,700
– Booth at annual trade show	22,250
– Redesign packaging	9,275
	Subtotal: $309,825
Projected Sales from This Program	$23,250,000
Minus Total Program Costs	– 2,463,025
Net Sales from This Marketing Program	**$20,786,975**

Figure 3-2:
A program budget, prepared on a spreadsheet.

© *John Wiley & Sons, Inc.*

Exploring Your Program's Details

A good plan is nothing without details, and a good marketing plan is no different. After outlining your marketing program (which I walk you through in the preceding section), you need to explain the details of how you plan to use each component in your program. Devote a section to each component, which means the details portion of your plan may be quite lengthy (give it as many pages as necessary to lay out all the facts). The more of your thinking you get on paper, the easier implementing the plan will be later — as will rewriting the plan next year.

Although this portion is the lengthiest part of your plan, I'm not going to cover it in depth here. You can find details about how to use specific components of a marketing program, from product positioning to web pages to pricing, in Parts III, IV, and V.

At a minimum, this part of the plan should have sections covering the Five *P*s — the product, pricing, placement (or distribution), promotion (how you communicate with and persuade customers), and people (salespeople, customer service staff, distributors, and so on). But more likely, you'll want to break these categories down into more specific areas.

Managing Your Marketing Program

The main purpose of the management section of your marketing plan is simply to make sure that enough warm bodies are in the right places at the right times to get the work done. This section summarizes the main activities that you and your marketing team must perform to implement your marketing program. Use this section to assign these activities to individuals, justifying the assignments by considering issues such as an individual's capabilities, capacities, and how the company will supervise and manage that individual.

Sometimes the management section gets more sophisticated by addressing management issues, like how to make the sales force more productive or whether decentralizing the marketing function is worthwhile. If you have salespeople or distributors, develop plans for organizing, motivating, tracking, and controlling them. Also, develop a plan for them to use in generating, allocating, and tracking sales leads. Start these subsections by describing the current approach and do a strengths/weaknesses analysis of that approach, using input from the salespeople or distributors in question. End by describing any incremental changes or improvements you can think to make.

Make sure you've run your ideas by the people in question *first* and received their input. Don't surprise your salespeople or distributors with new systems or methods. If you do, they'll probably resist the changes, causing sales to slow down. So schmooze and share, persuade and propose, maximizing their feeling of involvement in the planning process. People execute sales plans well only if they understand and believe in those plans. Getting them involved early with idea generation and strategy development also helps gain their buy-in and implementation.

Projecting Expenses and Revenues

At this stage of preparing your marketing plan, you need to put on your accounting and project management hats. (Perhaps neither hat fits you very well, but try to bear them for a day or two.) You need these hats to do the following:

- Estimate future sales, in units and dollars, for each product in your plan.

- Justify these estimates and, if they're hard to justify, create worst-case versions.

- Draw a timeline showing when your program incurs costs and performs program activities. (Doing so helps with the preceding section and also gets you prepared for the unpleasant task of designing a monthly marketing budget.)

- Write a monthly marketing budget that lists all the estimated costs of your programs for each month of the coming year and breaks down sales by product or territory and by month.

If you're part of a start-up or small business, I highly recommend doing all your projections on a *cash basis*. In other words, put the payment for your year's supply of brochures in the month in which the printer wants the money instead of allocating that cost across 12 months. Also, factor in the wait time for collecting your sales revenues. If collections take 30 days, show money coming in during December from November's sales, and don't count any December sales for this year's plan. A cash basis may upset accountants, who like to do things on an accrual basis — see *Accounting For Dummies,* 5th Edition, by John A. Tracy (Wiley) if you don't know what that means — but cash-based accounting keeps small businesses alive. You want to have a positive cash balance (or at least break even) on the bottom line during every month of your plan.

If your cash-based projection shows a loss some months, fiddle with the plan to eliminate that loss (or arrange to borrow money to cover the gap). Sometimes a careful cash-flow analysis of a plan leads to changes in underlying strategy. One business-to-business marketer I worked with adopted the goal of getting more customers to pay with credit cards rather than invoices as the primary marketing objective. The company's business customers cooperated, and average collection time shortened from 45 days to less than 10, greatly improving the business's cash flow as well as its spending power and profitability.

Several helpful techniques are available for projecting sales, such as buildup forecasts, indicator forecasts, multiple-scenario forecasts, and time-period forecasts. Choose the most appropriate technique for your business based on the reviews in the following sections. If you're feeling nervous, just use the technique that gives you the most conservative projection. Here's a common way to play it safe: Use several of the following techniques and average their results.

Buildup forecasts

Buildup forecasts are predictions that go from the specific to the general, or from the bottom up. If you have sales reps, ask them to project the next period's sales for their territories and to justify their projections based on their anticipated changes in the situation. Then combine all the sales force's projections to get an overall figure.

If you have few enough customers that you can project per-customer purchases, build up your forecast this way. You may want to work from reasonable estimates of the amount of sales you can expect from each store carrying your products or from each thousand catalogs mailed. Whatever the basic building blocks of your program, start with an estimate for each element and then add up these estimates.

Indicator forecasts

Indicator forecasts link your projections to economic indicators that ought to vary with sales. For example, if you're in the construction business, you find that past sales for your industry correlate with *GDP* (gross domestic product, or national output) growth. So you can adjust your sales forecast up or down depending on whether experts expect the economy to grow rapidly or slowly in the next year.

Multiple scenario forecasts

If you liked what-if stories as a child, you'll love *multiple-scenario forecasts*. They start with a straight-line forecast in which you assume that your sales will grow by the same percentage next year as they did last year. Then you make up what-if stories and project their impact on your plan to create a variety of alternative projections.

You may try the following scenarios if they're relevant to your situation:

- ✔ What if a competitor introduces a technological breakthrough?
- ✔ What if your company acquires a competitor?
- ✔ What if Congress deregulates/regulates your industry?
- ✔ What if a leading competitor fails?
- ✔ What if your company experiences financial problems and has to lay off some of its sales and marketing people?
- ✔ What if your company doubles its ad spending?

For each scenario, think about how customer demand may change. Also consider how your marketing program would need to change to best suit the situation. Then make an appropriate sales projection. For example, if a competitor introduced a technological breakthrough, you may guess that your sales would fall 25 percent short of your straight-line projection.

The trouble with multiple-scenario analysis is that . . . well, it gives you multiple scenarios. Your boss (if you have one) wants a single sales projection, a one-liner at the top of your marketing budget. One way to turn all those options into one number or a series of numbers is to just pick the option that seems most likely to you. That's not very satisfying if you aren't at all sure which scenario, if any, will come true. So another method involves taking all the options that seem even remotely possible, assigning each a probability of occurring in the next year, multiplying each by its probability, and then averaging them all to get a single number.

For example, the Cautious Scenario projection estimates $5 million, and the Optimistic Scenario projection estimates $10 million. The probability of the Cautious Scenario occurring is 15 percent, and the probability of the Optimistic Scenario occurring is 85 percent. So you find the sales projection with this formula: ($5,000,000 × 0.15) + ($10,000,000 × 0.85) ÷ 2 = $4,625,000.

Time-period forecasts

To use the *time-period forecast* method, work by week or by month, estimating the size of sales in each time period, and then add these estimates together for the entire year. This approach helps you when your program (or the market) isn't constant across the entire year. Ski resorts use this method because they get certain types of revenues only at certain times of the year. Marketers who plan to introduce new products during the year or use heavy advertising in one or two *pulses* (concentrated time periods) also use this method because their sales go up significantly during those periods.

Entrepreneurs, small businesses, and any others on a tight cash-flow leash need to use this method because it provides a good idea of what cash will be flowing in by week or by month. An annual sales figure doesn't tell you enough about when the money comes in to know whether you'll be short of cash in specific periods during the year.

Creating Your Controls

The controls section is the last and shortest section of your plan — but in many ways, it's the most important because it allows you and others to track performance. Identify some performance benchmarks and state them clearly in your plan. For example:

- All sales territories should be using the new catalogs and sales scripts by June 1.

- Revenues should grow to $75,000 per month by the end of the first quarter if the promotional campaign works according to plan.

These statements give you (and your employers or investors) easy ways to monitor performance as you implement the marketing plan. Without them, nobody has control over the plan; nobody can tell whether or how well the plan is working. But with these statements, you can identify unexpected results or delays quickly — in time for appropriate responses if your controls were designed properly.

Professor Scott Shane of Western Reserve University is probably the best person at crunching U.S. census data to compute survival rates for new businesses. He reports that, after five years, approximately half of all new businesses will fail. Ouch! Shikhar Gosh of Harvard Business School tracks a different group: start-ups with major venture capital financing. These start-ups have greater resources to help them out, and their failure rate is lower, about 25 to 30 percent, but that's still a scary number. After the average small business survives its first five years, it's failure rate is also better but still not great: 30 percent of survivors will go on to fail over the second five years. I'm not trying to discourage you — quite the contrary — but I do want your strategies and plans to be realistic. Don't budget more than 10 percent of your revenue toward marketing unless you have good reason to believe (from past experience) that the return on marketing investment will be there. And don't commit to a full year of expensive marketing. A first quarter plan is more cautious, and only commits you to a fourth of a year's spending. Take it one step at a time! You want to be in that special set of small businesses that actually survives from year to year and decade to decade.

Part II
Leveraging Your Marketing Skills

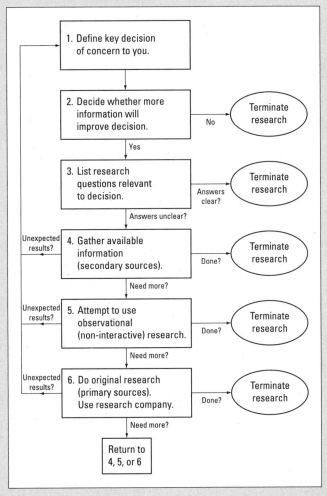

© John Wiley & Sons, Inc.

Visit www.dummies.com/extras/marketing to discover the contemporary elements of marketing success.

In this part . . .

- ✔ Analyze, analyze, analyze. Research what your competitors are doing, how the industry is looking, and what your customers really want in order to find the sweet spot for your company.

- ✔ Discover numerous ways of conducting low-cost (or no-cost) research, from conducting simple e-mail surveys and browsing databases to thinking outside the box and interviewing lost customers and children (they're naturally creative geniuses!).

- ✔ Find out how to craft a creative brief that presents the results of your brainstorming sessions in a format that allows you and others to turn creative ideas into a reality for your business.

- ✔ Appeal to customers' rational thoughts *and* their emotions in your marketing communications by developing an understanding how to engage the brain.

- ✔ Recognize — for once and for all — the true importance of excellent writing and compelling visuals in creating memorable and effective marketing communications.

Chapter 4

Researching Your Customers, Competitors, and Industry

*B*ig businesses hire research firms to do extensive customer surveys and to run discussion groups with customers. The marketers then sit down to 50-page reports filled with tables and charts before making any decisions. I rarely recommend this traditional approach, because people usually have far less time and money, let alone patience, than this approach demands.

Instead, in this chapter, I help you better understand your customers and competitors and, in the process, better understand yourself. I show you how to adopt an inquisitive approach by sharing simple, efficient ways of learning about customers and competitors. As a marketer, you need to ask questions and seek useful answers — something you can do on any budget. Often a resourceful marketer can learn something useful for free on the web and may even manage to avoid an expensive custom survey (although exercise caution with web data and opinions because they're not always accurate nor are they as likely to be relevant to your particular situation).

Knowing When and Why to Do Research

Research can tell you about your customers, competition, and industry. If you can get a better idea or make a better decision after conducting market research, then research is worth your while. Moreover, sometimes research helps you explore your identity to improve the way you position yourself in the market (see Chapter 2 for an explanation of positioning as a marketing strategy). Another key reason for conducting market research is to identify the attributes or prioritized needs your clients seek and/or value. Furthermore, research can tell you whether a communication strategy (the way an ad, website, or mailing talks to the customer) is appealing and clear. The following sections highlight the most common reasons for you to conduct market research.

Researching to find better ideas

Information can stimulate the imagination, suggest fresh strategies, or help you recognize great business opportunities. Always keep one ear open for interesting, surprising, or inspiring facts. Subscribe to a diverse range of publications, read interesting blogs, and make a point of talking to people of all sorts, both in your industry and beyond it, to keep you in the flow of new ideas and facts. Also, ask other people for their ideas.

Take advantage of the growing world of online social networking to talk to people about your product and how they view it. If you're on Facebook, Twitter, or a blog website, chat up your friends and virtual friends for opinions, suggestions, and ideas. Much of what you get back will be chaff, but you may find the grain of a great new marketing idea in there, too. Pinterest, Flickr, and Instagram are highly visual, with members' selections of photos, graphics, and other visual art rich in insights into how people are thinking, feeling, and living and how trends, needs, and concerns are evolving. A whole new art and practice of studying such websites is emerging, and you, too, can be an anthropologist of sorts, studying your own culture to seek business and marketing needs and opportunities, or even just to update the vocabulary (visual and verbal) you use in your marketing communications.

When asking for input and information on websites and in virtual web communities, be honest about who you are and why you're asking for advice. If you tell people you're in charge of marketing your product and want to know what they think of your new ad, many people will offer their views freely. If, however, you pretend to be someone outside the company who's just trying to insert business questions into an innocent chat, people will sniff you out and be angry with you for subverting their social network for business purposes. Honesty and transparency are the keys to successful research in online communities.

Don't fall into the trap of spending all your time online, though. Make a point of talking to people face to face, too. Carry an idea notebook in your pocket or purse and try to collect a few contributions from people every day. This habit gets you asking salespeople, employees, customers, and strangers on the street for their ideas and suggestions. You never know when a suggestion may prove valuable. Lee Iacocca kept an idea notebook in his early days as a marketing guy in the auto industry — and out of those jottings came the idea for the Ford Mustang, one of the biggest brand successes in history.

Researching to make better decisions

Do you have any situations that you want more information about before making a decision? Then take a moment to define the situation clearly and list the options you think are feasible. Choosing the winning ad design, making a more accurate sales projection, or figuring out what new services your customers want — these are the types of situations in which a little research can help you make important decisions. Table 4-1 shows what your notes may look like.

Table 4-1	**Analyzing the Information Needs of a Decision**		
Decision	*Information Needs*	*Possible Sources*	*Findings*
Choose between print ads in industry magazines and e-mail advertisements to purchased lists.	How many actual prospects can print ads reach?	Magazine ad salespeople can tell us.	Three leading magazines in our industry reach 90% of the market, but half of these aren't in our geographic region. May not be worth it?
	What are the comparable costs per prospect reached through these different methods?	Just need to get the costs for each method and number of people reached, divide cost by number of people, and compare.	E-mail is one-third the price in our market.

(continued)

Table 4-1 *(continued)*

Decision	Information Needs	Possible Sources	Findings
	Can we find out what the average response rates are for both magazine ads and e-mails?	Nobody is willing to tell us, or they don't know. May try calling a friend in a big ad agency; he may have done a study or something.	Friend says response rates vary wildly, and he thinks the most important thing is how relevant the customer finds the ad, not the medium used.
	Have any of our competitors switched from print to e-mail successfully?	Can probably get distributors to tell us this. Will call several and quiz them.	No, but some companies in similar industries have done this successfully.

Conclusions?

Seems like we'll spend less and be more targeted if we design special e-mails and send them only to prospects in our region. Don't buy magazine ad space for now; we can experiment with e-mail instead. But we need to make sure the ads we send are relevant and seem important, or people will just delete them without reading them.

Researching to understand love and hate

Consumer reactions to your product or service determine your success and your product's fate. Research can help you understand — and control — consumer reactions. Focus on the more extreme views that customers express — both positive and negative. If you collect a rating of all the descriptive features of your product from customers, many of those ratings will prove quite ordinary. A bank branch offers checking, savings, and money market accounts. So what? Every bank does. But a few of the features of that bank may be notably exceptional — for better or for worse. If the teller windows often have long lines at lunch when people rush out to do their banking, that notable negative stands out in customers' minds. They remember those lines and tell others about them. Long lines at lunch may lead customers to switch banks and drive away other potential customers through bad word of mouth.

On the positive side of the ledger, if that bank branch has very friendly tellers and a beautifully decorated lobby with free gourmet coffee on a side table for its customers, plus a counter where a local deli sells to-go sandwiches and salads for hurried individuals to grab lunch while getting their banking done, the bank's notable warmth and helpfulness sticks in customers' minds, building loyalty and encouraging them to recruit new customers through word of mouth.

If you gather customer ratings, you can draw a graph of all the features of your product, rated from negative through neutral to positive. Most features cluster in the middle of the resulting bell curve, failing to differentiate you from the competition. A few features stick out on the left as notably negative — you must fix those features fast! Other features, ideally, stand out on the right as notably positive. You need to nurture and expand on these features, and don't forget to boast shamelessly about them in all your marketing communications.

Do some research to understand your own *brilliance curve* (as I call it) by asking customers to rank you on a laundry list of descriptors for your business/product/service. The scale ranges from 1 to 10 (to get a good spread), with the following labels:

1	2	3	4	5	6	7	8	9	10
Very poor		Poor		Average		Good		Very good	

For example, the list of items to rate in a bank may include checking accounts (average), savings accounts (average), speed of service (poor), and friendliness of tellers (very good), along with many other factors you'd need to put on the list to describe the bank in detail. Getting customers to fill in a survey sheet is important enough that I'd consider offering them a reward for doing so. You can waive the fees on their checking account for the rest of the year if they mail in a completed form. Or (if you don't mind honest feedback) you can ask them to fill in a rating form while standing in a potentially long line.

Your high-ranking attributes from the survey represent the features customers think you do brilliantly. The low scores represent the features you need some work on. Sometimes you find yourself with a fairly long list of things (product attributes) that you don't score well on. To clarify which ones are most worthy of working on, you can ask customers to rate the importance of each listed item. Then you can focus your improvement efforts on the more important attributes.

Sometimes customers disagree about what's more and less important (some customers may value speed or convenience over price, while others want quality at almost any price, for example). When you notice a rift with some customers clearly having different priorities from others, then you have an opportunity to segment the market by catering to one specific group of customers and its high priorities (see Chapter 2 for more on segmentation strategies). You can also notice new market segment opportunities as they first emerge in real time by tracking what customers are saying about brands on social networking sites.

When you design your marketing communications, you definitely need to focus on leveraging your high-rated product attributes. Talk them up and invest even more in them to maximize their attractiveness.

Asking Really Good Questions

These days, you have an infinite amount of information at your fingertips. However, you probably don't want a million-page report, even if it's free. What you want is smart information that relates directly to important questions — questions that shape your marketing program and allow you to operate more successfully in the future.

Say you're in charge of a 2-year-old software product that small businesses use to do their planning and financials. As the product manager, what questions should you be asking? The following are the most likely:

- ✔ Should we launch an upgrade or keep selling the current version?
- ✔ Is our current marketing program sufficiently effective, or should we redesign it?
- ✔ Is the product positioned properly, or do we need to change its image?

A good question is thought provoking and affects your future actions and successes. If you come upon a really good question, research it carefully. You'll find that the first question breaks down into many more specific ones that, when answered, help you make a good decision.

How do you go about answering your question? Creative information-gathering is the key, and sometimes it helps to follow a formal research process. Figure 4-1 depicts the market research process in flowchart form.

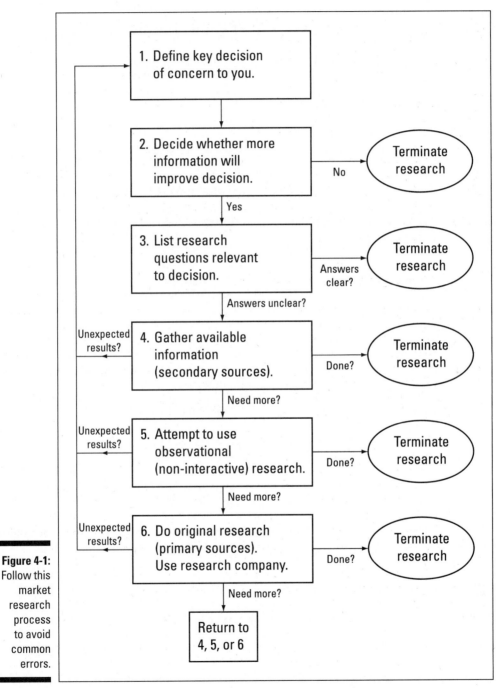

Figure 4-1:
Follow this
market
research
process
to avoid
common
errors.

© John Wiley & Sons, Inc.

Paying Wisely for Market Research

Most mid-sized to larger businesses hire market research firms to gather information for them. I'm not saying that this approach is dumb, but as a first step, it usually isn't the smartest because it guarantees an expensive, thick report when you probably just want a few clear answers.

Instead of doing a full-blown study of your own, try inserting a few questions into a *panel* — a regular survey of a group of people. A lot of vendors offer this option, including (in the United States) Darwin's Data, PaidViewpoint, BzzAgent, Viewpoint Forum, tellwut, Opinion Outpost, MyView, KidzEyes, OpinionPlace, and Panelpolls. Browse the latest lists of survey panels through a Google search, or look at sites like www.surveypolice.com, which ranks polls based on feedback from users, and then collect price points and proposals from several before choosing one to run with.

Also look into survey sites like SurveyMonkey (www.surveymonkey.com), Zoomerang (www.zoomerang.com), PollDaddy (www.polldaddy.com), Constant Contact's Listen Up option (www.constantcontact.com), and GutCheck (gutcheckit.com) for one-stop survey shopping. Working online, you can design survey questions, select a sample design, and (using your own database or, increasingly available, a sample arranged by the host site) send out your survey, collect data, and tabulate it. Does it make sense? Are you wiser as a result? Well, not every time. It takes practice and persistence to figure out how to extract useful findings from tables of survey responses, but at least it's less expensive to trial balloon some questions through these sites than through traditional full-service survey research firms.

If your website gets at least a few dozen visitors a day, it can produce free survey results for you. A question with general appeal (something everyone's invested in or curious about) may actually boost visitors at the same time it generates useful data for your marketing decisions. For instance, you could ask, "Should consumer product packages display honest information about the cost and environmental impact of the package?" A strong "yes" vote may really shake up packaging and display practices in your industry! The question would certainly attract interest from customers, bloggers, and the media in general.

Before you put out a request for proposals from research firms, ask yourself whether you can get your key questions answered in the same way you currently make your sales. If your customers order via a website, post questions for them there. If they talk to a call center, script some questions for the call center staff. If customers receive visits from salespeople or reps, brief the sales force about your questions and how to ask them without pressuring customers. However you currently talk to customers, use that channel to ask them helpful questions. It's the easiest way to gather market research for free (but not the only way; see the next section).

Researching the Low-Cost (Or Free!) Way

Knowledge is power. Power to make smart decisions that bring in customers and profits. Who wants what? Which markets are going to grow and be hot, and which aren't? It's amazing how many businesses and other entities lumber along, working hard but not stopping to gather enough information to know how to work smarter. The following sections provide a lot of ways — some cheap and others free — to boost your marketing intelligence.

Observing your customers

Consumers are all around you, and they're shopping for, buying, and using products. Observing consumers and finding something new and of value from doing so, isn't hard. And even *business-to-business marketers* (who sell to other businesses rather than end-consumers) can find plenty of evidence about their customers at a glance. For example, the number and direction of a company's trucks on various roads can tell you where its business is heaviest and lightest.

Despite all the opportunities to observe, most marketers are guilty of Sherlock Holmes's accusation: "You have not observed, and yet you have seen." Observation is the most underrated of all research methods. For example, when managers from the Boston Aquarium wanted to find out which attractions were most popular, they hired a researcher to develop a survey, but the researcher told them not to bother. Instead, he suggested that they examine the floors for wear and for tracks on wet days. The evidence pointed clearly to certain attractions as the most popular ones: The floors in front of those attractions had the most wear, and damp paths led to the attractions that visitors preferred to go to first. That was easy!

Find a way to *observe* one of your customers as he uses one of your products (note the emphasis on observe; don't just watch). Be nosey. Bring along a pad and pencil and take care to notice the little things. What does he do, in what order, and how long does he spend doing it? What, if anything, does he say? Does he look happy? Frustrated? Disinterested? Does anything go wrong? Does anything go right — is he surprised with how well the product performs? Take detailed notes and then think about them. I guarantee that by doing so you end up gaining at least one insight into how to improve your product.

In business-to-business marketing, the first step in really seeing your customers clearly may be simply to clarify what professional titles your target customers are choosing and using these days. If you're marketing technical tools for managing distributed databases, who should you target your message toward? Database managers, no doubt, but what if that function is being covered by people who don't have "database" in their titles, like systems administrators or technology managers? And how do these people think, what are they talking about with their peers, and what kinds of concerns and new training are they interested in these days?

Professional social networks like LinkedIn (with 5.5 million high-tech managers and counting) can provide a window for your online investigations if you take time to study what people are posting and how their professional peer-to-peer networks are constructed. And when you're clear as to which LinkedIn members are prospects, you can engage them through your own networking and also pay-per-click ads on LinkedIn.

Asking customers questions

Customer satisfaction changes with each new interaction between customer and product. If your product makes customers happy, they come back. If not, adios. Recruiting new customers costs anywhere from 4 to 20 times as much as retaining old ones (depending on your industry), so you can't afford to lose customers — which means you can't afford to dissatisfy them.

You can gather input from your customers in a variety of easy ways, because your customers interact with your employees or firm. You can put a stamped postcard in shipments, statements, product packages, or other customer communications. Include three or fewer simple, nonbiased survey questions, such as, "Are you satisfied with this purchase? no = 1 2 3 4 5 = yes." Also, leave a few lines for comments in case your customers have something they want to tell you. You generally get low response rates with any such effort, but that's okay. If someone has something to tell you, he lets you hear about it. And even a 5 percent response rate gives you a steady stream of input you wouldn't have otherwise.

Getting a customer's e-mail address is easy and natural. Send a follow-up e-mail after each purchase with a request to provide feedback and a handful of simple, quick questions, such as "What do you like most about the product you just purchased?" and "Did anything go wrong or frustrate you in the process of purchasing from us?" Customers with something to say often e-mail back a few well-chosen words telling you just what they think. But always make it specific and easy to respond, and always say what you will do with the response. People like to help out when they know what the cause or purpose is.

Find out (by asking or browsing) what social media your customers and prospects like and use. Do many of them use Flixster to watch movies or use Instagram to send photos and videos they make? Younger target audiences probably use both sites heavily. Or perhaps your prospects are older professional or academic people who use LinkedIn or Academia.edu. Wherever they're networking, you may be able to observe or even interact with them about their needs, attitudes, and brand preferences. And, of course, your blog can attract comments and subscribers (whose e-mails you then capture so you can ask them to comment on future blogs). Maintain a presence on the social media sites where your customers are, and offer a link to your blog there to draw in comments and followers.

Keeping up with customer opinion is a never-ending race, and you need to make sure you're measuring where you stand relative to those shifting customer expectations and competitor performances. The best way to do that is by asking questions directly of your customers. The next sections offer some advice for asking those questions and some sample questions you can use as models.

Posing your questions

Survey research methods are the bread and butter of the market research industry and for good reason. You can often gain something of value just by asking people what they think. Of course, survey methods have their shortcomings: Customers don't always know what they think or how they behave, and even when they do, getting them to tell you can be costly. Nonetheless, every marketer finds good uses for survey research on occasion.

Watch out for overly general questions or ratings. Any measure based on a survey that asks customers to "rate your overall satisfaction with our company on a scale of 1 to 10" isn't much use. What does an average score of 8.76 mean? Sure, that's pretty high, but are customers satisfied? You didn't really ask them. I favor asking a series of more specific questions, such as, "Was it convenient to do business with us?" Then track progress on each specific measure in a repeat survey after you make changes to see whether you've improved in ways that customers notice.

Considering some sample questions

Your customer satisfaction must be high, relative to both customer expectations and competitors' ratings, before that customer satisfaction has much of an effect on your customer-retention rates. Make sure you ask tough questions to find out whether you're below or above customers' current standards. You can ask customers revealing questions, similar to the following list:

1. **Which company (or product) is the best right now?**

   Give a long list with instructions to circle one, and give a write-in blank labeled *Other* as the final choice.

2. Rate [your product] compared to its competitors:

Far worse   *Same*   *Far better*
1   2   3   4   5   6   7

3. Rate [your product] compared to your expectations for it:

Far worse   *Same*   *Far better*
1   2   3   4   5   6   7

You can get helpful customer responses by breaking down customer satisfaction into its *contributing elements,* the specific aspects of service that customers notice and care about. (Focus groups or informal chats with customers can help you come up with your list of contributing elements.)

For example, you can ask the following questions about an overnight letter carrier:

1. Rate Flash Deliveries compared to its competitors on speed of delivery.

Far worse   *Same*   *Far better*
1   2   3   4   5   6   7

2. Rate Flash Deliveries compared to its competitors on reliability.

Far worse   *Same*   *Far better*
1   2   3   4   5   6   7

3. Rate Flash Deliveries compared to its competitors on ease of use.

Far worse   *Same*   *Far better*
1   2   3   4   5   6   7

4. Rate Flash Deliveries compared to its competitors on friendliness.

Far worse   *Same*   *Far better*
1   2   3   4   5   6   7

5. How likely are you to recommend Flash Deliveries to an associate or friend?

Not likely   *Neutral*   *Likely*
1   2   3   4   5   6   7

The final question addresses *word of mouth,* what the customer is likely to tell other prospective customers about your service or product. If you do well on specific questions about attributes of importance to the customer, then the customer will likely recommend you to others, thereby helping you build your market share.

Many marketers also pose questions or prompts about awareness (List the brands you've heard of), intent (Which brands are you interested in trying?), and usage and repeat purchase (Did you like it? Would you use it again?) to flesh out their research. Compare rates across this set of questions to see where your biggest challenge lies. If most people are unaware, promote! If they aren't repurchasing, then improve or retarget.

Comparing your approach to that of your competitors

When you compare your marketing approach to competitors, you easily find out what customers like best. Make a list of the things that your competitors do differently than you. Does one of them price higher? Does another give away free samples? Do some of them offer money-back guarantees? Make a list of at least five points of difference between your business and its major competitors based on an analysis of marketing practices. Now ask ten of your best customers to review this list and tell you what they prefer — your way or one of the alternatives — and ask them why. Keep a tally. You may find that all your customers vote in favor of doing something differently than the way you do it now.

Also gather information on your competitors' marketing programs, especially how they're getting their marketing messages out. Are they advertising a fast-growing social network you hadn't considered? If you have even a modest budget, consider the options for online research by firms like WhatRunsWhere (www.whatrunswhere.com), AdClarity's media intelligence (www.adclarity.com), Competitrack (www.competitrack.com), Adbeat (www.adbeat.com), or AdGooroo (www.adgooroo.com), all of which can help you benchmark your ads (especially online advertising) against top competitors or role-model marketers (larger companies with the resources to spot new opportunities and trends quicker than you).

Creating a customer profile

Collect or take photographs of people (from Facebook or e-mail thumbnails, and with the individuals' permission) who you characterize as your typical customers. Post these pictures on a bulletin board — either a real one or a virtual one like Pinterest (set this board to private because it's definitely not for sharing beyond your marketing team) — and add any facts or information you can collect about these people. Consider this board your customer database. Whenever you aren't sure what to do about any marketing decision, sit down in front of your bulletin board and use it to help you tune in to your customers and what they do and don't like. For example, make sure the art and wording you use in a letter or ad is appropriate to the customers on your board. Will they like it, or is the style wrong for them?

Entertaining customers to get their input

Entertaining your customers puts you in contact with them in a relaxed setting where they're happy to share their views. Hold a customer appreciation event or invite good customers to a lunch or dinner. Use such occasions to ask for suggestions and reactions. Bounce a new product idea off these good customers, or find out what features they'd most like to see improved. Your customers can provide an expert panel for your informal research — you just have to provide the food! (After they get to know you, they may be happy to give you ongoing quick feedback via a chat room, Twitter, or a group text message, especially if they use these media routinely themselves.) Another effective way to do this is to create a customer advisory board that recognizes top customers and makes them feel appreciated and heard.

Using e-mail to do one-question surveys

If you market to businesses, you probably have e-mail addresses for many of your customers. Try e-mailing 20 or more of them for a quick opinion on a question. The result? Instant survey! If a clear majority of respondents say they prefer using a corporate credit card to being invoiced because the card is more convenient, well, you've just gotten a useful research result that may help you revise your marketing approach.

Always ask people for their e-mails whenever you interact with them, through your website or in reality, so as to build a large e-mail list.

E-mailing your question to actual customers or users of your product is far better, by the way, than trying to poll users of social networking websites for their opinions. Sure, you may be able to get a bunch of responses from people on Twitter, but would those responses be representative of your actual customers? Probably not. Your best source for quick feedback about any marketing question is your in-house list of e-mails, especially if you market to businesses.

Surfing government databases

Many countries gather and post extensive data on individuals, households, and businesses, broken down into a variety of categories. In the United States, you can find out how many people earn above a certain amount of money a year and live in a specific city or state — useful if you're trying to figure out how big the regional market may be for a luxury product. Similarly, you can find out how many businesses operate in your industry and what their sales are in a specific city or state — useful if you're trying to decide whether that city has a market big enough to warrant you moving into it.

If you want to use the web to explore useful data compiled and posted by various agencies of the U.S. government, go to `www.census.gov`, the main gateway into U.S. Census data on households and businesses. This site is your portal to U.S. data from the economic census (which goes out to 5 million businesses every five years) and the Survey of Business Owners.

Another useful way to explore U.S. Census Bureau data is to go to `factfinder2.census.gov`, which has links on the navigation bar to the left. Click on People to see breakouts and trends by age, sex, disability, education, employment, income, relationships, and so forth, or click on Business and Government to find out how many of which types of employers, manufacturers, wholesalers, or retailers are where.

Establishing a trend report

Set up a *trend report,* a document that gives you a quick indication of a change in buying patterns, a new competitive move or threat, and any other changes that your marketing may need to respond to. You can compile one by e-mailing salespeople, distributors, customer service staff, repair staff, or friendly customers once a month, asking them for a quick list of any important trends they see in the market. (You flatter people by letting them know that you value their opinions, and e-mail makes giving those opinions especially easy.) Print and file these reports from the field and go back over them every now and then for a long-term view of the effectiveness of your marketing strategies.

If you don't work for one of the handful of largest and best-funded companies in your industry, then your trend analysis should also include careful tracking of what those giants are doing because they may be setting marketing or product trends that affect the rest of their industry. Tracking media coverage is easy on Google or other search engines. Also read their press releases on PR Newswire (`www.prnewswire.com`) to see what they have to say about themselves. Track changes on major competitor websites, too, either manually or (if you want to follow several) by using a service such as LXR Marketplace (`www.lxrmarketplace.com`), Watch My Competitor (`www.watchmycompetitor.com`), Competitor Monitor (`www.competitormonitor.com`), Compete (`www.compete.com`), Alexa (www.alexa.com), or Digimind (www.digimind.com). (You can also use these services to track competitor mentions in social media and compare them to mentions of your brand.) Benchmark your website against competitor stats on HubSpot's Marketing Grader (marketing.grader.com).

Note: Researchers wanting to do their own competitor monitoring at no cost may use Google Alerts to create customized search criteria for tracking competitor online activity (www.google.com/alerts).

Analyzing competitors' collateral

Print out or clip and collect marketing materials (brochures, ads, web pages, and so on) from competitors and analyze them by using a *claims table.* Open up a spreadsheet (or draw a blank table on a piece of paper or poster board) and label the columns of this new table, one for each competitor. Label each row with a feature, benefit, or claim. Add key phrases or words from an ad in the appropriate cell. Include one to three of the most prominent or emphasized claims per competitor. When filled in, this claims table shows you, at a glance, what territory each competitor stakes out and how it does the staking. One may claim it's the most efficient, another the most helpful, and so on.

Compare your own claims with those of your competitors. Are you impressive by comparison, or does a more dominant and impressive competitor's claims overshadow you? Do your claims stand out as unique, or are you a me-too marketer without clear points of difference? The claims table helps you see yourself as customers do — through the lens of your marketing materials and in comparison to your competitors. Using this table often delivers uncomfortable moments of truth that force you to rethink and improve your marketing approach. (But be careful to base your claims on genuine strengths, not just advertising fluff, by understanding what makes you strong — see the following section.)

Researching your strengths

Perhaps the most important element of any marketing plan or strategy is clearly recognizing what makes you especially good and appealing to customers. To research your strengths, find the simplest way to ask ten good customers this simple but powerful question: "What's the best thing about our [fill in the name of your product or service], from your perspective?"

The answers to this question usually focus on one or, at most, a few features or aspects of your business. Finding out how your customers identify your strengths is a boon to your marketing strategy. After you know what you do best, you can focus on telling the story about that best feature whenever you advertise, do publicity, or communicate with your market in any way. You can also concentrate your spending and improvement efforts on the factors customers like most about you.

Investing in your strengths (versus your competitors' strengths or your weaknesses) tends to grow your sales and profits more quickly and efficiently.

Probing your customer records

Most marketers fail to mine their own databases for all the useful information those databases may contain. Study your customers with the goal of identifying three common traits that make them different or special. This goal helps you focus on what your ideal customer looks like so you can look for more of them.

A computer store I'm a customer of went through its records and realized that its customers are

- ✔ More likely to be self-employed or entrepreneurs than average
- ✔ More sophisticated users of computers than most people
- ✔ Big spenders who care more about quality and service than the absolute cheapest price

This store revised its marketing goal to find more people who share these three qualities. What qualities do your customers have that make them special and that would make a good profile for you to use in pursuing more customers like them?

Testing your marketing materials

Whether you're looking at a letter, catalog, web page, tear sheet, press release, or ad, you can improve the piece's effectiveness by asking for reviews from a few customers, distributors, or others with knowledge of your business. Do they get the key message quickly and clearly? Do they think the piece is interesting and appealing? If they're only lukewarm about it, then you know you need to edit or improve it before spending the money to publish and distribute it.

Customer reviewers can tell you quickly whether you have real attention-getting wow-power in any marketing piece. Big companies do elaborate, expensive tests of ads' readability and pulling power, but you can get a pretty good idea for much less money. Just ask a half dozen people to review a new marketing piece while it's still in draft form. An even simpler (and very effective) technique is to make a list of possible headlines for an ad on a piece of paper and ask potential customers (or anyone in the industry whom you can talk into helping) to check the one they like best.

Interviewing defectors

Your company's records of past customers are an absolute gold mine of information that can be easily overlooked. Use these records to figure out what types of customers defect, when, and why. If you can't pinpoint why a customer abandoned you (from a complaint or a note from the salesperson, for example), try to contact the lost customer and ask him directly.

Tracking down lost customers and getting them on the phone or setting up an appointment with them may prove difficult, but don't give up! These lost customers hold the key to a valuable piece of information: what you do wrong that can drive customers away. Talk to enough lost customers and you see a pattern emerge. Probably three-fourths of them left you for the same reason (which can be pricing, poor service, inconvenient hours, and so on). That reason is for you to find out.

When your research reveals the most common reason for customers to defect from your product or service, do something about it. Plug that hole so you lose fewer customers down it. Keeping those customers means you don't have to waste valuable marketing resources replacing them. You can keep the old ones and grow every time you add a new one.

Asking kids about trends

In consumer marketing, it's best if customers think you're cool and your competitors aren't. Because kids lead the trends in modern society, why not ask them what those trends are? Ask them simple questions like, "What will the next big thing be in [name your product or service here]?" Or try asking kids this great question: "What's cool and what's not cool this year?" Why? Because they know, and you don't. For example, if teenage girls know what the next cool color combo will be, the way to find out is simple: Ask them what colors they want their room to be. (Or visit social media sites that skew toward younger members and see how they're decorating their pages.)

Even in business-to-business and industrial markets, kids and their sense of what's happening in society can be helpful, often giving you early indicators of shifts in demand that may have an impact all the way up the line, from consumers to the businesses that ultimately serve them.

Creating custom web analytics

Web analytics are readily available for your websites and blogs, but they're mostly traffic counts of various kinds. You probably want to know about sales, not just visitors. What are the most meaningful indicators of success on the web? Just as you (hopefully) do off-line, track online sales, repeat sales, lead collection, quality of leads (measured by rate of conversion), sign-ups, use of offers (such as you may post on a business site on Facebook, for example), and overall revenue and returns from e-marketing. These numbers tell the story of your marketing successes and failures online and give you something to learn from as you go.

Many firms now offer quite sophisticated and powerful research tools for tracking your brand and competitors on the web, especially in social media. It may be worthwhile to look into the costs and benefits of options such as Brandwatch Analytics (www.brandwatch.com) or The Social Studies Group (www.socialstudiesgroup.com), a firm that studies conversations on social networking sites to gain ideas about attitudes and trends.

Riding a Rising Tide with Demographics

Demographics — statistics about a population — are kind of boring to most people. Yet trends in the ethnic makeup of your market, its average age, its spending power, and its family structure provide you with good clues as to how your marketing ought to change. Aside from major new technologies, demographic trends are the biggest source of opportunities for businesses, yet they're not regular reading for marketers or managers. Here are some opportunity-laden demographic shifts or trends concerning women in the United States (by way of illustration, but you can find more trends by doing your own research):

- ✔ The pay gap between men and women is closing, and women in their 20s are making 93 percent of the income of men of the same age. Still a gap but far smaller than in previous decades, which suggests growing purchasing power for women and an opportunity to reorient marketing toward them in financial services, realty, travel, continuing education, and many other markets. (My source: a widely web-available press release from PewResearch, dated December 11, 2013.)

- ✔ More women than men are going to college, and the trend is growing over time. Add this to a slower trend toward pay parity, and the suggestion is that women will outpace men as the educated and leading gender at some point in the not-too-distant future. Headhunter firms, makers of power suits, and just about everybody else, are you aware of and ready for this shift in gender roles? (My source: a free-on-the-web chart from a Forbes.com article, which shows the trends in enrollment for men and women over several decades.)

✔ In the 2008 U.S. Presidential election, 70.4 million women voted, compared to 60.7 million men (my source: the Center for American Women and Politics [CAWP], which posts such data freely on their website). The pattern emerged again in 2012 gubernatorial races, with women outvoting men by between 3 and 11 percentage points, depending on the particular race (also sourced for free from CAWP in a November 9, 2012, press release).

Women outvote men, and they're also more likely to be socially liberal, which is producing (especially among younger voters) a big advantage for the Democratic Party, reinforced by the advantage it has with most minority voting blocks. But beyond politics, the voting power of women supports a general trend toward more active social and economic involvement and the likelihood that an emerging female social leadership trend is beginning that will have wide-reaching impacts on how people live, work, and shop.

✔ Women are having their first child (if they choose to have children) later than they used to, the mean age being 25.1 years. Record numbers are waiting to have children until their 30s or 40s. Also, births are declining slowly from year to year. These statistics are consistent with women going to college and pursuing professional careers at record rates. This tells you that you're better off introducing products for professional women than new mothers if you want to enjoy a growth market. (My source: "The Changing Demographic Profile of the United States," freely posted on the web by Congressional Research Service and a rich source of insight into dozens of interesting trends, from population growth to immigration to longevity.)

I've highlighted trends in one area, women in the United States, by way of example, but your demographic research should zoom in on a topic of your own choice. (For example, the U.S. Census Bureau projects a rapid increase in Hispanic Americans to 30 percent of the population by 2050, one of the hottest demographic trends.) Pick a growing group you think you may be able to tailor your offerings and message to. Back out of shrinking categories and regions. Go where the growth is, and you'll ride the tide to demographic success. For example, start a professional club or association for women in a growing urban or regional market in the United States, and you're guaranteed a fast-growing market for your services, which makes everything else about your marketing a *lot* easier!

Chapter 5

Engaging Your Marketing Imagination

In This Chapter
▶ Achieving breakthroughs by being creative
▶ Putting your creativity to use in advertising, product development, and brand building
▶ Making meetings and teams more creative
▶ Taking charge of the creative process, from initiation through implementation

*G*ood marketing depends on creativity. Marketers must always seek new approaches and reject assumptions and limitations. If circumstances aren't going your way — sales are slow, the boss rejects your proposals, customers complain about service, or your website isn't getting enough traffic — then remember to take some time out for creativity. The right creative idea at the right moment can turn the marketing tide your way. With the techniques I describe in this chapter, you can harness your organization's marketing imagination and spark incredible results — even if you're a small business owner wearing the hats of marketing, sales, service, custodial, and so on.

Turning the Tide with Creativity

Being creative can make a huge difference in your marketing in more ways than you may think. Not sure how to get started thinking creatively? I recommend checking your current level of creativity to see whether you're maximizing the benefits creative marketing brings. The next sections help you determine whether you're being as creative as you need to be and whether making creative changes is worthwhile.

Conducting a creativity audit

A *creativity audit* can help you see whether you're taking a creative approach as often as you should. Respond to each of the statements in Table 5-1 as honestly as you can, circling 1 if your answer is "rarely," 5 if your answer is "frequently," and the numbers in between if your answer is somewhere between "rarely" and "frequently."

Table 5-1	Marketing Creativity Audit
Marketing Creativity Actions	*Rating*
We make improvements to the selection, design, packaging, or appearance of our product(s).	1 2 3 4 5
We experiment with prices, discounts, and special offers to achieve our marketing goals.	1 2 3 4 5
We find new ways to bring our product(s) to customers, making buying or using the product(s) more convenient or easier for them.	1 2 3 4 5
We update and improve our brand image and the ways we communicate that brand image.	1 2 3 4 5
We experiment with creative new ways of communicating with customers and prospects.	1 2 3 4 5
We improve the look and feel of our sales or marketing materials.	1 2 3 4 5
We listen to customer complaints or objections, and we find creative ways to turn those complaints into our next business opportunities.	1 2 3 4 5
We change our marketing message before customers get bored with it.	1 2 3 4 5
We reach out to new types of customers to try to expand or improve our customer base.	1 2 3 4 5
We share creative ideas and have freewheeling discussions with all the people who are involved in marketing our product(s).	1 2 3 4 5

Add up all the numbers you circled to get a score between 10 and 50. Depending on your score, you can rate your marketing creativity as very low, low, medium, or high. You need to be in the medium range at minimum, but preferably in the high range, to gain bottom-line benefits from creativity.

- 10–19 = very low
- 20–29 = low
- 30–39 = medium
- 40–50 = high

As this audit points out, don't leave anything alone in marketing. If you can identify any unchanging elements of your sales, service, advertising, mailings, or anything else that touches the customer, you've just found your next marketing project, detailed in the following section.

Changing (almost) everything

The smartest move to make when you have a stunning, timeless, classic success in marketing is to leave it alone. But how many of those kinds of concepts can you think of? An orange paper box of Arm and Hammer baking soda. The Apple logo. A Swiss Army Knife. Coca-Cola in a classic bottle. I can't easily add many more items to this list, and I'm willing to bet your ad campaign hasn't generated concepts that are in this list of timeless classics. If you're not changing many of the aspects of your marketing program, I have to ask you a really tough question: Why not?

The most common reason marketers give for not changing their technique is that it takes too much effort. Nobody got around to thinking about it. As I bet you already guessed, I don't consider that much of a reason to leave well enough alone.

Mess with everything. In fact, why not make a quick list of the aspects of your marketing program that nobody has looked at or tried to improve for the last year or two? Jot down three to six aspects of your program that you tend to take for granted (such as your brochures, web home page, or price list). Tada! You've just made your creative to-do list. The remaining sections in this chapter can help you come up with creative improvements for the items on that list.

Are you working on the marketing for a start-up? If so, you still have to make that to-do list, but you get to backseat-drive for the established leaders in your new market. What do other marketers ignore or fail to change and improve? Perhaps they always mail the same kinds of catalogs to the same lists on the same schedule throughout the year (in which case, why not send yours two weeks sooner in a larger, more attractive format, with a link to special offers on your website?). Or maybe the industry you're entering always uses the web to support its sales but not as its lead marketing medium (you can try reversing that formula). Whatever the constants, list them now. Your list shows you the assumptions that you must question if you really want to become the next industry leader.

Getting creative with marketing

Need some help getting your creative energy flowing? Check out these tips and real-life examples:

- ✔ **Cross-promoting with a dissimilar business:** A nursery created a spring cross-promotion with a local bookshop. It provided the bookstore with bookmarks that featured garden plant identifications and photos, along with coupons worth 10 percent off all plant purchases. In exchange, the bookstore provided the nursery with a reference library of gardening books; the nursery included a sign on the rack thanking the bookstore for providing the books, along with coupons offering 10 percent off on purchases at the bookstore.

- ✔ **Creating an instant buzz in a target market:** The owner of a new pizza restaurant used *door-hangers* — small printed ads on heavy paper with a cutout at the top so they can be hung on front door knobs — to promote take-out dining. She hired kids from a local college to distribute the door-hangers in dorms and on houses and apartments in her neighborhood. The door-hangers included a summary of the menu, a phone number and website for placing orders, and a code for entering a contest to win a dozen party-sized pizzas and three dozen free sodas. The door-hangers and contest attracted a lot of attention, and soon business was booming.

- ✔ **Making a splash in public:** A chiropractor had one side of his car decorated with a gigantic picture of a comfortable-looking sleeping person. On the other side was a picture of the same person, shown as a skeleton to illustrate how well aligned her spine was. The car drew considerable attention and increased new patient inquiries by 200 percent in the month following its introduction.

Applying Your Creativity

Advertising — whether on the web, in print, TV, radio, outdoors, at the point of purchase, or elsewhere — is a key area of application for creativity. If you work in the advertising industry or use advertising in your marketing, you're dependent on creativity for your success. Too many other ads compete for their attention. Only the most creative ones cut through the clutter, attract attention, and make a permanent mark on consumer attitudes.

Think of the role of creativity in advertising as a vehicle for building relationships between your brand and your prospects. I find this a particularly powerful way to think about advertising's role in marketing — and you can make this role possible with the addition of creativity to your web communications and ads. Marketers use creativity to add something special and unique that accentuates a brand's differences and helps it stand out in consumers' eyes.

To apply creativity to your business, identify your best sources of creative ideas and give some thought to the constraints you'll bump into when applying creative ideas (such as budget limitations). Applied creativity has a purpose — to boost sales and profits and to help your marketing program succeed. The more sources you can work with, the better because you'll get a lot of creative ideas. Then you need to check those ideas against a list of your major constraints. Do they fit your brand and marketing message? Are they unique? Or has some competitor used them recently? You get the idea, so grab a chart pad and make a table like the one in Figure 5-1 to help you identify your own list of sources and constraints.

Sources	Constraints
- Metaphors and analogies	- Your brand's personality
- Word play	- Good taste
- Humor	- Your budget
- New trends	- What competitors have already
- New technologies	done
- Unmet needs	- Other people's patents,
	trademarks, and copyrights

Figure 5-1: Identifying your creativity sources and constraints.

© John Wiley & Sons, Inc.

To assist you with applying creativity to your marketing, the following sections provide different options for you to try.

Writing a creative brief

Any and all marketing materials, from advertisements and brochures to websites and packages, benefit from the use of a *creative brief,* a document that lays out the basic purpose and focus of a specific marketing piece and provides some supporting information that gives you grist for your creative mill.

Always include the following components in a creative brief:

✔ **Objective statement:** State what the marketing piece is supposed to accomplish in your objective statement. Make the goals or objectives clear and specific (note that one objective is easier to accomplish than many). The objective statement also includes a brief description of whom you're aiming the ad at, usually a group of customers. This target group's reactions determine whether you accomplish an objective.

✔ **Support statement:** Include the product's promise and the supporting evidence to back up that promise in your support statement. You use this point to build the underlying argument for the persuasive part of your marketing piece. The support statement can be based on logic and fact, or on an intuitive, emotional appeal — either way, you need to include a basis of solid support.

✔ **Tone or character statement:** A distinct character, feel, or personality is what you're going for in your tone or character statement. You choose whether the statement should accentuate the brand's long-term identity or put forth a unique tone for the ad itself that dominates the brand's image. The choice generally flows from your objectives, such as wanting to pull in a lot of shoppers for a special Labor Day sale. In this case, you, as a local retailer, want to give your event a strong identity, so you need to define an appropriate tone for your ad. In contrast, a national marketer of a new health-food line of sodas should build brand identity, so her creative brief needs to focus on defining that brand identity.

✔ **Constraints:** Perhaps you face budgetary constraints, or you need to avoid certain terms, concepts, or images that your competitors have already used. Your brand image or product personality may also constrain you to approaches that are consistent with it. Be sure to give your constraints careful thought and list them as clearly as possible. Ask important questions to ensure that you're aware of any potential constraints. Such questions include the following:

• Are there actions a designer can't do with your logo, like change the color?

• Are you trying to avoid looking like a particular competitor?

• Do you have to have vector art so that all images can be scaled up for big posters and scaled down for a blog or web page?

• Is it important to produce work that can be shown both in full color and in black and white, depending on the medium and variations in your budget, or that can be adapted easily from a still image to an animated one?

Clearly defining your constraints is perhaps *the* most essential part of writing your creative brief. Why? Because knowing the parameters in which your marketing piece needs to operate gives structure to your ideas and can prevent you from getting hung up on one that just won't work.

Say that you're asking a graphic designer to work up an ad concept. You need to let her know what the dimensions of the ad will be when it runs and what file format it needs to be submitted in. If you're not sure, have the designer talk to the ad rep who's selling you the ad space to make sure the design is consistent with the ad specifications. And don't forget that those specifications are more than just technical. They also include important do's and don'ts related to your brand image or personality, constraints imposed by the competition and their legal protection over intellectual property (such as a branded tag line you can't use), and so forth. (See Figure 5-1 for an exercise you can do to define constraints that should be mentioned in a creative brief.)

To put it all together, think about the task of designing a new booth for a trade show. If you write a creative brief first, you have to define what the booth should accomplish and what sort of customers you want to aim it at (the objective statement demands that you make these decisions). You also have to review (and maybe do some creative thinking about) the evidence available to support your company's claims to fame. What may make you stand out among exhibitors at a trade show? If you aren't sure, then use the demands of the support statement to do some research and creative thinking. Make sure you have your evidence at hand so your ideas for booth design can communicate this evidence effectively. Finally, you have to define the tone of your booth, or think about your company's overall image and how the booth can reflect that image in its tone. The tone or character statement requires this step.

As this example illustrates, the creative brief forces you to do some helpful foundational thinking about the booth before you actually start designing it. As a result, you've made your designs more focused and objective driven than they would be otherwise.

Including creativity in product development

After you have your creative brief in hand (see the preceding section for help writing one), you're ready to start brainstorming or using any other creativity tools you care to try (see the "Generating Rich Ideas" section, later in this chapter, for some helpful tools). The creative brief gives you a clear focus and some good working materials as you apply your creativity to product development. You can use your creative brief for any marketing communication or for any situation in which you must design something creative to communicate and persuade. Sometimes what you need to design is a new or improved version of your product.

New products must be innovative to stand out. Managing a product development team so that it's optimally creative and effective means first putting together the right team. That generally means a *diverse* team, one that includes the full range of knowledge that may be relevant. You need to include different functions, from sales and marketing to manufacturing and engineering, in the creative process. Why? Because they all have different knowledge bases that help generate good ideas. You need to bring them in eventually anyway, so why not now?

In mid-sized and larger companies, forcing closer interaction between research, business planning, marketing, and technical staff — as Kraft Foods does — is essential. That company (which generates several new products every year) uses a variety of conference-type events, training, and cross-functional teams to mix up its people and help them make those unobvious connections between their different knowledge bases. Small-business marketers need to pull together diverse development teams by reaching out to their distributors, customers, friends, and acquaintances to broaden their technical and social perspectives and fuel their imaginations.

Considering creativity and brand presentation

One of the most important steps you can take in marketing is to create a strong, appealing, distinctive, and easily identifiable brand image. Everyone knows the world's top brands, such as Google, Apple, eBay, or IKEA. Ferrari's rearing stallion logo and Nike's swish are unmistakable. How did these brands rise to the top? Partly by using creativity appropriately in the development of their brand images and logos. And they stay near the top because their logos are distinctive, appealing, and (something to think hard about) relatively timeless.

Many hot, new brands go through a boom and then fail to stick. They get modified or replaced. Take MeetMe, Inc., which was the fastest-growing brand in 2013 (www.meetme.com). It started life as MyYearbook.com but achieved breakout success by changing name and adding a smiley face to its logo. So is MeetMe soon going to be up there with classics like Coca-Cola? Maybe, but in 2014, the company is pushing a new video-dating service on www.getcharm.com, with a distinctive scripted version of the word *Charm* as its logo. Either the first two logos hemmed in the product developers, or someone in marketing is twitchily creative and can't leave the logo alone long enough to make it a classic.

Creativity doesn't play quite the role you may think in the creation of a powerful brand. Clarity, consistency, and strength seem to be more important than creativity when developing a brand name and logo, so you need to be careful to avoid being *overly* creative with your ideas. Try being creative in the following ways:

- ✔ **Start with a clear, simple, strong logo.** Logos are supposed to symbolize the product, so keep them clear and simple and use them consistently until they become highly recognizable.

- ✔ **Put the logo in front of consumers in association with appealing products.** You earn brand equity by doing a good job. Your product and service need to be valuable to customers.

✔ **Include a steady flow of good marketing communications to create a brand that everybody knows and respects.** This communication can include everything from packaging and ads to websites and good social media exposure. Always keep communicating. Never let your marketing program fall silent.

Interbrand (www.interbrand.com) is the largest consultancy specializing in branding, and it publishes an annual list of brands ranked by their value. For example, Interbrand still values the Coca-Cola brand identity highly but finds its value isn't growing rapidly, unlike more creative, faster-moving brands such as Google. Table 5-2 examines the ten top brands as of 2013 (you can check Interbrand's website for the most recent rankings). The style and coloring notes are based on my observations of these brands' marketing pieces.

Table 5-2	**Examining Elements of the World's Ten Top Brands**	
Brand	**Style**	**Coloring**
Apple	Friendly, distinguishable Apple design	White, gray
Google	Fun, unusual lettering	Multicolored, commonly blue, red, yellow, and green
Coca-Cola	Flowing, classic script	Red
IBM	Strong block letters	Blue with white
Microsoft	Plain, clean, modern lettering (changed after 25 years from black italic in 2012)	Gray lettering, small red-green-blue-yellow cube (derived from the Windows colorful logo and added to the corporate brand in 2012)
General Electric	Elegant, traditional monogram of initials (GE)	Blue with white
McDonald's	Curving, arch-like *M*	Yellow
Samsung	Off-center blue oval, with a unique letter *A*	White in print, often silver without the circle on phones
Intel	Lowercase modern letters in an energetic circle	Blue
Toyota	Clean block lettering combined with elegant modern logo of elliptical forms	Red in print, often silver on vehicles

As Table 5-2 shows, these top brands and their logos share two important common factors:

✔ **Simple, word-based designs and names:** By making the logo readable, the designers of these top brands made them especially easy to learn and recall. One exception to this simple and easy-to-read or say-out-loud plan is the top-ranked brand, Apple Computer, Inc. This company's logo, an apple with a bite taken out of it, defies the rule that great brands spell out their names, but the association between the image and the name is a no-brainer.

✔ **Simple, strong, conservative colors:** Blue and red dominate the top brands; yellow or gold, silver or gray, and green also appear. Brands that use two colors (such as 26th-ranked IKEA and 19th-ranked Amazon) usually draw from the conservative palate of blue, red, white, silver or grey, and black, with the occasional splash of yellow or gold. Having a creative mix of multiple colors is rare but not unheard of. Second-ranked Google does it, and so does 28th-ranked eBay, but most of the top brands favor a single color. Microsoft's corporate logo consisted of black type only, until in 2012 it was redesigned in a more modern gray type, with a colorful cube to leverage the strength of the Windows logo, while still keeping it clear and clean. Blues are usually navy (dark) but occasionally lighter (think HP and BMW). It's interesting that one could draw all the top 100 brands reasonably accurately with fewer than ten colors.

The goal of the top brand formula (which combines simple, word-based designs and strong, traditional colors) is to create a design that's highly readable and clear to anyone, anywhere, whether shown large or small, in print, on a product, or on the web. Although exceptions exist to every good formula, I suggest that you start forming your brand identity by following this formula and seeing how it works for you.

Although great brands usually stick to simple, clear lettering and a conservative color palate, they build their value through creative advertising, creative product designs, and creative distribution to make sure consumers are excited about them. Keep your creativity on a fairly short leash when designing your brand identity, but let your imagination have a good run when it comes to designing other elements of your marketing program.

Generating Rich Ideas

Artists practice creativity every day, but people in business generally don't. As a result, many businesspeople have remarkably few creative ideas in a day, or even in a year. So how can you start acting creatively? What's involved in generating unusually creative ideas?

First and foremost, give yourself permission to be creative in your work. After all, creativity requires you to let the mind's engine sit in idle, and you can't be creative if you're busy returning e-mails and phone calls or rushing to finish the day's paperwork. Go ahead and budget time for creativity, and use that time to open yourself up through new and different ways of working, asking questions, and exploring your marketing problems and opportunities. How much time? Well, if creativity is the most powerful and profitable of the marketing skills, how often do you think you should use it? One hour a month? One hour a week? One hour a day? One day a week? You have to figure out exactly how much creativity time you need based on what your product or company demands.

Additionally, seek out inspiration. Collect stories of creative marketing, using a bulletin board (in your office or on Pinterest), a large-sized index card box, a PowerPoint slide show, or another creative idea for how to store and display your examples. Jump the fence into other arenas, collecting creative actions from organizations and industries far from your own to make this collection more novel. Once a week (perhaps at Friday bag-lunch sessions), gather your team, pull out examples, and share your ideas. Which do you like best? Why? Could you try something similar (or creatively different) in *your* business? If your creative well begins to run dry after a few such sessions, consider opening up the group to virtual participants. Crowdsource creative examples and suggestions, and then review them at your weekly creative lunches. Oh, and don't eat the same old sandwich you always have. It's a creativity session! Take turns bringing in novel foods. When the taste buds are opened up, the mind usually follows.

The sections that follow can help you develop new ideas in all sorts of ways you may never have imagined. (For even more, see my companion title, *Business Innovation For Dummies,* published by Wiley.)

Coming up with new ideas from simple activities

Creativity isn't a science; it's a habit involving the use of a loose collection of flaky behaviors. Like soaking up information, questioning the problem, tossing ideas back and forth with an associate, and then setting the whole issue aside to incubate in the back of your mind while you do something else. So plan to work in different ways when exercising your creativity.

Here's a list of great activities that spur you to engage your imagination in new and unusual ways (when I lead creative retreats for marketers and ad agencies, I use dozens of ideas like these to get us going):

✔ **Seek ways to simplify.** Can you come up with a simpler way to explain your product or your business and its mission? Can you cut your two-page brochure down to ten words? Can you reduce the length of a headline in your print ad from eight words to one? Most marketing and advertising is too complicated and can stand to be simplified. Creative insight can help simplify and clarify all aspects of your marketing. Simple is good because simple helps make your message bold, attracting attention and zapping the key idea immediately into the customer's mind.

✔ **Think of a famous person from history and imagine that he or she is your spokesperson.** How would this person change your packaging, advertising, website, and so on? For example, what would George Washington do to sell more of your product? Can you tie your brand into Washington in some way? Might his famous crossing of the Delaware River become a metaphor for competitors' customers who need to be led over to your new and better product? "Follow me, customers. Victory awaits us on the other side of the river, where the new XYZ Brand has set up a more comfortable camp for you!" (Yes, that's a silly idea, but you'd be amazed how often great marketing starts with silly ideas.)

✔ **Cut out faces from magazine ads and look for one that expresses an appealing new personality for your product.** See whether you can use that personality in packaging and advertising or on the web. The process of matching people to your brand can help determine the look, feel, or tone of your branding.

✔ **Come up with ways to advertise or communicate to customers with really small messages.** This constraint forces you to clarify and codify your message in interesting ways. Try designing stamps, stickers, one-second TV or radio commercials, lapel pins, bumper stickers, or a miniature book that comes with a magnifying glass. See what else you can imagine. One of these ideas may actually prove useful for you. Even if you don't use any of them, the exercise may get you thinking in fresh ways about marketing communications.

✔ **Brainstorm ways to advertise or communicate to customers with really big messages.** Forcing yourself to change the scale of your thinking can free creative ideas, and if you communicate in unusual ways, you may attract more attention from customers. Could you advertise with dirigibles, oversized billboards or murals, or a message in which each word appears on a separate sign, spread along a one-mile stretch of road? (You can adapt this old-fashioned concept to e-mail with a series of one-word messages.) How about renting a large truck or bus and covering it with a marketing message or your brand name? Or maybe something simpler and zanier — like sponsoring a contest for who can bake and eat the largest cookie and then inviting the media to cover the event? Wait, I've got it! Why not make the largest alligator in the world into your mascot? Think big. You want to have a big impact, right?

✔ **Come up with interesting but inexpensive gifts you can give customers.** Everyone gets pens with the company name on them — that's boring. But what if your branded pens are different and better? Perhaps they're the only ones that glow in the dark? Or maybe they have riddles on them and consumers can win a contest by entering their answers on your web-site? Try to think of some novel gift ideas. Focus on items that make the customer say, "Wow!" or "Hey, that's cool; I can really use that."

✔ **Find new places to advertise.** Can you think of places to put messages to your customers that nobody in your industry has used before? An auto insurance agency could run an infomercial on the televisions that have been installed at some gas pumps. A men's health clinic could display its business cards in men's public restrooms. A computer repair service could offer a free laptop clinic under a tent in an urban park as a way to build awareness of its brand and abilities. The possibilities are practically endless.

✔ **Think of at least ten ways to get a famous person to use your product.** Go ahead, give this one a try. Maybe you can come up with an idea good enough to actually pitch to the celebrity. Celebrities can bring media attention to a new product if they decide they like it.

✔ **Cut out five stunningly beautiful, strange, or otherwise eye-catching pictures from an issue of *National Geographic* magazine.** Write a head-line for each one that relates that picture to your product. This exercise may lead you to a great new ad concept that you can then turn into a fin-ished design by obtaining the rights to use a similar photograph from a stock photography company. (If you want to use nice images like these in your advertising, you need to purchase the rights. See *Marketing Kit For Dummies,* 3rd Edition [Wiley], for my starter collection of photographs you can use in your advertising.)

Making creativity a group activity

When confined to a conference room for a morning, most groups of people do little more than argue about stale old ideas. Or even worse, somebody sug-gests an absolutely terrible new idea, and the rest of the group jumps on it and insists that the suggestion is great . . . thus eliminating the need for *them* to think. If you hope to get a group to actually be creative, use structured group processes. That means you need to talk the group into going along with an activity such as brainstorming.

In the following sections, I include some of the best group creativity techniques. I know that all these techniques work because I've used them often with a wide variety of groups. Note that these techniques generally produce a list of ideas. Ideally, it's a long and varied list, but it's still just a list. So be sure to schedule some time for analyzing the list to identify the most promising ideas and then develop those ideas into full-blown action plans. (Refer to my book *Business Innovation For Dummies* [Wiley] if you need further instruction on how to facilitate high-results creative sessions.)

Brainstorming

The goal of brainstorming is to generate a long list of crazy ideas, some of which may be surprisingly helpful. Brainstorming gets people to do *out-of-the-box thinking* in which they generate unusual ideas beyond their normal thought patterns. Don't let your group just go through the motions of brainstorming. To really get into the spirit of it, people must *free associate* — that is, allow their minds to wander from current ideas to whatever new ideas first pop up, no matter what the association between the old and new idea may be.

You may need to encourage your group by example. If you've stated the problem as "Think of new ideas for our trade show booth," you can brainstorm a half dozen ideas to start with, just to illustrate what you're asking the group to do: a booth like a circus fun-house, a booth shaped like a giant cave, a booth in the form of one of your products, a booth decorated on the inside to look like an outdoor space complete with blue sky and white clouds overhead, a booth like the Space Shuttle Launchpad featuring hourly launches of a scale-model of the Shuttle, a booth that revolves, or a booth that offers free fresh-popped popcorn and fresh-baked cookies to visitors.

These ideas aren't likely to be adopted by the average company, but they do illustrate the spirit of brainstorming, which is to set aside your criticisms and have some fun generating ideas. The rules (which you must tell the group beforehand) are as follows:

- ✔ **Quantity, not quality:** Generate as many ideas as possible.
- ✔ **No criticism of another member's suggestion:** No idea is too wild to not write down.
- ✔ **No ownership of ideas:** Everyone builds off of each other's ideas.

After you share the rules, set up a flip chart and start listing everyone's crazy ideas for the next trade show booth, catalog mailing, web-based promotion, or whatever else you want your brainstorming session to focus on.

If you need to narrow down a long list, give participants three votes and let them pick their favorites, and then tally the votes to find the top-rated ideas. Looking at the ideas one at a time, ask the group to try to build on each of them. If there isn't a clear winner after that, vote again, and then build again, but also allow each person to add a wild-card new idea at the beginning of or any time during this round.

Question brainstorming

Question brainstorming involves generating novel questions that can provoke your group into thinking more creatively. This technique follows the same rules as brainstorming, but you instruct the group to think of questions rather than ideas.

So if you need to develop a new trade show booth that draws more prospects, then the group may think of the following kinds of questions:

- ✔ Do bigger booths draw much better than smaller ones?

- ✔ Which booths drew the most people at the last trade show?

- ✔ Are all visitors equal, or do we want to draw only certain types of visitors?

- ✔ Will the offer of a resting place and free coffee do the trick?

These questions stimulate good research and thinking, and their answers may help you create a new and successful trade show booth.

Wishful thinking

Wishful thinking is a technique suggested by Hanley Norins of ad agency Young & Rubicam and one that he has used to train employees in his Traveling Creative Workshop. The technique follows the basic rules of brainstorming, but with the requirement that all statements start with the words *I wish.*

The sorts of statements you get from this activity often prove useful for developing advertising or other marketing communications. If you need to bring some focus to the list to make it more relevant to your marketing, just state a topic for people to make wishes about. For example, you can say, "Imagine that the Website Fairy told you that all your wishes can come true — as long as they have to do with the company's website."

Analogies

Analogies are a great creativity-inspiring device. You don't think I'm serious, I know, because the idea sounds so trivial. But many experts define creativity as making non-obvious combinations of ideas. A good analogy is just that.

 I once saw a great example of an analogy in a drug company's print ad. The ad showed a painting of a person about to put a huge, old-fashioned key into a keyhole in the wall. The caption next to this illustration read: "Imagine 'intelligent' drugs that could tell sick cells from healthy ones, and then selectively destroy the targeted ones." Illustrations often use metaphors or analogies when trying to communicate a complex topic such as selective drug therapies.

To put analogies to work for you, ask your group to think of things similar to the subject or problem you're thinking about. At first, group members come up with conventional ideas. But they soon run out of these obvious answers and must create fresh analogies to continue. For example, you may ask a group to brainstorm analogies for your product as a source of inspiration for creating new advertisements about that product.

Ads for the iPhone described it as having "a level of precision you'd expect from a finely crafted watch," which evokes thoughts of elegantly engineered gems of yesteryear — an interesting new way to describe a smartphone. But analogies can also miss their mark, so be careful. For example, a classic ad from the 1950s introduced DuPont's then-new miracle plastic, cellophane, by showing a stork delivering a baby wrapped up in a clear plastic bag. Apparently, nobody at the ad agency noticed that it looked like the baby was about to suffocate. And watch out especially for tasteless, biased, or offensive analogies, such as in a recent print ad for the Mercedes-Benz S-Class sedans that boasts about their high safety level by comparing their air bags (where more really is better) to a woman with eight breasts. Not as appealing an illustration as they hoped it would be, as you might imagine! Many analogies could be worth mentioning within a creative session in hopes of leading to more or better ideas, but in the end, only the good ones should be retained.

Pass-along

Pass-along is a simple game that helps a group break through its mental barriers to reach free association and collaborative thinking. You can read the instructions here, in case you've never heard of the game:

- One person writes something about the topic in question on the top line of a sheet of paper and passes it to the next person, who writes a second line beneath the first.

- Go around the table or group as many times as you think necessary.

This game can be done with any number of people, from 3 to 20. In general, you're trying to fill up a full page of lined paper, so bigger groups need fewer cycles. If people get into the spirit of the game, a line of thought emerges and dances on the page. Each previous phrase suggests something new until you have a lot of good ideas and many ways of thinking about your problem. Players keep revealing new aspects of the subject as they build on or add new dimensions to the preceding lines.

Say a team of marketing and salespeople meets to generate concepts for the product development department of a bank. Sure, that sounds like a tough assignment — what in the world can be new about banking? But you, the creative marketer, pick a subject and pass the paper around:

Subject: How can we make our customers' personal finances run better?

Pass-along ideas:

- Help them win the lottery.
- Help them save money by putting aside 1 percent each month.

✔ Help them save for their children's college tuition.

✔ Help them keep track of their finances.

✔ Give them a checkbook that balances itself.

✔ Notify them in advance of financial problems, like bouncing checks, so they can prevent those problems.

One idea leads to another. So even if the first idea isn't helpful, associating new ideas from the first one can produce useful thoughts. A bank probably can't get into the lottery ticket business (I'm sure there's a law against that). But after the members of this group thought along those lines, they came up with some practical ways of increasing their customers' wealth, like plans that can transfer money to savings whenever there's a surplus after regular bills have been paid.

Here's another fun pass-along idea: Ask people to help you find 20 words that rhyme with your company or brand's name in the hope that this list may lead you to a clever idea for a new radio jingle, YouTube video, or banner ad.

Managing the Creative Process

If you think of creativity as generating wild and crazy ideas, you're right — but only one-fourth right. Yes, you have to do some open-minded thinking to come up with creative concepts. But to actually benefit from your creativity, you need to have a mix of activities that includes exploring for new ideas and developing the best of them into practical applications in your ads, products, sales presentations, or other marketing activities.

In my creativity workshops, I show people how creativity needs to follow a four-step process to actually be of practical use in business. Here's the process:

1. **Initiate.**

   In this step, you recognize a need or opportunity and ask questions that launch a focused creative process. For example, you may take a look at your brochure(s) and ask yourself whether you can use an illustration and a catchy headline to make the brochure more exciting and powerful. Or if you run a women's clothing store, you may recognize the need for a January sale to clear out fall and winter styles and make room for new spring fashions. Thoughts like these stimulate creative thinking and give it a practical focus. A creative brief (see the earlier "Writing a creative brief" section) is useful at this stage of the process.

2. Imagine.

In this step of the creative process, you engage in the imaginative, wild-and-crazy thinking that taps into your artistic side. The brainstorming techniques I cover in the earlier "Brainstorming" section are good for this stage; your goal is to see how many wild ideas you can generate. It's a good idea to assemble a group to help you at this stage.

3. Invent.

Now you need to get more practical. Take a critical look at all of the wild ideas you imagined and choose one or a few that seem most promising. Work on them to see how to make them more practical and feasible for your application. For example, if you're working on a way to announce a 40 percent storewide discount at a women's clothing outlet, one of your creative ideas from Step 2 may have been "have nude models stand in the window, waving to passersby to attract public attention to the sale." It's an impractical idea at best, but can you use it as raw material for inventing a good promotion? One store I know of did by putting three full-sized mannequins in the window, each wearing only a poster board on a string around the neck. The first poster said "40%," the second one said "OFF," and the third said "EVERYTHING." It was an eye-catching display, and it communicated the message — but it took an inventor's persistence and practicality to translate a crazy idea into effective communication.

4. Implement.

Finally, you need to complete the creative process by pursuing successful adoption or implementation of your new idea or design. You may have a great design for a new brochure, but you can't make money from it until you carefully select a printing method and find a way to distribute that brochure to prospects (even an e-brochure, distributed only on the web). Or if you're designing a window display for a retail store, implementation may mean finding the right mannequins, signs, lighting, and so on and setting up the display according to the creative concept or plan.

You may need different sets of talents to imagine wild ideas and to implement them in a practical way. In fact, each of the four steps in the creative process (initiating, imagining, inventing, and implementing) requires different types of behavior. By knowing this fact, you can discipline yourself to change your style as you move through a round of creativity that follows the four steps of the creative process.

Alternatively, you may want to tap into the different creative styles of multiple people to take advantage of those who are particularly well suited for one or another of the steps in the creative process. When I work on creative projects in marketing, I'm particularly good at bringing imagination to the project, so I usually try to team up with someone who complements me by being really good at implementation.

Tapping Highly Creative Contributors

If you feel like creativity could be a bit of a blind spot for your organization, give yourself an A+ for honesty and then give some thought to assembling a special team or panel (they could be volunteers) to help you develop creative ideas. Most businesses don't have strong creative blood in their veins, so they fail to harness the full power of creativity. But many managers and marketers fail to recognize that they're lacking in this key dimension of success. Or even if you are quite creative, it can help to draw in other creative ideas to supplement your own.

To find out where you (or your organization) fall on the creative scale, ask yourself questions like the following.

Are you really a creative genius?

An April 2012 survey of 5,000 people funded by Adobe (maker of software used in many creative endeavors) revealed that 50 percent of U.S. respondents describe themselves as creative, a higher percentage than in other countries surveyed. Either Americans are (as usual) grossly overconfident in their abilities, or the sample was biased toward Abobe software users because most studies peg the incidence of highly creative personalities at far lower rates. I've done idea-generating and creativity training with people from hundreds of U.S. workplaces over the past 20 years, and in my experience, an incidence of 1 in 20 (5 percent) highly creatives is a generous estimate. But that's a different kind of statistic because it's based on *my* observations of people attempting to do creative work, which may be quite different from individuals' self-assessment of their ability. From these two data points, you could say that about half of Americans feel like they could and should be creative, but less than 1 in 20 apply creativity to work often enough for it to be a fluid, easy process for them.

Openness to experience (one of the "Big Five" personality dimensions and the one that correlates best with overall creativity and exploratory behaviors) is distributed on a bell curve, with less than 10 percent of people scoring in the top fifth of the scale. These outliers are likely to be innovative marketers or entrepreneurs, but most people won't be as naturally inclined toward seeing market opportunities or bringing creative energy to their marketing communications.

Some traits that mark an open, creative personality include inventive, curious, quick to understand new ideas, unconventional, and a tendency to become deeply absorbed in a creative task. Ask yourself whether your friends and family would naturally apply these descriptors to you. If so, you probably rate as exceptionally open and creative. If not, pull together a panel of people who sound more like those descriptors.

How do you tap into those crazy creatives when you need them?

Some marketers practice idea-generating techniques and strengthen their creative muscles so they can tap into their inner creative genius when needed. Others find it easier to outsource creativity. Because breakthrough marketing demands a much larger-than-average dose of creativity, you must flex yourself and think much more creatively than usual by adopting creative methods (see *Business Innovation For Dummies* [Wiley]).

Or you need to reach out to those whacky rarities who really are creative and open-minded to a fault, like me, I confess, which is why I always include the topic of creativity when I teach or write about marketing. However, business-school professors don't even cover the topic when they teach marketing or write textbooks; instead, these professors have personalities that measure closer to normal on the openness scale, making creativity a bit of a blind spot for them. Don't let it be a blind spot for you! Ad agencies seek out creative personalities, and often have "creative departments" to serve your needs. Or seek artists, inventors, and other people whose résumés demonstrate a high level of creativity, and ask them to consult or spend a day in a brainstorming session with you.

Chapter 6

Pumping Up Your Marketing Communications

- -

In This Chapter

▶ Grabbing attention with impressive communications

▶ Persuading by communicating to the whole brain

▶ Informing prospective customers with effective marketing materials

▶ Drawing customer traffic to your place, event, or web presence

▶ Rising above the marketing-writing muck and developing visual appeal

- -

You need to communicate constantly in marketing. The more effectively you communicate, the better you'll build sales and attract new customers. What's the difference between good and poor marketing communications? The single most important difference is *impact*. Good communications have the desired impact; poor communications don't.

The goals of your marketing communications should be twofold: to build awareness of your brand and offerings, and to stimulate interest in and purchases of them. You can accomplish these closely related goals by increasing the quality and quantity of your marketing communications. This chapter helps you do just that by showing you how to prioritize your communications, improve your writing, select stellar visuals, and more.

Pursuing Your Communication Priorities

The best marketing communications are frequent, clear, consistent, attention-grabbing, persuasive, and accurate. To gauge how well you're incorporating these priorities in your marketing communications, you need to conduct a *marketing communications audit*. This section goes into depth on these six priorities and how you can conduct an audit.

Perform your own marketing communications audit by first gathering examples of the ways in which you communicate with customers and the market in general. Include everything anyone sees, hears, or even smells and touches, including traditional advertising, mailings, web communications, packaging, signs, and so forth. Don't forget to add snapshots of public communications — or lack thereof — on your building and vehicles to the pile of samples.

After you have your samples of all the ways in which you communicate, create a spreadsheet or table with each type of communication down the left side as labels for rows (for example, blogs, Google ads, trade magazine ads, and trade show booths). Then create columns for the following items:

- Your estimate of what you spend per year on that type of communication

- The *frequency* (quantity) of that communication, rated as very low, low, medium, high, or very high

- The clarity of each communication (does it make its point sharply, quickly, clearly, well?), rated as very low, low, medium, high, or very high

- The consistency of the communication's message (does it reinforce a clear theme that can be seen in the other communications, too?), rated as very low, low, medium, high, or very high

- The *stopping power* of the communication (in other words, how attention-grabbing it is), rated as very low, low, medium, high, or very high

- The persuasiveness of the communication, rated as very low, low, medium, high, or very high

- The accuracy of the communication, rated as very low, low, medium, high, or very high

Anything that doesn't get high scores across the board should be dropped from the program or greatly improved.

Achieving high frequency without sacrificing quality

Quantity and quality are equally important in marketing communications. The goal of *quantity* (or *frequency,* as it's referred to in the marketing world) is to get your marketing message out repeatedly to the majority of people in your potential market. On the flip side, *quality* is the effectiveness of the communication (how powerfully it brings the message home to the target reader, viewer, or listener). You never want to trade quality for quantity by cutting back on writing, design, and production costs. The trick is to create high-quality communications that lend themselves to frequent, inexpensive placement.

Follow these steps to increase the frequency of your exposures:

- **Look for ways to piggyback a marketing message on anything and everything that has exposure.** For instance, at the bottom of all your e-mails, add a one-sentence marketing message (complete with live links to your website and Facebook page). Literally, anything that people see or hear, from your mailings to your building to the sound track while on hold or in the lobby, is a potential option for your marketing message.

- **Seek out new media that offer prime exposure at a very low cost.** New media — whether new social networking sites or blogs, or more traditional outlets that are just emerging on the scene — are a bargain until they mature, so take advantage of the low cost of advertising with them. Additionally, newly launched magazines (especially business-oriented titles and regional or city-oriented monthlies and weeklies) usually offer bargain rates on advertising for the first year or two of their existence. Also check out Twitter and Instagram. Instagram is currently a deal for advertisers because it's the latest new place to go. (Emerging social media often skew toward the young, by the way, so make sure the demographics work for your marketing program.)

- **Promote your website constantly.** The number of existing websites run into the billions, so don't think the various Internet search engines will do the job of driving customers to your web door. Instead, bid on key terms and spend a little money every month to drive searches your way. (See Chapter 10 for the inside scoop on web marketing tactics.)

- **Maximize your web exposure with multiple narrowly focused websites, blogs, and ads.** Many marketers think they need just one big, well-done website. Sure, such a site is the hub of your web marketing wheel, but don't stop there. Create informational blogs and web pages. Dedicate a website to one particular product. Join web communities with high traffic (such as eBay, Facebook, Pinterest, Twitter, and craigslist) and set up listings, stores, or auctions according to their rules. The web is an inexpensive place to communicate, so it's a natural avenue for increasing your frequency of exposures.

- **Give away helpful content.** The web is a great place to share helpful information and how-to advice that relates to your business and its expertise. Try websites, blogs (your own or ones you sponsor), Facebook business pages, Pinterest boards, or Twitter (which can summarize key points and let people know about a white paper on a website, for example). Giving away information builds trust and can generate brand recognition and sales leads. In the bad old days before the web exploded, it cost money to print up content, and businesses rarely gave anything away. Now it's free to post it, so the best strategy for any marketer is to become a publisher of useful content, not just ads and sales pitches. I'm going to call the chimney sweep whose website I've been using all along to discover how to optimize the performance of my wood stove (for a simple example).

✔ **Consider postcards for customer mailings.** Most postcards (except for the oversized ones) receive a lower postage rate and are quick and easy for the recipient to digest. Instead of mailing infrequent, expensive letters or catalogs, send creative, eye-catching postcards to your list every week and see what happens. Include URLs to web promotions and helpful content, or add QR (quick response) codes to each postcard so customers can scan them with their phones and be directed to a promotion or a source of richly useful, timely content.

✔ **Use QR codes to draw mobile customers to your website or attract leads and upsell with special offers.** Link QR codes to video, web store special offers, useful web content or other links (optimized for small scale display on phones), and place the QR code on packaging, store windows, mailings, signs, or display ads on the subway. People in transition or in cue are often willing to scan a code and see what the deal is. If you're a do-it-yourselfer, check out Kaywa (`qrcode.kaywa.com`) or alternatives like GOQR (`www.goqr.me`) and ScanLife (`www.scanlife.com`) for surprisingly easy-to-use QR code generation and management.

To keep your frequent marketing communications high in quality, avoid offering deals every time you communicate. When you mail coupons or advertise a special discount, you add the lost profit from the discounts to your costs of communicating. Make your core communications be about the brand, not the price. Build awareness. Build knowledge. Remind people of the one, two, or three things that make you special; then remind them that you're here and ready to do business. Coupons, special offers, blow-out sales, and other aggressive price-oriented messages should *not* be the main focus of your marketing communications. (I'm warning you because I see this mistake made all too often.) If you need to stimulate an immediate response, promote a special event that isn't about price cuts or discounts.

Being clear

Clarity is the first job of the marketer. Successful marketing communications have a clear, solitary marketing message: what's great about your brand or product. Sure, many people remember the highly attention-getting ads, but the more routine marketing communications do most of the heavy lifting in your average marketing program. And what makes these heavy lifters successful? Clarity.

To create your single, clear message that focuses on your brand's or product's best attribute, follow these steps:

1. **Position the product in your customers' minds.**

   You need the right positioning strategy as a foundation — along with products that follow through on the promises you make. A *positioning strategy* is a statement of how you want customers to think and feel about your brand, product, or service. It describes how you're positioned in their minds and hearts. You can describe your positioning with attributes and adjectives (such as *fast, helpful, reliable,* or *sexy*). You can also describe your positioning with comparisons to competitors *(faster than a BMW)* or metaphorical comparisons *(faster than a speeding bullet)*. See Chapter 2 for details if you don't already have a clear positioning strategy taped to the wall above your desk.

2. **Craft a basic appeal (motivational message) that gets that positioning across.**

   You need to figure out what you can say that clearly conveys the gist of your positioning strategy. Take the basic statement of how you want people to think of your product and convert it into a message that may actually convince them. For example, if you want to introduce a new, healthier kind of pizza made solely with organic and low-fat ingredients, your positioning statement may be: "healthier pizza that doesn't sacrifice taste." Okay, now craft the basic appeal that may convince others to see the pizza that way. Here's a possibility with appeal: "Instead of fighting to keep your kids from eating the unhealthy junk-food pizzas they love, why not give them healthy pizzas that are actually better tasting, too."

3. **Find a creative idea — something that packages your appeal in a message so compelling that people get it immediately.**

   The message should persuade people of your point or convince them to give your product or service a shot. Try to find a clear, simple way to state your message that's also creative enough to make it memorable. Continuing the example, you're marketing a pizza positioned for parents as healthy food that their kids will love. Now, what creative idea can you come up with to turn this appeal into a compelling communication? Here are some options:

   - Mother goes to pick-up window to get prescription for child and is shocked when the pharmacist reads the doctor's note and then pulls a fresh-baked pizza out of a big oven, boxes it, hands it across the window, and says, "Give him as many pieces as he wants, day or night."

   - Kids stare longingly through the glass-fronted case of a candy store, in such a crowd that it's hard to even see what has drawn their attention. It turns out to be the newest flavor of the low-fat, organic pizza.

   - A journalist is interviewing swimmers on a remote tropical island where the average age is higher than anywhere else in the world. In response to the question, "What's the secret to your amazing health and longevity?" a tanned and fit grandmother says, "We don't do anything special. We just order out for pizza every night." She then dives off a cliff into a pool of tropical water. The pizza, of course, is from a little old mud hut with the logo of your brand over its door and a crowd of village children outside a window, hands out, happily receiving slices of the magical pizza.

4. **Develop, edit, and simplify your creative idea until it's clear and fits the medium you want to communicate it in.**

   Note that your choice of medium is partially determined by your message — and by the creative idea you select to get it across. To tell a story, you may choose television advertising if your budget is large. A streaming video version for your website or a radio ad version of the story will cut your costs compared to TV advertising (see Chapter 9). If you prefer the really low-cost option, you can have a cartoonist do a series of drawings in comic-strip format and place them on your website or turn them into a print ad or flier. Even better, start with that series of drawings, and hire a whiz kid to animate them into an entertaining short film posted to YouTube and also displayed on your latest blog and on your website.

What if you can't come up with a really clever, creative idea that gets the point across clearly and simply? Then don't force it. Don't focus so much on creativity that you fail to make your point clearly. If you have to make a choice between creativity and clarity, opt for clarity. Simply communicate the basic message in clear language. Repeat a clear message often enough (see the preceding section, "Achieving high frequency without sacrificing quality," for more info), and people will remember it even if you haven't entertained or wowed them with your creativity.

For example, a web-based distributor of office supplies wanted to tell office managers that its warehouses were located all across the country and that it delivered on a next-day basis even though it didn't have traditional retail stores to make its presence visible. The distributor eventually settled on a simple but clear message — "We're always here when you need us" — and used it in all of its communications, from catalogs and packaging to the web.

Being consistent

After you craft your marketing message and come up with one or more ways to communicate it clearly, be consistent! If you repeat a clear, well-focused message, people will eventually get it. Make sure you ask yourself how consistent your marketing communications are.

To check your consistency, gather a diverse sample of your own marketing communications (mailings, website printouts, photos of signs, print ads, and so forth). Lay them out on a conference table or post them around a room. Enlist one or more helpers, preferably people who have keen eyes for detail and are good at editing. Examine your samples for variations and inconsistencies. Look closely at how you describe the product and its benefits as well as the verbal and visual style of each communication. If some are informal and others are formal, that counts as an inconsistency. If print ads use bold black Rockwell Extra Bold (a type style) for their headlines and your website uses blue Helvetica, note this inconsistency, too. Also look closely at how the brand name and contact information are presented. They should always appear in exactly the same form and style.

Even if an individual ad, web page, mailing, sign, or other communication is clear and well designed, it won't work well unless it's consistent with your other communications. Nobody remembers what you say in marketing unless you repeat yourself frequently, clearly, and consistently. Work on making your presentation more consistent, and you'll be amazed at how much better your results become. (Note that every single *For Dummies* book has the same yellow base color for its cover and the same typeface for the title. You wouldn't recognize the series without this consistency.)

Adding stopping power to catch the customer's eye

Stopping power is the ability of an advertisement or other marketing communication to stop people in their tracks or to make them sit up and take notice. Communications with stopping power generate "What did you say?" or "Did you see that?" responses.

You can be sure that thousands of other marketing messages beside your own bombard your customer. This high level of noise in the marketing environment means that most efforts go unnoticed by most of the people they target. That's why adding a little stopping power to your marketing communications is helpful.

Your stopping power can come from a really clever, attention-getting, creative concept, such as a great visual or a play-on-words type of headline. Some other realistic and easily achievable ways of getting stopping power on a daily basis include the following:

✔ Presenting your brand name and logo clearly and boldly whenever and wherever it appears

✔ Using strong, large type in ad headlines, brochure and catalog titles, and blog and web page banners, and surrounding that type with enough white space to make sure it pops out of the surrounding page or screen

✔ Placing ads and other forms of marketing communications where they aren't surrounded by similar messages from competitors, even if that means pioneering the use of new media for your marketing and advertising

You can achieve stopping power by using other methods as well, but these methods have their downsides:

- **Humor:** Most jokes fall flat, so building your entire marketing program around the idea of trying to be funny isn't realistic. (Even comedians can't be funny all the time!) However, if you think you have a really great joke that works perfectly for your marketing communications, give it a try by testing it on at least a dozen customers. If they also love it (and nobody's offended), then it may be worth a shot.

- **Celebrity endorsements:** Big-budget marketers use celebrity endorsements to gain stopping power (if you had Angelina Jolie, surrounded by her kids, promoting your new line of children's clothes, you can bet everyone would watch and remember your ads). But celebrity endorsements are expensive, and most marketers don't find them practical. (A fun, no-cost way to tap into the appeal of a celebrity is to run a tongue-in-cheek ad featuring a long-dead public figure such as a former president, but see my caution about humor in the preceding bullet.)

The following sections give you some do's and don'ts to follow when creating your ads to achieve greater stopping power without overdoing it.

Giving an ad greater stopping power

Incorporating stopping power in your ads doesn't have to be difficult. You can give your ads for magazines, the web, TV, or radio (as well as catalogs and websites) stopping power by

- **Being dramatic:** Tell an interesting story, create suspense, or draw the audience into an event in the life of an interesting character. The principles of good storytelling work well. After all, who doesn't love a good story? However, sometimes the story is more relevant to brand positioning and doesn't create a new, powerful reason to stop and stare. Consider whether a new chapter or a new story with a deadline (some amazing promo?) is going to be needed to bump up the stopping power.

- **Creating an emotional response:** Often people relate to an ad or other message on the emotional level first; their emotional response then draws them into the ad, encouraging them to take the time to digest its information. (This principle holds true even if you're making a rational appeal; see the later "Communicating to the Entire Brain" section for more on the concept of rational appeal). So give your ads emotional impact, by showing a beautiful picture of a tropical beach with footprints leading down it or by using a cute, charming child as a spokesperson.

- ✔ **Stimulating curiosity:** Your ad should make the audience want to know more. This desire gets viewers to stop and study the ad and follow up with further information searches afterward. One of the secrets to stimulating curiosity is not flooding each communication with information. Be brief. Use the least amount of info necessary to be persuasive; you'll leave viewers curious and looking for more.

- ✔ **Surprising the audience:** A startling headline, an unexpected visual image, an unusual opening gambit in a sales presentation, or a weird display window in a store — all have the power to stop people by surprising them. So, for example, a headline that says "We go out of business every day" has more stopping power than a headline that says "We have everyday low prices," even though both headlines communicate the same marketing message.

- ✔ **Communicating expected information in a *detcepxenu* way:** (Here's a hint: Try reading that mystery word backward.) A creative twist or a fresh way of saying or looking at something makes the expected unexpected. Yes, you have to get the obvious information in: what the brand is, who it benefits, and how. But you don't have to do so in an obvious way. If you do, your communication won't reach out and grab attention, causing your audience to ignore it.

Crafting an ad that has fresh, new drama or that says the expected in an unexpected way surprises people and takes creativity. When you need to get those creative juices flowing, flip to Chapter 5.

(Not) using sex appeal to attract attention

Advertising research reveals another secret of stopping power: sex. The word itself definitely catches the eye. So does showing someone who people think is sexy. Consequently, marketers often assume that they just need to give their ads sex appeal to give them stopping power.

Here's the hitch with that plan. The same research that shows sex-based ads have stopping power also shows that these ads don't prove very effective by other measures. *Brand recall* — viewers' ability to remember what product the ad advertised — is usually lower for sex-oriented ads than for other ads. So although these ads *do* have stopping power, they *don't* seem to have any other benefits. They fail to turn that high initial attention into awareness or interest, and they don't change attitudes about the product. In short, they sacrifice clear communication for raw stopping power.

The only exception to the rule that sexy ads are bad communicators is when sexiness is relevant to the product. If you're marketing a lingerie store, running some print ads of scantily clad, attractive models in the Sunday newspaper seems to make sense (although if they look more like real people and less like anorexic dolls, customers may identify more easily). However, I suggest you leave sexy models out of ads for hardware stores, lawn care, or office supplies.

Being as persuasive as possible

If you don't like being harangued, then you should assume your customers don't either. So you have a problem: You need to make your communications persuasive, but you also need to admit that most people don't like being persuaded. The solution? The very soft sell, in which you let people persuade themselves by giving them the information they need to make their own purchase decision.

Here are my favorite ways of making marketing communications persuasive without bugging people:

- ✔ **Avoid sales clichés.** Never say, "Have we got a deal for you!" or tell people they "won't believe their eyes!" Sounding like a charlatan or an old-fashioned, fast-talking, door-to-door salesman is all too easy. Take a thick black pen to your marketing communications and cross out every sales cliché you can find.

- ✔ **Steer clear of so-called "power words" from the books and seminars on how to be a super salesperson.** *Power words* are terms the so-called experts tell marketers to use (they also date back to the 1950s — talk about being out of style). Some examples include *incredible, guaranteed, amazing, unlimited, immediately, proven, limited time,* and *exclusive.* Such power words are so incredibly overused that I positively guarantee you'll receive amazingly poor results and be incredibly disappointed by them immediately.

- ✔ **Show the evidence through clear, simple language and illustrations.** The way to be persuasive is to *show* that your product is a success rather than tell people that it is. Share the statistics that show how good it is. Provide a sample of what it can do. Quote a happy customer's testimonial. Show and tell, with an emphasis on the "show" part, and your communications will be naturally persuasive. Just be sure to focus on the facts, not your opinions. YouTube videos demonstrating product use are a great way to show and tell. Embed them in your Facebook business page, your website, and a blog on the same topic to build awareness of the new video, and if they achieve popularity in social media, tweet about them to encourage more followers to find them.

- ✔ **Make your brand's personality appealing.** Give your brand a face that others will get to know, trust, and like. A sale always has an emotional component, and the best way to make people emotionally comfortable with their purchase is to build up a likeable, trusted brand personality through consistent presentation of that personality in all your marketing communications. Do so by first making a list of the things that contribute to your brand's unique and appealing personality. Then pick colors, type styles, words and phrases, photographs, and/or music that reinforce that personality. Delete anything that clashes with the personality profile you've chosen for your brand. (Check out the Big Five personality traits in Chapter 14 for specifics on how to define a brand's personality.)

If you do everything right, your communications will be naturally persuasive. Clear, concise, well-written copy is naturally compelling. Accurate, informative messages are persuasive. Professional, clean graphics and designs are convincing. If you look, sound, and read like a top brand or a leading professional in your field, people will assume you are. You don't have to tell them (nor should you). Let the professionalism of your presentation show how good you are. I consider this strategy as the *quiet dignity* strategy of communicating. Some marketers are parading down the sidewalk in sandwich-board signs handing out cheap fliers and shouting their pitch to anyone who'll listen. But the ones who wear neatly pressed business suits and make their presentations in conference rooms on the third floor of the office building above that sidewalk are the ones who go home with the most business. Be a pro, and people will find you naturally persuasive.

Checking the accuracy of your communications

Verifying that your communications are accurate may seem like a boring step, but I urge you not to neglect it. Marketing communications are full of errors, some of them obvious to the viewer or listener, others less obvious but equally damaging. Typos, incorrect prices and dates, misspelled web addresses and phone numbers, inaccurate specifications, and other factual errors plague marketing communications and cost billions of dollars a year for businesses that have to live with lost customers, angry customers, confused customers, and customers who can rightly claim that they were offered an absurdly low price due to an error in the production of a coupon.

To reduce errors, always check and double-check your work. In fact, check everyone's work! Be the irritating marketing manager with the red pencil who insists on reviewing everything. And check the final version of anything before it's released, just in case. Accurate communications are one of the essential priorities any marketer needs to pursue. For more information on editing your work, check out the "Tightening Your Writing" section, later in this chapter.

Communicating to the Entire Brain

When creating your marketing communications, you need to think about how your customers and prospective customers will respond to your ads. To do so, you need a basic understanding of the human brain. Essentially, the human brain has three parts (shown in Figure 6-1):

- ✔ **Left hemisphere:** This is the logical, analytical side of your mind.
- ✔ **Right hemisphere:** This is the creative, intuitive side of your mind.
- ✔ **Basal brain:** This is the equivalent of a storeroom for your feelings.

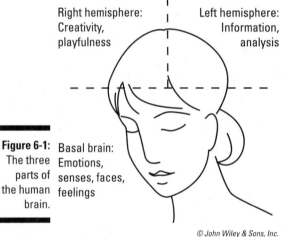

Right hemisphere:
Creativity,
playfulness

Left hemisphere:
Information,
analysis

Figure 6-1: The three parts of the human brain.

Basal brain:
Emotions,
senses, faces,
feelings

© John Wiley & Sons, Inc.

All human beings are mixtures of thoughts and feelings. Those thoughts derive from the left and right hemispheres of the brain, whereas those feelings come from the basal brain. To communicate fully and richly with your customers and prospective customers, you need to make people think, but you also need to balance all that thinking with some feeling. Not all marketing communications touch all parts of the brain, but the really great ones that have memorable impact certainly do.

Of course, you still need to select a part of the brain through which you want your message to enter. Any one of the brain's three parts can be your front door into a person's mind. You just need to decide which one promises the most effectiveness based on your target audience (see Chapter 4 for help determining your target audience).

For example, if you're selling industrial equipment to a very analytical, thoughtful buyer, you want to enter the left hemisphere of his brain by showcasing a large bar chart, an impressive performance statistic, or some other piece of factual information about your product. If you want to sell Caribbean vacations to families, you want to enter on the other side — the right hemisphere. Your appeal is probably dominated by a photograph of a happy family playing on a beach or by some other image designed to trigger a reaction from the brain's playful right hemisphere.

Here's an example of what the whole package can look like. The imaginary marketer has chosen an entry point (the basal brain) and crafted his message so that it touches all three parts of the brain.

> Imagine a short streaming video clip of a piece of cake sitting by itself on a plate in the middle of a corporate website's home page. Perhaps a stopwatch or timer is ticking down next to it. At zero, a puppy leaps into the frame and devours the cake in two huge, messy bites. Then a voice-over and scrolling text tell you, "Don't let the opportunity get away. Only three more days until the end of our Spring Sale."

This web ad engages the basal brain first (you salivate over the cake), takes a quick trip to the humor center in the right brain, and finally hits home with an informative message that the left brain can digest and remember.

Don't discount the basal brain as an entry point. It's one of the best ways to draw attention to your communication and gain entry into the busy inner world of your prospect's brain.

Exploring Four Strategies for Boosting Your Communications' Appeal

What else can you do to make your marketing communications more effective? Here are four good strategies, each of which takes a different approach to informing prospective customers and can be used to craft an effective marketing communication, such as an ad, brochure, mailing, or e-mail offer. The trick to using these strategies is to pick just one of them and then stick to it so that your communication has a sharp focus and does one thing well. Good appeals often rely on one of these strategies, so if you're stuck, give one of 'em a try:

✔ **Image strategy:** An *image strategy* shows people your product and its personality. It presents a good image of your brand, product, service, or business. For example, a day spa may develop a sophisticated logo and color scheme and work sophistication into everything, from its print ads and website to its decor, towels, bathrobes, and bottled water. To use this strategy, ask yourself these questions: What's our image? How can we communicate that image in an appealing way through all points of contact with our customers and prospects?

- **Information strategy:** An *information strategy* communicates facts that make you appealing. For example, a truck rental company may want to let prospects know how many of what kind of trucks it has available, in what condition it keeps those trucks, and how reasonable it makes its terms of rental. The facts should make the sale. And if you know you're particularly strong in a certain area, then communicate the facts of your brilliance instead of wasting effort on more ordinary information. To use this strategy, ask yourself these questions: What three facts are most impressive and compelling in trying to make a sale? How can we present and support these three facts effectively in our marketing communications?

- **Motivational strategy:** A *motivational strategy* builds a compelling argument or feeling that should lead prospects to take action and make a purchase. For example, a life insurance company may tell some stories about people who had insurance and others who didn't and what happened to their loved ones after they died. Prospects often experience strong emotional responses to such stories, so this approach should lead to new sales. To use this strategy, ask yourself these questions: What motivates our customers to purchase? What stories or facts can we use to tap into this motivation?

- **Demonstration strategy:** A *demonstration strategy* leverages the fundamental appeal of the product itself by simply making that product available to prospects. For many people, seeing is believing. If you don't already have a demonstration of at least one product up and running on your website, put one there today (or as soon as you can create a reasonably good-quality digital video of the demonstration). To use this strategy, ask yourself these questions: What forms of demonstration are most effective for our product? Where and how can we stage such demonstrations so as to reach the maximum number of prospects?

Pull Power: Building Customer Traffic

Pull power is the ability of a marketing communication to draw people to a place or event. Smaller or local marketers usually concern themselves with pull power more than *brand equity* (building the value of your brand) or positioning. After all, somebody has to actually *sell* a product at the ground level — in the local market and customer by customer. At this level, you really need to draw in those customers, which makes pull power important.

Pull power is often the primary goal of local advertising. (By *local advertising*, I mean advertising focused on a specific city or county — which includes almost half of all advertising in the United States.) Marketers use publicity, personal selling, direct mail, price-based promotions, and point-of-purchase spending to try to exercise effective pull power. Not only that, marketers use more than half of all the money spent on all forms of marketing communications to pull consumers in.

The trick to effective pull power is to include at least one call to action in every marketing communication. Having three calls to action is even better so long as each of the three is a little different to suit different needs and tastes. For example, a free-standing insert in the local newspaper's weekend edition can promote a garden center's master class on bonsai trees, which is a pull appeal based on a special event. But it can also include other calls to action, such as a reminder to purchase spring perennials before the end of June to receive a free bag of organic fertilizer and, of course, a basic reminder of the store's hours, location, phone number, and web address. With multiple, varied calls to action, this ad can generate increased store traffic and website visits. Product ratings and reviews are also a great way to get a response (and to gather customer data). But make sure you give easy options for responding, including active web links, a direct phone number, and a QR code. The impulse to action runs out of steam as soon as barriers to action appear.

For maximum pull power, give people a strong reason to act. Tell consumers your location and that you have what they need. Ask them to come by, call, return a coupon, or visit your website. And keep inviting them, sometimes in new and creative ways, so they never forget you. Also, make it easy for consumers to take action. Give them convenient hours, multiple locations, and the choice of buying however they prefer (in person, by phone, by e-mail, and so on). The more ways you offer for people to contact you and shop, the more traffic you can expect.

Tightening Your Writing

Marketing communications work mostly with words and pictures, and of the two, words are the most common. Although the right photograph or video clip can be powerful, even the most appealing image can be sabotaged by poor writing. A sure way to improve the impact of your marketing communications is to edit them carefully.

I've never met a website, ad, brochure, or press release that I couldn't cut by 30 percent and add an exciting introductory sentence and headline to in the first five minutes of editing. This is not a boast. Anybody who works all day with words may do as well or better. It's a testament to the truth of the saying that *the secret of great writing is rewriting*. Schedule less time for the first draft (dashing it off is often the best way because it comes out fresh). Then schedule plenty of time for revising, getting input, and revising again.

Also be sure to keep your writing simple and direct. It should reach out and grab the reader by relating directly to his concerns, experiences, and questions. If you tighten up your writing by putting everything in clear, simple, direct, present-tense sentences and by cutting anything extra, you can edit your way to success!

If you can find a novel way to make your point, do. Remember that you need originality and surprise if you want your writing to have stopping power (see the earlier "Adding stopping power to catch the customer's eye" section for more on this communications priority). But above all else, make sure you write simply and clearly.

You can only get to the essence of a communication by writing — and then rewriting and rewriting. Keep reworking, keep rethinking, keep boiling your words down until you have something that penetrates to your point with startling clarity. And then, after you make your point, shut up!

Creating Great Visuals

Pictures can truly be worth a thousand words. Imagine the following: A kid is playing tennis against a backboard when a dog runs up and steals the ball. The ball, bright yellow and fuzzy, overflows the dog's mouth as the camera zooms in to show the ball and mouth, filling the TV screen.

This visual image is simple, but it communicates a lot. Like how much fun kids, and dogs, have when playing with tennis balls. The image also offers drama. How does the kid feel when the dog takes his ball? How does the dog feel when he gets the ball? Most of all, the image reminds viewers that tennis is good fun for everyone, regardless of skill level, age, or even species!

The visual image I'm describing is at the heart of a U.S. Tennis Association television spot that promoted tennis. This spot illustrated the power of a good visual image or sequence of images to capture attention, tell an interesting story, and communicate a point. No words necessary. The spot also illustrated a key to successful visuals — a focus on one strong, relevant image. In this case, that image is the tennis ball, proudly framed in the dog's jaws. In your case, well, the image can be anything as long as it's (a) visually compelling, (b) easily recognizable, and (c) relevant to your appeal.

The next sections show you the best way to add punch to your visual marketing communications and explain how to keep your designs from looking amateurish and unprofessional.

Embracing hierarchy in design

A good rule of thumb when designing anything visual — be it a brochure, web page, logo, ad, sign, package design, label, and so on — is to know what you want people to see first, second, and third.

People see the visually dominant aspect of an image first. Therefore, this aspect needs appeal, to stop prospective customers in their tracks and draw them closer so they look at the second and third aspects of the ad. The second aspect they see should explain the basic appeal in a simple, clear way. And third, they should get some consistent, supporting evidence or feelings to back up what numbers one and two tell them. Now, with this hierarchy in mind, one image needs to be visually dominant. Not two images or ten images — one image. Always have a focal point or entry point for the eye.

What's the number-one image or design element in your existing ads, brochures, or other visual communications? Does it clearly dominate, or do many elements compete for primary attention? Is the dominant visual element appealing and attractive enough to deserve the top spot? And does it clearly show how your product benefits the customer? In most cases, existing marketing communications fail this hierarchy test and need to be redesigned. Most designers overdesign, most copywriters overcommunicate, and it's up to the brand marketer or business owner to get the hierarchy right. As you review and edit both the visuals and the words, focus clearly on a single, top-level message you want to convey.

Here's a simple and powerful suggestion: Make a visual image of your product the most visible feature of your design. If you have a physical product, get a really, really great photo of it and place that in a dominant position in your ad, brochure, web page, or other marketing device. If you provide an intangible service or process, give your service a visual identity by creating a really, really nice diagram, flowchart, picture of someone using or doing it, or a striking picture of something that can represent it (a rose can represent a dating service, for example). Now place that image as the biggest, most noticeable feature of your communication. (See Chapter 7 for details on laying out print ads and brochures.)

Relying on experience to avoid homemade design disaster

Unless you're an artist, you really need to work with one to create effective visual imagery. Some of the homemade designing I see coming off of people's desktop computers is embarrassing.

Still, you may find yourself having to take on some of the design tasks in your marketing department or business. A catalog sheet, brochure, store window display, or other visual design may have to be done right now, without the budget for a creative agency or graphic designer. If you have a Macintosh or PC running Adobe Photoshop software and Adobe Illustrator, along with a small budget for downloading images from stock photography vendors, you can play designer pretty effectively.

Doing design work yourself is now technically easy, but if you don't know much about design, you can get into trouble really quickly with the new technologies. I go into more detail about design (and provide ad and brochure templates) in my book *Marketing Kit For Dummies,* 3rd Edition (Wiley).

Part III
Advertising for Fun and Profit

Sans Serif	Serif
Helvetica	Century
Univers	Garamond
Optima	Melior
Avant Garde	Times New Roman

Who doesn't love something that's free? I tell you how to lure customers to your brand by providing free content at no cost to you at www.dummies.com/extras/marketing. Everyone wins!

In this part . . .

- Ensure clear, compelling, eye-catching, and easy-to-read text wherever it appears in your marketing materials, from traditional brochures and catalogs to websites, blogs, landing pages for promos, and web content optimized for phones, not just widescreens.

- Mix the best of traditional media, including outdoor signage, brochures, and mailings, with the impact of emerging media, from electronic signs to customized messages based on prospects' web-surfing interests or the proximity of their phone to your store.

- Tap in to the power of radio and streaming audio and video options as an alternative to traditional (and expensive!) television spots.

- Improve the efficacy of your marketing messages — and give them a more personal touch — by taking advantage of new advertising tactics that help you speak to the right prospects and avoid poorly directed (and costly) ad blasts.

Chapter 7

Perfecting Your Printed Materials

- -

In This Chapter

▶ Crafting great print pieces with good font selection and flow

▶ Creating brochures with focused impact

▶ Designing and testing effective print ads

- -

Marketers traditionally budget more for print advertising than for any other type of advertising, with the exception being the major national or multinational brands that market largely on television. For most local and regional advertising, print traditionally provided the most flexible and effective all-around advertising medium. Although print is shrinking due to the advantages of web-based advertising and promotions, it's still a major part of your marketing program and needs to be done right.

In fact, for the do-it-yourself marketer, trying to build sales for a very small business or promoting your own brand as a consultant or expert, under-standing the basics of a print campaign is essential. (You may still want to hire a local graphic designer to help you, though.) Not a do-it-yourselfer but rather a marketing manager or assistant who needs to get up-to-speed in a hurry because you're working on a campaign or plan for a mid-sized or larger organization? For your work, having a solid background in how advertising is made and placed proves immensely helpful in avoiding poor or overpriced services from vendors you may be working with, such as ad agencies and research firms.

No matter the size of your campaign, this chapter helps you integrate printed material, which may include print advertising as well as e-brochures, web-sites, and much more, into your business's marketing plan. Even if you're a very small business, you can make an impact on customers (both current and potential) with professional-looking printed communications that reinforce your brand image and overall marketing message.

When designing anything in print, your purpose is to stimulate a sale. Think ahead to that goal. If your product sells in stores, create signs, packaging, displays, or coupons that echo the ad's theme and remind the buyer of that theme. If the sale occurs on a website, make sure the ad sends prospects to a landing page where the offer from the ad is highlighted and it's obvious what to do next. If you make the sale in person, supply the salespeople or distributors with catalogs, order forms, PowerPoint presentations, e-brochures, or brochures (see the section "Producing Quality, Effective Brochures," later in this chapter) that are consistent with your design to remind them of the ad that began the sales process. Roll the ad's design forward to the point of purchase and beyond if you plan follow-up mailings, a mail-in warranty card, or other post-purchase contacts. Even if you're writing something that's informative or instructional (like a product manual), the professionalism and utility of the communication will make a strong impression that may bring customers back to your brand when they're next looking to purchase.

Designing Printed Marketing Materials

Many marketers start with their printed marketing materials (think ads, brochures, product literature as PDFs, and so on) and then work outward from there to incorporate the appeal and design concepts from their printed materials into other forms of marketing. Brochures, *tear sheets* (one-page, catalog-style descriptions of products), e-brochures, posters for outdoor advertising, direct-mail letters, catalogs, and even blogs and web pages all share the basic elements of good print advertising: good copy and visuals mixed with eye-catching headlines. They also all require a common look and feel that unites the separate pieces. Therefore, all good marketers need mastery of print advertising as a vital part of their knowledge base. The following sections cover the essentials of what you should know.

Including the eight necessary parts

Before you can create great printed marketing materials, you must dissect an ad, brochure, tear sheet, or similar piece to identify its parts. Fortunately, you won't find anything gross or disgusting inside most printed marketing materials. Just parts. And each part has a special name, as you can see from this list:

- **Headline:** The large-print words that first attract the eye, usually at the top of the page.

- **Subhead:** The optional addition to the headline to provide more detail, also in large (but not quite as large) print.

- **Copy or body copy:** The main text, set in a readable size, like what printers use in the main text of a book or magazine.

- **Visual:** An illustration that makes a visual statement. This image may be the main focus of the ad or other printed material (especially when you've designed an ad to show readers your product), or it may be secondary to the copy.

✔ **Caption:** Copy attached to the visual to explain or discuss that visual. You usually place a caption beneath the visual, but you can put it on any side or even within or on the visual.

✔ **Trademark:** A unique design that represents the brand or company (like Nike's swoosh). You should always register trademarks; see Chapter 14 for more info.

✔ **Signature:** The company's trademarked version of its name. Often advertisers use a logo design that features a brand name in a distinctive font and style. The signature is a written equivalent to the trademark's visual identity.

✔ **Slogan:** An optional element consisting of a (ideally) short phrase evoking the spirit or personality of the brand. Timberland used a series of print ads in which the slogan "Boots, shoes, clothing, wind, water, earth and sky" appeared in the bottom-left corner, just beneath the company's distinctive signature and logo — which marketers displayed on a photo of a rectangular patch of leather, like patches that appear on one of their products.

Figure 7-1 shows most of these elements in a rough design for a print ad (a brochure's layout is a bit more complicated and is covered later in this chapter). I use generic terms in place of actual parts of an ad (*headline* for the headline, for example) so you can more easily see all the elements in action. This fairly simple palette for a print ad design allows you endless variation and creativity. You can say or show anything, and you can do so in many different ways. (And even if you aren't buying space to run the ad in a magazine or newspaper, you can use this layout for a one-page marketing sheet to include in folders or as handouts at trade shows.)

Putting the parts together: Design and layout

Design refers to the look, tone, and feel (overall style) of your ad or other printed marketing materials. Design is an aesthetic concept and, thus, hard to put into precise terms. But design is vitally important: It has to take the basic appeal of your product and make that appeal work visually on paper (see Chapter 6 for details on how to develop appeal). Specifically, the design must overcome the marketer's constant problem: Nobody cares about advertising. So your design must somehow reach out to readers, grab their attention, and hold it long enough to communicate the appeal of the product you're advertising and attach that appeal to your brand name in readers' memories.

A memorable photograph is often the easiest way to grab the reader. If you don't have a better idea, try using a photo of an interesting face or of a child, as long as you can make the image relevant in some way to your product. Beautiful nature scenes are also good eye-catchers.

Catch attention with a

Headline
and explanatory subhead

Use a **Visual** that draws the eye

Include brief, crisp, focused

copy

that relates the headline and visual to one simple marking message, Check it for errors and typos, Shorten it as much as possible. Good work !

A caption explains the visual

Signature → (your name and logo)

B L A C K C A T *Designs*

Extra room for contact information, store location, or a call to action.

Figure 7-1:
A sample print ad featuring most of the eight elements.

Great advertising has to rise off the page, reach out, and grab you by the eyeballs. In the cluttered world of modern print-based marketing, this design goal is the only one that really works! So I want you to tape up a bunch of ads from the same publication(s) yours will go in (or use samples of competitor brochures, catalog sheets, or whatever it is you'll be designing in print). Put a draft of your design up along with these benchmarks and then step back — way back. Now, does your design grab the eye more than all the others? If not . . . back to the drawing board!

One good way to make your design stand out from the rest is to edit it down so you can have fewer words that are set in larger type. Less is often more when it comes to good print marketing design and writing.

Going with a professional designer

If you don't have the talent or desire to design ads and other printed materials, know that it's okay to delegate this work to skilled designers. This section walks you through the process of working with a designer. When selecting a designer, review their portfolio thoroughly. Only hire someone whose body of work matches your sense of style and quality. Past work is the best predictor of future work.

First, a designer crafts several *thumbnails,* rough sketches used to describe layout concepts. Traditionally thumbnails were created as small, quick sketches in pen or pencil, but nowadays designers are using computer programs such as Adobe InDesign to create more impressive-looking thumbnails. Younger designers call them *mockups* rather than thumbnails, but both serve the same purpose.

After you sign off on a thumbnail or mockup you like, the designer traditionally develops it into a *rough,* a full-sized sketch or high-quality computer-generated mockup with headlines and subheads set in an appropriate *font style* (the appearance of the printed letters). The rough may have sketches for the illustrations, or the designer may pull low-resolution pictures off the web to give you an idea of proposed illustrations. (To finalize the design, you'll probably need to either purchase the right to use a high-resolution image from a stock photography provider or hire a photographer or artist to create an image.) At this time, the designer also shows you where the body copy will go, but she won't use actual copy unless you already have some drafted that she can drop into the rough design.

Sometimes clients of ad agencies insist on seeing designs in the rough stage, to avoid the expense of having those designs developed more fully before presentation. I recommend that you ask to see rough versions of your designs, even if your agency hesitates to show you its work in unfinished form. After the designer realizes that you appreciate the design process and don't criticize the roughs simply because they're rough, you can give the agency more guidance and help during the design process.

After a rough meets your approval, the designer develops that rough into a *comp* (short for *comprehensive layout*). A comp should look pretty much like a final version of the design, whether it's created as a *full-color proof* on a computer or whether it's done by hand. Today, most comps are neatly printed on color laser printers, unless the designer is remote, in which case you may receive a PDF file by e-mail that you're expected to review from your end.

If you're working on a brochure or a special insert for a magazine, ask to see a *dummy,* which is a form of comp that simulates the feel — as well as the look — of the final design. By doing a dummy comp, you can assess the feel of the design while you're evaluating its appearance and decide whether you like the paper, ink, size, and any other physical elements of the design, such as folds, die cuts, or perforations.

Crowdsourcing designers through contests

Announce your design needs on the web and attract hundreds of professional proposals from graphic artists all across the e-world. You can even use sites set up to connect you to designers, such as Freelancer (www.freelancer.com), Crowdsite (www.crowdsite.com), LogoArena (www.logoarena.com), DesignContest (www.designcontest.com), Hatchwise (www.hatchwise.com), Logo Design Guru (www.logodesignguru.com), DesignCrowd (www.designcrowd.com), and 99designs (99designs.com).

For example, 99designs (99designs.com) had a recent logo contest for Alchemist Distilleries, which produced an elaborate and striking design for this local beer brewer from Waterbury, Vermont. The cost of the contest was less than $300, drastically less than most traditional logo designs. However, to date, the company hasn't rolled out its new logo, which gets at one of the limitations of crowdsourced design: It's easy and cheap to hold a contest and announce the winner, but unless you have the motivation and funding to revise all your marketing communications, from letterhead to signage to packaging, you may still find the costs of migrating to the new logo to be rather daunting. (Many of the crowdsourced design sites can be used for website design, packaging, or other design challenges, not just logos.)

Doing the design on your own

Anyone with a basic computer and printer can now set up shop and create his or her own fliers, brochures, business cards, and ad layouts. In fact, Microsoft Word and Pages both include a number of excellent templates that simplify layout and allow you to bang out a new brochure or other printed marketing piece quickly. Any graphic designer you hire will eschew Word and Pages and use the Adobe professional design programs (currently available at a fee of about $50 a month from Adobe Cloud at www.adobe.com/products/creativecloud.html). If you have experience using these programs, then you may want to design your own print materials (as well as websites and so much more), but if you've never used them, I don't recommend them. It takes a while to get really good, and your time may be better spent managing your marketing program. Do, however, take a look at Adobe Marketing Cloud, which many marketing departments now use to help them manage programs.

Small-scale marketers (such as independent consultants, landscape designers, and so forth) may want to try using a logo design website, where, for a usually quite modest fee, you can use easy-to-navigate software and a library of design elements to quickly make a clean, scalable logo that can be migrated to business cards, signs, your website, and so on. Take a look at the do-it-yourself options on sites like www.flamingtext.com, www.logogarden.com, and (my favorite) www.logomaker.com. A challenge may arise when design sites try to upsell you to their own printing and production partners and make it harder for you to work with your own vendors. You can easily buy a business card over the site with your new logo on it, but also find out whether you can get the actual file e-mailed to your own printer or web designer.

Designers often experiment with numerous layouts for their print ads or other printed materials before selecting one for formal development. Whatever approach you take to becoming a do-it-yourself designer, I strongly recommend that you experiment with layouts the way pro designers do. The more layouts you look at, the more likely you are to get an out-of-the-box idea that has eye-grabbing power.

Finding your font

Deciding on a font (not to be confused with a typeface) is perhaps one of the most important choices you make regarding your printed marketing materials. *Typeface* refers only to the distinctive design of the letters (Times New Roman, for example). *Font,* on the other hand, actually refers to one particular size and style of a typeface design (such as 10-point, bold, Times New Roman). It's the particular attributes for the *characters* (letters, numbers, and symbols) used in printing your design.

The right font for any job is the one that makes your text easily readable and that harmonizes with the overall design most effectively. For a headline, the font also needs to grab the reader's attention. The body copy (see the section "Including the eight necessary parts," earlier in this chapter) doesn't have to grab attention in the same way — in fact, if it does, the copy often loses readability. For example, a *reverse font* (light or white on dark) may be just the thing for a bold headline, but if you use the reverse font in the body copy, too, nobody reads your copy. It's just too hard on the eye to read more than a line or two in reverse font. The following sections help you find the font that will make your printed marketing materials pop.

Choosing a typeface

Finding the right font for your needs starts with figuring out what sort of typeface you want. You have an amazing number of choices, because designers have been developing typefaces for as long as printing presses have existed. Your word-processing software will have many of the basic options, including classics like Helvetica and Times New Roman. Check out Adobe Typekit (`www.typekit.com`) for nice displays of many more options, where you can call up most popular fonts or create lists by style and type.

A clean, sparse design, with a lot of white space on the page and stark contrasts in the artwork, deserves the clean lines of a *sans serif typeface* — meaning one that doesn't have any decorative *serifs* (those little bars or flourishes at the ends of the main lines in a character). The most popular body-copy fonts without serifs are Helvetica, Univers, Optima, and Avant Garde. Figure 7-2 shows some fonts with and without serifs.

© John Wiley & Sons, Inc.

Figure 7-2:
Fonts with
and without
serifs.

A richly decorative, old-fashioned sort of design needs a more decorative and traditional serif typeface, like Century or Times New Roman. The most popular body-copy fonts with serifs include Garamond, Melior, Century, Times New Roman, and Caledonia. Figure 7-3 shows an assortment of typeface choices, in which you can compare the clean lines of the sans serif typefaces with the more decorative designs of the serif typefaces.

Figure 7-3:
Popular
typefaces
for ads.

Sans Serif	*Serif*
Helvetica	Century
Univers	Garamond
Optima	Melior
Avant Garde	Times New Roman

© John Wiley & Sons, Inc.

In tests, Helvetica, Times New Roman, and Century generally top the lists as most readable, so start with one of these typefaces for your body copy; only change it if it doesn't seem to work. Research also shows that people read lowercase letters about 13 percent faster than uppercase letters, so avoid long stretches of copy set in all caps. People also read most easily when letters are dark and contrast strongly with their background. Thus, black 12-point Helvetica on white is probably the most readable font specification for the body copy of a printed marketing piece, even if it seems dull to a sophisticated designer.

Generalizing about the best kind of headline typeface is no easy task, because designers play around with headlines to a greater extent than they do with body copy. But as a general rule, you can use Helvetica for the headline when you use Century for the body, and vice versa. Or you can just use a bolder, larger version of the body copy font for your headline. You can also reverse a larger, bold version of your type onto a black background for the headline. Anything to make the headline grab the reader's attention, stand out from the body copy, and ultimately lead vision and curiosity into the body copy's text. (Remember to keep the headline readable, though. Nothing too fancy, please.)

Sometimes designers combine body copy of a decorative typeface (one with serifs, like Times New Roman) with headers of a sans serif typeface (like Helvetica). The contrast between the clean lines of the large-sized header and the more decorative characters of the smaller body copy pleases the eye and tends to draw the reader from header to body copy. This book uses that technique. Compare the sans serif bold characters of this chapter's title with the more delicate and decorative characters in which the publisher set the text for a good example of this design concept in action.

Making size and style choices within the typeface

Any given typeface presents a ton of choices, so selecting your typeface is just the beginning. How big should the characters be? Do you want to use the standard version of the typeface, a lighter version, a **bold** (darker) version, or an *italic* (right-leaning) version?

Believe it or not, making your style and size choices is really rather easy. Just look at samples of some standard point sizes (12- and 14-point text for the body copy, for example, and 24-, 36-, and 48-point for the headlines). Many designers make their choices by eye, looking for an easy-to-read size that isn't so large that it causes the words or sentences to break up into too many fragments across the page — but not so small that it gives the reader too many words per line. Keep readability in mind as the goal. Figure 7-4 shows a variety of size and style choices for the Helvetica typeface. As you can see, you have access to a wonderful range of options, even within this one popular design.

Figure 7-4:
Some of the many choices offered by the Helvetica typeface.

Keep in mind that you can change just about any aspect of a typeface. You can alter the distance between lines — called the *leading* — or you can squeeze characters together or stretch them apart to make a word fit a space. Assume that anything is possible and ask your printer, or consult the manual of your desktop-publishing or word-processing software, to find out how to make a change.

Now, having said that anything is possible, I want to warn you that your customers' eyes read type quite conservatively. Although most of us know little about the design of typefaces, we find traditional designs instinctively appealing. The spacing of characters and lines, the balance and flow of individual characters (with some white space around them or an appropriate illustration to break up the text) — all of these familiar design elements please the eye and make reading easy and pleasurable. So when you need to provide emphasis, try to do so in a conservative manner. For example, try simply bolding your body copy before resorting to a new style of type. Too many type styles may reduce your design's readability.

A good design uses two type families and varies the size of them, mixing in appropriate italics, bold, or reverse type if the overall design benefits from it. Figure 7-5 shows a black-and-white print ad laid out using Garamond and Helvetica, which are traditional, easy-to-read fonts. Some graphic designers avoid them because they like to be less traditional and more creative, but as the figure shows, these two type families lend themselves to clean, attractive, appealing, and (most important) *readable* designs.

Don't just play with type for the sake of playing (as all too many designers and do-it-yourselfers do). Stick with popular fonts, in popular sizes, except where you have to solve a problem or you want to make a special point.

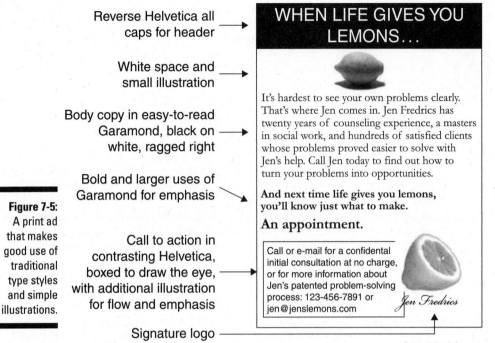

Reverse Helvetica all caps for header →

White space and small illustration →

Body copy in easy-to-read Garamond, black on white, ragged right →

Bold and larger uses of Garamond for emphasis →

Call to action in contrasting Helvetica, boxed to draw the eye, with additional illustration for flow and emphasis →

Signature logo

Figure 7-5: A print ad that makes good use of traditional type styles and simple illustrations.

WHEN LIFE GIVES YOU LEMONS…

It's hardest to see your own problems clearly. That's where Jen comes in. Jen Fredrics has twenty years of counseling experience, a masters in social work, and hundreds of satisfied clients whose problems proved easier to solve with Jen's help. Call Jen today to find out how to turn your problems into opportunities.

And next time life gives you lemons, you'll know just what to make.

An appointment.

Call or e-mail for a confidential initial consultation at no charge, or for more information about Jen's patented problem-solving process: 123-456-7891 or jen@jenslemons.com

Jen Fredrics

© John Wiley & Sons, Inc.

Selecting a point size

When designers and printers talk about *font sizes,* they're referring to a traditional measure of the height of the letters (based on the highest and lowest parts of the biggest letters). One *point* equals about 1/72 of an inch, so a 10-point type is 10/72 of an inch high, at the most.

Personally, I've never measured a character with a ruler. I just know that if the letters seem too small for easy reading, then I need to bump the typeface up a couple points. Ten-point type is the smallest size you can use for body copy, but you may want to use 11- or 12-point for brochures, especially if your readers are middle-aged or older.

Your eye can't distinguish easily between fonts that are only one or two sizes apart, so specify a larger jump than that to distinguish between body copy and subhead or subhead and headline. For example, if your body copy is set in 10-point Times New Roman, you need to set subheads at least two steps up (steps being defined by standard point sizes: 9, 12, 14, 16, 18, 24, 36, and 48, although in-between sizes can also be used).

Using (not abusing!) free fonts

You can find a variety of sources of free fonts, the biggest being, by far, Google Fonts (www.google.com/fonts). Free fonts arose because using proprietary ones, such as Times New Roman and Helvetica, includes a (fairly modest) cost. If you want to avoid all unnecessary costs, go ahead and set your printed matter or web banners with a free typeface, but don't just pick some novelty and think it will read well.

Following are a few Google fonts I find quite plausible:

- ✔ Open Sans
- ✔ Old Standard TT
- ✔ Volkorn

Red Hat, Inc., introduced a line of open-source fonts under the brand name Liberation that are quite superior options for anyone concerned with fees and restrictions associated with traditional purchased fonts. The Liberation line of fonts includes Sans (sub in for Arial and Helvetica), Serif (a good substitute for Times New Roman), and Mono (similar to Courier). You can use these fonts on the web or in print, without restriction (downloadable at `fedorahosted.org/liberation-fonts`).

More recently, some designers are enthused about the Google Croscore fonts. See what your printer or web designer recommends if you're not sure what the best font product is for your needs, but know that, even with all the new (and sometimes free) options, the basic font designs still matter, and fonts that mimic Times New Roman, Arial, and Helvetica are still considered excellent choices for their classic readability.

Bringing it all together in a perfect flow

As you put your ad together, think about your entire page as an artistic composition that has to have certain qualities. It must have balance, meaning that nothing should be so heavy or large as to prevent you from seeing the other elements. However, perfect balance is boring, so use differences in size and placement of type, white space, and illustrations to create flow. *Flow* is the smooth movement of attention from an entry point, around the page, and to an end point. In marketing, the entry point is almost always the headline, and the end point is either the brand name and logo, or a call to action, depending on whether you want to emphasize brand-building or generate traffic.

The ad in Figure 7-5 has great flow. The eye starts with the headline and is drawn down by the lemon to body copy that has a gentle sweeping curve to its ragged right side, until the eye is temporarily arrested by the bolder punch line. But it doesn't end there. The larger scale of the second lemon makes it jump up off the page, and the boxed, contrasting type of the call to action also demands attention so that the eye goes down and to the left for another batch of reading.

Notice how Figure 7-5 has a subtle flow cue in the way the second lemon has been cut. It seems to be telling a sequential story in which the service the ad describes has processed the "lemon" or problem and found the "lemon aid" or the solution within it. The flow doesn't quite stop at the call to action. The eye wants to finish the journey by moving to the right (a natural way to read), where it encounters the big lemon again before ending on the signature. The last thing you see in a list is the most memorable, so this exit point ensures maximum recall of the brand name.

In a really well-designed print ad, brochure, website, or blog page, the writing and the selection of type styles are just a part of the bigger-picture design, which ought to draw the viewer through a well-planned flow of reading and viewing experiences. Many designers lay out their designs on imaginary grids, where each section, like a headline or a column, fills a rectangular zone in the layout grid. However, ensuring good flow is more important than worrying too much about establishing an elaborate grid or underlying architecture. As long as the ad attracts attention and flows the reader through its component parts, the design is working.

Producing Quality, Effective Brochures

Word-processing or graphics software, a good inkjet or laser printer, and the help of your local photocopy or print shop (which also has folding machines) allow you to design and produce brochures, fliers, and more quite easily. In the sections that follow, however, I focus largely on the classic business staple: the basic brochure and its screen equivalent, the e-brochure (which follows the same core design and writing rules). Why? Because brochures provide an easy, effective way to market your company. (*Note:* Although I focus on brochures, the guidance provided in the following sections is also applicable to producing a variety of printed pieces, including fliers and catalog sheets.)

Knowing the purpose of your brochure

Marketers often order a brochure without a clear idea of what purpose the brochure should serve. They just think a brochure is a good idea. "Oh, we need them to, you know, like, put in the envelope along with a letter, or, um, for our salespeople to keep in the trunks of their cars."

Many brochure designs foolishly waste money because they don't accomplish any specific marketing goals; they just look pretty, at best. To avoid producing a pretty-but-pointless brochure that doesn't achieve a sales goal, know the answers to the following questions (which focus your brochure design and make it useful to your marketing):

- Who will read the brochure?
- How will they get the brochure?
- What should they do after reading the brochure?

Without a specific focus, your brochure can't be properly suited to any single use. It becomes a boring piece that talks generally about your company or product but doesn't hit readers over the head with any particular appeal or call to action.

A good general rule is to define up to three specific purposes for the brochure. Don't go past three, though, because your design can't accomplish more than three purposes effectively. The most common and appropriate purposes for a brochure are to

- ✔ Act as a reference on the product, or technical details of the product, for prospects.
- ✔ Support a personal selling effort by lending credibility and helping overcome objections (to find out more about sales, check out Chapter 17).
- ✔ Generate leads through a direct-mail campaign (I cover direct-mail campaigns in Chapter 13).

Say you want to design a brochure that does all three of these tasks well. Start by designing the contents. What product and technical information must be included? Write the information down or collect necessary illustrations so you have the *fact base* (the essential information to communicate) in front of you.

The next sections highlight the essential elements your brochure should contain to achieve its purpose(s).

A realistic acknowledgment of strengths and weaknesses

When creating your brochure, you need to be able to realistically address your product's strong points and weaker points. Organize your fact base to highlight your product's greatest strengths and overcome its weaknesses. The copy should read as if you're listening to the reader's concerns and needs and answering each one with an appropriate response. You can write subheads like "Our Product Doesn't Need Service" so that salespeople or prospects can easily see how your facts (in copy and/or illustrations) overcome each specific objection and highlight all the major benefits.

Also consider any of these options as you decide what to write to make your brochure's copy powerfully persuasive:

- ✔ The main benefits your product offers
- ✔ Key points of difference that make your product better than the competition
- ✔ Customers' favorite reasons for buying or aspects of your product
- ✔ Customer testimonials or case histories

Product benefits, points of difference, reasons for buying, and customer testimonials are all good ways of explaining why your product is great because they make the case based on evidence.

A clear, compelling appeal

A little basic appeal (see Chapter 6) communicated in a punchy headline and a few dozen words of copy, along with an appropriate and eye-catching illustration, help your brochure stand on its own as a marketing tool. The appeal needs to project a winning personality. It can be fun or serious, emotional, or factual — but it must be appealing. The appeal is the bait that draws the prospect to your hook, so you need to make sure your hook is well baited!

Laying out and producing your print brochure

An effective print brochure follows this standard layout:

- ✓ The appeal, with its enticing headline and compelling copy and visual, goes on the front of the brochure — or the outside when you fold it for mailing, or the central panel out of three if you fold a sheet twice.

- ✓ The subheads that structure the main copy (which responds to objections and highlights strengths, as explained earlier in this chapter) goes on the inside pages.

- ✓ The fact base, needed for reference use, goes in the copy and illustrations beneath your subheads.

If you don't know what each part of your brochure does, then you need to redesign it. Otherwise, that brochure becomes a waste of time and money.

Although you can lay out a brochure in many ways, I often prefer the format shown in Figure 7-6. It's simple and inexpensive because you print the brochure on a single sheet of legal-sized paper that you then fold three times. You can fit this brochure in a standard #10 or #12 envelope, or you can tape it together along the open fold and mail it on its own. This layout allows for some detail but not enough to get you into any real trouble. Larger formats and multipage pieces tend to fill up with the worst, wordiest copy, and people rarely read them. (For some actual brochure templates, check out *Marketing Kit For Dummies,* 3rd Edition [Wiley].)

To convert the design in Figure 7-6 into an even simpler, cheaper format, use 8½-x-11-inch paper and eliminate the *return mailer* (the left-hand page on the front, the right-hand on the back). It's the part that can be returned with the blanks filled in to request information or accept a special offer. If you do

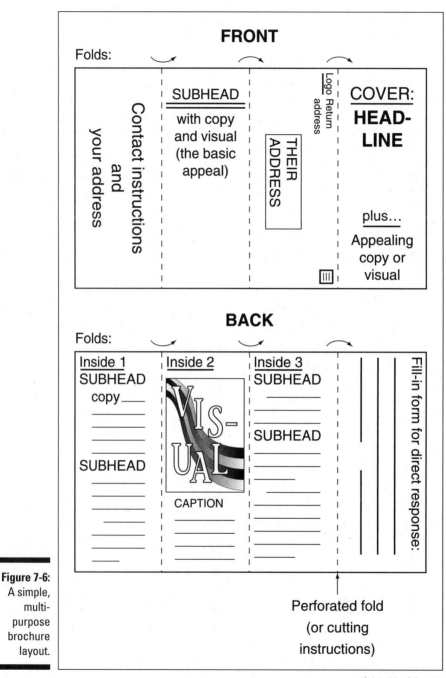

Figure 7-6:
A simple, multi-purpose brochure layout.

remove the return mailer, however, be sure to include follow-up instructions and contact information on one of the brochure's inside pages. You can point readers to a web address where you have a form they can fill in to receive more information. An electronic form can thereby take the place of the traditional return mailer.

You can print and fold a brochure at your local photocopy shop. Most copy stores now accept e-mailed copies of files and can produce short runs of your brochures (as well as pamphlets, catalog sheets, and other printed materials) right from your files. However, if you need thousands of copies, you should look into offset printing, which is a more cost-effective option at that quantity. *Offset printing* is how most books, magazines, and newspapers are printed. The printer makes a plate of each page, and the printing press automatically inks the plate, transfers or "offsets" the ink to a rubber blanket, and then transfers that to the page.

You can also do smaller runs (100 or less) right from your own color printer. Buy matte or glossy brochure paper designed for your brand of printer (HPs work well for this) and simply select the appropriate paper type in the print dialog box. Today's printers can produce absolutely stunning brochures, but you have to fold these brochures yourself, and the ink cartridges or toners aren't cheap, so print as needed rather than inventory a large number of brochures.

Publishing an e-brochure

Printed brochures will never entirely disappear, because handing someone a nicely printed brochure is always a good idea. However, in many cases, e-brochures now fill the need of a brochure less expensively, with the advantages of being easy to distribute through a website or blog or by e-mail and being easier to revise, able to be adapted to specific customers or market niches, and able to incorporate more content. Besides, people are looking for information on their computer, tablet, or phone screen these days, and an e-brochure can be optimized for both large and small screen formats.

Here are some additional features that make e-brochures a great new marketing tool:

- ✔ E-brochures can be created by using online templates or by uploading PDF files generated in more traditional typesetting and design programs or from your word-processing software (but invest in Acrobat Professional from Adobe so you can easily reduce the size of your PDF files until the e-brochure pages load and turn in fractions of a second, just like a real brochure).

- ✔ E-brochures can include embedded links, embedded video clips, and animation (such as an animated drawing showing how simple it is to assemble your product), giving you lots of options you don't have in print.

✔ E-brochure content, when posted on your website, can be reached by search engines, a major benefit you can't get from printed materials!

✔ Some e-brochure publishers (such as FlippingBook; check out www. flippingbook.com) give you good security options so you can direct confidential technical information or confidential proposals only to your intended audience.

Other than these special features, an e-brochure follows the design rules of any good print brochure and should be clear, interesting, well written, and visual as well as verbal. Rough designs can be built quickly in your word-processing program (click and drag in images and/or videos to approximate the final product). Select horizontal rather than vertical for the page setup so as to simulate an e-brochure's horizontal display.

In addition to FlippingBook, check out the following e-brochure publishing platforms, all of which offer a variety of templates:

✔ Digital e-Brochures at www.digital-e-brochures.com

✔ eBrochure at www.flash-ebrochure.com

✔ eBrochures.com at www.ebrochures.com

✔ Net Market at www.web-markets.net

✔ Snap at www.snap.ie/create-an-electronic-brochure.asp

When sports car manufacturer Maserati wanted to offer more photos and facts about its various models, it turned to the e-brochure format. A central website displays an array of e-brochures, each with more than a hundred pages of detailed photos and facts, allowing serious shoppers to really get to know each model before they even go to a showroom to take it for a test drive. Go to www.ebrochure.maserati.com to see how this company, known for its sense of style, makes e-brochures look as good as expensive Italian sports cars. One of Maserati's design secrets is the use of eye-wowing photographs on every page, some of them spreading across a two-page spread so that the e-brochure is light on text (hard to read on screen) and rich with high-resolution images (pleasing to view on any backlit screen). My only suggestion would be the addition of some video of the cars in action.

Placing a Print Ad

Ad agencies and the marketing departments of big companies have special-ists who do nothing but buy media, and some brokers specialize in it for mid-sized or smaller marketers. But if you're a smaller-scale marketer, you can easily figure out how to buy media space on your own. The following sections cover a marketing specialty called *media buying,* with an emphasis on buying print ad space.

Determining whether you can afford an ad

Print ads can be quite expensive, so before you run out and start placing them, you need to know whether buying one is a smart financial move for your business. Make sure you acquaint yourself with all the costs before making any decision.

If you're marketing a small business, start by collecting magazines or newspapers that you're sure your prospective customers read. Then look for the information in them that identifies the publisher and gives a phone number for advertisers to call. Call or visit their websites to get a *rate sheet* (a table listing the prices of ads by size of ad and also showing the discount rate per ad if you buy multiple ads rather than just a single one). If the publication is a magazine, also ask for the *schedule,* which tells you when ads for each issue need to be placed and what the topics of future issues will be.

After you've collected a selection of rate sheets from magazines or newspapers, take a hard look at the pricing. How expensive is the average ad (in the middle of the size range for each publication)? The answer may be a broad number. If a single ad costs one-twentieth (5 percent) or more of your marketing budget for the entire year, throw that rate sheet away and forget about advertising in that publication. You need dozens of ad placements per year to make a good print ad campaign, so don't begin with a publication unless you can easily afford to keep going.

In addition to finding a publication you can afford to advertise in regularly, use economical print media, such as brochures, blogs, mailings, and e-mails. (I help you figure out how to design a brochure earlier in this chapter.) If you operate on too small a scale or budget to afford print advertising, try turning your ad design into a good flier and mailing it. You can send it to 500 names and see what happens. That's a lot less risky and expensive than buying space in a magazine that goes to 200,000 names — some of whom may not care at all about what you're offering. Or you can search for smaller-circulation publications with a more local or specialized readership, where the rates may be much cheaper.

Finding inexpensive places to advertise

Every business looks for ways to save money on advertising. You may be surprised to know that several options are available to you if you're trying to save some cash. Consider the following less-expensive options for advertising:

✔ **Local theater program:** I recently went to the theater, and I noticed that many local businesses had purchased ad space in the program. What did this cost? Less than $100 for many of them. Compare that to an ad in a major magazine, which can cost $100,000. My point is this: If buying ads in the best publications to reach your market is too expensive, you can always find smaller-circulation publications that charge less, but be sure to pick publications your customers and prospects read.

✔ **A professional association's blog, e-column, or old-fashioned newsletter:** Professionals are people who have buying power, so even if you don't sell a product just for them, they may still respond to your ad. Some insurance agents have advertised successfully in newsletters that go to doctors, for example. Increasingly, such newsletters are published in web versions in addition to — or even instead of — print versions. With a web publication, you can take advantage of the larger reach of the web and the lower price of a small publication.

✔ **Local and small-town newspapers:** You can find hundreds of newspapers and weeklies with *circulation* (readership) only in the tens of thousands, which means that their rates for ads are one-fifth to one-tenth the price of big-city newspapers (and even less expensive when compared to major national magazines). Of course, you don't reach as many people, either. Advertising tends to be priced on a *cost per thousand readers* basis (the cost of buying that ad divided by the number of readers who read the publication and then multiplied by 1,000), so you generally get as much exposure as you're willing to pay for. But by buying ads in small-circulation publications, you avoid taking huge risks and minimize your investment. The challenge is that readership is declining for local papers, and many of them are folding or going to online-only formats.

Keep the scale of your print advertising (or any advertising for that matter) at such a level that you can afford to run an ad that may produce zero sales. Although zero sales certainly isn't your goal, it's always a possibility, and you want to base your buying decision on that possibility while you're experimenting to find an effective venue for your ads.

Selecting the ad size

What size ad should you buy? The answer depends in part on the design of your ad. Does the ad have a strong, simple visual or headline that catches the eye, even if it's only a third of a page in size? Or does the ad need to be displayed in a larger format to work well?

In addition to your (or your designer's) judgment about the specifics of your ad, also take into account some general statistics on what percentage of readers *notice* an ad based on its size. As you may expect, the rate goes up with the size — bigger ads get more notice (all other things being equal), according to a study by Cahners Publishing Co. (see Table 7-1).

Table 7-1	Selecting the Right Size Ad
Size of Ad	*Percent of Readers Noticing Ad*
Fractional (part-of-page) ad	24%
One-page ad	40%
Two-page spread	55%

The bigger the ad, the bigger the impact. But also consider the fact that the percentage of readers noticing your ad doesn't go up in proportion to the increase in size. Doubling the size of your ad gives you something like a quarter more viewers, not twice as many. That's partly why the cost of a full-page ad isn't twice the cost of a half-page ad. For example, a full-page, four-color ad in *Health* magazine costs 59 percent more than a half-page, four-color ad. The same ad, run at full versus half size, probably attracts, at most, about a third more reader notices, meaning your cost per reader exposed to the ad is higher for that full-page ad than for the half-page ad (although your impact on each of those readers may be greater with a larger ad, which is why the cost per reader can be set at a higher level for a larger ad).

Testing and improving your print ad

You may be wondering how you can tell whether anybody is actually reading your ad. If you run a *direct-response* ad (one that asks readers to take a measurable action, such as calling, faxing, or going to a store), then you should have a clear indication of that ad's effectiveness within days of its first appearance. Say you expect to receive a lot of inquiries and orders over the telephone or on your website's *landing page* (the page where you send readers of the ad; see Chapter 10) during the week the issue with your ad goes on sale. If you don't receive those calls, you know you have a problem. Now what? The next sections tell you what you can do.

Pretest your ad for a fee

Much brand advertising is indirect, leaving it to the retailer or local office to close the sale. No phones ring, whether consumers liked the ad or not, so to know whether your ad worked, you may need to go to a market research firm and have your ad tested for effectiveness. In fact, if you plan to spend more than $200,000 on print ads, you can probably consider the $15,000 or so needed to hire a research firm to pretest the ad money well spent. (*Pretesting* means exposing people to the ad in a controlled setting and measuring their reactions to it.)

Many research firms are local or regional, so inquire or consult directories in your area for vendors. For example, Q2 Insights (www.q2insights.com) offers pretesting in focus groups out of their locations in New Orleans and San Diego. Online panels can be less costly than face-to-face focus groups. G&R Researching and Consulting (www.gandrllc.com) is an example of the firms that now offer web-based pretesting. Also look at Readex Research (www.readexresearch.com) and PreTesting Group (www.pretesting.com); the PreTesting Group uses a hidden camera to track subjects' eye movement while they read magazines with a test ad in them, which is a good way to measure the ad's *stopping power,* or its ability to grab and hold reader attention.

Sometimes pretesting allows you to find a problem that can be fixed without starting from scratch. Maybe your headline and photo get high scores, but the body copy flunks. You can try rewriting and shortening the copy, and you may also try changing the layout or your choice of fonts. Perhaps the body copy is in reverse font, which consumers find hard to read. In that case, try switching the text to dark letters on a white or light background.

Conduct your own no-cost ad analysis

Usually pretesting, post-testing, and other forms of research are commissioned by ad agencies, who are familiar with the methods and suppliers. If your campaign is on a modest budget and you don't have an agency working with you, you may not really need to spend good money on a research service to find out whether your ad is working. Here are some free research alternatives that you can do all on your own:

- Run three variations on the ad and see which one generates the most calls or website visits (offering a discount based on a code number tells you which responses come from which ad).

- Conduct your own ad tests. Ask people to look at your ad for 20 seconds and then quiz them about what they remember. If they missed much of the ad, you probably need to rewrite it!

- Assemble your own panel of customers and ask them to rate your ad and give you feedback about why they do or don't find it appealing.

- Run the same ad (or very similar ones) in large and small formats and see which pulls in the largest number of consumers.

Compare traditional print with online options

Maybe you need to cut back on print and do more web advertising using Google AdWords, banner ads on high traffic websites such as Facebook, and YouTube advertising. Both consumer and business purchases are swinging strongly toward online (both computer-based and handheld platforms are growing), so print — no matter how well it tests — may not pull as well as electronic placements of the same message. Test web and traditional print side by side or in alternate months to see which has highest returns — most sales revenues for the cost — for your program. Head to Chapter 10 for details on online advertising.

Any experiments you can run as you do your marketing give you useful feedback about what's working and what isn't. Always think of ways to compare different options and see how those options perform when you advertise, giving you useful insight into ad effectiveness.

Chapter 8

Signing On to Outdoor Advertising

Although signs used to be a narrow category, today you have a broad range of options. You may choose to display your logo on traditional signage (think of the billboards you see while driving along the highway), or you may opt for portable signage, like all the reusable shopping bags you see at grocery stores now. You can also explore traditional outdoor advertising's new cousin, location-based media, which allows you to take advantage of all the screens people interact with in their day-to-day existence, from their smartphone to the pump at the gas station.

Although potential customers may see an ad you've placed in their favorite magazine once or twice, they're likely to see your signs over and over, making them a great way to get the message to these customers on a regular basis. That's why I devote this chapter to the many different ways you can use signs in your organization's marketing.

Heading Back to Basics: The Essential Sign

Signs are all over — if you're in an office right now, step to the nearest window, and you can probably see a handful with ease. Signs are also undeniably important. Even if they serve only to locate a store or office, they do a job that marketers need done. If your customers can't find you, you're out of business. And in many cases, signs also provide daily exposure to the brand name, helping to boost awareness and recognition. But most marketing reference books don't bother to cover signs. So why do marketers — or at least those marketing experts who write the books — tend to ignore signs?

No national or international set of standards for signs exists. Nor can you find a major association that promotes standards and champions best practices. When evaluating signs, I can't easily send you to the experts like I can with radio, TV, print, or other outdoor media. You'll probably end up working with a local sign manufacturer, which means you and your designer will have to specify size, materials, copy, and art. You need to take charge of the design and placement of your signs, because no one else seems to know or care how to do it well. The next sections show you how.

Knowing what your sign can do

Signs have a limited ability to accomplish marketing goals — but perhaps not as limited as you may think. You can use signs to help people find you, starting with a sign near the freeway exit and ending with signs marking the entrance to your store or parking lot.

Numerous businesses make finding themselves difficult. Case in point: My office in Amherst, Massachusetts, is near the main campus for the University of Massachusetts at Amherst, the biggest college in the state and home to a top business school. Why do thousands of visitors a year have to pull over in downtown Amherst and ask for directions to the campus? Well, no signs downtown point the way. Hmm. Maybe I should send a copy of this book to the president of the university with a bookmark stuck in this page.

Aside from their practical value (letting people know where you are), signs can and should promote your image and brand name. An attractive sign on your building or vehicle can spread the good word about your business or brand to all who pass by. Don't miss this brilliant opportunity to put your best foot forward in public every day — and night, if the sign is lit or in an indoor public space such as a mall or subway station.

Don't forget to maintain your signs! About a third of all commercial signs are in poor condition. Signs sit out in the weather, and when they fade, peel, or start to fall over, they give negative advertising for your business. Don't let your sign give the public the impression that you're going out of business. Maintain and refresh your signs at least four times a year.

Finding reputable sign producers

The best, most effective signs usually aren't do-it-yourself jobs. Take the time to seek out a reputable sign maker to ensure you spend your money wisely. Following are some suggestions for tracking down an expert who can produce your sign:

> ✔ **Consult local or regional directory listings when you need to have a sign made.** You should find several vendors in your area, but if they don't have the options or pricing you want, check the web for a wider range of options.

✔ **Explore web vendors that are able to service many signage needs from a distance.** Often, signs can be shipped (depending on size and whether they can be folded or rolled). Take a look at quick, simple options like SpeedySigns (`www.speedysigns.com`) or Staples (`print.staples.com`) for lawn signs, custom banners, and the like, and Build-A-Sign (`www.buildasign.com`) provides a large variety of signs. Sign Producers (`www.signproducers.com`) and Britten Studios (`www.brittenstudios.com`) do extraordinary custom work when you need a major wow. (Check out `www.brittenstudios.com/blog` for projects that will get your imagination going!)

✔ **Consider local copy shops for simpler jobs.** Copy shops increasingly provide cheap, high-tech solutions for smaller or temporary signs.

✔ **Have your sign designed and painted by an artist.** Most signs have little real art about them, so when a business hires an artist to carve its name and logo into a big piece of mahogany, the result is something truly special! Check craigslist for local artists or ask for suggestions from the art department of a local college.

Unusual and beautiful signs tell the world that your company is special, too. In fact, a really special sign that's well displayed in a high-traffic area has more power to build an image or pull in prospects than any other form of local advertising.

Writing good signs

As a marketer, you need to master the strange art of writing for signs. Too often, the language marketers use on signs is ambiguous or overly wordy. The following sections can keep you from falling into those traps.

All across the United States are millions of street signs that say *Ped Xing*. Who writes a sign using two made-up words? Only someone who wants to force the viewer to decipher his code. Ever notice that cars don't stop for people crossing? Why should they? The sign doesn't actually tell them what to do (lacks a call to action), doesn't give drivers a good reason to stop (lacks a benefit or cost), and doesn't even use any words they know (lacks clarity). In marketing, you can't get away with such bad writing. To make the meaning crystal clear, a marketer can use something like: "Always STOP for People in Crosswalk" or "Let people cross the road safely." Adding a smaller-print reminder of the fine for not stopping may add even more power to this clear call to action. If this wording requires a slightly bigger sign to be readable, then use a bigger sign! The sign's design must fit the message, not the other way around.

Before you approve any sign design, review the copy to make sure the writing provides a model of clarity. *Try* misinterpreting the wording. Can you read the sign in a way that makes it seem to mean something you don't intend to say? Also, try thinking of questions the sign doesn't answer that seem obvious to you — remember that the consumer may not know the answers. For example, some people have a terrible sense of direction, so a sign on the side of a store leaves them confused about how to enter that store. The solution? Put an arrow and the instructions "Enter from Front" on the sign!

Designing an informational sign

Marketers design some signs to convey substantial information — directions, for example, or details of a store's merchandise mix. Informational signs are often either too brief or too lengthy. To craft the most effective sign possible, divide the copy and design into two sections, each with a separate purpose:

- ✔ **Have a header.** The first section is like the header in a print ad (see Chapter 7). You design it to catch attention from afar and draw people to the sign. Be brief and use large, catchy type. (Often, the header is simply the name of the business, but if not, include the name and logo elsewhere on the sign.)

- ✔ **Communicate essential information.** The second section of the sign needs to communicate the essential information accurately and in full. If the first section does its job, viewers may go right up to the sign to read the informational part, so you may not need to make that type as large and catchy. The consumer should be able to easily read and interpret the wording and type, though. This section also needs to answer all likely questions.

Most signs don't have both a distinct header and essential info; therefore, they fail to accomplish either purpose very well. They neither draw people very strongly nor inform them fully. Unfortunately, most sign makers have a strong urge to make all the copy the same size. When pressed, the sign makers sometimes make the header twice as big as the rest of the copy. But going further than that seems to upset them. Well, to get a good sign, you may have to upset some people. As in many aspects of marketing, if you want above-average performance, you may have to swim against the current.

Getting creative to make your sign stand out

The average downtown street in the average city has more than 500 signs per block. Try walking such a block and then listing all the signs you remember seeing. One or two may stand out, but most go unseen. To avoid having your sign be lost in this sea of similar signs, you need to make yours stand out.

Signs permit innovation in two interesting areas. You can innovate in the copy and artwork, just as you can in any print medium. You can also innovate in the form of the sign itself. Experiment with materials, shapes, lighting (revolving or variable lighting is rare but amazingly eye-caching), location, and other creative ways of displaying signs. *Remember:* Signs should be creative and impressive!

Here are some of the many variations in form that you can take advantage of when designing a creative sign:

- ✔ Hand-painted (personal look and feel)

- ✔ Wood (traditional look; routing or hand carving enhances the appeal)

- ✔ Metal (durable and accurate screening of art and copy but not very pretty)

- ✔ Window lettering (hand-painted or with vinyl letters/graphics)

- ✔ Lighted boxes (in which lettering is back-lit; highly visible at night)

- ✔ Neon signs (real wow-factor here)

- ✔ Magnetic signs (for your vehicles)

- ✔ Electronic displays or digital signs (also known as *electronic message repeaters;* movement and longer messages, plus a high-tech feel; often these displays take the form of LED signs that make it relatively inexpensive to change your message at will)

- ✔ Small screen- or laser-printed boards with metal brackets for standing in lawns near roads (an inexpensive short-term option for promoting an event)

- ✔ Flat-panel TV screens (with shifting sign content and images or video)

If you want to quickly and easily place large lettering on a wall (perhaps the lobby of your office building?), you can contact firms such as Words Anywhere (www.wordsanywhere.com), one of many suppliers of custom vinyl letters. Figure a cost of around a dollar per letter for foot-high letters, and you won't be too far off in your budgeting. This fairly new medium is a great way to get a message posted quickly and at modest cost.

Each of the options presented in this section requires a different source or supplier, so you need to do some homework after you decide to explore a particular sign design. But have faith that you can find good commercial sources for any and all types of signs.

Researching the regulatory constraints before posting a sign

Many towns and cities regulate the display of signs in public places (you can usually get a list of the restrictions from local zoning boards). And if you rent retail or office space, your landlord may also have put some restrictions (or a *right of review*) into your lease. Research these possible constraints before spending money on design and construction of signs, and run a sketch or plan by the relevant authorities before you invest in having a sign made.

Going Big: Posters and Billboards

Posters and billboards are two of the most popular ways people use signs in their marketing. These two methods are popular because you can view them from a distance, and they can be displayed in public places where traffic is high. However, large posters on billboards, bus kiosks, and other such public spaces offer a difficult design challenge because they need to be readable from far away.

Innovative new LED billboards are spreading gradually through major urban markets. CBS Outdoor has them in more than 30 U.S. cities; see its website for great examples at www.cbsoutdoor.com (check out the options in digital media). The digital versions of billboards, urban panels (large screens positioned on subway station entrances in New York City), and other digital options can be programmed to change frequently, so you can chose time slots instead of having to commit to a static billboard or poster that's there all the time.

The next sections give you some important pointers to ensure that if you decide to include posters and billboards in your marketing, you do so successfully.

Deciding on formats for outdoor ads

You have several choices regarding the size of your outdoor ad and its distance from the average viewer:

- **30-sheet poster:** A standard *30-sheet poster* (a billboard-sized ad) measures 21 feet 7 inches wide by 9 feet 7 inches high in the United States. (With the advent of modern printing, they don't have to use 30 separate sheets anymore.)

- **Bulletin:** A *bulletin* is a huge version of the poster that usually measures 48 feet wide by 14 feet high (these ads may be 10 x 30 feet or 10.6 x 30 feet in places). You can extend bulletins with extra panels on the bottom, sides, or top (see Figure 8-1 for details). A bulletin is four times as big as a 30-sheet poster, giving it incredible impact close up. Bulletins also make the text readable from a greater distance, so they work well along high-speed roads where the viewer isn't near your ad for long enough to read anything requiring close attention.

✔ **8-sheet poster:** Also referred to as a *junior poster,* a standard 11-x-5-foot 8-sheet poster is perfect for sidewalk-level viewing. This poster is about one-sixth the size of the standard 30-sheet poster. But when you place an 8-sheet poster closer to viewers than a standard-sized poster can be, it's sometimes even more effective than the bigger formats. Advertisers seem to think so anyway; the format is very popular with them.

✔ **Spectacular:** If you really want to make an impression, you can choose something oversized (and not standard). In other words, you can use a huge *spectacular,* a custom-made, often building-sized display such as the ads that grace Times Square in New York City. These massive ads cost a bundle, and you should generally treat them as long-term, image-building investments. Few rules apply to spectaculars — aside from the rules of gravity and engineering — so you can have some fun with this unusual form of outdoor advertising.

Figure 8-1 shows the proportions and relative sizes of the standard outdoor ad formats. *Note:* Spectaculars don't have standard sizes, so they don't appear in this figure.

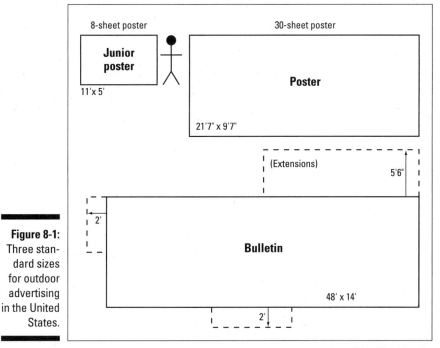

Figure 8-1: Three standard sizes for outdoor advertising in the United States.

You can also explore the growing number of variations on these standards. For example, do you want your message displayed on the floor of a building lobby, on a kiosk at a mall, or alongside the notice boards at health-and-fitness centers? Or how about on signs surrounding the arenas and courts of athletic events? You can use all these options and more by directly contacting the businesses that control such spaces or by using one of a host of ad agencies and media-buying firms that can give you larger-scale access.

Grasping the limitations of outdoor ads

Outdoor or public-space advertising must be kept simple because people view it from a distance and usually in a hurry. The message should be simple enough to grasp in a second; the art and copy must also be simple and clear.

Here's a useful exercise to help you understand the design requirements for a billboard. Draw a rectangular box on a sheet of blank paper, using a ruler as your guide. Make the box 2¼ inches wide and 1 inch high. That's the proportion of a standard outdoor *poster* (a large, printed advertisement posted on a signboard or building). Although an actual poster is much larger, from a distance it may look as small as the box on your sheet (see Figure 8-2). Now hold your paper (or Figure 8-2) at arm's length and think about what copy and artwork can fit in this space, while remaining readable to passersby at this distance. Not much, right? Be careful to limit your message to a few bold words and images — otherwise, your poster becomes a mess that no one can read. Perhaps you've driven behind a car with a bumper sticker you couldn't read. It's frustrating, but nowhere near as costly a design mistake as when a billboard is hard to decipher. Be simple, bold, and clear!

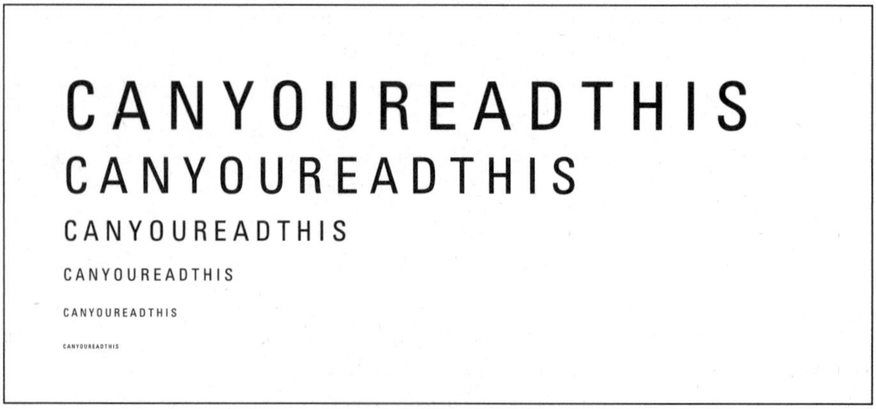

Figure 8-2:
From a distance, a large road-side poster looks no bigger than this image.

CANYOUREADTHIS
CANYOUREADTHIS
CANYOUREADTHIS
CANYOUREADTHIS
CANYOUREADTHIS
CANYOUREADTHIS

Maximizing the returns on outdoor advertising

The costs of outdoor advertising vary widely. In the United States, billboards typically range between $1,000 and $5,000 per month, depending on the quality and quantity of traffic. Digital billboards cost a little more but offer the advantage of lower production and setup costs. When you get down to it, you want to make sure you're getting your marketing money's worth out of this investment. The following sections help you do just that.

Making cost-effective billboard buys

Given the high traffic rates on many expressways, you can get a pretty good buy for a billboard on a cost-per-thousand-impressions (CPM) basis. The average U.S. 30-sheet poster reaches adults 18 years and older at a CPM of $1.50 per thousand impressions, which is cheaper than most other media. (Radio costs about twice that figure; TV and print ads cost at least three times as much.)

Of course, the CPM figures I give you are only the beginning point for cost estimates. Be sure to factor in your estimate of the percent of exposures that reach your target market, which may be small given the numbers of people the ad can potentially reach (in which case, the divisor in that CPM equation goes down, and the price goes up). For example, the average CPM for reaching women aged 25 to 49 with a 30-sheet poster is about $7 — more than four times as costly as when you don't care what sort of adults see your poster. If you need to target a specific customer and don't think the broad viewership of a billboard is for you, look into locational advertising instead.

Boosting your reexamination rates

Always consider the likelihood that your billboard exposures lose value after commuters have seen your billboard many days in a row. Do you get the same effect from the 30th viewing of a billboard as you do from the first half dozen? Will anyone even bother to look at the same billboard multiple times? Maybe not. In outdoor advertising, marketers talk about *reexamination rates* — the average number of times viewers bother to read the same outdoor ad.

The best billboards have higher reexamination rates because people find them interesting enough to look at again and again. If your ad is clear, easy to read, and attractive or amusing, its reexamination rate will be higher. Keep this goal in mind as you design any billboard (or any banner, sign, or poster for that matter).

Blanketing the area with a 100 showing

In most urban markets, you can readily purchase enough outdoor advertising to (theoretically, at least) cover the entire market. The out-of-home advertising industry calls this practice a *100 showing,* meaning you have enough billboards at viable locations to supposedly expose 100 percent of the people in that market to your message. (Similarly, a *50 showing* gives you a maximum of 50 percent coverage.)

If you're looking to introduce a product with a broad target market, such as a new restaurant or grocery store, then a 100 showing is a good goal. Search for an agency that handles outdoor advertising in your target city or cities and ask it for a proposal that includes 100 percent coverage. However, if you're targeting a more narrow market, such as business managers, don't worry about percentages. Instead, ask for placement where you can expect the largest concentrations of your target market, such as along a major commuter route.

Taking advantage of location to buy smaller, cheaper bulletins

As in print advertising (see Chapter 7), the costs of billboards vary based on both ad size and audience size. A bulletin costs about four times as much as the standard poster ad — reflecting the fact that a bulletin is about four times as big as a poster. A junior poster (which is about one-sixth the size of a standard poster) costs roughly a quarter of a poster ad.

Not all outdoor advertising is equal. Location makes a huge difference in the effectiveness of your ad. A smart shopper can find good locations that give a bigger bang for the buck than the average outdoor ad space. If you or your media buyer care enough to shop around (and possibly wait your turn) for locations with low-speed traffic, you can get a billboard that a higher percentage of passersby read more slowly and carefully.

Exploring the (Rather Creepy) World of Intelligent Locational Ads

When it comes to signs, it's kind of a creepy new world out there because outdoor advertising has a new shadow version of itself, coming to be called *location-based media.* These ads are all the remotely accessible screens at gas stations, hotel lobbies, stores, and other places where people are on the go, along with the tablets and phones they carry with them. You can now buy ads to target your leads (which are identified because they picked up a cookie — and I don't mean the edible kind — while visiting your store and talking on their phone or by visiting your website), and some services will place targeted messages when and where you want them.

So instead of a billboard reaching potential customers, you can pop up a custom ad at the gas pump, followed by an ad on customers' phones when they're near one of your stores. That may be a creepy way to get ads in front of a prospect, but it's actually quite effective at boosting retail sales. Another option for business-to-business marketers is to target prospects when they're commuting to work. Check out Vistar Media (www.vistarmedia.com), Verve (www.vervemobile.com), PayPal Media Network (advertising.paypal.com), or Millennial Media (www.millennialmedia.com) for location-based media options, or talk to your media buyer, ad agency, or broker. Foursquare, the online reference tool for restaurants, stores, and businesses, offers a feature for advertisers in which it rewards people for visiting with a Foursquare Special (see business.foursquare.com).

Prospects for customized outdoor or locational advertising and e-signs are often found through *retargeting* — follow-up advertising based on tagging people with a small code (a cookie) when they visit a website (or their phone visits your location). Don't worry about the technical issues — you don't have to write the code yourself! — media firms and online one-stop shops will do this for you. Think instead about whether you want to track people who visit your website, store, or trade show booth, and occasionally — that is, once every two or three days but not constantly, please! — send a follow-up message or reminder. After a half dozen to a dozen such retargetings, the rate of purchase is much higher than just from one visit to a website or store.

Be sure to specify (with whatever agency or media provider you use) that your retargeting ends when the customer purchases from you. The purchase adds another cookie, so you now can tell your buyers apart from prospects and not annoy the buyers with the same pre-buy ad message.

Putting Your Name on Portable Items

A broad definition of a sign may include any public display of your brand or marketing message. Your message can appear on quite a few items people carry around with them or even wear. To me, these messages are just as legitimate as a message on a signboard. And they're often a lot easier and cheaper to make. The following sections share simple, small-scale ways to get your message across, including T-shirts and bags.

Trying your hand at T-shirts

Your customers may think of a nice T-shirt as a gift for them, but you know the truth: That T-shirt is a body billboard! It's amazing how many people are willing to go around with your advertising messages on their clothes (or even on their bodies — temporary tattoos are also a marketing option). Don't overlook this concept as a form of outdoor advertising. In fact, use it as much as you can. People happily display marketing messages if they like them.

You can easily implement this quality premium strategy by looking for good-quality T-shirts made of good-quality fabric and by having a real designer create your compelling, fresh design. (A cool design on your T-shirt is practically guaranteed to get your target audience to want the shirt.) Make sure you use an experienced, quality-conscious silk-screener to put that fine design on those good T-shirts.

To find companies that provide customized T-shirts, search for listings of silk-screening shops near you. (Although silk-screening shops screen onto many different materials and products, directories generally list these shops under the T-shirts heading.)

Getting slapped on with bumper stickers

Don't overlook bumper stickers and car-window stickers. If you make your stickers clever or unique enough, people eagerly seek them out so they can deface their nice new cars with them. Don't ask me why. But because people do, and because the cost of producing bumper stickers is very low, why not come up with an appealing design and make stickers available as giveaways on store counters or as bill stuffers?

Commercial or brand-oriented bumper stickers appeal to people who think the brand is so cool that it enhances the car — a hard thing to achieve. An alternative is to keep your brand identity small and star an appealing message instead. A clever joke, an inspiring quote, or something similar is appealing enough to get your message displayed.

You can even include a nice bumper sticker in a direct-mail piece, where that sticker can do double duty — acting as an incentive to get people to retain and read the mailing and giving you cheap outdoor advertising when they display the sticker on their vehicles. (Contact local print shops, sign makers, or T-shirt silk-screeners; any of these businesses can produce bumper stickers.)

Putting your name on bags

Department stores believe in the importance of shopping bags as an advertising medium. But many other businesses fail to take advantage of the fact that shoppers carry bags around shopping malls, sidewalks, subways, trains, and buses — giving messages on those bags high exposure.

To use bags effectively, you need to make them far easier to read and far more interesting than the average brown paper or white plastic shopping bag. You should also favor designs with comfortable carrying handles, even though they cost two or three times as much. Why? Because if you do, people will carry the bags at their sides where they're easy to read instead of hugging them to their chests or stowing them in someone else's bag that has better handles.

A modern take is to order high-quality reusable shopping bags with your name and logo, plus attractive artwork or a message about green shopping, and give them to your customers. Reusable bags bring your message out shopping, not only in your store but in many others, time after time.

QR codes (those square versions of bar codes) belong on every bag, especially on reusable ones. When people scan the QR code with their phone, it links them to a web page offer or a website. Any signage you can reach with your cellphone should include a QR code, which allows the sign to become a doorway into creatively interactive offers, interesting or useful content, and whatever else you think may be a good way to help your customers and engage them with your business or brand. Check out Chapter 6 for tips on how to create QR codes.

Staying dry (or shaded) with umbrellas

Similarly, umbrellas (available from premium companies; see Chapter 11 for more on premiums) can broadcast your logo, name, and a short slogan or headline — although only in especially wet or overly sunny weather. The advantage of putting your logo on a high-quality umbrella is that people are likely to keep and use the umbrella for a long time. Plus, umbrellas are a lot more businesslike than T-shirts, so they make good gifts when formality is called for. (A bank could offer a free umbrella to each person who adds a new account, for example.)

Taking Your Message to the Streets

What better way to get your message to your prospective customers than to place it right in front of them as they walk around and do their daily business? Most marketers don't take full advantage of the many options for outdoor advertising. The most obvious one — the full-sized billboard beside a busy road — is great if you want to target drivers with a daily message and you have enough sales to justify the cost of giant signs (see the earlier section "Going Big: Posters and Billboards" for more info). But you can also consider other types of messages, including flags, awnings, and mobile signs on vehicles. The next sections take a closer look at these options and more.

Leveraging your vehicle fleet

Everybody likes free advertising, and you can get great free exposures from signs. A magnetic sign on the side of a car or truck, like those you see on the cars of real estate agents, can reach thousands of people a day at minimal cost. You basically have three choices if you want to use your vehicle fleet for signage:

- ✓ **A magnetic sign:** This sign is the cheapest and most flexible because it can be moved from vehicle to vehicle, but it doesn't make as strong an impression as a painted sign on the side of your vehicle.

✔ **A painted sign:** Airbrush artists are available through body shops and local web searches to decorate your car with durable painted lettering and images. Review a portfolio (photos of earlier jobs) first to make sure you like the artist's work. The cost ranges from a few hundred dollars for simple designs to more than a thousand dollars for elaborate images.

✔ **A shrink-wrapped sign:** Even more impressive, but also more expensive, is a shrink-wrapped sign that decorates most of your vehicle with your brand identity and marketing message. You can blow up a photo, a logo, or any other artwork as big as your vehicle can handle. The art is printed on special plastic sheets that are then shrink-wrapped right to the vehicle for high-quality art that makes a big impact. Although the setup costs are in the low thousands, you can apply the same design to multiple vehicles (such as a fleet of vans), and the cost per added vehicle is far less.

Figure 8-3 shows examples of these three options.

Shrink-wrap a vehicle with printed art and text

Use magnetic door signs

Magnetic Marketing Message

www.insightsformarketing.com

Figure 8-3:
Three strong options for vehicle signage.

Have a permanent message painted on

© John Wiley & Sons, Inc.

Flagging down your customers

I have a theory that the first branding by human beings took the form of a flag. Powerful back then, a *flag* (an outdoor message on canvas or synthetic cloth) is still a simple but strong way to communicate an identity or brand. Think of a flag as a more dynamic kind of sign and try to find ways to use it to build brand awareness, make your location(s) more visible, or get a marketing message displayed in more forms and places than you could otherwise. Also, note that the costs of cloth-based forms of advertising can be surprisingly reasonable.

If you find yourself in a community where you may encounter problems with public acceptance of a large billboard message, try a more low-key, decorative approach by using multiple flags and banners instead. Just know that you need to find lower, nearer locations to display them because they're smaller than a billboard. Check with a local realty firm to line up building owners willing to fly your flags.

A number of companies specialize in making custom-designed flags and banners. Of course, you see tacky paper banners — often produced by the local photocopy store — hanging in the windows of retail shops on occasion. But I'm not talking about those banners (because they probably don't help your image). I mean a huge, beautiful, cloth flag flapping in the breeze. Or a bold 3-x-5-foot screen-printed flag suspended like a banner on an office or trade show wall. Or a nylon table banner that turns the front and sides of a table into space for your marketing message. Or a streetwide banner, suspended from a wire cable, complete with air vents, tie-downs, and even sand pockets to keep the message readable in any weather. Figure 8-4 illustrates the most common standard options and terminology of the flag and banner industry.

Flag companies give you all these options and more. These businesses regularly sew and screen large pieces of fabric, and they can also supply you with cables, poles, and other hardware you need to display flags and banners. In recent years, silk-screening technology and strong synthetic fibers have made flags and banners brighter and more permanent, expanding their uses in marketing.

For superior outdoor performance, order a custom flag or banner printed on nylon. Some forms of nylon are protected from deterioration by the sun, so ask your supplier about that. If you want, you can also specify the method used to put your logo or message on the sign. An appliquéd sign is sewn and looks traditional and elegant from close up, but it may come apart in wind. Silk-screened signs are inexpensive and durable. Dye sublimation is a more expensive way to print on cloth, but it allows you to reproduce a photograph or other detailed piece of artwork, which can be very impressive.

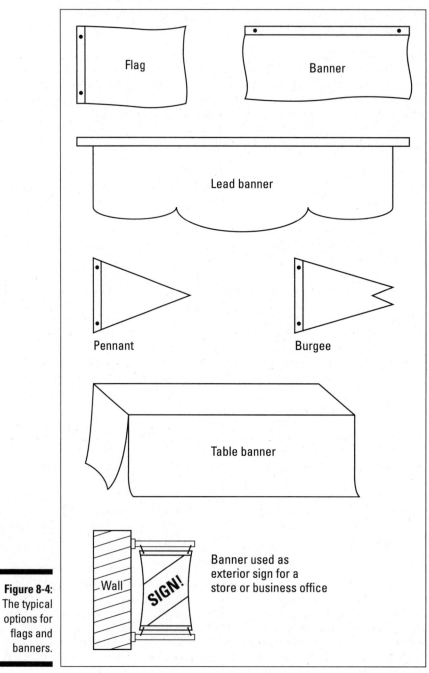

Figure 8-4:
The typical options for flags and banners.

Consider using a flag or banner as a sign for your store or business. So few marketers take advantage of this way to use a banner that it can help you stand out. A flag or banner is less static and dull than the typical metal or wood sign. Cloth moves, and even when it isn't moving, you know it has the potential for movement — giving the banner a bit of excitement. Also, flags or banners often seem decorative and festive. People associate flags and banners with special events because these decorations are traditionally used in that context rather than for permanent display.

You can find a full line of stock and custom products available from Arista Flag Corporation (www.aristaflag.com). US Flagstore (www.usflagstore.com) also offers custom flag production.

Capturing attention with canopies and awnings

If appropriate for your business, consider using an awning or canopy (most telephone directories list providers under the Awning and Canopy heading). For retailers, awnings and canopies often provide the boldest and most attractive form of roadside sign. Office sites may also find awnings and canopies valuable.

Awnings combine structural value with marketing value by shading the interior; they can even extend the floor space of your store by capturing some of the sidewalk as transition space. An awning can perform all the functions a sign can, and more, and it can do so in a way that's highly visible but not intrusive. Yards and yards of awnings don't look as crass and commercial as huge signs because your eye accepts an awning as a structural part of the building. So you get the same amount of advertising as with a big sign — without looking pushy.

Eyeing different alternatives

Although flags and awnings may be the main types of outdoor messages that immediately pop into your mind (see the previous sections), you can also maximize other types of outdoor advertising. Take a look around you to see some of the many creative, and often less expensive, alternatives available, including the following:

- Banners in metal stands (which can be placed temporarily at crowded events)
- Bicycles pulling small signs through downtown areas
- Carpet and rug graphics
- Cinema ads

✔ Fuel pump signs and handle markers

✔ Garage-door vinyls

✔ Hubcap ads

✔ Human statues (hired dancers) and pavement artists

✔ Inflatable signs, blimps, and models of your product

✔ Shopping center and kiosk signs

✔ Sports stadium signage

As you walk, ride, and drive around, take note of any such signs that catch your eye and may fit your marketing program. You may be amazed at how many options are available to you. If you can imagine it, you can probably find someone who brokers the option. All of the options presented in this section can probably be found in your city of choice with a short Internet search.

Keeping Your Message on the Move with Transit Advertising

Transit advertising is any advertising in or on public transportation systems. These ads can appear in buses, taxis, commuter trains, and subway systems, along with airport, bus, train, and ferry terminals. Transit advertising delivers high frequency of viewer notices in a short period of time. Public transit vehicles generally travel the same routes over and over, so almost everyone along the route sees an ad multiple times.

Standard options — the ones most easily available through media-buying firms and ad agencies — include shelter panels, bus and taxi exterior signs, and posters and back-lit signs in airports.

In most U.S. cities, *shelter panels* are 46-x-67-inch posters that appear at bus-stop shelters. (Different standards may apply in other cities.) You can mount them behind a Lucite sheet to minimize the graffiti problem. In many cities, designers have back-lit some of the shelter panels for nighttime display. A one-month showing typically costs anywhere from $500 to $1,500, depending on the city. You may need as many as 100 to 300 panels to achieve enough exposures to reach a 100 percent showing in a city, depending on the city's size (see the earlier section "Blanketing the area with a 100 showing" for more on this tactic).

Bus signs come with well-accepted standards in North America — although some local bus services now offer the option of full-bus painting or shrink-wrapping, too. Here are the typical bus sign standards:

- ✔ **Large bus poster:** Also called a *king-size ad,* a *large bus poster* is a 30-x-144-inch poster in a frame mounted on the side of the bus. This poster can be displayed on the street side or curb side (in the United States, the street side is generally the right-hand side).

- ✔ **Medium bus poster:** Sometimes called a *queen-size ad,* a *medium bus poster* is a 30-x-88-inch poster that's especially suited for the curb side of a bus. If you want to make sure bus passengers and other pedestrians on the route see your poster, then the curb side is for you.

- ✔ **Small bus poster:** Also referred to as a *traveling display,* a *small bus poster* is a 21-x-44-inch poster on the side of a bus. If you have a simple message and a tight budget, this format may be big enough to give you the visibility you need.

- ✔ **Front and rear bus displays:** These ads measure 21 x 70 inches and give high visibility to drivers near the bus. A front bus display can also go by the name *headlighter.* A rear-end poster (or *tail-light ad*) gives great exposure to people in cars behind the bus. But if the bus exhaust is messy, your ad may not look so great after a few days. Check that out before buying a rear bus display.

Want a relatively well-to-do audience with a rich mix of tourists and professional travelers? Then enquire about airport advertising options. Contact media firms such as Clear Channel Outdoor (`www.clearchanneloutdoor.com`), which can place your posters in hundreds of airports. Also, note that some airports are making video advertising available at baggage carousels to reach travelers while they wait for their luggage. (For tips on creating a video ad, flip to Chapter 9.)

When engaging in transit advertising, consider breaking the rule of outdoor advertising that says you have to make your design clear and simple. You may be better off layering your design so you provide a clear, large-scale, simple message for first-time viewers plus a more detailed design and message for repeat viewers to find within the poster. You can do something like hide a Waldo-like character in your ads for people to find or include a riddle or puzzle for viewers to solve. Do whatever you can to allow viewers to go deeper into the design each time they see it. This attraction should help keep the ad fresh and build viewers' interest in the ad and its message.

Chapter 9

Broadcasting Your Message

*M*any marketers are intimidated by video and audio and don't use these powerful communication channels enough. National television advertising is expensive, of course, and only one out of a hundred marketers has the budget for it. For everyone else, there's spot television and radio advertising (including in-store radio), Internet video advertising (including ads on YouTube and podcasts), demonstration videos on your website, video brochures whose links are sent to e-mail and digital cellphone addresses, large-screen TV displays at trade shows and conventions . . . the list goes on and on.

I want to encourage you to be open-minded about radio, video, and TV, because new and easier ways to produce in these media are emerging all the time, along with a growing number of low-cost ways to broadcast your ads. And even if you don't use these commercial media, you can quite possibly create your own ways to share audiovisual information with prospects. In fact, more and more marketers use websites that communicate in digital video or with PowerPoint-type slides and radio-style voice-overs. Modern technology is making these media more flexible and affordable for all marketers.

Producing Ads for Radio

Conventional wisdom says you have only three elements to work with when you design advertising for the radio: words, sound effects, and music. That's true in a literal sense, but you can't create a great radio ad unless you remember that you want to use those elements to generate *mental images* for the listener. And that means you can often perform the same basic plot on radio as on TV. Really. Radio isn't as limited as people think — it's just rarely used to full advantage anymore now that society's love affair with radio has been eclipsed by its love of TV and movies.

For example, I own a collection of old radio shows featuring that amateur sleuth known as The Shadow. My children and I used to listen to these classic radio dramas repeatedly. Why were these old radio dramas so engaging? Because you could see the action so clearly as it unfolded. The script and sound effects (*SF* or *SFX* in radio lingo) create a string of powerful visual images in your mind as the story unfolds (note that the script tells you what supposedly makes the sound effects to make sure you can picture what's going on).

> "Oh no, the giant black cat is coming toward us! My God, its eyes are glowing!" *(SF: Meeeowww. Snarl, snarl.)* "Help, it's backing me toward the edge of the roof of this ten-story building!" *(SF: Snarl, spit, snarl.)* "Look out, Margo. You'll fall off!" *(SF: Sound of falling, with a woman's scream fading into the distance.)*

You can see what's happening, can't you? A dangerous situation creates suspense with dialogue, sound effects, and narration just as well as if you could literally see the situation unfolding.

If you decide to create a radio ad, consider creating a story complete with sound effects, dialogue, and narration because these elements make your ad engaging and entertaining — which means people will listen to it and remember it. However, don't try to finalize a script or record an ad yourself. These are specialized skills requiring a sound studio technician. Instead, bring your concept to the staff of a local radio station for production (for local advertising) or to a production company or ad agency that does a lot of radio ads (for national radio network advertising).

The following sections provide you with helpful information and options you should think about if you're considering radio advertising for your business or product.

Recognizing the cost value of radio time

Radio offers a broader reach for less cash than other media in the United States (and many other nations as well), and I often find myself urging marketers to buy radio due to this incredible reach/value combination.

If you're targeting adults, your audience is probably served fairly well by radio ads. However, younger listeners are tending to tune out radio in favor of their own playlists, which they download from the web and play on MP3 players, cellphones, tablets, and computers. Consequently, traditional radio no longer reaches the under-30 crowd as well as it used to, but web radio can be used effectively instead.

You can target radio advertising quite narrowly — both by type of audience and by geographic area. This fact helps make radio a very good buy. The general lack of appreciation for this medium also helps by keeping ad prices artificially low. Radio ads are cheaper than television and newspaper ads in the United States. Radio programmers don't charge more for advertising slots, partly because of the problem that people may not be paying any attention to the radio they have on in the background. But a well-designed ad can often capture folks' attention for a few seconds.

Going the direct route with your goals

When creating your radio ad, you have the choice of being direct or indirect. *Direct-action advertising* aims to stimulate an immediate shopping response; on the flip side, *indirect-action advertising* informs listeners about a brand, store, or business. The most effective radio ads call for direct action (such as attending an event or picking up the phone), so you generally want to favor direct over indirect action goals for your radio ads.

The best way to go the direct route is to give out a web address (if the listener can remember that address easily) or a toll-free number in the ad. If you want to push people toward an event or blowout sale, use your radio ad to announce the event and drive attendance. Run announcements of events in the week leading up to them, not earlier. Early announcements are better made through print or web advertising (see Chapters 7 and 10, respectively), which allow people to clip or bookmark the ad. Radio ads tend to be forgotten after a few days, so keep them timely.

Put your brand name into your radio ad early and often, regardless of the story line. If you fail to generate the desired direct action, at least you build awareness and interest for the brand, which supports other points of contact in your marketing program. Radio is a great support medium, and not enough marketers use it that way.

Targeting your radio advertising

I like the fact that radio stations make a real effort to target specific audiences — after all, most advertisers try to do the same thing. With a little research, you can get good data, both demographic and lifestyle- or attitude-oriented, on radio audiences. And you can often find radio stations (or specific programs on those stations) that reach a well-defined audience that's rich in those people you want to target.

Arbitron, Inc., is the leading source of audited information about audience size and composition for television and radio stations in the United States. It now also provides information and assistance for those who want to purchase radio and video ad time on webcasts. Visit Arbitron on the web at www.arbitronresearch.com, or go to its parent's website, www.nielsen.com, for lots of market research options.

Prefer data straight from the source? Simply call any local station and ask for its audited report on its listeners, a document the station gives a potential advertiser free of charge.

One way you can target radio advertising is by running ads over the internal broadcasting systems used in many stores. This opportunity gives you another great way to target a particular audience, like advertising your brand of tires at an automotive store. Marketers call this kind of ad *in-store audio advertising*. It's an entirely different medium from a buying perspective because the store or a specialized service provider develops and controls the programming. As a result, most marketers don't know how to use in-store audio programming. An ad agency may be able to help you gain access, or you can turn to a specialized media-buying firm that handles this kind of advertising.

Looking into audio podcasts

An *audio podcast* is a radio program that people may download and listen to at their convenience (however, many are subscribed to and broadcast on specific schedules). Podcasts play on a variety of portable media players, such as iPods or other MP3 players. You can also listen to a podcast on your computer and store it in iTunes or a similar music management program. For marketers, podcasts are a way to make informational or educational radio-style broadcasts available for anyone interested in them. You can advertise on other people's podcasts (visit Podtrac's site, www.podtrac.com, and click on Advertisers at the top to find out how) or you can try your hand at creating your own podcast.

Podcasts are a good alternative to editorial publicity in traditional media because you get to create the content and produce the "show" without having to convince some journalist that your content is newsworthy. But, of course, your content should still *be* newsworthy! Keep your podcast informational and avoid hard selling, or else no one will choose to download and listen to it.

Here are some tools you can use to produce your very own podcast:

✔ **Final Cut Pro X:** Many professional web designers and audio and video producers favor this cool desktop production software by Apple. It'll set you back around $500 and require you to have plenty of memory

(I suggest a big external hard drive). But even if you have to upgrade your hardware to use the program, you'll be able to produce audio and video for the web for less than $1,000 in editing equipment, making this option a must-have for the contemporary marketer.

✔ **ePodcast Series:** Industrial Audio Software (`www.industrialaudio software.com`) offers this podcast producing software for less than $200.

✔ **Hipcast:** This audio and video podcasting service is perhaps the simplest way I've ever heard of to produce an audio recording. If you don't want to have to learn new software and make and edit your own recording, just contact the folks at Hipcast (`www.audioblog.com`) and let them record your podcast message.

Don't forget the obvious: Make your podcasts available on your website so regular visitors (who include your core customers) will notice them. Also consider linking to the latest podcast or video blog from a QR code.

You can also post your podcasts at a site like Podcast Alley (`www.podcast alley.com`), one of a new breed of sites on which you can post your podcast and make it available for members to rate and listen to. (You have to register on the site to post podcasts, but at the time of this writing, registration is free.) I recommend posting on such a site if you want to broaden your audience beyond your own list.

You can also create *video podcasts,* terminology sometimes used to refer to on-demand video clips and web television series. Check out the later section "Identifying Less Expensive Ways to Use the Power of Video" for more info on video podcasts.

Considering web radio

Web radio is audio programming delivered over the web on a regular daily schedule. It's very much like traditional radio except that traditional radio is delivered over the airwaves. Listeners like web radio because it gives them more control and selection than traditional radio. This is good for advertisers because it means that audiences sort themselves out according to tastes and interests, allowing advertisers to target very well-defined groups of listeners — which makes reaching these groups quite economical. Also, web radio is inexpensive to produce (no costly radio transmitters here); low production costs translate into low ad rates.

Web radio is an increasingly good advertising option, reaching hundreds of millions of people each week. Visit web radio leaders such as Slacker (`www. slacker.com`), Live365 (`www.live365.com`), iTunes (`www.apple.com/ itunes`), Spotify (`www.spotify.com`), or Pandora (`www.pandora.com`) to identify web radio stations that may match your customer base. These sites catalog thousands of web radio programs from the United States and elsewhere. Other companies act as brokers for radio ad buyers. TargetSpot (www. targetspot.com) makes it easy to place your own ads on appropriate web radio stations. Web radio ads can take the form of streaming audio or can be in the form of web page ads and banners, giving you multiple options. For instance, Spotify currently has seven different ad formats to choose from.

To get the most for your money, try combining traditional and web radio advertising. You can easily reach a larger audience this way than through print or TV advertising.

Identifying Less Expensive Ways to Use the Power of Video

If you're thinking of skipping this section because it's about video, consider this: Video can cost $2,000 per minute to produce — or even $20,000 if you're making a sophisticated national TV ad. But it can also cost $100 a minute or less. Most videos on YouTube are made for free by someone with a basic digital video camera. And although many YouTube videos look homemade, a surprising number of them are quite good.

If you've never shot and edited a video, you may not be the right person to do it for your marketing program, so consider hiring someone with experience and a portfolio you like. However, if you have some experience yourself, you may want to forge ahead on your own. If you're thinking of making your own video podcast, spot ad, how-to video, or video brochure, take the YouTube tutorial: Review a few dozen of the most popular YouTube videos to see why people are choosing to watch them. In doing so, you'll see a wide range of ways to win the interest of your audience. Sure, some of those YouTube videos feature people making fools of themselves, but others are good, solid pieces of video theater that may give you an idea for a good ad campaign.

Basically, if you think video is out of your ballpark, think again. You can (and probably should) make how-to instructional videos as well as video ads. The next two sections give you some helpful hints in preparing for your video shoot and making sure the actual shoot goes well — without you having to spend big bucks.

Planning your video shoot

Shooting good video takes more than competent lighting, sound, and camerawork. You need to do some advance planning to optimize the shoot. Here are some tips to keep in mind if you decide to shoot video yourself:

✔ **Write a simple, clear script and time it before you bother to shoot any video.** Keep your script brief because the typical spot ad's length is measured in seconds, not minutes (when you purchase ad time, you'll see the options, which usually range from 15 or 20 seconds to a minute). See the later "Designing Ads for TV" section for advice on how to write an effective video script.

✔ **Make sure you have the right supplies.** A fairly new hand-held digital video camera and a high-quality microphone are capable of producing effective video for your marketing, especially for use on the web where low-resolution video files are usually used, making camera quality less important. Additionally, plenty of software programs are available for editing video, although I recommend hiring an eager young videographer who already has the needed software and camera and can take direction from you but can do most of the technical work herself.

✔ **If you want actors, consider recruiting them locally and even asking people to volunteer.** I hate to promote this idea, but if you can avoid paying union rates for your actors, you're better off. Paying union rates and residuals is appropriate for major national campaigns but can be prohibitive for small marketers.

For information on video editing and production, check out the many *For Dummies* books that help you better understand what's involved. Or hire a media production firm (I've used MediaPro in San Francisco, California) that can do high-quality work at moderate rates. With plenty of smaller production firms around, try interviewing some in your area and getting samples of their work and price quotes — you may find that by the time you master the writing, shooting, and editing of a video, you'd rather have saved the time for other business activities and let an expert do it for a few thousand dollars or less.

If you want an easy way to produce a video suitable for podcast or website use, go to Hipcast's site, www.audioblog.com, and click on the Create Video link. You can record video footage of you delivering a message into any digital video camera, send it to this website, and simply follow the instructions to turn your footage into a video podcast. The result may not be stunningly high quality, but it'll be done in a short while and cost almost nothing to make. Most marketers prefer something with higher production quality, but it's nice to know you can do video production for cheap (or even free!) if you're willing to use your computer to do it yourself.

Shooting your own high-quality video

Poor video quality due to lack of light. Inferior sound quality. Shaky camerawork. These are just some of the common problems plaguing amateur video.

Avoid these pitfalls and create good-quality video (even if you're using a camera that costs just a few hundred dollars) by doing the following:

✔ **Clean up the background.** Most amateur efforts to shoot video podcasts or ads are plagued by stuff that shows up in the background. Eliminate trash cans, competitors' signs, and anything else that's unsightly.

✔ **Light the subject brightly and well.** Cameras need more light than your eyes do, and any camera will give you good results if a lot of light is available. Bright, hazy sunlight (through a light cloud cover) is optimal if you're shooting outdoors. Indoors, the low-budget producer can use high-powered but low-cost halogen work lights (careful, they get too hot to touch). Put two lights at about 45 degrees from your subject's face, preferably on her right (the viewer's left). This is your main source of light. Then fill with a lower-powered light on the subject's other side at about the same distance and angle. If you have a backdrop (such as a cloth or a set of some kind), you can light that with smaller lights from the side, top, or bottom, which helps reduce the impact of shadows from the main lights.

✔ **Use a dedicated microphone close to anyone who's speaking.** Don't use the video camera's built-in microphone. You need to be much closer to pick up good-quality sound than you do to take a good still or video picture.

✔ **Set the camera on a solid surface.** Ideally, this means a heavy, nonwiggly tripod. If you don't own one, use a heavy table instead.

✔ **Do multiple takes.** Capture enough footage so you can edit out the bad and use the best.

If you're making a simple, low-cost or free video podcast, you may be tempted to simply sit down in front of your computer's built-in camera and start recording. However, the rules of good video production still apply. Check the lighting! Make sure you look good! After all, you're representing your brand.

Don't shoot faces from a low angle. Many video podcasts show way too much chin, distorting the speaker's face oddly. The camera should be at or slightly below your eye level if you don't want to look like an alien.

Designing Ads for TV and YouTube

Video ads must use great drama (whether funny or serious), condensed to a few seconds of memorable action. Think of a really powerful, moving, and memorable scene from a movie. How about (if you're a Bogart fan) the scene from *To Have and to Have Not,* in which Lauren Bacall tells Humphrey Bogart, as she slinks out of his hotel room, that all he has to do is whistle if he wants her back. It's one of the most well-known sequences in the movies.

These few seconds of drama etch themselves into the memory of anyone who watches that film because they feature a good script with just the right touch of just the right emotion, great acting, good camerawork, and a good set, plus the most important element of all — the suspense of a developing relationship between two interesting characters. You don't need to achieve this level of artistry to make a good video ad, but you certainly need to achieve a higher-than-average level to stand out. The following sections cover important points to help you create compelling video ads.

Proceeding with TV ads

Video ads look simple when you see them, but don't be fooled — they aren't simple at all. If you want to advertise with video, you need to make sure you know what you're doing. Consider the following tips to help you as you begin the process:

- ✔ **Hire an experienced producer or production company to help you do the ad or hire a big ad agency (at big ad agency dollars) to design and supervise the production of your ad.** Hiring experts does add to your costs, but it ensures quality work. Just remember that *you* ultimately decide whether the script has that star potential or is just another forgettable ad. Don't let the production company or ad agency shoot until you have something memorable to make the investment worthwhile.

  Strapped for cash but still want some assistance? Film students at the nearest college with a film or media department are usually eager to help produce ads. To them, it's an opportunity to show that they can do professional work. For you, it may be an opportunity to get near-professional work at very low prices. Just make sure the students and their professors agree upfront (in writing) that you own the finished product and can use it in your marketing.

- ✔ **Aim for an ad that looks high quality and professional.** Sure, you can go to a local cable station and shoot your own talking-head ads in its studio at little cost, or even sit down and talk at your computer's digital camera to make a podcast-style ad. But boy do those ads look cheap when shown on the local network affiliate right next to expensive ads from national advertisers. Without high-quality production, even the best design doesn't work. Why? Because people watch so much TV that they know the difference between good and bad ads — and they don't bother to watch anything but the best. This is true of ads on podcasts, too, because podcast viewers are often downloading high-quality movies or TV shows.

Michelle Phan, a modern marketing success story

If you ever wonder whether YouTube, Twitter, and other new web media can really build brand identity as effectively as traditional television and radio spot ads, consider Michelle Phan's phenomenal success story. I reported in the previous edition of this book that in July 2009, more than 190,000 people had subscribed to Phan's YouTube *channel* (the term for a YouTube home page), and channel visitors had viewed her how-to makeup videos more than 6 million times. The college student started posting videos when she was a teenager, and by the time she turned 21 and decided to launch her own skincare line, she was already a minor celebrity. Now as I write the fourth edition of this book, Michelle Phan has more than 800,000 followers on Google+, and her YouTube channel has more than 5 million subscribers. Posting a new video every Friday, she often gets views in the millions. She has uploaded several hundred videos, proving that her initial flash-fame social media campaign is enduring and has no need to shift to more traditional media to keep growing her personal brand, which she has now (with the

help of L'Oreal Group) translated into a line of cosmetics under the brand name EM (a reflection of *ME*... get it?).

Phan started making how-to fashion videos for YouTube as RiceBunny and also used the name on Twitter, but when she began to market makeup in her own name, she migrated her social media followers to her real name, too (MichellePhan on YouTube and Google+, and @MichellePhan on Twitter). The principle is simple, and one that all marketers can learn from: Invest consistently in a single, clear brand across all the many social media platforms.

Phan combines a chic personal presentation with a nerdy brilliance about her topics, offering unique tips, such as how to make a better face mask out of aspirin and honey. She also tackles real-world problems, like how best to apply makeup if you wear glasses. And her demonstrations of how to, say, make your eyes look bigger and more flirty are just the sort of how-to advice that her followers need. If she sometimes pumps a product along the way, so much the better!

✔ **Create a spoof ad if you're on a shoestring budget.** A *spoof ad* makes fun of one of the silly video ad genres, like the one where an overenthusiastic salesman does a frantic 30-second sell. Because the whole point is to make a campy spoof, you don't need (or want) high production value, but you do still need help from someone with experience in setting up shots and handling camera and lights, plus a good enough actor to make the ad entertaining.

Getting emotional

As you may already be aware, emotion makes for highly effective advertising. Videos can do emotion better than any other medium because they can showcase the expressiveness of actors' faces. So when you plan to use TV as your marketing tool, always think about what emotion you want your audience to feel.

Select an emotional state that fits best with your appeal and the creative concept behind your ad. Then use the power of imagery to evoke that emotion. (This strategy works whether your appeal is emotional or rational.) Always use the emotional power of video to prepare your audience to receive that appeal. Surprise. Excitement. Empathy. Anxiety. Skepticism. Thirst. Hunger. The protective instincts of the parent. You can create all these emotional states and more in your audience with a few seconds of good TV. A good ad generates the right emotion to prime viewers for your appeal. For instance, the classic Prudential commercial ("Own a piece of the rock") is a strictly emotional appeal, designed to give viewers a feeling of permanence and dependability about the investment products the company pitches.

Some marketers measure their video ads based on warmth. Research firms generally define *warmth* as the good feelings generated from thinking about love, family, or friendship. Emotions, especially warm, positive ones, make TV ad messages far more memorable. Many marketers don't realize the strength of this emotional effect because it can't be picked up in the standard measures of ad recall. That is, in day-after recall tests, viewers recall emotional-appeal video ads about as easily as rational-appeal ads. But in-depth studies of the effectiveness of each kind of ad tend to show that the more emotionally charged ads do a better job of etching the message and branding identity in viewers' minds.

Being visual: Show, show, show

Be sure to take full advantage of video's other great strength: its ability to show. In a video ad, you can demonstrate a product feature, show a product in use, and do about a thousand other things just with your visuals. I recently went to YouTube to view a series of tests of blenders and juicers and discovered that I didn't need to buy a higher-priced model to get good performance. I was able to see, right there on the screen, that some of the cheaper models outperformed their fancy counterparts. Seeing really is believing.

Some people in your audience think visually, whereas others favor a verbal message, so you have to cover both bases by using words *and* images in your advertising. In a video ad, you must *show* and tell (note the emphasis on showing). Compare this with radio, where you show by telling, or with print, where the two modes balance each other out, so the rule becomes simply to show and tell. The visual and verbal modes reinforce each other.

To make sure you keep the "show" part of the formula top of mind, do what TV ad designers do: Rough out your ideas in a visually oriented script, using quick sketches to indicate how the ad will look. You — or preferably the competent agency or scriptwriter you hire — should prepare rough storyboards as you think through and discuss various ad concepts. A *storyboard* is an easy way to show the key visual images of film, using pictures in sequence. The sketches run down the center of a sheet of paper or poster board in most standard storyboard layouts. On the left, you write notes about how to shoot each image, how to use music and sound effects, and whether to superimpose text on the screen. On the right, you include a rough version of the *script* (the words actors in the scenes or in a voice-over say). See Figure 9-1 for a sample storyboard.

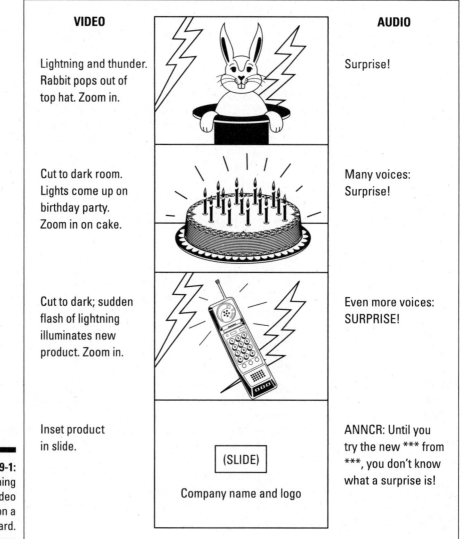

VIDEO

Lightning and thunder. Rabbit pops out of top hat. Zoom in.

Cut to dark room. Lights come up on birthday party. Zoom in on cake.

Cut to dark; sudden flash of lightning illuminates new product. Zoom in.

Inset product in slide.

(SLIDE)

Company name and logo

AUDIO

Surprise!

Many voices: Surprise!

Even more voices: SURPRISE!

ANNCR: Until you try the new *** from ***, you don't know what a surprise is!

Figure 9-1: Roughing out a video ad on a storyboard.

Answering the question of style

You can use a great variety of styles in your video advertising. A celebrity can endorse the product. Claymation fruit can sing and dance about it. Animated animals can chase a user through the jungle in a fanciful exaggeration of a real-life situation. Imagination and videotape know no limits, especially with the growing availability of high-quality computerized animation and special effects at a reasonable cost. But some of the common styles work better — on average — than others in tests of ad effectiveness. Table 9-1 shows styles that are more and less effective.

Table 9-1	Comparing the Effectiveness of Common Ad Styles
More Effective Styles	*Less Effective Styles*
Humorous commercials	Candid-camera style testimonials
Celebrity spokespeople	Expert endorsements
Commercials with children	Song/dance and musical themes
Real-life scenarios	Product demonstrations
Brand comparisons	

Most studies show that both the humor and celebrity endorsement styles work best. So try to find ways to use these styles to communicate your message. On the other hand, making ads that are the exception to the rule may give you an edge, so don't give up hope on other styles. Just make sure your ad lands well above average if you don't want the rule of averages to apply to it.

Purchasing ad time on TV

Although it's possible you may do TV ad buying, most marketing managers never do. Instead, they use a media buyer or ad agency and provide only general guidance as to where the ads should be placed. To manage media buying or direct buying ad time on TV, you need to know the answers to questions such as these: Which television venues work best for your ad? Should you advertise on a network or cable station? Should the ad run in prime time, evening, or late nighttime slots? What programs provide the best audience for your ad?

Audience size and characteristics are tracked and reported by Nielsen Media Research (nielsen.com). Nielsen's viewer studies provide the following statistics by geographic area:

- ✔ How many TV sets are in the market in all (television households, or TVHHs)
- ✔ How many TV sets are turned on at any given time (households using TV, or HUTs)
- ✔ What percentage of the HUTs are tuned to a specific program (audience share)
- ✔ What percentage of the TVHHs are tuned to a specific program (rating)

For example, say that a city has 800,000 TVHHs. If 200,000 (or 25 percent) of these TVHHs are tuned to a particular program, that program gets a rating of 25. If half of all televisions are on, then HUT equals 400,000 households (or 50 percent), and that program's share of market is 200,000 ÷ 400,000, or 50 percent.

In general, advertisers pay more attention to ratings than to share of market data, because ratings tell them how big the audience is, and they usually try to reach the largest audience possible with their ads.

A *gross rating point* (GRP) is the total rating points achieved by your *media schedule* (all the times you run an ad over a specific period). When media buyers purchase a series of time blocks on TV for your ad, they add up all the ratings from each of the times/places where your ad runs and give you the total — your campaign's GRPs. The number is big, but it doesn't tell you very much.

The GRP number doesn't distinguish between new exposures *(reach)* and repeat exposures *(frequency)*. Maybe your ad reached 10 million television households, but did it reach the same 1 million households, ten times over — or did it reach 10 million households, one time each? The answer probably lies somewhere in between. You can find out the exact answer by getting reach and frequency estimates for any TV ad schedule. In some campaigns, you may want 50 or 100 repetitions. In others, 10 or 15 repetitions may be your goal. Let your agency or media buyer know what your goal is.

I recommend adding one further refinement to audience data. Rating points emphasize the size of the program's audience, not the match between the audience and your target market. So be sure to convert — or ask your ad agency to convert — ratings into figures that represent reach into your target market and exclude those households outside of your target market that you don't need to advertise to. When you look at the TV-buying decision in this way, you often end up advertising on a wider variety of channels and programs than if you relied on straight rating points.

Buying spot television and web video ads on a shoestring budget

Spot advertising runs in local markets instead of nationwide. You can buy spot ad time for your commercial from a local TV station or you can ask for localized broadcast from a cable TV company. Web video ads aren't spot advertising because, in theory, they can be seen by anyone on the Internet anywhere in the world, but in practice you can target them fairly specifically by viewer interests and geography. Consequently, they offer much the same benefits of traditional spot advertising: narrow targeting to specific audiences, often at modest prices.

Here are some options you can try if you want to consider spot television and web video ads:

- ✔ **Spot Runner:** This media planning engine (found at `www.spotrunner.com`) creates custom media plans, targeting customers by demographics, networks, and neighborhoods. Use it to purchase 15-, 30-, and 60-second spots on prime time, local broadcast, and cable channels. Many spots cost less than $100. For a local campaign in a modest-sized market, a budget of $10,000 is sufficient to run a spot ad more than 100 times. Major cities cost more, but they offer more customers, so they're worth the added expense.

- ✔ **Apple TV:** This service connects any high-definition television to the Internet and provides access to a wide range of video programs and broadcasts, both live and on demand. The user base is growing rapidly, making this a great new advertising medium. To place your ad on Apple TV alongside movies, YouTube videos, TV shows, podcasts, and other Internet video content, as well as to tap into iPod-using podcast viewers, look into advertising options offered by Blip.tv (`www.blip.tv/advertise`).

- ✔ **YouTube ads:** Users of YouTube may post their videos for free, but you'll have to pay a modest fee to show your ads on the site. Fortunately, it's easy to place ads (either embedded text or video) on YouTube, which has millions of viewers each day. Access YouTube video ads easily (as one of many options) through Google AdWords (`www.adwords.google.com`).

- ✔ **Hulu:** Viewers watch their favorite shows and movies on demand, on the platform of their choice, and you, the advertiser, can target your ad based on Nielson market areas (the industry term being *designated marketing areas,* or DMAs, which are just ways of defining geographic markets) and also by state or zip code. At the moment, a Hulu ad stands out better than a TV ad because Hulu has half as many ads per show (the so-called ad load is lower).

- ✔ **InVideo advertising:** Google offers this option, which allows you to embed an ad message in any web video based on its content, thereby allowing you to target your ad more effectively to people with a specific interest in it. The ad pops up as an overlay in the bottom fifth of the video viewing area if there's a content match — hence the name InVideo.

Another way to cut costs (on any kind of ad but especially on high-cost ads and TV spots) is to look for last-minute opportunities to buy *remnant TV* — ad time that hasn't been sold. Just like hotels deeply discount rooms at the last minute, advertisers may also slash prices to sell excess inventory, but often it's the big advertisers' media buyers who swoop in on these opportunities. Either get in touch with your local television stations to let them know you have funding and an ad ready to go or work with a media buyer who understands the needs of smaller and mid-sized advertisers and ask them to look out for deals. For example, Converze Media Group, which works with small-budget advertisers, is a remnant broker and can facilitate your search (www. converzemedia.com or 800-880-6722).

Using vlogs in place of TV ads

A *vlog* is editorial content in short video format, designed to run on free web channels or YouTube. Vlogs take their name from blogs, being the video equivalent. If your content is interesting and useful, consider making videos and offering them basically as free programming for those with an interest in your topic. The strategy may be used for a business-to-business marketer to good advantage, for example, by offering a tutorial on how to design leadership trainings for the workplace. The goal is to inform viewers and, by so doing, get them to know you and your brand.

Part IV
Finding Powerful Alternatives to Advertising

Five Easy Options for Face-to-Face Marketing

- ✔ **Sponsor a community event.** A community event is a great way to draw a crowd and mingle with prospects as well as boost visibility and good feelings for your brand!

- ✔ **Attend trade shows.** Your presence (even if you don't want to go to the expense of renting a booth) can build visibility and create natural opportunities to mingle and network.

- ✔ **Create an advisory board.** Draw members from your market and industry. People who have influence and visibility will help boost your presence and build your brand.

- ✔ **Offer a free or low-cost workshop.** The topic should be something that highlights your expertise and addresses a common need among your customers and prospects. What a great way to draw prospects to you at the same time that you impress them with your knowledge.

- ✔ **Post how-to advice on the web.** A blog addressing common questions and concerns or a series of demo videos on YouTube may bring you a big spike in online followers, some of whom may be converted to customers.

Help customers navigate their way through the marketing jungle to your brand with the advice I share at www.dummies.com/extras/marketing.

In this part . . .

✔ Revamp your website to give it more visibility and power and then begin using it as the hub of a vital range of web-based communications activities that includes social media.

✔ Realize the numerous ways you can make an impression in customers' minds without spending much at all. Sending press releases and blogging are just the beginning of the story.

✔ Create referrals and stimulate sales by going where your customers are and making personal contacts. Better yet, bring them to you by staging your own public event!

✔ Figure out the secrets of direct-response mail and advertising as well as how to craft a telemarketing script that's guaranteed to keep people on the other end of the line interested in what you (or your company's representatives) have to say.

Chapter 10

Maximizing Your Web Marketing

*W*hen I wrote the first edition of this book, *twitter* was for the birds and *hash* was for the kitchen. Nobody thought about the role of Twitter and hashtags in lead generation. Web marketing was more passive, with most marketers having just a single, central website, usually informative but occasionally with a shopping cart. You needed to be good with HTML to create and manage a good website. Now you don't. There are so many user-friendly options for every aspect of web marketing that the do-it-yourself web marketer is in clover (and, no, that's not a new app — at least not yet).

The paradox of web marketing is that even though it's all so much easier to do, there's so much you *can* do that I still don't recommend you try to do everything at your own desk. Working with specialized web services and sites that automate or template-ize tasks is wise. You may even find it helpful to hire specialists.

Just make sure you budget something toward web marketing — ideally 20 percent of your total marketing budget, whether that's $600 or $60,000 — because the web is too big a marketing opportunity to miss out on. If you want to find out more about the many options the web offers, including website development and web advertising, this chapter has you covered. (Also check out Chapter 21 for some tips on boosting web sales.)

Creating and Managing a Web Identity

Your *web identity* is the sum of your appearances on your own and others' websites, including search engines that may list your websites, any banner or other ads you may be running on the web, and blogs and other online conversational or social appearances. Just like in good real-world brand management, you need to have a clear, consistent name and image in the virtual world of web marketing.

The core of your Internet marketing strategy (literally!) is a good *hub website,* the main website for your business or product that supports a range of uses, from general customer inquiries to press visits, and that also provides access to your online store. Your hub website's structure should stay relatively constant. Don't worry about it getting old because you'll always be updating it with new products, new press releases, and banners or boxes that highlight any special promotions you may be doing elsewhere on the web or off of it. Around this hub and connected to it through reciprocal links, you may have a wide range of smaller and/or shorter-term web pages for specific promotions, as well as pages you may maintain on social networking and blog sites. Your ads on high-traffic websites and in web directories are additional spokes that direct traffic to your hub. (See "Developing Your Hub Website," later in this chapter, for help with the design of your site.)

The next sections take a closer look at what you can do to set and manage your web identity.

Standardizing your web identity

When establishing your web identity, make sure the message you're sending is clear and consistent. To achieve the latter, remember that you want your brand to be recognized and reinforced *everywhere* people run into you, both on the web and off. Start with your *URLs* — the web addresses that identify and link people to your web pages — as well as any corporate or personal business names you may use on blogging sites and social networking sites. These web identities need to match and reinforce your brand identity. If you can't create web identities that are exactly equal to your brand name (the product or company name you want to promote), then embed that name in a longer name so it's still visible.

If you use a variety of names on the web that don't really add up to one simple, clear, single identity, then you need to pick the strongest name and migrate the others toward it. For instance, if your business is named Forest and Stream Natural Landscaping, having your main website address be www. forestandstream.com and your blog name be ForestandStreamGardener may make perfect sense. You can even create a Facebook page using this same name and also load lots of photographs of your successful landscape projects on Flickr (www.flickr.com) under the same moniker. If you're using Gmail or another common e-mail platform, you can add e-mail capability to your hub website address so that anyone who sees your e-mails will see the brand name and know what your web identity is, too.

Using the top inch to advantage

When creating your web identity, maximize the amount of screen space your customers see. The top of your web page is where you get to hammer home a consistent, memorable, clear brand identity on the web. In fact, web designers and users generally accept that the top inch or two of every web page is branding space for whoever controls that page. You want to use that top inch or two to present your brand name plus a short tag line, logo, and special promotional links and messages. Be careful, though, because this space can easily get cluttered with multiple logos, messages, and promotions.

To ensure that you're taking full advantage of this top inch or so, select type, colors, and a visual logo that tie into your overall branding. Repeat this banner design with only minor variants whenever you control the appearance of the top of a web page. You can do a quick audit of your web brand identity right now by looking at the top inch of every page you control. Is it as consistent and as strong as it can be? If not, clean this area up immediately.

Registering domain names

If you don't have the right *domain names* (also called web addresses or URLs) already, you need to create one or more new ones. Select candidate names based on your off-web brand name, which can be combined with a descriptive word or short phrase if need be to make it more unique. To test the availability of a possible domain name, go to sites such as www.register.com and enter the domain name in question to see whether it's available.

As you search for potential domain names for your hub site, remember that a good domain name has the following characteristics:

- **Relates to your business or brand:** I can register the domain name www.lookmanohands.com if someone else hasn't already. It's catchy. It amuses me. Should I use it for my website address? No. It fails my first test because it doesn't relate to my business or brand.

- **Is memorable:** Using your company or brand name makes the website memorable to anyone who knows the name of your business. (For instance, customers can easily remember that Crayola's website address is www.crayola.com.) Or you can simply combine two or three easy words and make the string into a memorable URL. A firm selling UV filtering glass and Plexiglas for framing valuable art could choose a sufficiently relevant and memorable domain name like www.uvprotectionglass.com.

- **Is unique:** If your company name is similar to others, add a unique term or word in your domain name to make it more unique. For example, Ford Insurance Agency has to avoid accidentally losing web visitors to Ford Motor Company's www.ford.com, so the agency uses www.fordinsurance.net. Also, make sure your domain name doesn't violate someone's trademark. Check web addresses against a database of trademarks (in the United States, you can do this search for free by going to www.patents.uspto.gov, clicking on the Trademarks link at the top of the page, and clicking on Trademark Search or ask a lawyer to do a more detailed analysis if you think you may run into an issue. The trademarked domain name you want may be available, meaning you can register it at a site like www.register.com because nobody else has yet, but if you begin using it, the owner of the trademark may sue you.

✔ **Morphs into other identities, such as your e-mail names and a blog name:** Assume that you'll be creating domain-name-based e-mail identities (so don't pick a long or awkward domain name), and at least one general-purpose blog in which you share your expertise and news of interest to prospective customers. Pick a blog name that's based on or relates clearly to your domain name for your website so it's easy to recall and see the relationship between both. Then purchase the blog name (at a host such as WordPress, Bluehost, or iPage).

Many web-hosting platforms now support both websites and blogs, making the integration of them easier than it used to be. For example, FatCow (www.fatcow.com) offers inexpensive hosting for website development, plus integration with WordPress for blogs, and easy links to promote the site on Google, Bing, Facebook, YellowPages.com, nextiva, and so on. It also has the unique feature of its hosting equipment being run entirely on solar and wind power, a good match to alternative and sustainable marketers. Aside from any special promo pricing you may find, expect to spend around $10 a month for hosting, with shopping carts often costing additional but generally with unlimited disk space.

After you have your website registered, take steps to protect your new domain name. Purchase options such as multi-year registration and protection against lapsing due to late payment. Consider purchasing private domain registration, in which your host doesn't give out your personal details as the owner of the site. Also, and this is especially important, if you can afford to, purchase extremely close domains, — that is, pick up domain names with different extensions such as .net and .info. If an obvious misspelling for your site exists, register that, too. The alternate names can be set up as simple redirects, and they'll keep a competitor from owning a domain that may receive some of the traffic you generate.

Developing Your Hub Website

Your *hub website* is your main site where you provide broad coverage of all-important topics, each under a separate tab. If you plan to sell products online, it's also home to your e-commerce site. Your hub website should look and feel a lot like a traditional business website, because it's the all-in-one site for customers, employees, the media, and the just plain curious. What makes it a *hub* is that it links all of your smaller, single-purpose sites and places, including landing pages to support web ads, your blog, your Facebook page, your Flickr albums, and your YouTube videos.

Whether you ask for professional proposals from design firms or design your own site by using templates, make sure your website has a custom look built around your logo. Your website needs to put your logo and business name or brand name out there consistently and clearly. Don't compromise your brand identity just to accommodate a cheap template or a snazzy design concept. (See the earlier "Standardizing your web identity" section for more on the importance of consistency in your brand's presentation online.)

No matter whether you design your own hub website or have someone design one for you, you should also consider adding an online shopping cart. Many basic hosting plans include a shopping cart, so you can implement this feature fairly easily by using theirs. And note that you need to have a dedicated merchant banking account linked to the shopping cart. Talk to your banker about this. If he looks at you blankly when you ask, then you need a more modern bank — switch at once.

Designing a hub website on the cheap

Creating your hub website doesn't have to cost you thousands of dollars. If you want to save a little money, just try creating it yourself.

To create your own hub site, start small and consider the following:

- ✔ **Look for providers of website templates and select the one that offers the features, style, and pricing you like best.** Examine the many sources closely to determine which one is the best fit for you. Some options include

  - **Google:** I like the options that Google offers, including an assortment of easy-to-use, professional-looking templates.

  - **Firms that register domain names, such as Register.com:** These companies generally offer do-it-yourself packages.

- ✔ **Hire an Internet service provider (ISP).** You can find an ISP to host your site quite easily. In fact, dozens of ISPs may be trying to find *you* to make a sale. Pick one that offers the fee structure, services, and flexibility you want — and change ISPs if that ISP winds up not satisfying you. If you're planning to build your own site using a template, then search for an ISP (working with only one is easier, if possible) that offers a template you like. Also, if you plan to set up a store on your website, look for an ISP that offers a shopping cart template. Many of the basic website templates do *not* include a shopping cart, so make sure you find one with a cart you like. (A low-cost alternative is to use an eBay store for your shopping cart function and link to it from your hub site.)

Consider using your domain name and ISP to provide your own e-mail addresses, too. Having your e-mail done through your own domain looks more professional and helps you promote your brand name and web address. For example, if you register www.excellenthairproducts.com, you may also want to have your personal e-mail be yourname@excellenthairproducts.com.

✔ **Check out the latest edition of** *Building Websites All-in-One For Dummies,* **3rd Edition (Wiley).** This book by David Karlins and Doug Sahlin gives you the essentials of website construction as well as information on mobile site planning and social media integration.

Using responsive design for mobile devises

A traditional website is programmed in HTML with lots of tables — some of them managing the content, and others managing its positioning and look on the page. Such sites don't change size and look when displayed on a smaller screen, like a tablet or phone. Although it can be a real hassle to peek through a tiny window on your phone's screen, trying to move around a giant website designed for a computer screen, many websites are still unresponsive to this need for flexibility of scale.

A good solution is to insist on working with a web developer or development platform that avoids lengthy HTML style tables but instead uses cascading style sheets (CSS) to specify the look of the site. (No, you don't need to know much more than this. You likely won't be programming your own website unless you already know all about CSS and HTML. But you *do* need to insist that your site be responsive to the highly varied screen sizes it will encounter.)

Sometimes it may make sense to create a special website optimized just for smaller screens. For instance, a landing site for a promotion that will be marketed to cellphone users may be designed for phone use as its priority, with a fill-in form to capture the participants' information. A bidirectional link should connect this special landing site with the home website (it's bidirectional not only for user convenience but also to allow Google and other search engines to "see" the relationship between them). However, building parallel sites for phones and home computers is costly, and I'm not sure it currently makes sense for most marketers to do so. It depends on where the trend goes as more and more people access the web primarily via their hand-held devices. Perhaps by the fifth edition of this book, smaller-scaled websites will dominate, with huge ones offered for home computers that have gigantic entertainment-oriented screens. Then two parallel website designs may be the norm.

Hiring a professional designer or firm

A sophisticated website design may be beyond the reach of a do-it-yourself marketer and the available templates. If that's the case for you, you pretty much have two options when hiring a professional:

- ✔ **A young freelance designer:** If you need a good custom site and can afford at least a few thousand dollars for it, look for a young freelance designer who's about to finish college and has already designed a number of good commercial websites on the side. I've used several up-and-coming designers on web projects and saved my clients a lot of money this way. *Note:* I find young freelance designers need fairly close supervision, so if you don't have the time or patience for that, look elsewhere.

- ✔ **A professional design firm:** If you have a relatively large business already (that is, you gross at least half a million dollars a year), then don't mess around with amateur website designers just to save money. Instead, visit several dozen design firms' websites and look at their sample work. Choose a handful of firms that have good examples of the kind of web work you want. Past work is the best predictor of future work.

After you have some candidates in mind, ask these firms to provide detailed proposals based on a specific list of objectives you provide. The clearer you are about your objectives, the more focused and affordable your candidates' proposals will be. Don't let any firm talk you into three times as much work than you think you need. Stick to your objectives. If a firm can't offer a proposal that addresses your needs specifically, cross that firm off your list. No matter how impressive its proposal, the firm's inability to follow your instructions will only end in over-budget disaster if you go ahead and work with it.

Looking at the core elements of a good hub site

The best hub websites are easy to navigate and feature clean, uncluttered, appealing design, despite having a great many options embedded in them. Be sure to include the following elements in your site if you want to increase your chances for success:

- ✔ **Simple, clear navigation:** Before you do any designing, you want to ensure that people who visit your site can find what they need. To guarantee your hub site is easy to navigate, make a list of between three and six main categories or topics around which your site will be organized. In my opinion, when a home page has too many tabs or buttons, nobody can find anything, and viewers tend to get frustrated and migrate away to some competing site that's easier to use. Also help visitors click from one section or page to another in your site based on content-oriented links (for example, under the topic Warranties, link to Submitting a Claim).

✔ **Streaming video, animation, and database management:** You can use these technologies as important delivery methods, like showing a speaker in action, demonstrating a new product or providing services, and supporting the consumer online.

✔ **Photographs:** If you have good photos of your product in use, candid shots of customers, or any other relevant pictures, post them to illustrate your site. Or budget another $500 to $1,000 to add stock photographs to your site. Sites with relevant images — especially of real people — are graphically more appealing and hold the visitor's attention longer. Stock photography houses sell low-resolution images (at a lower price I might add) that are optimal for the web and load quickly. Check out stock photography sources such as Corbis (www.corbisimages.com), Getty (www.gettyimages.com), iStock (www.istockphoto.com), or Shutterstock (www.shutterstock.com). Also look for useful images on Flickr, where photographers set up pages to share their work. If you like an image, contact the photographer directly. You may be able to use it for a modest price or even for free. The body of work there is growing rapidly.

✔ **An About Us button or tab:** This button or tab links to a simple page featuring contact information, company history, customer testimonials, media clips, and photos and bios of key personnel. Try substituting short video statements for those boring photos of key people. The video footage can live on YouTube (www.youtube.com) and be called to your hub website when someone wants to view it — this is a cheap and easy way to offer streaming video.

✔ **Bestsellers and special offers:** This element is important if you're selling products on your hub site. Feature bestsellers and special offers on the first page, along with links (in the form of buttons or tabs) to the handful of main product categories.

✔ **A call to action:** Let customers rate or review the product or service. Offer e-mail sign-up for special content like white papers, how-to tips, or discounts (check legal requirements, of course). Run a contest for the best or funniest photo of the product in use. Offer a two-for-one day once a week, only redeemable over the website. The idea of such web events is that they stimulate some sort of action in which the customer or prospect participates, and you capture, if not an actual order, at least the contact information on a prospective future buyer.

Fashioning a registration-based site

A *registration-based site* is one that locks visitors out of the bulk of its pages until they input their name and some identifying information, such as an e-mail address, title and business, or other useful information for your marketing activities. A registration-based site builds a list of visitors for you. You can then use this list to send marketing messages by e-mail or regular mail.

Think about what you want to do with the names before deciding what information to ask people to provide. If you may want to mail or call visitors, collect their full addresses and phone numbers.

To do so, create a form for visitors to fill in, linked to a database that captures each field (a *field* is a specific bit of information, such as name, title, street address 1, street address 2, state, zip code, e-mail address, daytime phone, evening phone). HTML programmers know how to program these forms, or you can use an off-the-shelf version from an ISP.

People won't register on your hub website unless you offer them something that (a) reduces the perceived risk they may feel they're running by giving up their contact information, and (b) seems worth the minute or two registration takes. A credible, well-designed site and a well-known brand or business name reduces the sense of risk. As for what you give them to reward them for registering, that's up to you — apply your marketing imagination to the challenge. If you have useful information, you can allow people access to it after they register. If you normally charge a fee for some service, offer a discount for visitors who register. A frequent-customer discount is another great way to entice people to fill in your form.

Following Simple Rules for Higher Traffic

So much of the success of a website lies in whether it's designed to be visible and easy to use. Many websites fail to follow the basic rules of navigation that ensure easy use and frequent, happy visitors. They also tend to break the golden rule of content, which states that content should have two main aims — to communicate on a clear, simple, compelling marketing position, and to encourage direct action (such as going to a store or placing a web order). So many websites are like vastly overgrown, interactive brochures, or maybe more like a rack full of competing brochures, each on a different topic. A website like that won't pop up at the top of searches, and it won't provide easy navigation or purchase options. Follow these rules to make your website a success:

- ✔ **Test and refine the copy (written content).** Think of most of the website's writing as plain and simple *sales copy,* writing that's designed to generate a sale. Sure, it's good to offer tabs with information and help, but layer those behind the top level of the site, and keep the home page clear and simple, with a focus on generating action. Your goal isn't to become a popular but starving blogger. Your goal is to have visitors to your site become shoppers who buy your products or services.

- ✔ **Offer a clear entry to a very simple order process on the first page of your site.** If I want to say yes to the call to action on your website, how many clicks do I have to go through? It's common for the answer to be a dozen or more. That's a terrible impediment to purchase! Try to simplify to the point that no more than three clicks are needed to get you face to face with an order amount and the option of offering your credit card. Adding more to the shopping cart then becomes an add-on option, not a barrier.

✔ **Ask visitors to opt in right away.** Any opt-in offer is any deal that entices a website visitor to fill in a form and give you their contact information. It could be an offer to qualify for a consumer discount, an upgrade, an informative B2B newsletter, or a high-value, closed section of the website. A frequent buyer membership or professional club registration can also generate opt-ins.

✔ **Make a simple, easy sale right away.** Past purchase is the best predictor of future purchase, so there's nothing quite as valuable in the world of leads as someone who's already become a customer, at least on a small scale. If your sales or adoption process is multistep and complex, consider whether you can make some simpler, smaller sale initially. Can a college sign up website visitors as prequalified candidates, for a small fee, and offer in exchange a discount off the admissions fee should they decide to apply within the next two years? You get the idea.

✔ **Clean up your site navigation.** Most websites start out with a pretty good navigation plan and then get modified to shoehorn in more tabs, add a shopping cart, link to a blog or a Facebook page, showcase a special offer, or incorporate content from a partner business or new acquisition. Talk about messy! Take stock of your site's navigation and clean it up, pruning less important tabs and options and simplifying the top level of navigation. That way, the visitor who's serious about making a purchase or requesting a quote or proposal doesn't have to wander in the website wilderness, clicking madly, lost, until she gets fed up and goes to a competitor's website.

✔ **Take control of recruitment.** The idea that Google and other search engines will consistently rank you high and send you good traffic is a bit naive. How many hundreds of thousands of web addresses do you have to beat out to be at the top of any particular search? Google and other search engines offer key word and searcher profile driven advertising, and you should budget for some of this, at least part of the time, to see how much you can elevate your traffic and bottom line results. Also use QR codes on your signage and packaging (see Chapter 8), do blogging, social marketing, and other publicity with links to your site (see Chapter 11), and direct-response advertising in a variety of web and other media (see Chapter 13). Run an ongoing campaign, with a budget and careful tracking of results, whose single purpose is to promote your website and produce elevated sales there.

✔ **Make sure you have a strong presence on the web and then manage that presence.** A strong, consistent brand, with well-selected web addresses and other identifying names (such as YouTube, Facebook, a blogging host of your choice, and Flickr), can help make you visible on the web. Refer to the earlier section "Creating and Managing a Web Identity" for more.

✔ **Provide a site map.** The fewer links a search engine has to navigate to find content relevant to a specific search, the higher it'll rate your site. A well-designed site map cuts the search engine's journey down to just two links. A large website needs a separate page for its site map, whereas simpler pages can place the map on a navigation bar that's visible from every page. On your map page or navigation bar, list all pages by title or topic and provide a direct link to each one.

✔ **Communicate directly with your customers to build traffic.** Search engines look at traffic when ranking pages, so anything you do through direct communication with your customers to build traffic can help. Offer free informational or entertaining content people will want to visit and download. Consider hosting a bulletin board about your industry or product. Make your website a resource for customers and noncustomers alike, so as to maximize the amount of interaction with visitors.

✔ **Collect, post, and update a page of links to related sites to improve your ranking.** Put a tab or button on your home page that's labeled Links, or if you want to pump up its appeal, label it The Best Links, Recommended Links, Our Pick of Links, or something like that. To find sites to link to, do your own searches and see what sites appear in the top ten listings. Then visit each of them and see whether you can find appropriate places and ways to link to them from your site (and vice versa, if possible). A company that distributes products for you or a professional association in your industry is a natural to link to your site. Build such links and the higher-ranked sites tend to draw yours up toward them. But make sure you have useful content to justify those links! Very brief reviews of the linked-to sites may increase the value of your links page and thus build usage and traffic.

✔ **Build a family of sites and social networking site pages around your hub website.** Doing so may capture traffic out on the rim of your web presence and direct it toward your hub. Include single-purpose, single-topic satellite pages and optimize the META tags for these pages so they rank higher than your hub site in searches specific to their topics. Check out the "Adding Satellites around Your Hub Site to Draw Visitors" section, later in this chapter, for more info.

✔ **Advertise steadily enough to amplify search engine traffic.** Traffic increases rank on most search engines, so a promotion that drives traffic to your website gets amplified by follow-on traffic that comes from search engine visibility, which in turn creates more visibility. I cover advertising options in the later "How to Advertise on the Web" section.

It's arguable that the previously listed points are almost all you really have to know to be a fairly good website manager. However, there are additional concerns and options that an excellent marketer may want to consider, so if you want to have a way-above-average web marketing presence, check out the following sections.

Driving traffic with content

To increase the length of time users spend on your website, and to ensure high involvement and return visits, you need to think like a publisher, not an advertiser. For this reason, I consider strong content to be the hidden factor for increasing website traffic. Unless you have valuable and appealing content, you may have difficulty building up traffic on your site. If you don't know how to write (or film) and publish great content for the web, enlist the help of eager young writers, videographers, and others who do. However you do it, make sure you enrich your hub site (and/or satellite sites) with valuable content visitors will want. But be careful to keep this content relevant to your sales goals. As long as you're attracting people who browse then buy, you're on the right track!

Today's most exciting web content is often published in social media first and then linked into the main website from Twitter, YouTube, and so forth. Traffic is out there on dozens of social media sites, so it makes sense to get out there, too, and try to attract some of it your way.

You basically have two kinds of content you can offer on your site. I've coined these terms because no other appropriate terms seem to exist in the web lexicon. (You may need to explain these terms and the content strategies they represent if you're working with a web designer.) They are as follows:

- **Durable content:** It holds its value and may be kept on your website in an easy-to-access archive.
- **Ephemeral content:** It's useful for a few days to a week but has to be replaced regularly, or else it gives your site an abandoned, neglected feel.

I suggest you try to have a mix of durable content (such as useful facts for your customers) and ephemeral content (such as commentaries on recent events or the latest how-to or demonstration video). Update the durable content at least once a year and renew the ephemeral content every day or week, deleting out-of-date content as you add the new stuff. (Most websites have a lot of out-of-date ephemeral content on them; don't let yours be one of them.)

If you don't have a ton of time to keep updating ephemeral content, focus on putting durable content on your websites. This useful information accumulates on your sites and builds traffic more durably than ephemeral content. And unless you're a journalist or an insomniac tweeter and blogger, it's hard to do your real work and also post fresh new content on the web every day. Durable content works for you while you ignore it. I like that. Your durable content should include reference materials of use to your customers, such as

- A glossary of technical terms
- A list of readings, web pages, and other useful references

✔ White papers and how-to instructional pages and blogs

✔ Instructional videos and photos (which you can post on YouTube or Flickr and call up to display on your hub website)

The useful or interesting content you add to your site to boost visits isn't the same as that call to action that drives sales. Keep the call to action and the compelling sales copy top level and nest supportive content below it in the navigation hierarchy, so as not to set up obstacles to quick sales or opt-ins.

Reaching your traffic tipping point

The *tipping point* concept applies to web visibility. You have to do a lot of work initially to build traffic, and that hard work often seems difficult and costly. But as soon as you begin to be one of the more visible sites in your topic area, the traffic starts to sustain itself. So have faith and keep plugging away until your site's traffic is high and you appear among the top dozen sites for key searches relating to your product or service.

What if you do everything you can to build traffic but your website continues to be ignored? Then you may be tempted to hire one of the many companies that offer search engine optimization (SEO) consulting services. Most of these firms (such as Wpromote, which has a service called QuickList; see `www.wpromote.com/quicklist` for details) work for a fairly reasonable fee, and there's little harm in trying them for a month or two to see what happens.

Succeeding as a niche web marketer

If you're a specialty marketer and need to have only a few hundred or thousand customers, the rules of mass web marketing don't apply to you. Instead of building traffic, you need to focus on people who are interested in your specific offerings. Do so by using keywords effectively and bidding on Google search terms that are highly specific to your *niche* (small, specialized) market and therefore cost less to bid on. Tailor your web copy to your niche market by using the jargon your audience uses and offer sophisticated, specialized informational content on your website(s).

As a niche marketer on the web, you may also find it more effective to emphasize your own expertise as the spokesperson for your brand.

Blog in your own name and post a short video seminar or how-to demonstration on YouTube. Don't worry whether the average YouTube viewer thinks your video is boring or can't follow it technically, giving it a low YouTube ranking; you're targeting the people in your niche market, not everyone who visits YouTube for the latest humorous take-off of "Wrecking Ball" (if you recall the hit song that was parodied so effectively on YouTube). In addition, look for ways to build visibility in professional online venues, perhaps by offering content to newsletters and signing up to be listed with professional associations and then linking those sites to your hub website.

Adding Satellites around Your Hub Site to Draw Visitors

Many opportunities are available for increasing your web reach and presence. For starters, you can put smaller or more specialized websites and pages in orbit around your hub site to attract more and different types of visitors and draw them toward your hub. Interested in knowing more about how such satellite websites can help your main hub site? The following sections have you covered.

Using landing pages effectively

If you advertise on the web (and I suggest you do; see the later "How to Advertise on the Web" section for tips), then you probably need one satellite web page for each ad campaign. A campaign is a *run,* also referred to as a *flight,* of ads that deliver the same basic message or offer but may do so in different formats or styles depending on where they're placed. Because the campaign has the same basic message or offer, all the ads can include a link to one *landing page* (the name for the satellite website that supports an ad campaign).

Two types of landing pages exist. Pick the one that supports your ad campaign best:

✔ A *transactional* landing page (also called a *lead capture page*) finishes the job the ad started by persuading visitors to complete some kind of transaction, such as making a purchase or signing up for a membership or special offer. Special trial offers are often effective on transactional landing pages. Write a transactional landing page like you would any good ad or catalog copy (see Chapters 6 and 7), but keep the copy simple and short because people don't like to read at length on the web. Also keep in mind that a majority of those folks who click on the ad and arrive at your landing page will then move on without taking further action. You may want to give some of these defectors a lower-level way to engage (like offering to send them free information if they simply sign up for your database).

✔ A *reference* landing page aims to fill the visitor's informational needs by providing useful content, such as links, reviews, and professional listings. Marketers for associations and nonprofits tend to use reference landing pages more than for-profit marketers do, but this type of page can be helpful in a wide range of ad campaigns. If you build a reference landing page that has rich enough content to attract a steady flow of thousands of visitors a month, you can sell advertising on it and turn it into a revenue stream.

Use Google AdSense to sell ad space on your website or go through broker sites such as Banners Broker (`www.bannersbroker.com`), Internet Ad Brokers (`www.internetadbrokers.com`), Orange Soda (`www.orangesoda.com`), or Turn (`www.turn.com`). Marketers with valuable information may be able to subsidize their own advertising by selling ads on a reference page. Or just contact brokers to buy ads that drive traffic to your transactional website's landing page. They can help with either type of site.

Regardless of the type of landing page you employ, be sure to track visitor statistics with an eye to *conversion rate* (the percentage of visitors who sign up for your list, accept your special offer, or make a purchase). Ultimately, you want to optimize this ratio. Experiment with ads that attract people who are easy to convert; also experiment with the copy, layout, and offer on your landing page. The more you experiment, the more you discover about how to convert visitors at a good rate.

Conversion rates on successful landing pages may range from 1 to 50 percent depending on the type of site, offer, and visitor, so there's no magic number to shoot for. The best way to know you're succeeding is to document an improvement over your own past performance.

Note that you don't always have to create a physically separate site for your satellite. A page within your hub site that can be linked to (and that offers navigation to a registration page, your home page, and a shopping cart page) can provide an appropriate landing page. The key is to create a dedicated landing page that draws people further in by getting them to sign up or begin using something right away.

Building relationships by blogging

Many of my readers are experts in their fields with interesting viewpoints, anecdotes, and tips. In other words, they're people who can write good columns or blogs. A *blog* is really just a modern-day column posted on a website rather than printed in a newspaper. I recommend blogs over traditional columns because they're easier to set up and because they tend to attract more readers, thus creating new marketing relationships with prospective customers. However, note that the average blog — a personal rant that doesn't seem very professional — isn't what I'm talking about. Most marketers need *professional blogs,* which take the same form as personal blogs but with content that's more consistent and professional (think how-to advice, tips, and interesting facts aimed at potential customers).

To help you get your own business blog started, compare blog services (such as `blog.com`) to find one that offers the platform you want. Many are free, but if you upgrade to fee-based blogs, you can get rid of the ads that pop up on the freebie services — and on a corporate site you may not want other companies' ads mixing with your message.

Take a look at Adobe's blogs (`blogs.adobe.com`), where the software company aggregates technical and how-to blogs by many of its employees. The look is amazingly simple and clean considering this company makes software such as Illustrator and PhotoShop. (I don't know why Adobe uses a simple text format for its blog site; perhaps the goal is to emphasize that the blog is all about serious content.) Many designers and artists visit these blogs regularly for ideas and tips, making them an important link to the customer community.

Also look at airplane maker Boeing's blog (`boeingblogs.com/randy`), which is written by one of its top executives and speaks to employees as well as customers and the general public. This is a good example of brand management on a blog page. The banner features the Boeing logo on the left and a product — an airplane in flight — along with the more specific brand name for this blog: Randy's Journal.

My favorite example of a corporate blog is the one maintained by the photography website Flickr (`blog.flickr.net/en`). It features interesting examples of photographs on Flickr, and it has a simple, clean column down the left side with all the action and navigation options, from subscription, following, and searching, through community events down to archives. Small call-to-action display ads are also run in that left-hand column. You can count on visitors scrolling and seeing the whole column, because the photos displayed on the main panel of the page are so compelling that you can't resist browsing through them. I recommend following Flickr's lead on blog page design, including the addition of a subscription option to your blog so you can capture readers' names for your marketing activities.

Getting active on social networking sites

If you're targeting a younger audience, a social networking site, such as Facebook, Twitter, or Pinterest, can be the core of your web marketing strategy. But even if you're not aiming your product at 20- or 30-somethings, I urge you not to overlook the value of social networking sites. The acid test is, do your customers use a site? If so, then you can do good recruitment and brand-building there.

To brand yourself on these sites, make honesty your number-one priority. Regular users of social networking sites quickly see through fake personas and reject insincere and inappropriate friend requests. Don't engage in *astroturfing,* the term for marketers who try to create fake grassroots buzz on social networking sites. Leave astroturfing to ruthless political campaign consultants whose huge budgets make up for their lack of morals. Real marketers don't create a buzz unless there's genuine in them and their message.

The foundation of brand development on the various social networking sites is either to create and maintain pages in your own name or in the name of your brand. Any number of businesses, ranging from destination resorts to local hair salons, have Facebook pages where they post fun information, photos, or videos about their work and customers.

If you're already communicating with peers and friends on a social networking site, then you shouldn't have a problem creating a brand presence there, too. On the other hand, if hopping on Twitter or Facebook is totally foreign and unappealing to you and your typical customer, then you're probably not going to succeed in integrating your business or brand into the site's web community.

After you have one or more pages set up on social networking sites, you can use them as a platform to launch a *viral marketing campaign,* which is simply the introduction of some piece of content that others will enjoy or find useful enough to pass along. An obvious option is a how-to video that demonstrates one or more of your products. Post it on YouTube and then link to it on your blog, website, and/or Facebook page. Tada! It's now available for anyone on the web. If the video has *legs* — appeal that makes others want it — then links to it will begin popping up on other people's websites and social networking pages; in other words, the video will *go viral* (spread on its own). If it doesn't, make another video with more appeal. Making something that lots of people love isn't easy, so be persistent if you want to use this strategy to good effect.

How to Advertise on the Web

To make your hub and satellite websites (see the earlier sections in this chapter for the scoop on these specific sites) visible to anyone searching for them, you need to spend some advertising dollars. In fact, most marketers have to turn to web advertising at some point. If you're one of them, the sections that follow can set you off on the right foot.

As with all advertising, start small with your web campaign, look for profitable returns, and scale up *only* when you're fairly sure you have a winning ad that won't lose money for you.

Starting with pay-per-click search ads

People punch in search terms millions of times a day, so a great way to attract prospective customers is to make sure your website pops up when they do an Internet search. A few of the largest search engines are Google, Yahoo!, and Bing, although many others exist. Cover these sites with your advertising, and you'll reach many millions of potential viewers. Also consider YouTube, which has grown into the second largest search site (after Google) because of the popularity of its content. Amazon is also a giant (but it won't release its figures, which doesn't matter much to advertisers because they pay per click rather than for audience exposure).

To see what comes up when someone searches for a product or business like yours, make a list of the sorts of key terms a prospective customer may use and punch them into any of these search engines. You'll get pages and pages of listings, some of them commercial in nature. The commercial listings are usually paid for on a usage basis, meaning that the marketer pays a fee each time someone clicks on his listing. Basically, you never pay for ads unless they're used.

Pay-per-click advertising (also sometimes referred to as *key-term advertising*) can form the foundation of your web advertising because it reaches people when they're actively looking for something — either information or a product or service to buy. The fact that they're actively searching means they're likely interested in buying, which means you can turn them into your customers relatively easily.

Here's how pay-per-click ads generally work:

1. **You write a very short (one-line only) text-based description of your product, service, or special offer.**

   This is the foundation of your pay-per-click ad.

2. **You link your ad to key terms you think people will use in searches.**

   Do this by following a specific search engine's instructions for advertisers and entering your bids for specific search terms in the relevant form.

3. **You tell the Internet search engine how much you'll pay for a click on your ad.**

   This is your *bid*. For example, I may commit to a bid of 50 cents for a click on the search term "marketing advice." So if someone follows my link from his search to my website, I owe Google 50 cents. If my bid is higher than anyone else's bid, my listing appears before any other commercial listings at the top of the searcher's screen, which increases the probability of that person clicking on my listing.

4. **You track the results.**

   Based on your findings, you may have to adjust the wording of your ad, the selection of key terms, and the amount you bid on them. Keep experimenting day by day until you find a formula that works for you. Then revisit your formula once a week or so to make more minor adjustments as needed.

All Internet search engines these days offer pay-per-click advertising. I suggest you start by experimenting with Google AdWords (`adwords.google.com`). Google has the biggest share of the search engine market, so you'll probably reach more prospective customers through Google than any other search engine. Also, it's easy to look at monthly and year-to-year trends in searches on Google by using Google Trends (`www.google.com/trends`). This site can alert you to slow periods (searches for many business-oriented terms fall off sharply in December), allowing you to time your pay-per-click advertising to peak search periods.

Adding banner ads to your repertoire

Banner ads (those brightly colored rectangles at the top of popular web pages) are the web's answer to display advertising in a print medium or outdoor advertising on a billboard. They're good for building awareness of your brand, but not much more than that.

The goal of your banner ad is to get across a simple, clear, and engaging message, usually a call to action. Use only a single, brief headline, perhaps supported by a logo and a couple lines of body copy. Alternatively, you can use a brand name and an illustration. In either case, the ad must be simple and bold — able to attract the viewer's attention from desired information elsewhere on the screen for long enough to make a simple point.

Whatever you do, don't let your banner ad get too lengthy; web viewers don't want to read a ton of copy, and you'll lose their interest in a flash if you use more than a handful of engaging words.

You can create your own banner ads by searching for and selecting any of the many banner ad templates that are for sale over the web. Or you can hire a web design firm to create a banner ad that's designed to fit your marketing program more exactly. A good web design firm often adds enough value because of its experience and expertise to make paying the firm's fees worth it, so don't be afraid to ask for proposals and consider the option of hiring a pro.

If you decide to use a banner ad for direct-action advertising, be sure to include a clear call to action in your ad. Typical web banner ads don't give enough information about the product to stimulate an urge for immediate action. Nor do they make taking action easy.

After you design a good banner ad, you need to give even more thought to where it sends the interested viewer. Usually a dedicated landing page is necessary (see the earlier section "Using landing pages effectively" for more on landing pages). You also need to determine the best sites on which to place your banner ad. The three criteria to keep in mind are traffic (favor sites with lots of visitors), a good fit with what you do (favor sites where your customers are likely to be), and cost (compare sites where traffic is high and the fit is good, and shop around for the best ad rates).

Check out advertising options on Facebook by going to `www.facebook.com/advertising`. The interface is simple and clear, with good examples to help you see how to optimize the results by targeting your ad effectively. You may be able to reach a billion people through Facebook, but most of them aren't prospects, so follow its instructions and narrow your audience as much as you can. Doing so keeps your costs lower and your response rates higher, which are the two key variables that drive return on your advertising investment. (Also consider advertising on Twitter; check out `ads.twitter.com` for details.)

Furthering your web campaign with creative display ads

The best online advertising campaigns integrate multiple forms of advertising, including

- **Buttons:** Very small, clickable ads.
- **Half-banners:** Half-sized banner ads that provide significant cost savings.
- **Square pop-up ads:** These open on top of the active web page in their own small browser windows.
- **Pop-under ads:** These open as larger windows beneath the current web page.
- **Skyscrapers:** These are tall, thin ads that look like vertical banner ads.

In addition, web ad agencies offer lots of creative options, including interactive ads such as *widgets,* which are banners with an overlay of a pop-up interactive box that usually asks for an e-mail address in exchange for a chance to win some contest or prize. You can also animate a pop-up or regular display ad or include video in it. Or you can use one of the skyscraper formats to create something that looks like an old-fashioned printed coupon, with the addition of a live form for entering an e-mail address and linking to a landing page where the offer's details are provided and the deal is sealed.

Then there's the *interactive,* a web display ad that invites the viewer to try his hand at something entertaining or useful. For example, a kitchen design company may run an interactive display ad on websites whose content is aimed at homeowners and remodelers. The copy may say something like "Click here to use our kitchen design software for free." The trick with interactive web ads is to quickly send people to a landing page where they fill in a short registration form, allowing you to capture their information before you give them access to the free tool or toy.

If your initial experiments with web advertising (pay-per-click ads, banner ads, and other display ads) are at all encouraging, consider hiring a web design and advertising firm to develop a more extensive program that includes a wide variety of web display ads. Search for a firm in your area so you can sit down face to face and make sure you like and trust the personnel involved. Then set very specific objectives and budgets so the campaign doesn't get out of control. Of course, if you really want to manage your own web marketing campaign, you can, but it takes time and a willingness to roll up your sleeves and learn how to do it yourself. I recommend using display ad templates unless you want to spend all of your days programming in HTML rather than running your marketing campaign.

As for where to place your web display ads, follow the same general criteria that you would for placing web banner ads (see the preceding section): Target high-traffic sites that are a good fit with your brand and offer competitive ad prices.

Knowing How Much to Budget

When asked how much of a marketing budget should be set aside for web marketing, I tell people to strive for between 10 and 25 percent. However, this is a very broad generalization. I've suggested to some clients that they spend 100 percent of their net profits on web marketing for a year or two, in order to boost themselves up to national or international visibility. For clients whose business comes largely from word of mouth, I've recommended they keep their total web spending at 1 or 2 percent of revenues.

You have to determine what percentage is right for you by trying different marketing initiatives and seeing what happens. If you're a fairly small business right now and you run a banner ad that swamps you with great leads and orders, then maybe you should borrow money to run that banner ad all over the place and scale up your business to meet the demand it produces. If so, then you may actually decide to spend more than your last year's revenue on this year's web marketing. Sounds radical, but in the right circumstances, it can be sensible. No point allowing opportunity to pass you by!

The one thing I can say with absolute certainty about ad budgets is this: Don't send good money after bad. If you run an ad, invest in a website, or do any other web marketing that loses money and doesn't seem to boost your leads and build your brand, admit defeat and refuse to spend more on the same kinds of activities. You can and should see positive results from your web advertising. Increase your spending in response to positive feedback from your market. If an ad doesn't work on a small scale, it's not going to work on a big scale. Try something else — on a small scale, of course — and keep experimenting until you find an approach that produces positive results.

Understanding E-Mail Etiquette

You can create, or hire your website designer to create, an e-mail that looks like a well-designed web page, with animation and clickable buttons linking to your site. Then all you have to do is blast it out to millions of e-mail addresses and surely you can make millions overnight.

Not so fast! Okay, so you have this great marketing message or sales pitch, and you want to send it to everyone in the world who has an e-mail address. You can do that, but I don't advise it. The more specific and narrow your use of e-mail for marketing, the better. And U.S. marketers must be careful to avoid violating federal restrictions on *spam* (junk e-mails). I help you stay on the sunny side of these laws in the following sections.

Sending appropriate individual e-mails

The best marketing e-mail is a personal communication with a customer you know, sent individually from you with an accurate e-mail return address as well as your name, title, company name, full mailing address, and phone number. It may read as follows:

> Subject: Thanks for your order!
>
> Dear So-and-so,
>
> I wanted to follow up after your purchase of (your product) on (date) to see how it's working out for you and to thank you for your continuing business. If you have any concerns or questions, please let me know by return e-mail, or feel free to call my private cellphone number, (xxx) yyy-zzzz. Thanks!
>
> Best,
>
> Your Name

Your customer is going to receive, open, read, and appreciate an e-mail like this one. He may even respond to it, especially if he has any current concerns or questions or has another order on its way. Even if he doesn't reply to it, however, he appreciates that e-mail. And that message doesn't bug anyone or look like spam.

Use e-mail as much as you can for legitimate, helpful, one-on-one contact and support of customers or prospects.

Going over the guidelines for mass e-mails

Sometimes sending an e-mail to a list rather than an individual is appropriate, but make sure you have a clear purpose that benefits everyone on the list. Also make sure your list is as focused as possible to avoid angering people. Goodwill is a valuable asset, so don't destroy it!

Like much you do in marketing, you can sub out the task of e-mailing a promotional message to a large list of prospects. It's something of a specialty, and dedicated firms may do it better, or at least cheaper. Take a look at vendors such as ExactTarget (www.exacttarget.com), iContact (www.icontact.com), Benchmark (www.benchmarkemail.com), or Constant Contact (www.constantcontact.com).

The following list has some additional guidelines for good mass e-mailing that I think all marketers should follow. My inspiration for them comes from the Association for Interactive Marketing and the Direct Marketing Association, which have guidelines for the responsible use of e-mail. These guidelines for bulk e-mailing also take U.S. federal regulations into account:

✔ **Send e-mails only to the people who ask for them.** Your bulk e-mails should ideally go only to those people who've given you permission to contact them. You get the most solid form of consent when someone asks you to include him in your mailing. You can get these requests by creating a useful e-newsletter and advertising it on the web as a free subscription. Those people who sign up really want it, and they're happy to see the next issue arrive.

✔ **Remove addresses from your list immediately when people ask to be removed.** Why? See the earlier rule about not angering your customers and recall that in the United States, refusing to allow people to opt out is illegal. Also, people have such widespread distrust of web marketers that you may consider writing the person a brief, individual e-mail from you (identify yourself and your title for credibility), letting him know you've eliminated him from the list and are sorry if you've inconvenienced him. Don't say any more in the e-mail or try to make a sale — you'll just make the person even madder. By being so responsive to his complaint, you generally leave a positive impression, so don't be surprised if your special attention to his request leads him to initiate a sale later on.

✔ **Test purchased e-mail lists before using them.** This guideline is applicable only if you absolutely insist on buying a list. If you do, try e-mailing a very simple, short, nonirritating message to the list, like an offer to send recipients a catalog or free sample, and ask for a few pieces of qualifying information in return. See what happens. Cull all the many bounce-backs and irritated people from the list. Now your list is a bit better in quality than the raw list was. Save those replies in a separate list — they're significantly better and more qualified and deserve a more elaborate e-mail, mailing, or (if the numbers aren't too high) a personal contact.

✔ **Respect privacy.** People don't want to feel like someone's spying on them. After all, real people live at the end of those e-mail addresses and deserve to be treated as such! Never send to a list if you'd be embarrassed to admit where you got the names. You can develop an e-mail list in plenty of legitimate ways (from customer data, web ads, inquiries at trade shows, return postcards included in mailings, and so on), so don't do anything your neighbors would consider irritating or sleazy.

✔ **Send your bulk e-mails just like you send individual ones.** Use a real, live, reply-able e-mail address. I hate it when I can't reply to an e-mail — it makes me mad! And as any good marketer knows, you don't want to make customers and prospects mad.

✔ **Include your company name and a real mailing address.** If you're in the United States, federal law now requires that you include this contact information. Also give recipients an easy way to opt out of future e-mailings — another legal requirement in the United States.

✔ **Make sure the subject line isn't deceptive.** U.S. law now requires you to make your subject line straightforward (that's just good sense anyway). In marketing, you want to know right away if someone isn't a good prospect instead of wasting your time or his when he has no interest in your offer.

✔ **Keep your e-mail address lists up to date.** When you get a *hard bounce-back* (a notice that a message was undeliverable) from an address, remove it and update your e-mail list for the next mailing. A *soft bounce-back* is an undeliverable message resulting from some kind of temporary problem. Track it to see whether the e-mail eventually goes through. If it doesn't, eliminate this address from your list.

People change their e-mail addresses and switch servers, so you can easily have bounce-backs on your list who may still be good customers or prospects. At least once a year, check these inactive names and try to contact them by phone or mail to update their e-mail addresses. Some of them are still interested and don't need to be cut from your list; they just need their e-mail addresses updated.

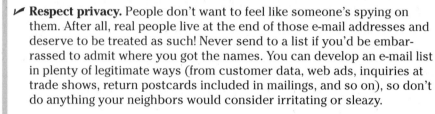

If you're e-mailing to an in-house list of people who've bought from you, gone to your seminar, or asked for information in the past, remind them of your relationship in the e-mail. They may have forgotten.

Chapter 11

Making a Positive Impression in Low-Cost Ways

In This Chapter

▶ Using viral marketing to generate buzz

▶ Thinking like a journalist to score positive publicity from traditional media and bloggers

▶ Knowing how to choose quality premiums with high impact

*I*f you can work your way into the environment of prospective customers in positive ways that don't have the costs and stridency of advertising, you can make a positive impact in an effective, low-cost manner. In this chapter, I present three complementary ways of winning the right to be visible and liked. If managed well, each tactic can make a positive impression for surprisingly low cost.

✔ *Word of mouth* is what people say about you to others. If you give good service and make a friendly, positive impression on people, they'll be motivated to share their enthusiasm with others. *Viral marketing* is a current word-of-mouth trend that I cover here.

✔ *Publicity* works you into the editorial part of the media, where exposure to or mention of your company, service, or product can become a part of the news.

✔ *Premiums* are products identified with your brand (and often with your company's contact information). If people like the premiums, they hold, use, and share them, generating considerable positive exposures for you, again without you having to pay for each exposure.

All three tactics have one very powerful commonality: They get people talking about your product or brand. Many marketers ignore or give only minor attention to them, but all three belong in the front lines of your marketing program because of their ease of use, simplicity, low cost, and potential.

Making the Most of Word of Mouth

If you survey customers to find out why they decided to buy a product, you generally find that answers like "my friend told me about it" outnumber answers like "I saw an ad" by ten to one. When customers talk, other customers listen.

Word of mouth gives a consumer the most credible source of information about products, aside from actual personal experience with those products. What consumers tell each other about your products has a huge impact on your efforts to recruit new customers. Word of mouth also has a secondary, but still significant, impact on your efforts to retain old customers.

Most marketers spend somewhere from 5 to 25 percent of revenues on their marketing activities. Every now and then, I meet people who say they don't have a marketing budget. They don't even have a brochure. They just get referral after referral, and they rarely if ever lose a customer. Must be nice to send that normal marketing expense straight down to the profit margin! What's their silver bullet? How can they avoid marketing costs? It's simple: They've been doing a consistently impressive job in their industry for a long time, and they have a really strong following and great word of mouth. They've probably spent more on quality (great product, great people, and good pay) to maintain their superior reputation. Usually, they market locally or regionally to a relatively tightly defined customer base, which helps build that strong reputation.

The bottom line is, quality and reputation are the best marketing tools ever, and if you're the best, you may not need to do much marketing. Offer the best service, develop loyal customers, and grow from their referrals. It's cheap, it's simple, and it can be written on a single scrap of paper. Now, that's a powerful — and low-cost — marketing plan!

The following sections give you the lowdown on word of mouth and explain what you can do to keep some control over it. I also cover viral marketing, which is akin to word of mouth but tends to live online.

Engaging with customers and followers on social media

Go to your Facebook home page, and look at the Trending box to see whose pages are particularly popular at the moment on Facebook. All too often, it's a celebrity with a scandal, but sometimes it's a business identity or brand. Right now as I write, Coca-Cola has the top spot, trending up, because of the chatter about its 2014 Super Bowl commercial, celebrating the diversity of the nation. Some people were deeply moved and loved it; others were offended by American citizens singing in languages other than English. I doubt the marketers at Coca-Cola thought that would get anyone's dander up, but it's hard to overestimate the vigor of extreme politics. From a marketing perspective, this is a kind of a social media gold mine. Coca-Cola corporate at the top of the charts on Facebook and Twitter? Hey, who could ask for anything more! Even if some of the hits are from haters, it's still an opportunity to present the brand with dignity, compassion, and class.

Almost any coverage is good coverage in social media. The trick is to contribute — in meaningful and well-intentioned ways — to the national conversation. What do you and your brand have to contribute to the week's conversations? Has something happened that you can speak to in some way? Do you want to step forward and share information, sponsor someone, or take a stand? Don't wade in with a negative position; try to take the high ground with constructive comments. A positive, constructive tone is always appropriate for a professional identity, regardless of whether you get peppered on occasion by people who hate your ads.

How much is enough when it comes to Twitter and Facebook comments and contributions? Remember that social media is all about dialogue. If you're not generating retweets on Twitter, comments on Facebook, pins on Pinterest, and so forth, then you're not in the conversation. The alternative to conversation is a monologue, and people soon get tired of that. So let the reactions be your guide, telling you what's of interest and showing you where the conversation should go.

Marketers aren't generally going to be the leaders of social media conversations. They are (they hope) well-mannered guests, chiming in when the social cues suggest it's appropriate but stepping back when it gets more personal and less corporate or professional in nature. But that doesn't mean marketers go unheard. Take a look at the leader board on Twitter to see which brands or professionals are getting a lot of retweets, and then track them back to see what content got picked up as a way to train yourself to be more savvy about how to plant the root of a good viral conversation.

When consumers interact with you on your social media properties, make it a priority to respond to any questions or feedback within one business day — even shorter if possible. For more on how to use social media, see *Social Media Marketing For Dummies,* 2nd Edition, by Shiv Singh and Stephanie Diamond (Wiley).

Managing word of mouth

Many marketers automatically assume that there's no way to effectively encourage customers to say nice things about a product or prevent them from slamming it. However, you actually can influence word of mouth to a considerable degree.

Here are some ideas for how to manage word-of-mouth communications about your product:

- **Make your product special.** A product that surprises people because of its unexpectedly good quality or service is special enough to talk about. A good product or a well-delivered service wins fans and turns your customers into your sales force.

- **Do something noteworthy in the name of your product or company.** If no aspect of your product is incredibly wonderful and surprising, do some cool activity and associate that activity with your product. Get creative and think of some way of helping improve your world that surprises people and makes them take notice of the good you're doing in the name of your product. Support a neat nonprofit organization in your neighborhood. Stage a fun event for kids. Let your employees take short sabbaticals to volunteer in community services. All of these strategies have worked well in the past to generate positive publicity and word of mouth. And don't forget to post a couple minutes of video footage of the event on YouTube and your website (just be sure to get permission if there are any close-ups of individuals).

- **Use exciting sales promotions and premiums, not boring ones.** A 24-cent coupon isn't worth talking about. But a sweepstakes contest in which the winners get to spend a day with the celebrity of their choice can get consumers excited. A premium like that generates positive PR and a *lot* of word of mouth. As an added bonus, if you can think of something really unusual to give winners, that item becomes a talking point, especially if folks can wear or prominently display the premium in their home or office. Why? Because people are guaranteed to ask them about it!

- **Sponsor an online sweepstakes that's publicized with hashtags on Twitter.** Putting a hashtag (pound sign) before a word or phrase points back to earlier Tweets or postings on the topic, which is helpful for following the thread of a conversation. You can also sponsor a contest on Twitter, giving it a hashtag such as #yourfreegiftfromourbrandf orbestetphoto. People wanting to submit their pet photo (or their cheer for their favorite sports team in a big game, or whatever you want to make the topic of your contest) simply Tweet, using your hashtag. If the contest attracts interest, a lot of people will retweet it, and it may go viral. (Services such as www.offerpop.com can help you run such contests.)

Capturing the power of viral marketing

Viral marketing aims to build word of mouth by giving people something (either in the real world or on the web) that they'll pass on to multiple other people because they like it. The object is to get your message to spread naturally, like a cold virus, except with many more positive benefits for society — and your business, of course!

Good viral-marketing campaigns target *decision influencers,* also known as *alphas.* These are the folks whose opinions matter the most. In business-to-business marketing, the decision influencers are often obvious. A handful of prominent executives, the top bloggers in your industry (also check for top microbloggers), a few editors working for trade magazines, and some of the staff at trade associations probably exert a strong influence over everybody else's opinions. Often, you can tap into the Facebook pages of leading thinkers. And you can find plenty of identifiable decision influencers in consumer markets. For example, in the soccer-equipment market, youth coaches, league managers, and the owners of independent sporting goods stores are important decision influencers, and loads of bloggers, YouTube posters, or Instagram personalities also address topics to do with the sport. Some of those bloggers will have huge follower lists, making them your best starting point.

To take advantage of decision influencers, develop a list of the people who fall into that category for your product or service and then make a plan for cultivating them. Match them with appropriate managers or salespeople who can take them out to lunch or to events. The goal is to get people associated with your business into the decision influencers' personal networks.

Alternatively, why not consider developing a series of giveaways and informational mailings to send to these folks? For example, if you want to sell a new soccer cleat to youth players, send free samples to youth coaches. You may even hold a contest (with daily updates on Twitter and video coverage on YouTube) for which team striker can score the most goals in the new cleat in one season. When you know who's talking and who's listening, you can easily focus your efforts on influencing the talkers.

You can reach the decision influencers of your viral content through any medium, from the web and giveaways to local newspapers and sales of products containing or displaying your viral content. The trick to viral marketing is to come up with something that people will think is cool or useful enough to share with others. A giveaway in exchange for their signing up with e-mail address (which then links you into their social media) is a good way to feed your CRM database.

Here are some examples of viral marketing:

- A great design incorporating your logo and additional art or text that people think is fashionable enough to wear or use in public (think T-shirts, temporary forehead tattoos, shoulder bags, or caps). If the design "gets legs" and starts to become fashionable, everyone will want one, and soon you'll see your logo on the chests of teenagers everywhere.

- An amusing, fascinating, or beautiful digital video of one to three minutes in length that attracts a large number of viewers and copycats.

- A fun or clever hashtag that links your product or brand to a situation or occurrence everyone can identify with, perhaps using a fun or startling photo to maximize pickup.

These examples of viral-marketing content illustrate the simplicity of viral marketing and its range of possibilities. **Remember:** Something simple and appealing can always spread, especially if you take care to launch it in ways that make it easy for the right decision influencers to find and share.

Using Publicity to Your Advantage

Publicity is coverage of your product or business in the editorial portion of any news medium. If, for example, *Consumer Reports* runs an article praising your product as best in a category, that's publicity. Good publicity. If, in contrast, the evening television news programs run a story saying that experts suspect your product caused numerous accidents, that's also publicity — the bad kind.

These examples illustrate two common reasons for journalists to cover a product as a story — because the product is better or worse than expected. In both cases, product quality is the key to the publicity. If you have a unique product or service and can make any interesting performance or quality claims, they may be newsworthy, so share them with local, industry, or national media and bloggers.

Public relations (PR) is the active pursuit of publicity for marketing purposes. You use PR to generate good publicity and minimize bad publicity. For example, you may send editors a *press release,* which is a letter summarizing a suggested news story. Or you may write a short, informational e-mail summarizing your newsworthy claim to fame and send it to your favorite bloggers for a more modern spin on releasing your content to the news media.

Many businesses hire *publicists* or *PR firms* — experts who do PR on a free-lance or consulting basis. A regional or smaller PR firm can often do a decent job for you on a retainer of $1,000 to $3,000 a month. If your marketing budget is at least ten times this much, then you can probably afford PR representation. If not, then you need to write your press releases and communicate your stories to the media yourself. (But first, however, you have to come up with something newsworthy to send.)

The following sections help you identify which stories are worth promoting and how to go about putting together a press release that will get you results.

Sniffing out good stories

To a journalist, a *good story* is anything that has enough public interest to attract readers, viewers, or listeners and hold their attention. A good story for a journalist covering the plastics industry must hold the attention of people in that industry. I'm sorry to say that most of what you want to communicate to your market (the great features of your product, why your service is better than your competitor's, and so on) doesn't fall into the category of a good story.

To get good publicity, you have to give reporters what they want. Sniff out a good story, put together sufficient information to back it up, and script a version of the story that reporters in your target media can run, almost without doing any work.

Although the specifics of what the journalists you're targeting want vary depending on the beat they cover, here are a few standard characteristics of a good story:

- **Timeliness:** Pay attention to trends and current events and weave your product or service into them. You don't want to be the marketer pitching the benefits of high-quality parkas in July (unless of course you live in Alaska).

- **Solid information:** The story you pitch needs to have the right facts and quotes within a clear, well-written narrative.

- **Novelty:** Your story should be something that hasn't already been talked about. If it is, try to give it a fresh twist. Old news isn't news.

Reporters and editors do *not* want stories about

- Your new product or service and how it differs from previous models or your competitors' product or service (unless that's their coverage specialty)

- Why you or your company's senior executive think your products are really great

✔ Your version of an *old story* — one that they've covered in the same way before

✔ Anything that seems boring or self-serving to anyone who doesn't work for your firm

Finding the hook: Think like a journalist

Journalism is all about finding the hook that makes your story appealing. Basically the *hook* is a fresh, interesting piece of information that catches and holds attention. When you start sniffing out good stories, you have to look for something interesting, new, and news- or gossip-worthy because without a hook, you don't have a real news story, and the press more than likely won't pick up your story. Journalists don't want to help you communicate with your target market, but they happily use any good stories that you're willing to write for them. And often your product gets mentioned or you get quoted as a result of the good story you pitched.

So what's the secret, the key, the essence of good publicity? Develop stories with effective hooks and give those stories away to journalists and bloggers, both of whom eagerly accept a little help from time to time.

Looking at the situation logically, you need to design hooks to convert your marketing message into stories that appeal to journalists. Your hooks need to be just like the ones that attract your attention to interesting news stories, with one exception: You need to somehow tie them to your marketing information. You have to make sure that at least a thin line exists, connecting the hook to your brand identity, the news that you've just introduced a new product, or whatever else you want the public to know. That way, when journalists use your hook in their own work, they end up including some of your marketing info in their stories.

Try this simple exercise to help you get an idea for your story's hook. Scan today's newspaper (whichever one you like to read) and rank the top five stories based on your interest in them. Now analyze each one in turn to identify the one thing that made that story interesting enough to hold your attention. The hooks will differ, but each story will have one. And I guarantee that all five hooks you find will have certain elements in common:

✔ Hooks often give you new information (information you didn't know or weren't sure of).

✔ Hooks make that new information relevant to your activities or interests.

✔ Hooks catch your attention, often by surprising you with something you hadn't expected.

✔ Hooks promise some benefit to you — although the benefit may be indirect — by helping you understand your world better, avoid something undesirable, or simply enjoy yourself as you read the paper.

If coming up with newsworthy hooks proves challenging for you (and you don't have the budget to hire an expensive PR expert), consider hiring a journalist who has written dozens of stories for one or more media outlets in the past. Writers don't cost that much to hire, so run an ad saying you're looking for a writer with journalism experience to develop press releases and see who responds. I bet you'll find plenty of people are eager to help you come up with interesting content about your business or brand and turn it into usable stories that the media will pick up.

Communicating a story to the media

To effectively communicate your story to the media, you need to keep both format and content in mind. Put your story into an appropriate and professional format so reporters and editors can know the subject of the story and find that story easy to work with. The most important and basic format for communicating a story is the *press release* (also called a *news release*), a short, written document with a clear headline at the top, sufficient facts and quotes to support a short news story, brief supporting background on the company/product involved, a date, and contact information for journalists who want to follow up with a phone call or e-mail to get more info or to arrange an interview. If you include all of these elements — and you have a good hook to start with, as explained in the preceding section — you can write an effective press release.

Reporters and editors throw away more than 90 percent of the releases they receive. Beat the odds with proper formatting and good content (as explained earlier in this chapter). Also, always do the following to help you secure *pickup* (coverage) in the media:

- ✓ **Include something helpful that the media can quote, such as a list of tips, rules, or principles.** For example, a chiropractor's practice may offer five ways to have a healthier back, or a home inspection firm may give ten tips to avoid costly surprises when buying a home.

- ✓ **Offer yourself as an expert commentator on industry-related matters in case the reporter needs a quote for another article.** She may just include one sentence from you, but if she mentions your company name, you just got some good publicity.

- ✓ **Keep it brief.** Journalists are quick on the uptake and work fast, so let them call or e-mail if they need more information.

- ✓ **Post your press releases on your website.** Your press releases can do double duty on the web, providing information for both curious journalists and potential customers.

- ✓ **Send releases to every local editor in your area, no matter how small the publication or station.** Local coverage is typically more attainable than regional or national coverage, and that local coverage can be surprisingly helpful.

✔ **Include a short introductory paragraph in your electronic release that includes a half dozen or more well-chosen (specific) key words so that web search engines like Google can find it.** Someone looking for information with those keywords may go directly to your release, bypassing the need for media or a blogger pickup of the story.

✔ **Deliver your release electronically as an e-mail attachment unless you know that a particular reporter or editor prefers the old-fashioned printed release sent by mail.** Most journalists like electronic releases because they can directly cut and paste text.

✔ **Collect examples of good coverage of your type of product or service and build a mailing list of journalists and media that cover your type of business.** Sending your releases to these people makes sense because they've already proven they give similar stories coverage.

✔ **Check electronic databases of media contacts to see whether you can send your release to more names.** You can expand your list by using services such as Cision MediaSource (us.cision.com/ products_services) and Burrelles*Luce* (www.burrellesluce.com/ Media_Contacts).

Whatever you do, be sure to avoid these common press release errors that journalists complain about:

✔ **Don't send inappropriate or late releases.** Target the right contacts. The food critic doesn't need a release about a new robotic factory. And if the facility opened two months ago, the business correspondent doesn't need the release either because it's old news.

Take the time to build up an accurate database of media contacts. E-mailing your release can be sensible because journalists work on tight deadlines, so include a field for e-mail addresses in your database. Think about developing a list identifying authors of stories you like that may be similar to stories related to your business. Now you have a smaller list that's a much tighter match with your content and target audience.

✔ **Don't make any errors.** Typos throw the facts into question. You want the journalist to trust you to do her research for her, which means she really has to trust you. Prove that you're worthy.

✔ **Don't give incomplete contact information.** Always include up-to-date names, addresses, and phone numbers. Also, give journalists instructions for how to reach you directly by phone or e-mail. (***Note:*** Your personal cellphone is easier than a company phone that rings to a directory.)

✔ **Don't ignore reporters' research needs.** The more support you give them, the more easily they can cover your story. If you want to e-mail a photo, make it a TIFF format of 300-dpi resolution or higher. Also, consider offering plant tours, interview times, sample products, or whatever else may help journalists cover your story.

✔ **Don't pester journalists.** You won't get your story picked up by being a salesperson for it. After your targeted reporters or editors have your pitch, let them do their job without frequent, interrupting phone calls from you.

✔ **Don't bother reporters or bloggers who actually pick up your story.** Journalists don't want to send you clippings of the articles they write, so don't bother asking. Nor do they care to discuss with you why they didn't run a story or why they cut off part of a quote when they did run a story. They're busy with the next story. You should focus on the next story, too.

✔ **Don't forget that journalists work on a faster clock than you do.** When a journalist calls about your release, return the call (or make sure that somebody returns it) in hours, not days, or she'll have found another source by the time you get back to her.

Sending press releases to website editors and (especially) bloggers

Realistically, most publicity programs today are going to get ten or more online pickups for every off-line or print pickup. The web simply has so much more editorial content than print these days that you must plan to run a largely online publicity campaign. People are reading news online, so that's where you want your story to appear. Major newspapers and many magazines run active and interesting websites, so make sure you submit a release electronically per the instructions for publicists on their website.

Online magazines are outpacing print magazines, to be sure. But the real winners of the race for audience are the bloggers, many of whom post their content (at least initially) for free, although if they build a following, they may enjoy selling ad space, just like newspapers and magazines. Blogs exist for just about every conceivable audience and topic.

To send a press release to a blogger, first build a list of blogs that address your topic and have enough audience and/or influence to have an impact. One way to cold-search for blogs is to go to directories, many of which are available online (just do a search for "blog directory"; add the country or a state or region if you want to refine the search geographically). Here are a couple of directories worth investigating:

✔ **Technorati** (www.technorati.com) tracks more than 1 million top blogs by readership and shows their momentum by dividing them into risers and followers; it also cuts the blog deck by topic.

✔ **Top Blog Directory** (www.top-blogs.org) also provides data on blog readership and topic.

PR Newswire and Business Wire

PR Newswire is the premier site for online press releases and a good starting point for do-it-yourself economical publicity. For pricing information, head to `www.prnewswire.com`, and click on Send a News Release, which brings you to the member login or signup. If you expect to use the service regularly, joining is worth the modest fee. You then see a menu of options for submitting releases, ranging from the low hundreds of dollars up. Or if you're a less frequent poster of information, try iReach (`ireach.prnewswire.com`), which allows you to submit a release quickly and easily for as little as $129. Business Wire (`www.businesswire.com`) provides quite similar coverage at a comparable price point but asks you to become a member before posting releases. The Expert Advice on this site includes helpful thoughts on how to write winning press releases and white papers.

Don't waste time (yours or the bloggers') on blogs that are a mismatch with your topic. A business press release may go to some of the 41,000 business bloggers in the Technorati directory but not to anyone else.

After you build a list of blogs for your release, visit each blog to make sure it fits your release topic (or vice versa), and see whether the blogger accepts releases. If so, there will almost always be some instructions for how to submit a release. Occasionally, a blog may require you to pay a small fee in order to submit. If the fit is good and the blog has a lot of readers, it may be worth your while to pay to submit, at least the first few times — but if it never picks up your stories, cut it from your distribution list. You don't need to become an unwitting, anonymous supporter of the blog.

Considering the hodgepodge of video releases and wire services

E-mailing or mailing a traditional press release to a reporter isn't the only way to get your story out there. You can generate a video release with useful footage that a television producer may decide to run as part of a news story. Video works well for stories that have a strong visual component. Opt for video if you can provide the media with footage that viewers will find compellingly interesting. (Hint: It should involve plenty of action.) You can also put a written press release on PR Newswire, or any other such service that distributes hard copy or electronic releases to its media clients — for a fee, of course. You can even pitch your stories to the Associated Press and other newswires (but I recommend hiring a major PR firm before trying to contact a newswire).

When it comes to online distribution of a news story, a photo or short video clip is helpful for attracting attention if (but only if) there's clearly something worth illustrating. If the story doesn't need an illustration, then leave out the photo or video clip for fear of annoying journalists with extra content they don't want in their inboxes. PR Newswire offers the option of online photo or video distribution in which your headline and visual are displayed on the websites of major newspapers (such as the *Los Angeles Times*), MarketWatch, and even the Reuters sign above Times Square in New York City.

Going directly to readers with a blog

If you are (or have on staff) a good writer with a flair for the fun and clever (or, for B2B, a flair for making the technical interesting and clear), consider sponsoring a blog on a topic of general interest. Note that "why our brand is the best" is *not* of general interest, but "what's the best way to have fun when you go out on your own?" or "how are smart small businesses beating the pants off bigger rivals?" may be. Creating an interesting blog is akin to writing a good press release, except it has a higher standard of general interest. For example, a medical consultant I know spends 30 minutes each day blogging and tweeting, exchanging interesting thoughts about medical research and, incidentally, building her network of prospective clients.

When you go the blogging route, think of yourself as an online journalist and/or entertainer first and a publicist only second, or else your blogs will be so marketing-plan serving that readers won't become regular followers.

After you have at least a handful of good blog entries posted and are clear on your writing formula and ready to write a dozen more good ones, start publicizing your blog. WordPress (wordpress.com), an excellent platform for posting blogs, also has (under the Social Tools category) a Publicize option that does a decent job of finding potential readers (based on demonstrated interest in the topic) from Facebook, Google+, Twitter, Tumblr, Path, and LinkedIn, which, added up, spans a huge swath of the online reading community.

Premiums: The Most Abused and Misused Medium of All!

A *premium* (referred to in some circles as a *giveaway*) is any product with a marketing message somewhere on it that you give away. (Actually, sometimes you may want to sell a valuable premium, but you need to at least make getting it easy so as to spread your message as widely as possible.) Classic premiums include T-shirts, coffee mugs, pens, wall calendars, and baseball caps with your company name or logo on them. But you don't have to confine yourself to these choices by any means. In fact, businesses have used these classics for years, so offering something more innovative may be just the route you want to take. The next two sections focus on identifying the premiums that work best and how to make sure people notice whatever premiums you choose to use.

Creating an impact with your premiums

As with any other marketing initiative, you want a premium to change someone's behavior. And you can't do that very easily with a cheap pen or ugly mug. To make a premium really work, you must think through an *impact scenario,* which is a realistic story about the premium and its user in which the premium somehow affects that user's purchase behavior.

An impact scenario starts with your wish list of what the target customer should understand and do. It ends with you thinking of ways that premium items can accomplish your wish list goals. For instance, perhaps your goal is to stimulate and strengthen feelings of pride in a brand. If you're doing marketing for a college or museum, simply putting the institution's name and logo on a mug may accomplish this purpose. Some examples of impact premiums include coffee mugs, pens, T-shirts, calendars, notepads . . . the list is endless.

Say you're marketing a new set of banking services for small businesses, and you want to spread the word about these services to business owners who currently have checking accounts with your bank. Specifically, you want to let these businesses know that you've made a variety of helpful new services available, and you want the business owners to call or visit their branch offices to find out more about these services.

Why not have the bank's name and the slogan "Servicing small businesses better" printed on pens, which you can then distribute in the next mailing of checking account statements? Sounds like this premium item will give you an easy and cheap marketing tactic, but try to imagine the scenario before jumping the gun:

> *The small business owner opens her bank statement, and a pen falls out. She grabs the pen and eagerly reads the slogan. Then, curious about what the slogan means, she immediately dials her local branch and waits patiently on hold for a couple minutes. When she finally gets someone on the phone, she says, "Hey, I got your pen! Please tell me all about your services for small businesses!"*

Somehow that scenario doesn't seem too plausible. In fact, I think most people would just toss the pen into a drawer, or even into the trash can, without reading the message or thinking about what the slogan means. And if you really look at most premiums, you see that they're a part of equally unlikely scenarios. Sure, they often cost little, so marketers often fall for them. But they usually don't work too well, causing even that little bit of money to go to waste.

Don't give up hope! You *can* find some way to use a premium so that people actually get the message about your business or product and, as a result, take some action. In the earlier bank example, a coffee mug may work better than a pen. A mug gives you room to print more information about the services you offer, such as a "Did You Know?" headline followed by short, bulleted facts about the problems the bank can solve for a small business owner ("Miser National Bank offers automatic bill paying" and so on). A customer, drinking coffee from that mug at the office, sees the information you print on it more often and may become curious enough about one of the services listed to ask for details the next time she goes to the bank. But why will she keep the mug at the office and use it? Because it's attractive, and perhaps because it has something appealing (a nice picture, for example) on the opposite side of your marketing message.

Prizing premium quality over quantity

A premium is a gift from you to your customer — which means it tells your customers a great deal about you and what you think of them. A cheap, tacky gift may look good when you run the numbers, but it doesn't look good to the customer who receives it. Yet most premiums are of low or medium quality. Few are as good as, or better than, what you'd buy for yourself. Make sure whatever premium item you choose is of good quality.

You can make your premium stand out by simply selecting an item of higher-than-usual quality. One health spa, for example, orders the nicest terry-cloth robes money can buy, with an elegant embroidered version of its logo on the chest, and sells them at cost to customers, who view them as prized possessions. A customer remembers a better gift more easily, and that gift creates a stronger and more positive image of the marketer. And more customers keep and use higher-quality items for a lengthy period of time.

Of course, a better premium usually costs more. But you can justify this cost by selecting a premium that makes a greater impact — and reduce the cost by distributing it to a better-quality, more selective list. Consider the following example:

✔ **Premium A (Cheap premium with direct-mail solicitation)**

- Cost of Premium A = $5 each, or $5,000 for a distribution of 1,000.

- Response Rate (customer orders within 1 month) = 1.5 percent, or 15 per thousand.

- If profit from each order is $1,000, *premium gross* = $15,000.

- Return = gross of $15,000 per thousand minus cost of $5,000 per thousand = $10,000 per thousand.

✔ **Premium B (Expensive premium with direct-mail solicitation)**

- Cost of Premium B = $25 each, or $25,000 for a distribution of 1,000.

- Response Rate (customer orders within 1 month) = 12 percent, or 120 per thousand.

- If profit from each order is $1,000, *premium gross* = $120,000.

- Return = gross of $120,000 per thousand minus cost of $25,000 per thousand = $95,000 per thousand.

If the $25 premium is of significantly higher quality, you can expect a more positive impact on your customers — and higher response rates in any direct-response program. Thus, the return is often considerably higher on a high-quality premium — provided you target the premium to the right customers (those likely to respond according to your scenario) and don't just blast it out to a poor-quality list.

For a quality take on some classic premiums, plus a broad assortment of high-quality clothing and luggage options, try Lands' End Business Outfitters (visit www.landsend.com and click on the Business Outfitters tab or call 800-587-1541). It offers everything from aprons and sweaters to canvas bags and beach towels; it can even neatly embroider your logo and message. I recommend the company for screen-printed T-shirts, too. And although it's known for clothing, it carries higher-end mugs, water bottles, and other good premium items as well. I keep hoping someone will send me a good reusable water bottle as a premium gift, so I don't have to go buy one for myself!

Chapter 12

Leveraging Face-to-Face Marketing Opportunities

*T*here's an old saying that goes like this: Half the secret of life is simply showing up. It may not be true in all aspects of life, but it certainly applies to marketing. To be a successful marketer, you need to be where things are happening and make yourself and your brand visible and accessible to both prospective customers and others in your industry and community. If you're not sure how to maximize your brand's visibility, never fear. This chapter gives you the lowdown on making the most of face-to-face marketing opportunities for your current and prospective customers. (*Face-to-face marketing* describes all the many ways of having a personal impact on individuals and groups.)

Harnessing the Power of Face-to-Face Marketing

Face-to-face marketing has a personal, warm, human element to it that gives it special marketing leverage and considerable drawing power. Sometimes, it's akin to theater — a performance that entertains or stimulates people in a satisfying way (and sometimes includes people as participants, not just an audience). Other times, it's more like family — a long-term relationship where you take care of your customers and they take care of you. Business used to be trade, and trade used to be based on mutual benefit and personal trust.

Why not go back to these core principles and earn the trust of your customers one by one? Face-to-face commerce is more enduring and durable than electronic arms-length impersonal e-transactions, that's for sure!

The possibilities for face-to-face marketing are endless and varied, but no matter what you do, they should all attract people and hold their attention. After all, you need that attention to communicate and persuade as a marketer. The next sections help get you started making the most out of your face-to-face interactions with customers by highlighting some options you can try and by showing you how to keep marketing events interesting.

Considering your options

Face-to-face marketing can take a number of forms, which can be simplified by placing them into one of two categories: You may either participate in someone else's event (such as a trade show) or stage your own event. Here are several ideas for face-to-face marketing that you may want to promote:

- ✔ **A trade show:** Trade shows allow you to buy exhibitor space and get in front of a lot of prospects in a hurry. If you can't afford booth space, plan to attend anyway and do plenty of informal networking. After all, the more visible you are at your own industry events, the more customer attention and credibility you can generate. (See the later "Exhibiting at Trade Shows and Exhibitions" section for more.)

- ✔ **A client-appreciation event:** A party aimed at entertaining and recognizing your customers can be a great way to strengthen relationships. If you invite a broad range of people, they may enjoy the event's friendship and business networking opportunities.

- ✔ **A musical performance:** Sponsoring a concert your customers and prospects may like, or organizing your own concert or other performance, can be a great way to draw a crowd and get a chance to mingle with prospects. For maximum marketing impact, add a food and/or beverage counter in the lobby along with a table or counter where you give out information and answer questions about your products or services.

- ✔ **A weekend at a golf resort for your top customers, along with prizes for the winning golfers — and everyone else, too:** Many business-to-business marketers find that their prospects enjoy golf and find such events entertaining opportunities to socialize. Make sure your staff is visible and mingling during the event to maximize networking. (The later section "Putting On Your Own Public Event" offers ideas to help make your event manageable.)

- ✔ **A fundraising dinner for an important charity:** Philanthropy is a great unifier, drawing people together and making them feel good about their contributions. Participate in or sponsor social events that benefit nonprofits, and you may find the brand visibility and networking opportunities worthwhile. (See the "Sponsoring a Special Event" section, later in this chapter, for direction on choosing an organization to get involved with.)

✔ **A community event, like a fair or children's workshop:** If you market to families, events that attract and entertain or educate children are a great opportunity for sponsorship and volunteering because they get you in front of your target audience in a positive way.

✔ **A community talent show:** The idea is to think of creative events that attract publicity and draw crowds, raising your visibility and creating natural opportunities to meet and network.

✔ **A client advisory board:** Invite a select group of good customers to join your advisory board and offer them quarterly dinners at a nice restaurant (private room recommended) in exchange for their input, feedback, and ideas.

✔ **Local supply chains where you wholesale to your neighbors and local stores that sell to their own communities:** Sounds like old-fashioned village life, and that's the point! Face to face and person to person, the traditional way, without the trappings of advertising and promotion.

✔ **A how-to or expert commentary video on your blog page:** The web can extend your face-to-face marketing by bringing your smiling face to prospects and other interested parties. However, a video isn't interactive, so invite people to e-mail their questions to you.

✔ **A workshop in which you share your expertise or solve problems for participants:** This workshop can be in person or it can be an interactive web workshop. For example, if you own a store, you can bring in an expert and hold a day or weekend workshop. If you run a consulting firm, this advice may mean offering a special one-hour seminar, led by your principals, that's accessible to all clients and prospects via the web.

Whatever the business-oriented opportunity, keep in mind that you're still trying to attract and hold the attention of people, not businesses. You're interested in the people in any business who make the purchase decisions. Make sure your business-oriented events interest the people involved.

Avoiding boredom to ensure interesting events

If you're planning your own event and want it to attract customer attention, keep in mind that it needs to be entertaining as well as professional and informative. Getting stuffy and businesslike is very easy, but no one really wants to sit through two days of lectures on the impact of new technologies in the industry. You're better off offering optional, one-hour panel discussions on the topic, with a backbone of outdoor sports and recreation events or a visit to a nearby golf course. And, yes, it's true: Attendance is always high at conferences and other corporate events if you hold them in Las Vegas or any other venue that attracts tourists in high numbers, but you don't have to get on a plane to find interesting things to do. Look around your community for interesting field trips or entertaining local talent to feature at your next event.

Some events and sponsorships become staples that gain visibility and impact with each repetition. However, the majority of face-to-face events are one time only; don't repeat them because they'll fail to attract as much attention after people view them as outdated and their novelty has worn off. Creativity adds impact in face-to-face marketing, just as it does in other aspects of your marketing program.

Sponsoring a Special Event

One great way to create face-to-face marketing opportunities is to sponsor a special event. (Think of event sponsorship as piggybacking on others' investments.) The right special event — that is, an appropriate one that's well publicized — is often many times more effective than a paid advertisement.

Sports get the biggest share of sponsorship spending (about 70 percent), but there are lots of other options, too, including entertainment, tours, attractions, festivals, fairs, and the arts. To decide what sort of event is best for your marketing program, think about your customers and what events they like to go to or watch. If your product, service, or customer base is related to the arts, or if you happen to be interested in the arts, you may want to ignore sports events and sponsor the arts, leaving your competitors to compete over more costly sports sponsorships. The key is to have a good reason to be sponsoring the event, some sort of tie-in story that relates the event to your product or brand.

The following sections break down the four actions you should take if you're considering sponsoring a special event. If you follow them, odds are your experience will be worthwhile.

Whatever special event you decide to sponsor, make sure you get a clear, detailed agreement in writing about where, how, and how often the event identifies your brand name. That identification is the return on your sponsorship investment. Too often sponsors end up complaining that they didn't get as much good exposure as they expected, so make sure you and the event directors understand the exposure level upfront.

Know your options

Your first step when determining whether a sponsorship is a good idea is to look at all of your options. The more informed you are, the better a decision you can make. The following sources can help you discover and identify your options:

- ✔ **IEG:** IEG is the International Events Group. It publishes a sourcebook listing many of the special event options out there, including just about every large-scale event. Check out www.sponsorship.com for more info. (*Note:* IEG's emphasis is on U.S. sponsorship opportunities.)

- ✔ **Local chambers of commerce:** Chambers offer lists of local events that may be the biggest things in town, even though you've never heard of them.

Supporting cause-related events

You can attract a lot of positive attention from the media and the community by sponsoring a fundraising event for a charity. This type of event sponsorship is, for obvious reasons, called *cause-related event sponsorship.* Businesses in North America alone spend an unbelievable $5 billion on cause sponsorship per year. You can generate extremely valuable goodwill through cause sponsorship — so long as the cause and event are appropriate to your target market.

Be careful to pick causes that appeal not only to you and your associates but also to your target customers. Maybe your CEO gets really excited about those United Way campaigns. But have you checked with your customers to see what charities they're excited about? Don't throw your money away by forgetting to take into consideration the causes your customers hold dear.

Also, make sure to carefully examine a charity's books and tax-exempt status before sponsoring it or running an event to benefit it. Make sure it has full charitable status (defined as a 501c3 corporation in the United States, for example) and that its audited financial statements show it has relatively low overhead and moderate-looking executive salaries. You don't want to support a charity that turns out to be poorly or dishonestly run. I'm on the board of a charitable foundation that gets hundreds of applications for funding from charities, and I've gone through this due-diligence process many times. It has taught me that some charities are more effective and well run than others and that you never really know until you look. A charity's records and financials should be available for public inspection, so all you have to do is ask. If an organization hesitates to share this information, don't get involved with it.

If you think the event sponsorship is more credible and convincing than an ad because of its affiliation with an appealing cause, you can adjust your cost figure to compensate. Doing so is called *weighting the exposure.* For example, say you decide one exposure to your company or brand through a cause sponsorship is twice as powerful as exposure to one of your ads. Just multiply the number of people the event reaches by two before calculating the cost. That way you compare the cost of reaching 2,000 people through the sponsorship to the cost of reaching 1,000 people through advertising, which adjusts for the greater value you attach to the cause-related exposure.

Don't have the marketing budget to sponsor a local charity? Consider donating your time instead. You can join the board of a charity and offer your energy and business savvy rather than your cash.

- ✔ **Organizations that seem like a good match with your product and customer base:** These groups may know about or put on special events that are appropriate for your sponsorship. For example, if you market sports equipment, educational games, or other products for kids, you may want to call the National Basketball Association to see whether you can participate in one of its many events geared toward children (perhaps a stay-in-school event featuring popular musicians and basketball stars?).

- ✔ **Schools and colleges:** These institutions usually have a strong base of support in their communities, and some add a broader reach through their alumni, sports teams, prominent faculty, and the like. So try calling their public relations offices to see what kinds of events they have that may benefit from your sponsorship.

- **The web:** A number of web-based companies now help you locate possible events to sponsor. For example, check out www.eventcrazy.com for hundreds of possibilities in everything from sports and the arts to reenactments and museum shows. At this site, you can enter your zip code and limit the distance away from your location if you want to find smaller, local events to sponsor.

- **Local television stations:** Call the local television stations and ask them what local events they expect to cover in the coming year. These events are naturals for your sponsorship because television coverage makes the potential audience bigger.

Run the numbers

When deciding on a special event to sponsor, you need to be careful to choose one that reaches your target customers effectively. Carefully analyze the marketing impact of each candidate for sponsorship. Cut any from your list if their audiences aren't a good match with your target market. You may also want to cut controversial events that are likely to generate negative publicity. Last (but certainly not least), axe any events that don't seem to have strong positive images. (After all, a strong nonprofit brand combines well with your goal of building your own brand.) Now compare what's left by calculating your cost per thousand exposures for each one.

Like any marketing communication, an event sponsorship needs to deliver reach at a reasonable cost. So ask yourself how many people will come to the event or hear of your sponsorship of it. Then ask yourself what percentage of this total is likely to be in your target market. That's your *reach*. Divide your cost by this figure, multiply it by 1,000, and you have the cost of your reach per thousand. You can compare this cost with cost figures for other kinds of reach, such as a print or radio ad or a direct mailing (see Chapters 7, 9, and 13, respectively, for more information on the costs of these types of reach).

Screen for relevance

Relevance is how closely the event relates to your product and its usage by customers, and it's the most important yet least considered factor. A chance to use the product, or at least to see the product in use, makes any event highly relevant. And the more relevant the event, the more valuable those exposures. Make sure you pick events that tie into your product or service in some obvious way. For example, a healthcare organization may logically sponsor a blood drive, and a bank can reasonably sponsor a first-time homebuyers' clinic. These events clearly reinforce the sponsor's brand image in its industry.

Sometimes going beyond direct relevance is okay, especially in community-based business, but always consider the pros and cons first. For example, an area savings and loan institution may sponsor a local youth soccer team, contribute to a campaign for the local homeless shelter, and help fund the preservation of conservation land, purely because these are good local causes and the managers of the savings and loan institution care about them.

Express your values and convictions

Whatever charities you support, make sure they're working on issues that matter to you. Sponsorship is a great way to align your personal values with your business interests. For example, sponsoring events and charities aimed at making business greener may excite you — and also attract like-minded customers.

Of course, you don't always have to have a profit-focused agenda. The more genuine your concern about a cause, the more honest and real the support will be. Often, community members pick up on this and appreciate your concern and commitment. In such cases, toss the reach statistics out the window and just budget something you can afford to contribute. One good turn deserves another, as the old saying goes, and the big-picture return on investment on charity is real, even if it doesn't drop down to this year's bottom line.

Putting On Your Own Public Event

Sometimes the best alternative is to stage a special event yourself. Perhaps none of the available sponsorship options fit your requirements. Or maybe you really need the exclusivity of your own event, a forum in which no competitors' messages can interfere with your own. If you want to put on your own special event, check out the following sections for some sage advice.

Selling sponsorship rights

Many of the events you may want to hold — such as a workshop, open house, or clinic — are small in scale and easy to stage on even a small budget. However, if you want to put on a larger event, you'll inevitably run into bigger costs and may want to find ways to defray those costs. A possible way to make your event pay for itself is to find other companies that want to help sponsor it (not your competitors, of course). Many companies often have an interest in the same event as you do but for different reasons; these firms make good cosponsors. Basically, if the event is relevant, novel, and likely to draw in those companies' target audiences, then you have a good pitch. Now you just need to go out and make sales calls on potential sponsors.

Be sure to publicize your event well by listing it in *Advertising Age* (check out adage.com) and your industry's trade magazines and by posting it on the web. You can also consider hiring an event management firm that sells sponsorships in addition to helping organize and run events and send out press releases to local media, including bloggers, to generate editorial coverage of your event (see Chapter 11 for the scoop on sending press releases).

Getting help managing your event

Large events are challenging, and even if you can run one by yourself, doing so probably will take most of your time for several months, leading you to neglect your other duties. That's why I recommend bringing in an event management specialist to help you design and manage any event that involves a lot of people, shows, speeches or activities, meals, conference and hotel room reservations, security, transportation, and all those sorts of details that you have to do right when staging a major event. The Event Planners Association (EPA; www.eventplannersassociation.com) posts a member directory by category on its website, so you can check out categories such as Event Planner/Producer/Coordinator and Event Marketing for leads as well as advertise or network in your region for someone with a proven track record and good references.

For inspiration and lots of benchmark-level examples, read the Event Planning blog by Cvent at blog.cvent.com. (Cvent sells software for event marketing and management, hence its interest in sponsoring a blog on the topic.) I also recommend Event Manager Blog (www.eventmanagerblog.com) for examples, ideas, and promotion strategies.

Expanding the event online

For every person who attends your event, you may find ten or even a hundred people to follow it virtually on the web. Every event ought to have an event website (that's set up in advance and runs throughout the event itself) with live feeds, YouTube videos, and postings of interesting content from the event. Of course, you can promote the event website on your own website, on your Facebook professional page, and even on an event-focused special Facebook page.

Tweets are a natural tie-in with events, too, because a good event gives people something to talk about, so link a Twitter feed into Facebook and web page coverage. Better yet, take advantage of the relatively new Custom Timelines option on Twitter, which gives you, as the event manager, more control over how you display present tweets about your event. Also, set up a hashtag associated with the event so that tweets about it become an identifiable (and displayable) common thread. If these terms and strategies sound like Greek to you, explore the Twitter website and/or consult the appropriate *For Dummies* titles. It's not all that complex to do it yourself, or you can simply hire someone with experience in online publicity and event promotion.

Exhibiting at Trade Shows and Exhibitions

A traditional way to get face-to-face contact is through trade shows and exhibitions. If your industry has regional or national trade shows or other professional events, you may want to attend them at least once to see whether the leads and/or sales justify the costs of attendance.

Some retail or consumer industries also have major shows. For example, boat manufacturers use boat shows as an important way to expose consumers to their products. County fairs attract exhibitors of arts and crafts, gourmet foods, and gardening supplies. Computer shows showcase new equipment. If your industry has a major show for the public, I highly recommend that you try to exhibit there. Send your in-house list of customers and friends an invitation, too — the more traffic you can get in your booth, the better. (In fact, you should plan to begin direct marketing to announce the event and give people incentives to come, starting at least two months before the show!) And don't forget to create a temporary website or section on your regular website devoted to the show. Treat your presence (especially if you have a booth or are presenting) just like any promotable event (see earlier sections). Tweets and Facebook postings about the event should include a link to your event website landing page.

The sections that follow explain how you can take advantage of trade shows to get more face-to-face contacts.

Knowing what trade shows can accomplish for you

You can generate leads, find new customers, and maintain or improve your current customers' perceptions of you at trade shows. You can also use trade shows to introduce a new product or launch a new strategy. You can even introduce back-office people (like the sales support staff or even the company president) to your customers in person. At a minimum, trade show presence makes you visible, building awareness of your brand that helps with future sales. Make sure you bring lots of marketing materials and samples to hand out (if at all possible) to help build your visibility and seed future sales.

Use trade shows to network in your industry. You usually find the best manufacturers' representatives and salespeople by making connections at trade shows. And if you're secretly hoping to find a better employer, a little mingling may yield an offer at the next big trade show. Also, be sure to talk with a lot of attendees and noncompetitive exhibitors to find out about the newest trends and what your competitors are doing in the market. The information a good networker gleans from a trade show is often worth more than the price of attendance. Never mind selling — get out there and chat!

Building the foundations for a good booth

Marketers traditionally focus on the booth when they think about how to handle a trade show. But you should consider the booth just a part of your overall marketing strategy for the show. Develop a full-blown show strategy by answering each of these questions:

- How do we attract the right people to the show and to our booth?
- What do we want visitors to our booth to do at the show and in our booth?
- How can we communicate with and motivate visitors when they get to the booth?
- How can we capture information about them, their interests, and their needs?
- What can we send visitors away with that will maximize the chances of them getting in touch with us after the show?
- How can we follow up to build or maintain our relationship with our booth visitors?

Your strategy has to start by attracting a lot of prospects and customers, and the easiest way to do so is to just go with the flow by picking a show that your potential customers already plan to attend. Find out what shows your customers are going to attend. ***Remember:*** You need to see high numbers of your target customers; otherwise, the show wastes your marketing time and money.

Don't overlook the drawing power of simple things, like fresh flowers or food. At a trade show where my publishing business rented a booth, we offered free fresh-baked cookies each day. It was a simple gesture but a remarkably effective one in terms of drawing traffic to our booth and putting visitors in a positive mood! Other times, we've used comfort as our draw by setting up some cushy seats in the booth. A massage chair or bottles of cold spring water can also draw weary visitors to your booth.

Locating trade shows

Your most reliable source for trade show info is your customers. The whole point of exhibiting at a trade show is to reach customers, so why not just ask them where you should exhibit. Call or drop by a selection of your best customers and ask them for advice on where and when to exhibit. They know what's hot right now and what's not.

Here's where else to look for the scoop on trade shows:

- **Virtual Press Office:** For recent listings and press announcements of trade shows and other industry events, visit www.virtualpress office.com.

> ✔ **Exhibit & Event Marketers Association (E2MA):** This association can provide you with information about shows in your industry. The association also offers a great source of information and training for trade show booth designers and exhibitors. Find out more at www.e2ma.org.
>
> ✔ **Trade Show News Network (TSNN):** This organization's website (www.tsnn.com) is a useful clearinghouse of listings for vendors and companies involved in the trade show industry. Check out the list of top 250 U.S. trade shows for venues that may be good for your marketing program.

Renting the perfect booth

If you decide to rent a booth, you need to select a location and booth size. You want to aim for anywhere near a major entrance, the food stands, bathrooms, or any other place that concentrates people. Being on the end of an aisle can also help. And bigger is better — in general, you should get the biggest booth you can realistically afford.

Even if you end up with a miniature booth in the middle of an aisle, don't despair. Many shoppers try to walk all the aisles of a show, and these locations can work, too, provided the show draws enough of the right kind of customers for you. In fact, smart buyers often look at the smallest, cheapest booths in the hope of discovering something hot and new from an up-and-coming entrepreneurial supplier.

Setting up other kinds of displays

The firms that make trade show booths can also help with many other kinds of displays, such as lobby and conference room kiosks and tabletop displays. These smaller-scale displays can be effective in the right spot and often cost you less than a trade show booth, so explore all the options before you decide what fits your marketing program and budget best.

Experts can help you design and build your booth or other display, manage your trade show program, and handle the sales leads that result from it. Freeman of Dallas, Texas (800-453-9228; www.freemanco.com), builds exhibits, manages leads, and coordinates international and domestic trade show programs. Many firms provide booth design services, so consult business directories or cruise the Internet for leads. And don't count ad agencies out; many of them handle trade shows as part of an overall marketing communications program. (Another option is to search for used booth equipment that you can convert to your needs.)

Be sure to get opinions and quotes from multiple vendors (and ask for credit references and the contact names of some recent clients) before choosing the right company for your job. Also, share your budget constraints upfront to find out whether the company you're talking to is appropriate for you. Some can do very economical, small-scale projects with ease, whereas others are more oriented to large-scale corporate accounts.

Doing trade shows on a dime

A major booth at a big national convention or trade show is costly (somewhere between $15,000 and $50,000, depending on scale), so if that's beyond your current budget, look for more modest ways to participate, such as the following ideas:

- ✔ **Share a booth.** You may want to consider sharing a booth with a similar (but not closely competing) business if the expenses are too high and you aren't sure you can get a good return on the cost of a booth. We use this money-saving strategy at my firm. We buy half-booths at some regional human-resources meetings by working with our regional affiliates, smaller local training companies. These affiliates show our products, and they also sell themselves and their own services. We both get good leads — at half the regular cost. However you do it, make sure you show up so you can do some face-to-face marketing.

- ✔ **Work with a sales rep.** If you can't afford even a shared booth, you may still be able to appear in the exhibit hall of a trade show by working with a sales representative. If your industry has any sales reps, consider contracting with one and letting him include your products in his wider assortment at the next major show. (Flip to Chapter 17 for more on working with sales reps.)

- ✔ **Make a presentation at the show.** Start early with a proposal to speak at the event. Many trade shows are coupled with conferences, so get in touch with the person in charge of selecting presenters and pitch a workshop during regular conference hours (but avoid the final morning of a multi-day conference because attendance is usually very low then). Speakers are selected as much as a year in advance, so plan ahead. You can wait to decide how big of a booth to rent until you find out whether you'll also have an opportunity to present, because your presentation can help drive traffic to the booth and make your investment more worthwhile.

Passing out premiums

Premium items, as the industry calls them, are gifts you give to your customers, clients, prospects, or employees. Trade show booths usually give away premium items, so think about what you can give away if you exhibit at a convention or trade show. I recommend a fun or interesting premium (a puzzle, joke book, or toy, for example) as a token of appreciation for filling in a registration form. You want to focus your marketing resources on finding and qualifying leads, so focus everything you do, from advance mailings and e-mailings to booth design and signs, on this goal.

Demonstrating your wares

Seeing is believing. This old saying contains wisdom, and if you think a demonstration is applicable to your goods or services, you should definitely consider giving one. Demonstrations are often the most effective ways of introducing a new product, or even introducing an old product to new customers. When *Weddings For Dummies* launched at a publishing industry trade show called Book Expo America, the PR staff gave out slices of wedding cake in the *For Dummies* booth. Talk about a big hit! Everybody wanted a piece, and everybody became aware of the new book.

You can do a demonstration anywhere. Really. Even when you sponsor someone else's event. If you ask early on, that person can often find a time and place for you to stage a demonstration. And when you control the event or a part of it, you have considerable freedom to design demonstrations.

Giving everyone who wanders by your booth a premium is silly and requires such a large volume of premiums that you can't afford something nice. But there are exceptions to this rule. Free bottles of cold spring water, cookies, or other draws can be offered to all as a way to attract people to your booth. Then add a more durable premium as a thank-you gift when you give out brochures and collect information from serious leads. (For help calculating the cost of and return on premiums, see Chapter 11.)

If you're selecting premium items for a trade show or other event to which people travel for long distances, stick with easy-to-carry items. Keep premiums small, durable, and suitable for airport security. Also make an effort to keep your marketing materials (such as brochures) compact and durable enough that they won't be left in the hotel room or ruined in someone's luggage. Heavy catalogs are usually deserted, but informative, compact brochures stand a better chance of making it home with the prospect — especially if they contain special offers for samples or introductory discounts.

If you use giveaways at a trade show, harness social marketing to get the word out by using a hashtag on Twitter to alert customers that they can pick up the gift at your booth. The trick is to link this event (in fact, all your events) more broadly to your marketing program. If people opt into an online form to get their ticket or coupon to bring, your CRM database can capture their information as they sign up, for example.

Chapter 13

Going Direct with Your Marketing

Doing direct marketing is easy, but doing it well is difficult. You have to master it to the degree that you can beat the odds and get higher-than-average response rates. I share multiple ways to achieve this goal in this chapter as I help you review the varied problems and practices of direct marketing. This chapter focuses on conventional media: print ads, conventional mail (versus e-mail — that's covered in Chapter 10), and the telephone. These media can all be integrated with (or sometimes replaced with) web-based marketing, which I fill you in on in Chapter 10.

Beating the Odds with Direct Marketing

Direct marketing, relationship marketing, one-to-one marketing, and interactive marketing: They're all the same thing at heart, so I don't care what term you use. To me, *direct marketing* occurs whenever you, the marketer, take it upon yourself to create and manage customer transactions through one or more media.

The odds of success in direct marketing aren't particularly good. The average direct appeal to consumers or businesses goes unanswered. If you can up the response rate even a little bit over the average, you can make some serious money in direct marketing. Make sure your marketing message is well targeted at prospects when they want and need to buy. Your message should also be well crafted, meaning professional, clear, and with an appealing hook and call to action.

To get you started on the right foot, the following sections point out how to maximize your direct marketing and minimize your risks.

Recognizing that practice makes perfect

Practice makes perfect in direct marketing, if you make sure to keep records of what you do and track the responses. That way, you can tell when a change improves response rates. Even if you have little or no experience in direct marketing, have faith that a small initiative can generate enough information for you to get a grip on how to direct market better and on a larger scale. The best way to become good at direct marketing is simply to start doing it.

Ease into direct marketing with a modest program to minimize your downside risk and start growing from there. This principle is true, whether you're big or small, a retailer or wholesaler, a for-profit or nonprofit business. Include a registration card with shipments of product and add a registration option to your website to begin building your in-house list. Also, consider buying a list of prospects from an established list broker and testing it with a mailing or e-mailing. Positive responses to this test mailing may be added to your in-house list. Then keep mailing and e-mailing your in-house list regularly so as to keep it fresh and up-to-date.

The importance of civility in direct marketing

Many marketers are rushing to direct marketing in the often-mistaken belief that they can handle their customers better than any intermediaries can. But if you aren't accustomed to dealing directly with customers, you can easily offend them rather than win them over. If you're in your customers' faces, you're probably getting on their nerves — the exact opposite of what you want to accomplish.

Ultimately, direct marketing should build a permanent bridge between you and the customer. No matter what direct marketing you do, always keep it civil and polite. If you do, you'll get much better results. Avoid impolite calls, errors on labels, and anything else that may offend the average person. Cull lists to eliminate duplications and errors. Also, avoid using the cheapest call centers to handle your outbound or inbound telemarketing calls because they tend to have high employee turnover and low quality.

You have to make a positive impression if you want to achieve high response rates, so keep this mantra in mind: It's better to contact a hundred people well than a thousand people poorly.

Knowing what you're up against

Failure is the most common outcome of direct-response advertising. So your real goal is to minimize failure. Direct marketing basically doesn't generate very high response rates, which means you need to make realistic projections before deciding to pay for a program. Check out these average statistics to see what you're up against:

- A full-page magazine ad typically pulls between 0.05 and 0.2 percent of circulation (the *pull rate* is the percentage of readers who respond to the ad by calling or mailing, according to the ad's instructions). So you can expect only two responses per thousand from a decent ad. Pretty bad, huh?

- An individually addressed direct-mail letter typically pulls between 0.5 and 5 percent of the names you mailed to. So you can expect, at most, 50 responses per thousand from a decent letter. Better, but still pretty bad. By the way, the cost per thousand (or *CPM,* from the Roman numeral M meaning "one thousand") of a letter is often higher, so you don't necessarily get a better deal from direct mail than from magazine ads.

- A direct-mail showing of your product in a portfolio of products, as in a catalog or card deck, pulls far less. Divide that 50-per-thousand figure by the number of competing products for a rough idea of the average response rate (prominent placement does improve the rate; so does any tendency of customers to make multiple purchases from the catalog). For example, if your product is on one postcard in a shrink-wrapped deck of 50 cards, the maximum response may be 1 per thousand. That's really bad, unless you happen to be selling something expensive enough to give you a good return at low numbers.

- A telemarketing center making calls to a qualified list can do somewhat better. The center may pull in the 0.75 to 5 percent range for a consumer product, but that pull can get as high as 10 to 15 percent for some business-to-business sales efforts. However, the CPM of telemarketing is often higher than direct mail because it's more labor intensive.

- An e-mail offer may have an open rate of 10 to 20 percent. However, a big fall-off usually occurs from opening to click-through, which is typically in the 1.5 to 3 percent range for consumer marketing and as high as 4.5 percent for business-to-business (where the focus of the list tends to be more specific). In general, you may also anticipate some "unsubscribe" requests from each e-mailing, typically less than 1 percent.

Before you despair, know that good direct-marketing programs can be highly profitable. And if you're looking to build up a list of good customers, you may be happy just to find them now and wait for them to reorder before you see profits from your direct-marketing campaign.

Focusing on tactics that create high response rates

To boost sales from your offers, you need to be focused on the goal of generating high responses to your direct marketing. Here are some tips that can help:

✔ **Send a letter, special announcement, small catalog, or brochure by first-class mail once in a while to find out how well your mailing list responds.** The U.S. Post Office returns undeliverables if you use first-class mail, so you can remove or update out-of-date addresses.

✔ **Run a very small ad in an appropriate magazine.** Limit yourself to 15 words or less. Describe in a simple headline and one or two brief phrases what you have to sell and then ask people to contact you for more information. Here's a hint: Including a simple photo of the product eliminates the need for wordy description. (See Chapter 7 for tips on designing and placing your print ad.)

✔ **Create a landing page on the web with a more detailed direct-response ad on it and bid on key terms on Google to drive leads to your landing page.** A *landing page* is a dedicated web page where you explain your offer and guide customers to a form to fill out or a shopping cart to fill up. Check out Chapter 10 for more info.

✔ **Use testimonials on your web landing page and in direct-mail letters and direct-response ads.** *Testimonials* are quotes either from happy customers praising your product or firm or from news coverage discussing your firm or product. These comments attract more buyers because they seem more believable than positive things you say about yourself.

✔ **Trade customer lists with a related business to boost your list size for free.** For example, a magazine specializing in your industry may be willing to exchange its readership list for your customer list.

✔ **Give away a simple, useful, or fun gift.** You can give the gift in exchange for placing an order or simply as an inexpensive *premium* (giveaway product) in your mailing. Nicely decorated pens, pencils, stickers, refrigerator magnets, or anything with utility can boost response rates by making your mailing more interesting and memorable. After all, who doesn't love receiving gifts? (Check out Chapter 11 for some premium ideas.)

✔ **Send a thank-you note or card to customers by mail or e-mail after they place a purchase.** This polite gesture often wins a repurchase. It also lets you test your contact information and habituates customers to reading your messages so they're more likely to pay attention to a sales-oriented message later on.

✔ **Send birthday or holiday greetings in the form of cards or gifts to your in-house list.** If you consider them valuable customers, let them know it. You may be surprised at how many contact you afterward to place a new order, even though your mailing to them was noncommercial.

✔ **Change the medium or form of your communication every now and then.** If you always send a sales letter, try a color postcard or an e-mail newsletter once in a while. Such variations can increase customer interest, and you may also find that different customers respond best to different forms of communication.

✔ **Include a photograph of a person's face, looking directly at the viewer with a friendly expression, in print ads, mailings, web banner ads, and web landing pages.** The person should represent a user or an expert on the product, or relate to the product or offer in some other way. A face attracts attention and increases sales for most direct-response ads and direct-mail letters. (On the web, streaming video and audio permit you to upgrade to a video spokesperson.)

✔ **Use a clear, appealing photo of the product in your ads, mailings, web banner ads, and web landing pages.** Showing what you have to sell attracts appropriate customers simply and effectively. And if some details don't show up in the photo, add close-up photos. Seeing is believing, and believing is a prerequisite for buying! Few businesses use largely visual direct-response ads, though I can't tell you why. Visual direct-response ads can outsell wordy ones by a wide margin.

✔ **Post a short how-to or demonstration video on the web.** The video can feature a new product, and you can end the video with a link to a special trial offer.

✔ **Try an old-fashioned radio advertisement using a lot of amusing sound effects and asking people to call a toll-free number or visit a website.** Radio ads can be fun! Flip to Chapter 9 for help constructing one.

Behind every effective direct-marketing program stands a well-managed database of customer and prospect names. (If you need some help with your database, see the nearby sidebar.)

Maximizing direct response on the web

The web is a brilliant place to be doing direct-response marketing because you can develop profiles or indicators of purchase interest from the data collected on sites such as Google and Facebook and hone in on the most likely prospects quite easily. Yet a lot of the direct-response advertising done online yields unsatisfactory results and frustrates the advertisers. How can you make sure your ads do well?

First things first: Test and refine your campaign so you have a good idea of the performance to expect before you give the okay to scale up. For example, try a few hundred e-mailings, or run an ad for a day on Google, and look at the results. Then, if you're not satisfied, make some adjustments and do another short, cheap experiment. Scale up to larger lists or longer runs when you have a good idea that your ad is a winner.

Clarify how prospects are selected when you purchase or approve a direct-response campaign to make sure the campaign targets high-level prospects. If you're designing or selecting a direct-response ad campaign, ask what level of interest the prospects have shown. They may be selected based on the following:

- **Profile:** At the lowest level is just a general demographic or other profile. In other words, they seem similar to customers, so maybe they'll become customers.

- **Interests or likes:** The next level, an improvement in terms of response rate, is prospects chosen because they've demonstrated an interest.

- **Keyword search matches:** The third level of web prospect has superior response rates and is generally the best target: people who are actively searching for key terms associated with your product or service. Their interest is more active and immediate than those who have indicated a general interest or liking.

- **Past purchasers:** The fourth and highest level of prospect is anyone who's made a similar purchase in the relatively recent past. So be sure to fold in your own customer lists as well as look for ways to reach out to competitors' customers if you can.

Smart selection of your target audience is just step one in managing a good direct-response campaign on the web. Ad purchase criteria and algorithms on the various sites used will determine how often prospects are exposed — whether the ad, should it become popular, will then be run too often and create burnout and whether prospects will be pulled from the pool after they make a purchase (if not, continued advertising may annoy them). You don't need to be a leading expert on these matters, but you do need to ask questions and make sure the ad's performance on the web is being managed sensibly. If not, do it manually by limiting the exposures and not allowing the same ad to run endlessly.

Also, pull back on low-performing ads and shift to high-performing ones. The web offers very rapid feedback about performance, so request and review the stats often. An interesting statistic that sometimes can be tracked (for example, with the newest Facebook advertising support) is *viewthrough,* which is the percent of people who view your direct-response ad and then, say, within the hour, visit your website. They don't have to click on the ad itself for you to get a sale, so that's why it's interesting to track viewthrough along with ad response. Sometimes the ad gets people thinking, even though they didn't click it, and they go visit your site later.

Expanding your command with demand side platforms

A *demand side platform* (DSP) is a website serving advertisers by giving them the ability to buy, track, and manage electronic advertising across multiple platforms and websites. Sophisticated DSPs have only recently emerged, and they're quickly assuming an important role in online advertising. Using one, you may target your audience with real-time buying of ad display space on many different sites, from Google and Facebook to more obscure ones, shifting your ad buying in response to performance measures like click-throughs and sales. Imagine having the command of Google AdWords but for many different advertising venues. That's what a DSP provides. It's leading to an increased ability to do it yourself when it comes to web advertising, and to do it well.

For example, using a DSP, you may test your ad on Facebook's News Feed, along with placement on various other news platforms, and compare to see which does best, and then shift your spending to the optimal choice. All in a day. The feedback can be that quick and accurate.

Here are some of the current DSPs you may want to look at if you decide to experiment with managing a direct-response ad campaign through a demand side platform:

- AdRoll, `www.adroll.com`
- Google's DoubleClick Bid Manager, `www.google.com/doubleclick`
- SiteScout, `www.sitescout.com`
- The Trade Desk, `www.thetradedesk.com`
- Turn, `www.turn.com`

Whether you have the expertise to bring ad bidding and placement entirely in-house or you choose to manage electronic advertising through an agency or outside consultant, consider shifting your e-media buying to a DSP platform and make sure your campaign is optimized by real-time or nearly real-time tracking, comparing, and buying. And stay on top of the shifting rules and algorithms of the sites where you advertise or take advantage of the DSPs, which stay up-to-date. If you're a marketer who has to wear many hats, tracking the latest on Facebook and Google yourself can be too time-consuming.

Using computerized marketing databases

A drawer of customer folders and a box of index cards make up the simplest forms of marketing databases, but nowadays almost all direct marketers use computerized databases. The old-fashioned system is just fine for many smaller businesses, but if your business has more than 100 customers, I strongly encourage you to manage your lists electronically.

A wide variety of customer relationship management (CRM) software platforms are available. You'll need to do your own research, based on your budget and specific requirements, to know which one is right for you, but here's a starting list of some of the best-known brands to consider:

✔ **MarketingPilot** (www.marketing pilot.com) offers a host of specialized software applications for all aspects of marketing, including list management. Many ad agencies use these programs.

✔ **Prophet** is a leader in CRM software, which can be used for direct sales as well as for mailings and e-mail contacts. It integrates with Microsoft Outlook now, which is handy for those using Outlook already. See www. avidian.com.

✔ **Sage** offers its *Act!* software for customer list management; many small businesses find this product useful. Check it out at www.act.com.

✔ **Vision 6** has a customer list program (appropriately named *Vision 6*) that emphasizes e-mail contact management and marketing. Find out more at www.vision6.com.au.

If you're unfamiliar with the use of CRM and database programs, you may want to take a workshop on database management for marketing. Or consult the *For Dummies* product line, which contains reference books on a wide variety of computer programs at www.dummies.com.

Making Your Direct-Response Ads Work

Direct-response ads stimulate people to respond with an inquiry or purchase, exactly like the printed examples you probably receive in the mail on a too-frequent basis. The people who respond to direct-response advertising are self-selecting as customers or prospects. You need to do two things with them:

✔ Try your best to close the sale by getting them to buy something.

✔ Find out as much as you can about them and put the information in your database for future direct-marketing efforts.

Many businesses build a direct-marketing capacity through this very process. They place ads in front of what they hope is an appropriate target market and wait to see who responds. Then they attempt to build long-term direct-marketing relationships with those who respond (for example, by sending them catalogs, e-mails, and letters). Over time, the businesses add respondents to their direct-marketing databases, information about the respondents builds up, and many of those respondents become regular direct purchasers.

The high failure rates of direct-response ads (presented in the earlier "Knowing what you're up against" section) make sense if you consider how much more these types of ads must do than the typical image-building or brand-oriented ad. A direct-response ad must create enough enthusiasm to get people to close the sale, on their own initiative, right now. How do you accomplish this goal? By making sure your direct-response ad does the following:

- ✔ **Appeals to target readers:** A good story, a character they can identify with and want to be more like — these factors make up the timeless elements of true appeal (I cover appeal in greater detail in Chapter 6).

- ✔ **Supports your main claim about the product fully:** Because the ad must not only initiate interest but also close the sale, it has to give sufficient evidence to overcome any reasonable objections on the reader's part. If you think the product's virtues are obvious, show those virtues in a close-up visual of the product. If the appeal isn't so obvious (as in the case of a service), then use testimonials, a compelling story, or statistics from objective product tests — in short, use some form of evidence that's logically or emotionally convincing, or better yet, both.

- ✔ **Speaks to readers in conversational, personal language:** Your ad must be natural and comfortable for readers. Don't get fancy! Write well, yes. Polish and condense, yes. Seek better, catchier, clearer expressions, yes. Just don't be stiff or formal.

- ✔ **Targets likely readers:** Your ad's readership dramatically affects your response rate. In fact, the same ad, placed in two different publications, can produce response rates at both ends of the range. So the better you define your target consumers, the easier it becomes to find publications relevant to those target consumers, and the better your ad performs.

Highly selective publications and websites work better for direct-response advertising. A special-interest magazine may deliver a readership far richer in targets than a general-interest magazine or newspaper. If you're focusing on women, select a publication or website read by them. That specification ups your response rate by 50 percent right off the bat! *Good Housekeeping,* for example, reaches more than 5 million readers in print — most of them women. Combined with its e-mail edition, the total readership is about 24 million, a rather impressive number if you're looking to sell something of interest to women who take an active interest in their homes. (The magazine amplifies its print readership by offering content over iPad, Nook, Zinio, Kindle, and Google play.)

- ✔ **Is timed correctly:** The right prospect is no use if the timing is off. Don't sell lawn and garden care in December, or tropical vacations in August. Getting the timing right can greatly increase response rates.

- ✔ **Makes responding easy:** If readers can make a purchase easily, ask them to do so. If the product is complicated or difficult to buy (because it's technical, for example), then just ask people to contact you for more information and try to close the sale when they do so. Sometimes, you need an *intermediate step* (a way for the customer to find out more about the product before making the final decision to buy). When in doubt, try two versions of your ad: one with an intermediate step and one that tries to make the sale on the spot. Then see which one produces the most sales in the long run.

✔ **Promotes your brand name clearly:** Let viewers know who's advertising, and don't let your name or logo get squeezed out of the ad for space reasons. Also, keep in mind that a lot of people will see the ad but not respond. For these people, the brand identity may still make an impact, raising awareness of the brand and what it stands for, which may convert to a response or sale sometime in the future.

REAL WORLD

Levi's finds its fit with direct-response marketing

Levi Strauss & Co. (also known as Levi's) provides a great example of effective online direct-response marketing. A simple Google search for "Levi's jeans" produces a flurry of direct-response messages, from the top promo slot occupied by www.levi.com, the company's official site, to the top AdWords result on the right, which (depending on day, time, and location) is usually a retailer near you with a Levi's promotion of some sort. For example, I get a fairly typical AdWords top result: "Levi's Jeans Sale" from Sears, where the link takes me to a page full of options, including Fit Finder, direct-purchase options for various styles of Levi's jeans, and a store finder. The rest of the Google results in my sample search are dominated by similar ads from retailers and e-retailers, all eager to engage shoppers and capture information about them by dangling valuable memberships, promotional pricing, free shipping, or other inducements to action.

The array of ads online for Levi's jeans may change each time you search, but I find them to always be instructive because this well-known brand is the focus of competitive, leading-edge advertising and well worth studying for direct-response ideas. Also check out the maker's website at us.levi.com/home for good examples of direct-response promotion on a website. At the time of this writing, there's a "Stay Connected" section on the bottom of the page with options to connect to Levi's through Facebook, Twitter, YouTube, Instagram, Pinterest, or its blog (at explore.levi.com). Next to this list of social media options, Levi's offers a way to Subscribe & Save, adding the explanation, "Sign up for our email newsletter and we'll send you a promo code for **free shipping.**" Following that is a link for a student discount.

Levi's student discount (accessed from its main website) usually has a special offer to entice college students to register or, if already registered, log in to shop. The direct-response promo tells students to register and verify their student status with UNiDAYS, a company that provides support for student-aimed promotions, not just for Levi's but for anyone wanting to directly target this market. See www.myunidays.com for its main site. (E-mail to info@myunidays.com and ask for information on advertising if you want to try a student-oriented promo yourself.) For more information on how to do direct-response advertising on the web, check out Chapter 10.

Both print and television advertising have fairly successful track records when it comes to direct response. Radio may work, too, but you have to innovate to overcome the problem of people rarely writing down what they hear on the radio. In other words, you need to convert the otherwise passive medium of radio into an action-oriented medium by making your call to action easy to remember. A memorable website address may do the trick. And web advertising is quite good for direct response because many people have grown accustomed to purchasing on the web and are willing to enter a credit card number and complete their transaction while online.

Delivering Direct Mail

Direct mail is the classic form of direct marketing — in fact, the whole field used to be called direct mail until changing practice forced marketers to adopt a broader term. *Direct mail* is the use of personalized sales letters, and it has a long tradition all its own. Direct mail is really another form of print advertising. No more, no less. So before you design (or hire someone to design) a direct-mail piece, think about it in this context (and refer to Chapters 6 and 7).

A direct-mail piece isn't like *a* print ad; it's more like *two* print ads:

✔ **The first ad is the one the target sees when the mail arrives (usually an envelope).** This ad has to accomplish a difficult action goal: Get the viewer to open the envelope rather than recycle it. Most direct mail ends up in the recycling pile without ever getting opened or read! Keep this fact in mind and devote extra care to making your envelope

  • Stand out (it *must* be noticeable and different).

  • Give readers a reason to open it (sell the benefits or engage their curiosity or, even better, promise a reward).

  Note: If you're sending a color catalog with a stunning front and back cover that people can't resist, make sure the recipient can see the catalog's exterior. Don't hide it under a dull envelope.

✔ **The second ad goes to work only if the first succeeds.** The second ad is what's inside, and it needs to get the reader to respond with a purchase or inquiry. In that respect, this ad works in much the same way as any other direct-response ad. The same rules of persuasive communication apply — plus a few unique ones that I present in the sections that follow. (And if you're writing an e-mail letter, note that the subject line takes the place of the old outside-of-envelope message, and the body of the e-mail is analogous to the letter; the next section also applies to e-mail.)

Unlocking the secrets of great direct mail

A great many so-called formulas exist for successful direct-mail letters. None of them work, so avoid the temptation to make anything about your letter formulaic. Your letter must have creative copywriting and design at its best. It needs to use the secrets of direct-response advertising design (as described in the earlier "Making Your Direct-Response Ads Work" section) and employ the principles of creative marketing and good communications, which you can find in Chapters 5 and 6, respectively. However, certain strategies can help you employ these principles of good design in a direct-mail piece.

The most effective direct-mail letters generally include several elements, each with its own clear role:

✔ **Bait:** You should include some sort of bait that catches the reader's eye and attention, getting her to read the letter in the first place.

✔ **Argument:** You then need to provide a sound argument — logical, emotional, or both — as to why your great product can solve some specific problem for the reader. Marketers devote the bulk of many letters to making this case as persuasively as possible, and you should keep this sound practice in mind when drafting your direct-mail letter.

✔ **Call to action:** Finally, you should make an appeal to immediate action, some sort of hook that gets readers to call you, send for a sample, sign up for a contest, place an order, whatever. As long as they act, you can consider the letter a success. Your call to action is really the climax of the letter, and you need to design everything about the piece to ensure your call works.

These three essential elements are sometimes called the *star, chain,* and *hook.* Although the terminology — and metaphors — differ, the basic concept is the same: You need to include something attractive (the star or bait) to catch attention, followed by something substantive to arouse enthusiasm (the chain of argument that pulls the reader through the copy), followed by some kind of call to action that hooks the reader into responding.

These formulas refer specifically to the text of your letter itself, but that doesn't mean you should forget about what else goes into your mailing. The outside of the envelope needs to entice readers and get them to open your letter in the first place. Following are some techniques to make your envelope enticing enough to open:

✔ **The stealth approach envelope:** You disguise your letter so it looks like a bill or personal correspondence — or so that it can't be identified at all. The theory is that the reader will open the envelope just to find out what's inside.

✔ **The benefits approach envelope:** You include a headline, perhaps a little supporting copy, and even some artwork to let people know what the mailing is about and to summarize why you think your offer is worthy of their attention. I like this approach best because it's honest and direct (this is direct marketing, after all!). Furthermore, this method ensures that those who do open the envelope have self-selected based on interest in your offer. But this technique only works if you have a clear benefit or point of difference to advertise on your envelope. If you can't say "Open immediately for the lowest price on the XYZ product ranked highest in *Consumer Reports,*" then this ploy may not work.

✔ **The special offer envelope:** This envelope entices with your call to action — never mind your offer. By letting consumers know that they can enter a sweepstakes to win a billion dollars, or get free samples, or find valuable coupons or a dollar bill enclosed, this envelope gives them a reason to read the letter inside. But the envelope doesn't try to sell the product; it leaves that to the carefully crafted letter inside.

✔ **The creative envelope:** If your mailing is unique enough, everyone wants to open it just to find out who you are and what you're up to. Consider an oversized package in an unexpected color, an envelope with a very funny cartoon or quote on the back, or a window teasing readers with a view of something interesting inside. Or how about an envelope that reads "Don't open this envelope!" You can make your envelope the most exciting thing in someone's mailbox by using any number of creative ideas. Yet this strategy is the least common, probably because creative envelopes cost more. But don't be penny wise and pound foolish. If you spend 25 percent more to double or triple the response rate, then you've saved your company a great deal of money on the mailing by spending more on the envelope!

What else should go into your mailing? In general, a letter combined with a *circular* — a simple catalog-style description of your product(s) — pulls more strongly than a letter alone. Circulars don't work for all products (don't bother for magazine subscriptions), but they do work well for any product or service the consumer sees as expensive or complex. Be sure to make the circular more elaborate, involving, glossy, colorful, and large where involvement should be higher. Think big circulars for big-ticket items and little ones for simple items.

Also include reply forms that allow readers to easily get in touch with you in multiple ways. Give readers some choices about what offers they want to respond to, if possible. Postage-free (or prepaid) reply forms generally ensure a higher response rate and thus justify their cost many times over. Don't skimp on the form because, after all, getting that response is the whole point of your mailing.

A coupon offer helps keep the reader reading by giving them an incentive, and coupons often improve response rates (read: increase sales). If the coupon is redeemable at stores, the customer has another way to benefit from the mailing other than making a direct purchase, and you can get data from coupon redemptions (give it a unique code number) to show you how many readers used this option.

Always include ways to switch over to the web through a computer, phone, or tablet. A scannable code, a web address, or an offer to register and receive a special benefit (such as a discount or free shipping) on the web will swing some people over and simplify the capture of their information. Why not try to pull people to a web landing page registration option on the outside of the envelope and on every page of the letter. (If the letter is going as an e-mail, these options can be embedded as links.)

The final design issue is deciding how to send the letter. Should you use the U.S. Postal Service's standard mail (what used to be called third class) versus first class? Should you use an overnight air service for an offer to business customers? Perhaps you need to send the letter by e-mail? In general, the U.S. Postal Service is still best. And, on average, standard mail (which costs less) pulls as well as first class, so save your money unless timeliness is important or you want to check your list (first-class postage means the envelope comes back to you if the address is no good).

When writing a direct-response e-mail, include the bait, the argument, and the call to action, just as you would in a traditional mailing. However, when writing the copy, think computer screens, not pages. It takes as much effort (and involvement) to click on the next screen as it does to turn the page, yet a screen holds less than a page. So be more precise and less wordy, or else your e-mail can't pull as well as the same letter in printed form. And pay attention to each transition between screens. Break the text in a way that creates suspense and gives viewers a reason to click or scroll onward toward the final offer (the call to action or hook).

Getting your letter mailed

One little detail often puzzles first-time direct mailers: how to actually get their mailing printed, folded, stuffed, and mailed. If you don't know, you need to hire someone who does. Your local telephone directory lists some companies that do this kind of work under Mailing or Marketing headings. Commercial printers regularly do this type of work as well, and they can often handle anything from a small envelope to a major catalog. Talk to various printers to get an idea of the range of services and prices.

If you're planning small-scale mailings — say, less than 2,000 a pop — you may find doing the work in-house offers you a cheaper and quicker route. Many local businesses and nonprofits do small-scale mailings, and they'd be throwing away money by hiring printers. If you want to set up this in-house capability, talk to your local post office to find out how to handle metered or permit mail. And consider purchasing mailing equipment, such as the following (all of these items can process standard-format mailings): feeders, sealers, scales to weigh the mailings, and meters. Combine this equipment with your local photocopy shop's ability to produce, fold, and stuff a mailing, and you have an efficient small-scale direct-mail center!

Purchasing mailing lists

Thousands of vendors offer lists. Search the web or ask your broker for a list that fits your customer profile. However, don't expect purchased lists to work very well — response rates can be low, and you may get high returns or undeliverables. That's okay, though, because you're just using the purchased lists to build up your own higher-quality in-house list of purchasers. So plan to send relatively inexpensive mailings with easy-to-say-yes-to offers and then focus on the replies. If you get any calls, faxes, or postcards from these purchased lists, qualify them as leads or customers and move them to your own list.

I recommend buying one-time rights to mailing lists, with phone numbers or e-mail addresses to make replying to a response easier for you. *One-time use* means you're just renting the list; you don't actually own it. You do, however, own the replies. As soon as someone contacts you from that mailing and you begin to interact with her and gather information about her, you can add that person to your own list.

List suppliers usually have minimums. I recommend buying the minimum (usually available on sticky mailing labels or in a database, depending on what's easiest and cheapest for you to use). Then test the list with a mailing and see what happens. If you get some good customers out of it, go back and buy a larger number of names. Or if you're disappointed in the response, buy a different list next time. And if your mailing is too expensive to test on the minimum — which is often 1,000 names — just mail to the first 250. That's enough to find out how the list performs.

You have so many lists to choose from that you can keep shopping until you find one that works for you. But remember the basic principle of list-buying: The best indicator of future purchase is past purchase. Try to find lists of people who've purchased something similar to what you're selling, preferably through the mail, rather than people who fit your customer profile in other ways.

Establishing and Running a Call Center

A *call center* is the place where telephone calls from your customers are answered. It can be a real, physical place: a big room full of phones staffed by your employees. Or it can also be a virtual place: a telephone number that rings to whatever subcontractor you're currently using to handle telemarketing for you.

Every business is a call center, but most don't realize it. If you have telephones and people calling in and out on them, you need to manage this point of customer contact very carefully. Small businesses may not operate on a big enough scale to hire or build a dedicated call center, but they still must manage this function wisely if they want to win customers, rather than lose them, on the phone.

When you use the telephone in your marketing, you need to follow the common-sense principles that I cover in the following sections.

Make your brand available by phone

In the United States, three-fourths of all consumers use a toll-free number at least once each year. And more than $500 billion in sales take place over the phone. In spite of the growing dominance of web commerce, many services are still purchased by a consumer over the phone. Don't lose control of your inbound calls just because the web is hot. The phone may still be your most powerful tool for finding and closing on new prospects. Answer it!

Although telemarketing requires nothing but a telephone, combining it with toll-free, inbound calling may make it more effective (but the rise of cellphone plans with national calling has reduced the value of free long distance numbers). In the United States, you can offer free calling to your customers and prospects on numbers with prefixes of 800, 888, 877, or 866. Toll-free numbers are available in similar forms in other countries as well.

Here's a little-known alternative to the toll-free number that's particularly effective if you're in a business that values local relationships (such as pest control, lawn care, or computer repair): You can arrange for most phone companies to list a local number in each local market you sell to and then have the phone company bill you the added cost of transferring that call to your nonlocal office. That way, people pay only for their local call and feel that they're dialing a local business rather than an impersonal national business. List the local number in the local phone book, Yellow Pages, or other phone directory for local visibility.

Be accessible to desirable customers when they want to call you

Being accessible to your customers in part means having staff by the phones. If you service businesses, then you can use business hours to answer business calls (but make sure that you cover business hours in the customers' time zones, not just your own). If you service consumers, be prepared to take calls at odd hours. Some of the best customers for clothing catalogs do their shopping late at night — just before bed, for example.

Of course, you also need to make sure nobody gets a busy signal. Your phone company offers a variety of services to help solve this problem; ask it for details. If you answer your phone faster than the competition does, you can gain some market share from them. (***Note:*** A hidden advantage of keeping your call center in-house is that managers can keep an eye on the accessibility issue and add more lines and staff quickly if a problem arises.)

You'll inevitably need to put some callers on hold some of the time. An outgoing message that includes an upbeat, attractively professional voice delivering your brand name and thanking callers for waiting is therefore essential. Also include your website address and let callers know what functions the site supports so that if they don't want to bother waiting on the phone, they may still place an order on the web.

Whatever you do, always measure and minimize customer wait time. Don't leave people sitting on hold for more than what they perceive to be a moderate amount of time. Depending on the nature of your product and customer, that time limit is probably less than two perceived minutes. A *perceived minute* is the time period a customer on hold thinks she has waited for a minute — and that time typically comes out to be more like 40 seconds when you measure it on the clock. You have to convert actual wait times to perceived wait times in order to appreciate the customer's perspective.

If you don't want to set up a call center yourself, you can either hire a consultant to design a call center for you or simply use a service firm to perform the function for you. Following are some recommended service providers:

- ✓ **24-7 Intouch:** This Canadian company (available at 800-530-1121 or `www.24-7intouch.com`) operates call centers and has recently added the capacity for online support and chat centers.

- ✓ **AnswerNow!:** This Arizona-based company (which you can reach at 866-506-5663 or `www.answernowinc.com`) can provide a simple virtual receptionist or a full-blown order handling center with credit card processing capacity.

- ✓ **CallCenterOps.com:** This provider features an information-rich website at `www.callcenterops.com`.

Trade associations may also be able to provide you with information, referrals, and training. Try contacting the International Customer Service Association (ICSA; www.icsatoday.org) and the Association of TeleServices International (ATSI; www.atsi.org).

Capture useful information about each call and caller

One of the most important functions for your call center is to field inquiries or orders from new customers as they respond to your various direct-response advertisements (think magazine ads, letters to purchased lists, and your web page). These callers are hot leads that you need to gather information about. Have operators ask each caller how she heard of your company, perhaps along with a few other qualifying questions. Also, the operators need to determine what type of call it is. Categories may include complaint, sales inquiry, service request, technical question, warranty question, and so on. The handling of each call will depend on this categorization.

The best way to capture callers' info for your customer database is to have your operators online so they can type the data directly into your database as they get it. At the very least, give them a printed information form they can fill in. If you're the one answering those customer calls, make yourself a form so you don't forget to capture useful information about the prospects, their needs, and how they found your number.

Putting your operators online also solves the related problem of recognizing repeat customers. Repeat customers' names pop up on-screen for the operator's reference. That way, the operators don't have to ask stupid questions, and they can surprise customers with their knowledge. (Refer to the "Using computerized marketing databases" sidebar in this chapter, or go to your favorite online search engine and look for "providers of call center management software" if you don't already have software that supports your sales and service function.)

Gather data on the effectiveness of direct-response ads and direct mail

I'm often amazed by how little information marketers gather about the effectiveness of their own work. What you don't know *does* hurt you in marketing! You can easily find out which direct-response ads (both print and web), call scripts, or mailings pull the best. Just have your call center operators or staff ask every new caller where he or she heard about you and ask repeat customers what prompted this latest call. (For web-only customers, include a checklist so they can report where they first heard about you.) You can track the performance of each individual ad, letter, or promotion by giving it a unique code so you can discover which approaches pay off and which don't.

Everything you send out should have your phone number and web address on it plus social contact information, such as where to find you on Facebook, Twitter, or Pinterest. It's amazing how often I find myself staring at a catalog page, package, product, website, bid, bill, or memo trying to find a phone number that just isn't there. Then what? I may just call the competition instead. The solution? Audit and order.

- First, *audit* your mailings, web pages, search engine ads, packaging, and other customer communications to find those holes where you've accidentally left out contact information.

- Next, *order* up some simple contact information stickers with your brand or business name, phone numbers, address(es), and website and e-mail information. Pop those stickers on folders, boxes, cards, products, scribbled notes, or anywhere else anyone may conceivably look when thinking of calling you with a question or order.

Drumming Up Business by Phone

If you decide to prospect for new customers by phone (in other words, if you choose to engage in *outbound telemarketing*), you can do so in a couple of ways:

- You can do a little bit of outbound telemarketing informally as part of a broader routine of contacting customers and following up on leads.

- You may have a full-blown outbound telemarketing program set up in a call center that you either run yourself or contract out.

One way or the other, though, every marketer makes some calls to customers and prospects and must be prepared for the reality that outbound telemarketing yields plenty of rejections. In fact, I don't generally recommend outbound telemarketing for *cold call* lists, or lists of strangers who've never done business with you before. You can buy such lists from list brokers easily, but expect lower response rates than from lists you build yourself.

The next sections explain in more depth how you can use a phone to garner business while keeping legal.

Developing a good call list

You can improve the success rate of outbound telemarketing dramatically by developing a good list before you start calling. Preferably, this list is of people who've had some contact with you before (they've purchased, returned an inquiry card, tried a sample, or responded to an ad). With a good list, you can afford to put competent salespeople on the phones so that your company puts its best face forward.

I don't know why most telemarketers haven't figured out that the first contact between their company and a prospective customer shouldn't be in the hands of a temp worker who can't even pronounce the name of the product correctly. To avoid such problems, you need to develop good call lists and a script that gives your callers at least a 10 percent success rate — about ten times the average for typical bottom-feeder consumer telemarketing operations.

Writing a winning telemarketing script

Before you call someone, you absolutely must make sure you know what you're going to say — and that means crafting a script. Always write, role-play, revise, and test a script before asking anyone to make an outbound telemarketing call. Keep your script upbeat, simple, short, and clear. Demonstrate the script to your telemarketers by making a few calls yourself and remind them to stay friendly and positive (by smiling into the phone) no matter what happens.

Here's a seven-element template for writing a simple and effective telemarketing script with sample text for a magazine subscription offer (but substitute your own offer and text to make this script work for your marketing program):

1. **Introduce yourself.**

   For example, "Hello, I'm [full name], and I'm calling from [company name]. . . ."

2. **Give the caller a very brief explanation about why you're calling.**

   For example, " . . . to offer you a chance to extend your subscription at a 50 percent discount."

3. **Request permission.**

   "May I tell you about our special offer? It will take only 30 seconds."

4. **If the person on the phone gives you permission, provide a longer yet succinct explanation about why you're calling.**

   "When your subscription expires next [month], we will extend it for another year at half the price of a regular subscription, if you will confirm now by phone. This offer is good only for orders placed by phone, because it is more economical for us to process subscriptions this way."

If she doesn't give you permission, thank her for her time and be professional.

5. **Pause for questions and answer them with simple facts, using as polite of manners as possible and remembering to smile when speaking.**

   For example, "Yes, the regular subscription is $40 per year, and our special offer costs you only $20."

6. **Close the deal.**

   "Very well, then shall I sign you up for another year's subscription to [name of magazine]?"

7. **Confirm the details.**

   "Good. We're almost done. Now I just need to confirm your name, address, and credit card information."

When crafting your script, be careful to avoid anything deceptive or misleading. Failing to do so is just opening yourself up for trouble.

Keeping legal

Make sure you're honest and accurate about who's calling and avoid using deceptive scripts. Deceptive telemarketing is all too common, and it sours the market for honest telemarketers. I'm sure you've hung up on inappropriate callers many times. I have, too.

Unfortunately, many telemarketing scripts are improper and may lead to legal complications. Why? Because the pressure is on. Selling anything over the phone is much harder than it used to be, whether it's a magazine or a long-distance telephone service. People are getting sick of these sales calls and adding their names to "do-not-call lists" by the millions, and businesses are setting up impenetrable phone systems to duck telemarketing calls. Consequently, marketers are experimenting with stealth techniques, and these techniques lead them into dangerous ethical and legal territory. The next section offers some sensible alternatives to persisting with deceptive calls when you find it too hard to close the deal with normal lists and scripts.

Looking at new telemarketing strategies

Telemarketers need to find new strategies for their increasingly mature medium. Some of these strategies include

✔ **Using the phone to follow up on leads, not to find them:** Whenever possible, use your web marketing activities (see Chapter 10), events (check out Chapter 12), and advertising (see "Beating the Odds with Direct Marketing," earlier in this chapter, plus all of Part III in this book), to generate telephone or personal sales call leads. When you generate inquiries about your product or service, you have permission to call. The prospect takes your call gladly in 99 percent of these cases, and you close a sale in many of them.

✔ **Not overusing the phone:** Save calls for issues that really deserve personal contact from the prospect's perspective and try to call people who actually know you or your firm or will welcome the call for some other good reason. If you have something truly important to talk about, then you don't need a misleading hook to keep people on the phone. Remember that every marketing program should use a balanced mix of media and methods. You can't do all jobs with one tool. Also remember that even when telephoning is appropriate, your customers and prospects don't want you to call constantly. Give them a little breathing room.

✔ **Scripting a message to leave on voice mail:** Write a short (less than 30 seconds) script for a voice mail message in which you introduce yourself, provide a brief explanation of the offer, and then give the person two or three options for follow-up (your return number, your e-mail, and a web address to a page with details of the offer).

✔ **Being respectful:** Remember that you're interrupting anyone you reach by phone. If someone clearly doesn't want to talk with you, don't be a jerk. Get off the phone politely, thanking her for her time, so that you at least leave behind a positive impression of your firm or brand.

✔ **Compensating telemarketers for building relationships, not frying them:** If telemarketers are paid only by the kill (commission on sales), then they can get frustrated and start berating and hanging up on your prospects and customers. Note that this rule means you shouldn't use *subcontractors* (specialized companies that telemarket for you) if they pay by the kill — and most of them do.

✔ **Guarding existing customers from bad telemarketing:** Deceptive, high-pressure, or irritating phone sales tactics may produce a good-looking end-of-day sales report, but they're guaranteed to increase customer turnover. Why? Because they bring in deal-prone customers who can be taken away by the next telemarketer, and they irritate rather than reward your loyal customers. At the very least, use two different strategies and scripts: one for existing customers and one for deal-prone prospects. At best, focus your telemarketing on building existing customer loyalty; for example, by calling to see whether you can improve the product or service quality.

Part V

Selling Great Products to Anyone, Anytime, Anywhere

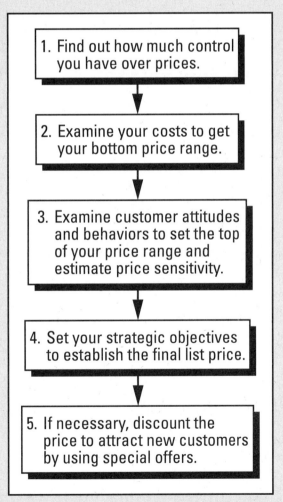

1. Find out how much control you have over prices.

2. Examine your costs to get your bottom price range.

3. Examine customer attitudes and behaviors to set the top of your price range and estimate price sensitivity.

4. Set your strategic objectives to establish the final list price.

5. If necessary, discount the price to attract new customers by using special offers.

© John Wiley & Sons, Inc.

web extras

I give you a tool for determining how credible, visible, and distinct your brand is at www.dummies.com/extras/marketing. After you know how you score, you can begin making improvements or pat yourself on the back for a job well done.

In this part . . .

- ✔ Build a stand-out brand identity that's compelling, clear, and consistent across all marketing and communications platforms and venues.

- ✔ Use pricing and promotions more effectively, both to generate sales and to maximize profits.

- ✔ Rethink distribution channels to reach more prospects and reduce steps, whether through traditional channels, on the web, or through hand-held devices.

- ✔ Design or manage a sales force or network of sales representatives.

- ✔ Maximize customer retention and referrals by optimizing customer service.

Chapter 14

Making Your Brand Stand Out

In This Chapter

▶ Creating a powerful brand identity

▶ Naming your brand well

▶ Fitting your products into branded product lines

▶ Pumping up current products and introducing new ones

▶ Knowing when it's time to improve or replace a product

*T*he brand is the heart and soul of any marketing program. If the product is good and has a strong, appealing identity (the brand), then the marketing program has a high chance of success. In this book, I use the word *product* as an umbrella term that means a product, a service, or anything else your company wants to sell. The *brand* is the special identity you give this product, or line of products, through your marketing. You may even think of yourself as a branded product at times — for instance, when applying for jobs or running for office. The marketer's approach to branding products is a powerful one, and this chapter has tons of great tools and techniques you can use, whatever your current marketing challenge may be.

Burning Your Brand into Your Customers' Minds

The term *brand* comes from the old practice of burning a permanent mark, or brand, onto the flanks of cattle to identify a herd. It was a common practice in the Western United States because cattle roamed widely and an owner could easily lose his valuable herd without a durable, unique identifier. Today the term is used a bit differently. A brand is no longer burned into the skin. However, marketers still hope to burn their brand into their customers' minds.

You may get some clues to successful branding from looking at the history of branding by ranchers. A traditional cattle brand took one of three forms: the name in simplified form (usually two initials), the initials plus a simple symbol, or a symbol alone. Today's business, consumer, and nonprofit brands still take one of these three simple forms, and yours should, too. Whichever form it takes (name alone, name plus symbol, or symbol alone), your brand needs to be clear, distinctive, appropriate, and appealing; you also need to repeat it consistently and frequently so people can recognize it instantly.

Whether you're starting from scratch or have been in business for some time, taking a closer look at your brand and how you use it in your marketing can pay off. The following sections help you do just that.

Getting tough about your brand identity

Many businesses fail to control their brand presentation and allow more variation than is good for their marketing. In fact, this is the most common problem I find when I do marketing strategy consults with small- and mid-sized businesses as well as nonprofits, such as museums, schools, colleges, and social service agencies. It's not that these marketers disagree about the need to manage brand presentation; it's just that there are so many different facets to one's communication with the outside world and so many opportunities for small problems to accumulate into a big problem of brand inconsistency.

You need to have a standard for your brand that's as hard, clear, and unwavering as an iron brand. If your brand isn't iron-hard, then you need to review it and settle on a single, strong identity that you can use in all media at all times. (Sometimes this requirement necessitates a review of the name itself. If you find you've had to develop multiple names or name variants for different purposes, that's a sure sign your name isn't a comfortable fit and needs updating or out-and-out changing.) Variation in your brand presentation confuses people, reduces recognition, and dilutes the strength of your brand. Get tough about your branding and stick to your guns!

Narrowing logo options down to one strong design

Indecision is the enemy of effective branding. Think about the brands you know best, such as Coca-Cola, Nike, Starbucks, or IBM. You may see minor (and highly intentional) variations in how their logos are presented, but generally, they're as clear and consistent as if they were burned by an iron brand. Is yours?

To ensure that customers and prospects recognize your brand immediately, you need to have a single, strong logo design in place. But first you need to choose that winning design from a variety of options. If you hire someone to help you define or refine your brand, ask him to give you a broad selection of possible logos. Most designers do this on their own, but sometimes designers just want to come up with one design, which is why you need to push them to develop good alternatives (not just straw men for you to knock down).

REAL WORLD

Unifying the branches of your identity tree

Business growth is good, but sometimes an organization grows so many branches that branding them recognizably is difficult because those multiple branches have evolved into different brand identities that fail to reinforce and promote each other fully.

A great example of this branching brands phenomenon is a nonprofit I'm involved with located in the famous colonial village of Old Deerfield, Massachusetts. The organization was founded so long ago that its name doesn't make all that much sense with what it does today: Pocumtuck Valley Memorial Association. The term *memorial association* used to be more common for civic groups formed to memorialize people or places from history with statues and plaques. That was its first charter, its trunk. Then it branched out by archiving and presenting historical artifacts at the Memorial Hall Museum in Old Deerfield — another brand name, one that appears over the door and on the organization's website and many of its pamphlets, grant applications, and other communications. The website is www.deerfield-ma.org, which reflects the historical interest in the town of Old Deerfield itself, another brand identity. Then there's the Indian House Children's Museum, a popular place for visitors and another brand identity. Plus the fascinating work the organization does to educate teachers in how to better teach

history, nested on the brand branch, Deerfield Teacher's Center. And did I mention the crafts fairs the organization puts on, known in the region for many years by the brand name Old Deerfield Craft Fairs?

To try to unify these many brands, the organization is using PVMA Deerfield as a new umbrella identity, which retains the traditional name as an acronym but adds in the Deerfield identity that pops up in so many of the sub-brands. Still, there's an apparent need to continue to promote the sub-brands, because each has an identity and a function of its own. Should this organization think of itself like a consumer brand marketer, where each brand is a separate marketing asset and doesn't dovetail with others? Or should it continue to try to unify its marketing presentation by migrating every sub-brand toward a more unified identity? This is the key strategic question, and its answer will affect the amount of resources put behind each brand. My thought is that because every activity really is rooted in the same deep interest in history, the migration toward a single, unified brand should continue. Perhaps a single word and image can be incorporated into every sub-brand, showing clearly that it comes from the same brand tree. How would you tackle the rebranding of this multifaceted nonprofit?

If you're not sure how to determine what makes a strong logo, put yourself in the shoes of Herb Chambers Business Consulting, a case study I developed for marketing classes I sometimes teach at the Eisenberg School of Business. (The case is based on a real client but features a fictitious name so students can't find "the answer" online but rather must solve it themselves.) Herb Chambers Business Consulting is trying to come up with one clear, bold, appealing version of the firm's brand identity to use in all of its marketing communications. Even though the firm has been in business for many years, its brand identity isn't a marketing asset, so the company is asking a marketing team to come up with some suggestions for a new logo. The first suggestion many teams arrive at is to simplify the name to Chambers Business Consulting. Figure 14-1 shows a selection of first-round ideas for a Chambers Business Consulting logo, including a variety of ways to brand the name using different typefaces and some ideas involving the use of the business's initials.

Figure 14-1: A selection of design ideas for branding a consulting firm.

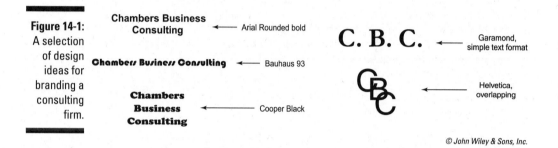

Chambers Business Consulting ← Arial Rounded bold

Chambers Business Consulting ← Bauhaus 93

Chambers Business Consulting ← Cooper Black

C. B. C. ← Garamond, simple text format

CBC ← Helvetica, overlapping

© John Wiley & Sons, Inc.

After you have an initial selection of design ideas for your logo, take a week or more to evaluate them and make sure one really stands out as superior and meets all your needs. If no one option really stands out, identify what you like and dislike about the top three designs and send the designer back to come up with another set of options. Sometimes it takes many of these design-and-review cycles to come up with the perfect logo, so don't be impatient.

The perfect logo appeals visually to everyone involved in marketing, stands out from competitors and other well-known brands, contributes to a strongly positive brand image or personality, and makes your brand name memorable when shown on letterhead, packaging, brochures and e-brochures, or the top left corner of a web landing page.

In the case of Chambers Business Consulting, none of the initial designs were as strong as hoped, so the marketing team went back to the drawing board. The main objections were that the logos based on the name alone (refer to Figure 14-1) lacked visual strength and appeal, while the logos based only on the initials were visually stronger but failed to remind people of the firm's name. Also, some of the designs seemed too modern, because the marketing team wanted to project a solid, traditional look that clients would view as highly trustworthy and professional.

Figure 14-2 shows a second-generation design for the new Chambers Business Consulting brand identity. This logo presents the company's brand name in a distinguished font called Engravers MT, which, as its name implies, is based on traditional engravings in stone and metal. The idea was to convey a sense of solidity and traditional reliability through the brand's appearance. On stationery and business cards, the logo may be shown in plain black ink. However, when color is an option (like on the web, in PowerPoint slide presentations, or in full-color brochures), the logo can appear as if it's carved into a bronze plaque (the firm could also use a real bronze plaque as the sign in its office lobby). The firm's new logo presents a strong, easily recognized brand identity in a consistent manner wherever the firm's name appears.

Figure 14-2:
The final
design
improved
upon the
initial
concepts.

To help you keep your brand consistent, maintain a master style sheet specifying the font size and type style and how the design elements relate to each other. Don't permit any variations beyond the style sheet; otherwise you're failing to protect your logo.

The Chambers Business Consulting case is a good model for you to follow as you examine your own brand identity and make sure it's as strong and consistent as possible. Is your brand presenting strongly and well with a good clear logo that you repeat everywhere you can? Figure 14-3 shows two additional brand identities to give you more ideas about how to approach the important challenge of designing the strongest logo you can for your brand. Note that both logos include a clear, simple visual element along with the brand name written in a standardized type style. The relationship between the type and the art should be fixed — relative spacing and size should never vary, even when the logo is enlarged for signs or reduced for business cards.

Figure 14-3:
Distinctive
brand
identities
for small
businesses.

Developing your brand's iconography

Iconography is the study of visual images; in marketing, iconography is the development of a family of images or imagery that make the brand appealing. Iconography isn't as tightly planned and specified as the design of the logo, but it should also be thought about and described through illustrations and examples. For example, since 1971, Adidas has had the Trefoil brand with its three petal-like shapes radiating upward, bisected by three lines (the three stripes that have appeared on all Adidas shoes since 1949). That Trefoil symbol is rendered with identical proportions whenever it appears (for example, on the Adidas Originals collection). That's an important logotype, but what iconography, or supporting images, should be associated with it? For some years, Adidas used simple action figures neatly silhouetted in black, performing athletic movements.

Over time, the Adidas action images began to feel a little too static, so Adidas retained EIGA Design (of Hamburg, Germany) to update them. The new versions are also action figures in black and white, but the originals are hand-drawn in felt tip pen, with exciting lines adding to the sense of dynamic movement and grace of each action figure. You can see the updated iconography in animated sequences in some Adidas commercials or by doing an Internet search for "Adidas brand iconography."

In developing your brand's iconography, you may want to create a family of artistic images to illustrate it, as Adidas did. Or you may want to take a more general approach, collecting a handful of the sorts of images you think work well to guide designers of marketing materials. For instance, a natural, old-fashioned cookie brand may have a set of images of traditional farms and farm kitchens, drawn from Flickr or stock photography houses. The exact images need not be used in marketing, but they help advertisers, packagers, point-of-purchase display designers, blog and web designers, and other marketers zoom in on a general look and style, perhaps even a setting, for displaying the cookies.

Focusing on your website

Because a strong Internet presence is now more critical for marketing success than ever before, pay special attention to making sure your brand is displayed effectively on the web. Every landing page and website home page must present a noticeable, simple, clear, memorable, brand mark in the top left corner of the screen. This is a pretty good general rule, but one that's often violated. Even expert marketers too often flub their web branding.

At the time of this writing, Adobe, maker of software used to design almost all brand identities, does a poor job of presenting its own brand: a horizontal red rectangle with an inner white square against which a boxy red *A* appears. The logo itself isn't my favorite because it fails to capture the sophistication and elegance of the company's software; however, setting that concern aside, the bigger issue with Adobe's web displays is that its logo is very small and seems secondary to the tabs across the top of the web page.

You want to make the logo big and bold, and give it some personal space to show that it's powerful! A good example of how to highlight your logo is provided by Web Designer Depot, whose website (at `www.webdesignerdepot.com`) includes a large gold circle on the top left corner with the black cursive *W* — that is, the company's logo virtually leaping out of it due to the contrast of the bold black letter against the bright gold background color. To add more interest and memorability, the *W* is animated, so if you accidentally brush across it with your mouse (or finger on a device with a touch screen), it rotates clockwise — a surprise that makes you stop and look at it long enough to commit it to perpetual memory.

The logo can be a letter or symbol (such as a stylized drawing of a mountain or tree), or it can be a name, set in a distinctive typeface and color or colors. eBay epitomizes the latter strategy, on web and off. Open any page in eBay, and you'll always see the distinctive eBay logo in four colors, with plenty of white space around it to make it pop visually.

Branding throughout your "herd"

As a marketer, you need to be just as systematic and strong about your branding as an old-fashioned rancher branding his herd. You can think of your modern-day marketing herd as all the (possibly hundreds) of different ways you may communicate with customers, prospects, and the world at large.

Whether you're marketing through your blog, a YouTube video, signs, stationery, brochures, or other means, you need to burn your brand into these initiatives clearly and strongly, without variation in the essentials of its design. Evaluate your brand identity to make sure it's presented consistently and that it appears everywhere possible. If you already have a distinctive brand, stick with it and focus on rolling it out consistently everywhere you can. If it suffers from weak design or is virtually unknown, then redesign it before rolling it out aggressively.

Your brand name and logo don't have to be the most beautiful, sophisticated, or clever to be successful. In fact, many top brands are strikingly simple. What sets them apart from other brands is that they're recognizable and known, which in turn gives them value and helps them sell products. Rolling your brand out consistently and strongly is even more important than perfecting your logo design. Choose something that's clear and simple and then stick to it no matter what. Pretend your brand identity is an old-fashioned iron brand. If you see it as carved in metal, you'll resist any efforts to treat it as something flexible.

Many websites fail to present a brand properly and well. Don't let yours be one of them! Make the web design match your brand, not the other way around. And when your designer lays out a new blog, web page, or other page, insist that it be designed to showcase your logo. See the preceding section for details.

Coming Up with a Brand Name

When branding your company or new product, you want to make sure it has a name that customers can easily identify with you. You have several important factors to consider, and the next sections can help.

Naming your brand with personality

Branding a product or company is a little like giving a new puppy a name. You want to get a feel for its personality first so you can give it a name that fits. You can call a standoffish poodle Fifi, but that name doesn't fit a playful mutt. When naming your brand, you want to give it a clear personality that becomes its intangible signature. Customers get to know the brand personality when it's reflected in everything, from choice of fonts and colors to the style and approach of advertising copy.

The Ford Mustang is presumed to have the personality of the fast, tough horse of the American plains from which the car took its name. The idea is that the driver is a modern-day cowboy, akin to the real cowboys who broke and used the mustangs for their work. This strategy has a powerful effect because it uses existing terms whose meaning marketers apply to their products. And the fact that Mustang is a 50-year-old brand with truly famous models dating as far back as the 1960s means that the brand equity is worth more than its current 3 percent of Ford's sales. In fact, Ford Motor Company is promoting the 2014 Mustang heavily, both in the United States and abroad, with the expectation that it will boost overall Ford brand strength. It is, after all, the *Ford* Mustang, not just the Mustang, and that gives the parent company a halo effect it can use to promote other Ford lines, too. You may not be ready to ride a mustang this year, so the theory goes, but perhaps a Ford with a bit more cultured of a personality will be a good fit and allow you to keep in touch with that latent wild side to your own personality.

How can you ensure that your brand name exudes a winning personality? Try one of these two simple exercises to help you start to define your brand's personality:

> ✔ **Select an animal that's most like your brand or what you want your brand to be.** What animal did you come up with? An elephant — big, powerful, intelligent, and long lasting? A bee — busy and industrious? A cat — quick, sleek, attractive, and smart? An eagle — a natural leader

flying high above the rest? A butterfly — delicate and light, spreading beauty where it flies? Don't laugh at this exercise. Many brands receive the personalities commonly associated with animals. For example, the United States is branded as an eagle for its intended leadership role on the world stage.

✔ **Ask yourself what your brand would be like if it were human.** Would it be female or male? An adventurous teenager or a wise elder? What personality would it have? Human personality traits appeal to humans, so it makes sense to position your brand using dimensions of real personalities.

Identifying your brand's personality traits

Research psychologists rarely agree on anything, but they do agree that human beings have five broad dimensions to their outward personalities. Every person can be defined by where he or she falls on these five dimensions. To define your brand more clearly, you may describe it by using these five factors of human personality: extroversion, agreeableness, conscientiousness, emotional stability, and openness to experience.

Table 14-1 shows the range of options. Circle one of the answers on each row to define your brand's characteristic personality. Then reference this table whenever you design anything, from a logo to a letter, and make sure your marketing communications are consistent with the brand personality you've chosen. Over time, you'll teach the market about your brand's unique personality, and consumers will become increasingly comfortable with your brand because they'll feel like they really know it.

Table 14-1	Defining Your Brand's Unique Personality	
Does Your Brand Seem . . .	*Your Answer*	
Extroverted: Outgoing. Makes friends easily. Sociable. Takes charge.	Yes	No
Agreeable: Makes people feel at ease. Is on good terms with nearly everyone. Trusts people. Thinks of others first.	Yes	No
Conscientious: Does a thorough job. Well prepared. Gets chores done right away. Does things according to a plan.	Yes	No
Emotionally stable: Relaxed. Calm. Handles stress well. Not easily bothered.	Yes	No
Open to experiences: Imaginative. Creative. Intelligent. Has many interests. Quick to understand things.	Yes	No

Source: Alex Hiam, The Big Five Personality Test, Trainer's Spectrum, 2009

Unlike humans, brands may have simple, one-dimensional personalities, so if you check only one "yes" in Table 14-1, that's okay. Perhaps you define your brand simply as conscientious. This trait would be perfect for a line of file cabinets, for example. Or you may create a richer personality for your brand by adding one or two additional traits (your line of file cabinets could also be stable or even imaginatively styled if they're designed to be visible to the buyers' customers). With these traits, designers and writers can consistently present a calm, organized but also stylish personality for your brand of file cabinets.

You can't change your own personality very easily, but you do get to pick the traits you consider most helpful for marketing your brand. For instance, a new line of cosmetics may be portrayed as extroverted and open to experiences. Dynamic, exciting colors and sounds will help convey this sociable, creative, enthusiastic personality to consumers, who'll buy the brand in order to add those traits to their own lives when they feel the need for them.

Giving a memorable and meaningful name

Would a rose by any other name really smell as sweet? In poetry perhaps, but not in marketing. The name *rose* is a wonderful brand identity for the flower. It's short and simple yet smooth and pleasant to speak, and it has come to be associated with the most popular and romantic of all flowers. But what if your brand name isn't as appealing? For example, someone who has just purchased a small business called Franz Gingleheimer Heritage Rose Nursery may find it prudent to change the name to Antique Roses, which has a nicer sound and is easy to remember. How do you pick a new or improved name that makes your brand as appealing as a rose?

Following are some approaches you can take to name your brand so readers can remember and identify with your product:

- ✔ **Give your brand an informational name.** Doing so makes spreading the word about your offerings easier. For example, a business called Amherst Gallery of Figurative Art is clearly an art gallery selling figurative works. If it were called The Amherst Salon, some people would think it was a hair salon, not an art salon. Is your name informative? If not, consider making it describe your business more accurately. If you can add information power to your brand name easily and without making it too big of a mouthful, then do.

- ✔ **Pick a name for your brand that's clear, simple, short, and easy to say.** How a brand feels and sounds when spoken is very important. Say "Coca-Cola" and think about the feel of it in your mouth as you speak.

It's satisfying to say. It moves through and out of the mouth in a nice way. Root beer is harder and less pleasant to pronounce, which helps explain why it's less popular than cola.

✔ **Select a brand name that has good visual appeal.** The look of a brand is also important, so give careful thought to the imagery evoked by a name and choose a name that has good visual associations. People are very visual, so visual recognition and appeal can add tremendously to the impact of a brand. For example, *star* is a nice word. It evokes the image of a symbolic star, usually a five-pointed geometric form. Star Computer Repair sounds good and can easily be made to look good with a logo that includes a star along with the name. Many logos tap into the visual appeal of a simple symbol, and you can, too. Shell Oil Company benefits from the strong visual appeal of its logo, a golden scallop outlined in red. The company is usually known simply as Shell due to the power of its visual logo.

✔ **Make up a brand-new word that has no prior meaning and hasn't been used before.** This approach gives you something you can more easily protect in a court of law, but it isn't necessarily effective at communicating the character of your product. Also, you have to invest considerable time and money in creating a meaning for the new name in consumers' minds.

When you use meaningful components for your made-up names, they're called *morphemes,* which NameLab, Inc. (a San Francisco–based leading developer of such names), defines as the semantic kernels of words. For example, NameLab started with the word *accurate* (from the Latin word *accuratus*) and extracted a morpheme from it to use as a new car brand: Acura. The company also developed Compaq, Autozone, Lumina, and Zapmail in the same manner. Each one is a new word to the language, but each word communicates something about the product because of the meanings consumers associate with that word's components.

Many new brand names are formed by semi-scientific re-combinations of root syllables, which make them sound semi-scientific. Consider asking poets and songwriters for input, too. Perhaps one of them will come up with a unique new word that is appealing to the ear when heard and, when spoken, forms nicely on the tongue. Melodious words are more memorable than technical or awkward ones. (Hence the enduring popularity of any bar drink that is baptized with a melodious name: Wouldn't you want to try a Singapore sling? It's been popular since the 1930s. Before that, it was called the gin sling and didn't enjoy the same global popularity. I attribute the difference entirely to its renaming.)

Updating your brand

Many brand identities look and feel out-of-date. In fact, large companies commonly hire top designers and agencies to study their brands and come up with upgrades. You should keep an eye on your brand, too, and make sure it isn't looking outdated. However, be careful not to throw away its most distinctive qualities. Brand updates have a rather low success rate, even when the pros do it and bill in the hundreds of thousands of dollars.

Consider what happened with The Gap, which switched from a distinctive GAP logo, white on a deep blue square, to a generic-looking Gap logo on black with only a small remnant of the old blue square. Instant loss of brand equity. Nobody liked it. Now the old logo has quietly reasserted itself, and the new one has been retired. A few years ago, Kraft Foods had an all lowercase "kraft foods: make today delicious" logo with some sort of complex rainbow colorburst thingy behind it. Have you seen it? It's hard to spot these days. Oddly, the Krafts Food Group website (www.kraftfoodsgroup.com) currently has no corporate logo and no banner at the top; instead it features simple text and a scrolling viewbar of all the food brands the company owns, many of which are strong, iconic designs. In other rebranding news, USA Today's distinctive white caps logo on a blue box was scrapped in favor of dull black letters next to a strange light-blue circle. I bet the old one will come back soon.

On the other hand, sometimes brand updates take off. American Airlines' updated logo is powerful, simple, and dynamic, looking like an eagle just ghosting into view against a blue and red slash. It's so strong visually that I expect it will really stick. (However, the recent merger with US Airways may lead to an eventual combining of the two brands. So stay tuned, eager brand-marketing experts . . . .)

If you want to stay on the pulse of brand updates that hit it big or flop spectacularly, look up logo designs by searching for "brand name + logo design" in your favorite Internet search engine. These changes get a lot of online attention from the design community, so there are always plenty of images and editorial chit-chat to review on the topic.

Designing a Product Line

A *product line* is any logical grouping of products offered to customers. (**Remember:** Products can be goods, services, ideas, or even people — such as political candidates or movie stars.) You usually identify product lines by an umbrella brand name with individual brand identities falling under that umbrella. After you establish a strong brand (see the earlier sections in this chapter for help doing just that), you can extend it to a line of products. The stronger the brand (if people know and like it, of course), the longer the line of products. A really well-established brand name has the strength to make a wide range of products appealing.

The sections that follow provide valuable insight about what to consider when developing your product line, how to manage the product line after you develop it, and what to do to protect its identity.

Eyeing depth and breadth

You have two key issues to consider when designing your product line:

- ✔ **Depth:** How many alternatives should you give customers within any single category? For example, should you make a single T-shirt design in a range of sizes? How about offering the design in a variety of colors? Both of these options increase depth because they give customers more options. Depth gives you an advantage because it improves the likelihood of a good fit between an interested customer and your product. You don't want to miss a sale because somebody was too big to wear a size large.

  Increase depth when you're losing customers because you don't have a product for them. Increasing your depth of choice reduces the chance of disappointing a prospective customer.

- ✔ **Breadth:** Breadth comes from offering more types or categories of products. For example, if you sell one popular T-shirt design, you can increase your product line's breadth by offering more T-shirt designs or (to go even broader) by adding sweatshirts, baseball caps, and other items that can be silkscreened with designs. When you add anything that the customer views as a separate choice, not a variant of the same choice, you're adding breadth to your product line. A broad line of T-shirts includes dozens and dozens of different designs. A broad and deep product line offers each of those designs in many sizes and on many different colors and forms of T-shirts.

  Increase breadth whenever you can think of a new product that seems to fit in the product line and that you believe will increase your sales without sacrificing profits. By *fit,* I mean that customers can see the new product's obvious relationship to the line. Don't mix unrelated products — that's not a product line, because it doesn't have a clear, logical identity to customers. But do keep stretching a successful line as long as sales continue to grow. Doing so makes sense for one simple reason: You sell new products to old customers. Of course, the line may also reach new customers, which is great. But you can sell to your old customers more easily (read: less costly), so you definitely want to do more business with them in the future; offering them new products within a popular product line is a great way to do this.

Managing your product line effectively

The secret to good product management is the motto "Don't leave well enough alone." But if you keep growing your product lines, you can obviously bump into some practical limits after a while. How do you know when the pendulum is going to swing the other way — when it's time to do some spring-cleaning? (One easy indicator: Too much variety in your lineup to fit on your main website anymore.)

You should decrease your depth or breadth (or both; see the preceding section for more on these concepts) if you find that certain items never or hardly ever sell. Also prune back if your distribution channels don't display the full product line to customers. Often distribution becomes a bottleneck, imposing practical limits on how big a product line you can bring to the customer's attention.

When I consulted for the Kellogg Brush Company some years ago, I was amazed to discover it made many hundreds of different items. Yet the grocery and hardware stores selling its products never displayed more than a couple dozen items. Obviously, the company's product line was far broader and deeper than its end customers ever realized. I recommended that the company either develop a direct catalog- or Internet-based distribution channel to bring these choices to customers or cut its product line back to the top items purchased by retailers and try to make those items better and cheaper. (It chose the latter option.)

Protecting your product line and brand

You can gain legal protection for your product, a specific line of products, or even your entire company by using, and getting legal recognition for, a unique identifier. This protection can apply to names, short verbal descriptions, and visual symbols. All of these forms of identification are marks that can represent the identity of the thing you apply them to. A tangible product's name and/or visual symbol is a *trademark*. A service name is termed a *service mark* (U.S. law treats a service mark similarly to a trademark). A business name is a *trade name* (again, with similar protection under U.S. law).

In the United States, you establish and protect your rights to exclusive use of any unique trademark by using it. Yes, you should register it (with the U.S. Patent and Trademark Office — contact any law firm handling intellectual property to find out how). But registering the trademark isn't nearly as important as *using* the trademark. In other countries, usage and registration also matter, but sometimes governments reverse the emphasis, meaning without registration, usage gives you no protection. So check with local authorities in each country where you plan to use a trademark.

For more information on establishing and strengthening trademarks, contact your lawyer, any experienced ad agency that does brand marketing, or a name lab. More detailed coverage of the topic can be found in *Patents, Copyrights & Trademarks For Dummies,* by Henri Charmasson (Wiley). Additionally, free information is available at the U.S. Patent and Trademark Office's trademark-specific website (www.uspto.gov/trademarks/index.jsp). There, you can download a free book, search the database, and discover info about U.S. trademark law. You can also file a trademark application online using the Trademark Electronic Application System (TEAS), although I don't really recommend doing it yourself unless you have working knowledge of trademark law.

To register your trademark in other countries, you must contact a lawyer who specializes in intellectual property. Most of the countries in which you may want to do business (including the United States) subscribe to the Berne Convention, which means your legal protection for a published work (even a label or ad) in one participating country is also honored in other participating countries.

Strengthening an Existing Product

Your existing products have some degree of brand identity and a certain amount of customer loyalty already. Often your best investment is to boost the strength of their brand image or improve their design or packaging. Doing so takes advantage of any existing brand equity, which is easier than starting from scratch.

Here's a list of simple and quick actions you can take to build customer loyalty and grow sales by working on your product:

- ✔ **Update the appearance.** Many companies present good products to the world in poorly designed exteriors that don't dress those products for success. Look at the product itself (colors, attractiveness, and visibility of brand names).

- ✔ **Freshen up the packaging.** A consumer product that sits on a shelf waiting for someone to pick it up should be highly visible and appealing. Can you add a brighter color to the packaging to attract the eye? Can you mention key features on the outside? Perhaps you can add a clear window to show the actual product? If you can possibly do so, you should convert to *green* (recycled or recyclable) packaging and promote this fact on the packaging. More and more buyers are looking for green brands.

- ✔ **Make sure the product is attractive and easy to use.** Your product should also feel nice — smooth, polished, soft, or whatever texture is appropriate to the product's use. Even very minor changes in your product's look, feel, and function can improve its appeal as well as customers' satisfaction.

- ✔ **Refresh any printed materials that come with the product.** Can you improve their appearance? Dress them up? Make them clearer or more useful? Whatever you do, make sure these printed materials instill pride of ownership in the product. A professional, attractive web page should also support the product. Refresh it periodically so it doesn't start to look out-of-date or neglected.

- ✔ **Choose your product's best quality.** Coin a short phrase to communicate this best quality to the consumer and put that phrase in prominent places on the product, its packaging, and its literature. Have simple (but attractive) color-printed stickers made up for this purpose, if you want — that's the quickest and cheapest way to add a marketing message to something.

- ✔ **Eliminate confusion about which product does what for whom.** If you have more than one product, clarify the differences and uses of your products by pricing and naming them distinctly (to make them obviously different). You'd be amazed how confusing most product lines look to the average buyer.

- ✔ **Make your logo beautiful.** Apple Computer, Inc., switched from a somewhat dated-looking rainbow-colored version of its distinctive apple-shaped logo to a sophisticated version made of a clear plastic panel backlit with diffused white light. This logo sits on the top of all of its newer laptops, giving those computers a more sophisticated appeal. Can you upgrade your image by improving the appearance of your logo on your products? (For help updating your logo, see the earlier "Narrowing logo options down to one strong design" section.)

- ✔ **Pick up a related but noncompeting product from another company and repackage and distribute it as part of your product line.** Adding another good product your customers like can increase their average purchase size significantly. I recommend that you use distributor-style arrangements that eliminate the investment of product development, giving you a good way to expand your product line in a hurry if you so choose. Selling a new (or new to you) product to an existing customer is often easier than finding a new customer for an existing product.

I hope this list of simple ideas for action has your marketing blood circulating! As you can see, you can do a lot with and for your products, even if you don't have the cash or time right now to develop and introduce an entirely new product. Of course, in the long run, you're only as good as your products, so you also need to try to update, upgrade, or perhaps even replace your current line of products. It's a long-term but vital activity that most marketing plans need to include, just as gardeners have to remember to plan the next planting along with their more routine weeding and watering duties.

Identifying When and How to Introduce a New Product

If your market is like most, innovations give you a major source of competitive advantage. A competitor's major new product introduction probably changes the face of your market — and upsets your sales projections and profit margins — at least once every few years. So you can't afford to ignore new product development. You should introduce new products as often as you can afford to.

Okay, you think you need a hot new product. But where do you get the idea? First, check out the basic creativity skills covered in Chapter 5. That chapter offers a host of brainstorming and idea-generating techniques you can use. If you and your fellow marketers are stale, bring in people from the sales field, production department, repair area, or service call center. Or try bringing in some customers for a brainstorming session. There's no single formula for inventing new products. You just need to engage in a new and different thinking process. *Remember:* Do something new to produce something new.

The following sections highlight various ways of coming up with new products as well as a suggestion for making your new product stand out as something noticeably new and different.

Making the old new again

Old ideas are any product concepts that you or another company have previously abandoned. They may have been considered but rejected without being marketed, or they can even be old products that have fallen out of use but can be revived with a twist. Because people have been struggling to develop new product concepts for decades in most markets, many abandoned ideas and old products are around.

Often companies fail to keep good records, so you have to interview old-timers and poke through faded files or archived catalogs to discover those old ideas. But old ideas may be a treasure trove, because technical advances or changing customer taste may make yesterday's wild ideas today's practical ones. Even if you can't use any old ideas you find, they may lead you to fresh ways of thinking — perhaps they suggest a customer need that you hadn't thought of before.

Stealing — er, borrowing — ideas

You can often profit from other people's ideas through licenses. A private inventor may have a great new product concept and a patent for it, but he may lack the marketing muscle and capital to introduce the product. You can provide that missing muscle and pay the inventor 5 or 10 percent of your net revenues as reward for his inspiration. Many companies generate inventions that fall outside of their marketing focus. These companies are often willing to license to someone specializing in the target market. That's the official way to use other people's ideas.

Unofficially, you can simply steal ideas. Now, by steal, I don't mean to take anything that isn't legally yours. A *patent* protects a design; a *trademark* protects a name or logo; and a *copyright* protects writing, artwork, performances, and software. You must respect these legal rights that protect other people's expressions of their ideas. But often the underlying ideas are fair game so long as you implement them in your own fresh way (when in doubt, check with your lawyer!). I call this activity "stealing" in humor. It isn't really, *if* you do it legally. Some people call it "benchmarking"; others call it "being inspired by others." Whatever you call it, be aware of new concepts and keep your product offerings up-to-date with them.

If the ideas make it to your ears or eyes through a legitimate public channel of communication, then you can often use them. Just don't bug your competitor's headquarters, go through its dumpster, or get its engineers drunk — doing so may violate *trade secrecy laws;* ask your lawyer about any questionable research.

Although a competitor may be upset to see you knocking off or improving upon its latest idea, nothing can stop you as long as your source was public (not secret) and you aren't violating a patent, trademark, or copyright. In most markets, competitors milk each others' ideas as a matter of routine. Also look at other industries for inspiration you can apply in your industry.

Picking your customers' brains

A final source of new product ideas comes from your customers. Customers are actually the best source, but they don't know it. Ask a customer to describe a brilliant new product you should provide for him, and you get a blank stare or worse. Yet frustrations with the existing products and all sorts of dissatisfactions, needs, and wants lurk in the back of all customers' minds. You may be able to introduce a new product that helps them with their gripes.

How do you mine the treasure trove of customer needs, many of them latent or unrecognized? Collecting customers' words helps you gain insight into how they think — so talk to them and take notes that use quotes, or record and transcribe their comments. Get them talking and let them wander a bit so you have a chance to encounter the unexpected. Also, watch customers as they buy and use your product. Observation may reveal wasted time and effort, inefficiencies, or other problems that the customer takes for granted — problems that the customer may happily say goodbye to if you point them out and remove them.

Using the significant difference strategy

New product development has a downside: Almost all new products fail. To achieve real success, you have to introduce something that really looks new and different to the market. The product needs a clear point of difference. Innovations that consumers recognize quickly and easily provide the marketer with a greater return. Researchers who study new product success use the term *intensity* to describe this phenomenon. The more intense the difference between your new product and old products, the more likely the new product can succeed.

The Product Development and Management Association (PDMA) publishes reviews of good new books on product development via its website, www.pdma. org. PDMA also offers conferences, training, and other services to its members.

When to Upgrade an Existing Product

Some products are so perfect that they fit naturally with their customers, and you should just leave them alone. For example . . . well, I suppose the formula for Coca-Cola is one example, but I'd be hard-pressed to come up with another. That alone tells you something important about product management: You'd better modify your products to improve performance, value, and quality with each new season and each new marketing plan.

You're competing on a changing playing field. Your competitors are trying hard to make their products better, and you have to do the same. Always seek insights into how to improve your product. Always look for early indicators of improvements your competitors plan to make and be prepared to go one step further in your response. And always go to your marketing oracle — the customer — for insights into how you can improve your product. The next two sections describe tests that a product must pass to remain viable. If your product doesn't pass, you need to improve or alter it somehow.

Passing the differentiation test

At the *point of purchase* — that place or time when customers make their actual purchase decisions — your product needs to have something special. It must pass the differentiation test by reaching out to at least a portion of the market and being better than its competition on certain criteria due to inherent design features. Or it needs to be about as good as the rest but a better value, which gives you a sustainable cost advantage. (Do you actually have such a cost advantage? Marketers generally underestimate the rarity of them! Don't slash prices unless you actually have lower costs to support the low prices.) Or the product needs to be the best option by virtue of a lack of other options.

Don't assume your lack of special features means that your product isn't special. You can be special just by being there when customers need the product. You can justify keeping a product alive just by having a way of maintaining your distribution advantage. But a product at the point of purchase must have at least *something* special about it if you expect it to generate a good return in the future. Otherwise, it gets lost in the shuffle.

If your customers don't think your product is unique in any way, then you may need to kill that product. But don't set up the noose too quickly. First, see whether you can work to differentiate the product in some important way. (See the "Strengthening an Existing Product" section, earlier in this chapter, for help reinvigorating your current product offerings.)

Passing the champion test

Champions are those customers who really love your product, who insist on buying it over others, and who tell their friends or associates to do the same. Champions are great to have, but they're also rather rare.

The championship test is tougher to pass than the differentiation test (described in the preceding section). Many products lack champions. But when a product does acquire them — when some customers anywhere in the distribution channel really love it — then that product is assured an unusually long and profitable life. Such high customer commitment should be your constant goal as you manage the life cycle of your product.

Products with champions get great word of mouth, and their sales and market shares grow because of that word of mouth. Even better, champions faithfully repurchase the products they rave about. And this repeat business provides your company with high-profit sales, compared with the higher costs associated with finding new customers. (This is one of the principles of good marketing, which you can read more about in Chapter 1.)

The hook? The repeat buyer must *want* to repeat the purchase. He needs to be a dedicated fan of the product. Otherwise, you need to think of each sale as a new sale that costs you almost as much as selling to someone who has never used the product before.

If your product doesn't seem to have champions and sales aren't growing, the product itself may be holding your brand identity hostage. Upgrading your brand image in your marketing may not be enough. You may need to improve or replace the old product so you actually deliver as much excitement to the user as your well-crafted brand identity promises. Don't be afraid to renew your product offerings regularly. Strong brands outlive individual products.

Chapter 15

Finding the Right Pricing Approach

In This Chapter

▶ Facing the facts about pricing

▶ Establishing or modifying your list price

▶ Crafting price-based special offers in traditional media and via the web

▶ Staying out of legal hot water

*G*etting the price just right is the hardest task you face as a marketer, but finding the right pricing approach makes success much easier to achieve. The bottom line is that the customer needs to pay — willingly and, you hope, rapidly — for your products or services. But how much will he or she pay? Should you drop your prices to grow your market? Or would raising the price and maximizing profits be better? What about discounts and special promotional pricing? Getting the price part of your marketing plan right is hard, but this chapter helps you through it by giving you a clearer idea about the many questions you may have about pricing and what it means to your bottom line.

Eyeing Pricing Opportunities and Constraints

Many companies fall prey to the myth that customers choose a product based on its *list price* (the published selling price in a catalog, on a price list, or on the product itself). Setting your list prices lower than you need to is tempting. So is trying to boost sales by offering discounts or free units. However, being too liberal with price cuts, discounts, and free offers is a mistake as well. So where exactly do you set your prices? The following sections provide you with some strategies you can undertake when setting your pricing, including increasing the price to sell more, staying clear of underpricing, and looking at how pricing affects what your customers buy. The goal is to feel that you're in control of your margins and able to make plenty of sales at the price points you choose.

Raising your price and selling more

If you insist on selling your product or service on the basis of low price, your customers will get in the habit of shopping for the lowest price. To counteract that, take appropriate action by combining conservative pricing with aggressive branding to win a higher net price and a bigger profit margin. *Remember:* Your goal should be to see how much you can sell your product for, not how little.

To raise your price *and* sell more, you may decide to

- ✔ **Build brand equity:** Better-known brands command a premium price.

- ✔ **Increase quality:** People talk up a good product, and that word of mouth earns the product a 5 to 10 percent higher price than the competition.

- ✔ **Use prestige pricing:** Giving your product a high-class image can boost your price 20 to 100 percent.

- ✔ **Create extra value through time and place advantages:** Customers consider the available product worth a lot more than the one they can't get when they need it. (That's why a cup of coffee costs twice as much at the airport. Who's really going to leave the terminal, get in a taxi, and go somewhere else to save a couple bucks?)

Sometimes my readers tell me that competition and/or their distributors force them to lower prices to the point where they barely make any profits. If this situation happens to you, then face the fact that you've lost control over your own pricing. You should be able to price fairly, meaning fairly to both you *and* your customer. If you're forced to slash costs and lose money, then you can't control your own pricing. Either get out of that line of business at once or lower your costs by changing your business model (cut out a middle man, for example).

Avoiding underpricing

You're always going to have an easier time lowering a price than raising it. In general, you want to set price a bit on the high side and see what happens. You can take back any price increase with a subsequent price cut — just be wary of underpricing your product or service because you may find you've given away your profits.

Exploring the impact of pricing on customers' purchases

Price sensitivity is the degree to which purchases are affected by price level. You need to estimate how price sensitive your customers are. Specifically, you want to be able to predict how many sales you'll lose or gain from a specific increase or decrease in your sales price. This information can tell you whether you'll profit from a change in price.

You can estimate customers' price sensitivity through observation and tests. For example, if you think a 5 percent increase in prices won't affect sales, try that increase in a test market or for a short period of time, holding the rest of your marketing constant. Were you right? If so, roll out the increase nationwide (or townwide if you're part of a small business).

If customers think your pricing is reasonable, and if no cheaper competitors exist that customers think are comparable, then they won't be especially price sensitive. You'll face little or no pressure to cut prices. In fact, you may even be able to raise prices modestly without hurting sales.

However, if you find new competitors with lower prices than yours and they're taking some of your business, then you can conclude that your customers are price sensitive. You need to match the competitive prices to stop losing customers. That's too bad, but it happens often, and when it does, you have to turn to cost controls if you want to save your profit margins.

Finding profits without raising prices

When you think about profits, you may assume that your focus should be on the price. But many factors drive your company's cash flows and profits, not just the list price of your products. Here are some ways to boost profits without raising prices:

- ✔ **Check to see how quickly you're making collections.** Cutting that time may make up the needed profits without any price increase.

- ✔ **Look at all the discounts and allowances you offer.** These factors affect your revenues and profits, so you need to review them before assuming that price is the culprit. Are customers taking advantage of quantity discounts to stock up inexpensively and then not buying between the discount periods? If so, you have a problem with your sales promotions, not your list prices.

✔ **Examine how you assess fees.** Perhaps your company is failing to collect the appropriate fees in some cases. (This one is particularly important if you're in a service business that charges a base price plus fees for special services and extras.)

✔ **Determine whether your fee structure is out of date.** If it is, your cost structure likely isn't reflected accurately. For example, a bank that charges a low price for standard checking accounts, plus a per-check processing fee, may well find its profits slumping as customers switch to automated checking over the bank's computers. Why? Because banks often set the introductory fees for this service low or waive them to stimulate trials. If so, the problem isn't with the base price of a checking account; it's with the nature of the fee structure.

Setting or Changing Your List Price

If you need to establish a price, you're stuck with one of the toughest tasks anybody does in business. Surveys of managers indicate they suffer from a high degree of price anxiety. The sections that follow take you through the process of setting or changing your price logically, step by step. (Figure 15-1 illustrates the process that I describe in the following sections.)

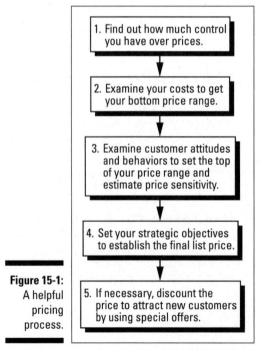

Figure 15-1:
A helpful pricing process.

1. Find out how much control you have over prices.

2. Examine your costs to get your bottom price range.

3. Examine customer attitudes and behaviors to set the top of your price range and estimate price sensitivity.

4. Set your strategic objectives to establish the final list price.

5. If necessary, discount the price to attract new customers by using special offers.

Step 1: Figure out who sets prices

The step of determining who sets the price isn't obvious. You, as the marketer, can set a list price. But the consumer may not ultimately pay your price. You may encounter a distributor or wholesaler as well as a retailer, all of whom take their markups. Furthermore, the manufacturer generally doesn't have the legal right to dictate the ultimate selling price. The retailer gets that job. So your list price is really just a suggestion, not an order. If the retailer doesn't like your suggested price, she sells your product for another price.

As you determine the price of your product, involve these parties in your decision making by asking some of them what they think about the pricing of your product. They may tell you that you have constraints to consider. Know what those constraints are before you start. For example, if you're setting the price for a new book, you may find that the big bookstore chains in the United States expect a 60 percent discount off the list price. Knowing that, you can set a high enough list price to give you some profit, even at a 60 percent discount rate. But if you don't realize that these chains expect much higher discounts than other bookstores, you may be blindsided by their requirement.

Marketers who operate in or through a *multilevel distribution channel,* meaning that they have distributors, wholesalers, *rack jobbers* (companies that keep retail racks stocked), retailers, agents, or other sorts of intermediaries, need to establish a trade discount structure. *Trade discounts* (also called *functional discounts*) are what you give these intermediaries. They're a form of cost to the marketer, so make sure you know the discount structure for your product before you move on. Usually, marketers state the discount structure as a series of numbers, representing what each of the intermediaries gets as a discount. But you take each discount off the price left over from the discount before it, not off the list price. See the nearby sidebar for more detailed advice.

Step 2: Examine your costs

In practice, you may not have good, accurate information on the true costs of a specific product or service. That's why you need to carefully examine your costs. Take some time to try to estimate what you're actually spending and remember to include some value for expensive inventories if they sit around for a month or more (assume that you're paying interest on the money tied up in those products to account for the loss of having your capital wrapped up in inventory).

After you examine your costs carefully, you should have a fairly accurate idea of the minimum amount you can charge — at the very least, that charge should be your actual costs. (Okay, maybe sometimes you want to give away a product for less than the cost to introduce people to it, but don't use this ploy to take customers from competitors or you can be sued for dumping. See the later "Staying Out of Trouble with the Law" section for the dirt on

---

Determining discount structures

Here's how to compute prices and discounts in a complex distribution channel: Say that you discover the typical discount structure in the market where you want to introduce your product is 30/10/5. What does that mean? If you start with a $100 list price, the retailer pays at a discount of 30 percent off the list price (0.30 × $100 = $70). The retailer, who pays $70 for the product, marks it up to (approximately) $100 and makes about $30 in gross profit.

The 30/10/5 discount structure tells you that other intermediaries exist — one for each discount listed. The distributor, who sells the product to the retailer, has a discount of 10 percent off the price that she charges the retailer. That's 0.10 × $70 = $7 of gross profit for the distributor.

And this distributor must have paid $70 – $7, or $63, for the product to another intermediary (probably a manufacturer's representative or wholesaler). The marketer sells to this intermediary. And the 30/10/5 formula shows that this intermediary receives a 5 percent discount: 0.05 × $63 = $3.15 in profit for her.

Subtracting again, you can also determine that the marketer must sell the product to this first intermediary at $63 – $3.15, or $59.85. You, as the marketer, must give away more than 40 percent of that $100 list price to intermediaries if you use this 30/10/5 discount structure. So you have to calculate any profit you make from a $100 list price as costs subtracted from your net of $59.85. That's all you ever see of that $100!

---

dumping.) More often, you need a price that includes the cost plus a profit margin — say, 20 or 30 percent. So that means you have to treat your cost as 70 or 80 percent of the price, adding in that 20 or 30 percent margin your company requires.

This cost-plus-profit figure is the bottom of your price range (see Figure 15-2). Now you need to see whether customers permit you to charge this price — or even (if you're lucky) allow you to charge a higher price.

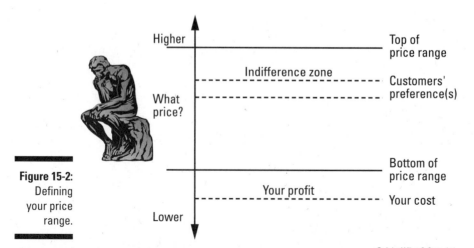

Figure 15-2:
Defining your price range.

Step 3: Evaluate customers' price preferences

Your costs and profit requirements impose a lower limit on price, but your customers' price preferences impose an upper limit. You need to define both of these limits to know your possible price range. That means you need to figure out what price customers are willing to pay.

In Figure 15-2, I label the price that customers favor as *customers' preference.* Note that customer preference may not be the upper limit. If customers aren't too price sensitive, they may not notice or care if you set your price somewhat higher than their preferred price.

Pricing experts sometimes call the difference between the customer's desired price and a noticeably higher price the *indifference zone.* Within the indifference zone, customers are indifferent to both price increases and price decreases. However, the zone gets smaller (on a percent basis) as the price of a product increases. How big or small is the zone of indifference in your product's case? (See the earlier "Exploring the impact of pricing on customers' purchases" section for help gauging your customers' price sensitivity.) The zone is small if your customers are highly price sensitive; the zone is large if they aren't that price sensitive.

You can also get at customer preference by looking at the current pricing structure in your market. What are people paying for comparable products? Does a downward or upward trend exist in the prices of comparable products? Are prices stable? Go shopping to figure out the existing price structure; you get excellent clues as to how customers may react to different prices for your product this way.

In many markets, web prices are beginning to set the standard by undercutting traditional distributors while still maintaining quality, so you may want to make a list of all the prices of competing products from web vendors.

Through these sorts of activities, I assume that you have at least back-of-the-envelope figures for your customers' preferred price and how much higher you can price without drawing attention. Guess what? You've established the top of your price range!

The simplest approach to pricing is to set your price at the top of the range. As long as the price range is above your bottom limit (as long as your preferred price plus the indifference zone is equal to or greater than your cost plus your required profit), you're okay. But you can't always set your price at the top of the range. In the next step of the pricing process, I show you how to figure out what your final price should be.

Step 4: Consider secondary influences on price

Your costs and your customers' preferred prices aren't the only factors you need to consider when trying to set or change your price. Yes, they're your primary considerations, but you also need to examine secondary influences. These factors may influence your decision by forcing you to price in the middle or bottom of the price range rather than at the top, for example.

Following are the key secondary influences you need to consider:

- ✔ **Competitive issues:** Do you need to gain market share from a close competitor? If so, either keep price on par with your competitor's pricing and do aggressive marketing or adjust your price to be slightly (but noticeably) below the competitor's price.

- ✔ If you're tempted to undercut a key competitor, be careful not to start a *price war* in which you and the competitor keep trying to undercut each other's prices until you're both giving your products away.

- ✔ **Likely future price trends:** Are prices trending downward in this market? Then you need to adjust your figures down a bit to stay in sync with your market.

- ✔ **Currency fluctuations:** Any fluctuation in currency may affect your costs and, consequently, your pricing options. If you're concerned that you may take a hit from the exchange rate, better to be safe than sorry and price at the high end of the range.

- ✔ **Product line management:** This factor may dictate a slightly lower or higher price. For example, you may need to price a top-of-the-line product significantly higher than others in its line just to make it clear to the customer that this product is a step above its competition.

Step 5: Set your strategic objectives

You may have objectives other than revenues and profit maximization. That's fine, but you need to clearly understand what those other objectives are. For instance, many marketers price near the bottom of their price range to increase their market share. (They price low because a high market share later on will probably give them more profits. It's an investment strategy.)

This low-price strategy only makes sense if the customer is fairly price sensitive! If not, you're throwing away possible revenues without any real gain in market share. You should be pricing at the top of the range and using the extra revenues to invest in product and service quality along with brand-building marketing promotions to increase market share (see Chapter 2 for details on these and other strategy options).

Sometimes marketers price high because they want to minimize unit volume, like when they're introducing a new product. They may not have had the capacity to sell the product to a mass market at first, so they *skimmed the market* by selling the product at such a high price that only the very wealthy or least price-sensitive customers could buy it. Then they lowered prices later on, when they'd made maximum profits from the high-end customers and had added production capacity.

Don't use a skimming strategy unless you're sure that you're safe from aggressive competition in the short term.

Step 6: Master the psychology of prices

To effectively set or change your price, you must possess a clear understanding of how customers perceive price. Believe it or not, psychology plays a big role in this process. What you set as your price and how customers perceive that price can have a significant impact on your level of sales. The following sections help you understand the psychology behind three different pricing methods available to you.

If you're in the service business, set a price that's consistent with your quality. Don't accidentally cheapen the perceived quality of your service by setting your price too low.

Odd-even pricing

The *odd-even* pricing method lowers the rounded-up price of an object by a cent or so, which people perceive as significantly lower than the rounded-up price. For example, if the top of your price range for a new child's toy is $10, you probably want to drop the price down to $9.99 because most customers think this price is much cheaper. Assuming your customers are in any way price sensitive, they buy more of the lower-priced product, even though the price difference amounts to only one cent. Why? Because people perceive prices ending in 9 as cheaper — generally 3 to 6 percent cheaper in their memories than the rounded-up price. It's just something about the way your customers see your price, and you can take advantage of it.

Odd-even pricing used to be confined largely to quick retail purchases where the consumer glanced at the price and didn't register it in detail, so the beginning number stuck in her mind and she didn't round up and recognize that she was paying significantly more. Maybe most people these days are getting more hurried (or worse at math?) because odd-even pricing is becoming more effective with big-ticket items, too. Use odd-even pricing for consumer products when you want to make the price more enticing and blunt the impact of a round number. In other words, it's generally better to price at $1.99 or $199 than at $2 or $200.

The only catch to using odd-even pricing is that customers sometimes associate prices ending in 9 with cheap products that have worse quality and are hyped with aggressive advertising. So don't use odd-even pricing when your customers are quality sensitive and cautious. For example, odd-even pricing may cheapen the image of an original work of art for sale in an art gallery. If you really think you need to make a list price for an expensive, important product more appealing, drop it by a significant amount. Don't play around with pennies. A collectible painting worth approximately $7,000 could be priced in a gallery at $6,900, for instance. But don't price it at $6,899.99 because doing so may make people wonder whether it's really a valuable antique or just an overpriced consumer product.

Price lining

The *price lining* method fits your product into a range of alternatives, giving the product a logical spot in customers' minds. By adjusting your price to make it fit into your product line or into the range of products sold by your retailers or distributors, you make it clear what the competition is and how consumers should think about the product's value.

When you shop for a MacBook laptop (made by Apple Computer, Inc.), you find that the pricing is fairly easy to understand. Two product lines (the MacBook Air and the MacBook Pro) include different screen size, processor, and memory options, laying out a price ladder from under a thousand dollars up to several thousand dollars, depending on your preferences and budget. The biggest cost variables for Apple are the size of the screen and gigabytes of memory; Apple uses these features to define the price points in the product line. Take a tip from Apple and present your consumers with simple, clear options at several price points based on your biggest cost variables (which depend on what you produce and sell).

Notice that Apple uses two other strategies along with its price lining strategy — and you can, too. First, Apple uses odd-even pricing for the individual prices ($2,499 versus $2,500). Doing so makes the line of products appear at first to be a bit more affordable. Second, Apple uses the phrase "starts at" to describe its list prices. By doing so, Apple encourages purchasers to add extras, such as memory upgrades and software that often add hundreds to the list price. Apple could've integrated more options into its line at firmer list prices, but the result would've been far more confusing and would've given consumers less choice. Choice equals control, and consumers of complex products like laptops often prefer to feel in control of the details.

Competitive pricing

The *competitive pricing* method calls for you to set your price relative to that of an important competitor or set of competitors. Should you price above or below a tough competitor? That decision depends on whether you offer more or fewer benefits and higher or lower quality. It may also depend on the relative values of your brands. If you're facing a larger competitor with a famous brand name, recognize that you may need to price 5 to 10 percent less just because your brand isn't as well known.

In the competitive pricing model, if you offer your customer fewer benefits or less quality, you must make your price significantly lower so you look like a better value. If you offer greater benefits, you can make your price a little higher to signal this fact — but not too high because you want to be sure your product seems like a better value than the competition. And if you want to distinguish your product on the basis of some subtle difference, price exactly at your competitor's price so that customers' attention is focused on the difference rather than the price.

If you want to appear significantly superior to the competition, make sure your prices are significantly higher. If Tiffany & Co. priced its jewelry too low, the jewelry would lose its prestigious image. In fact, this loss of image is just what happened when Avon bought Tiffany. Avon tried to mass-market the Tiffany name by putting it on inexpensive jewelry. Millions of dollars of losses later, Avon sold out, and Tiffany went back to success — by reverting to its exclusively high prices. These events happened nearly 20 years ago. Since then, Tiffany & Co. has resisted the temptation to cheapen its brand name. The rise of Internet shopping has created a myriad of websites pretending to sell Tiffany products, often with clever variations on the Tiffany name. Many of these sites have been driven out of business by Tiffany & Co.'s complaints, but they'll probably reemerge under new names. They sell cheap pseudo-Tiffany products to deal-hungry consumers, but Tiffany & Co. continues to offer a premium shopping experience to more quality-conscious consumers through its stores and its website, www.tiffany.com (thereby avoiding using cheaper distributors). The company seems to have learned its lesson from the Avon experience.

Some competitors try to convince customers that their product is better but costs less than the competitors' products. Nobody believes this claim — unless you present evidence. If you do, customers will love you. After all, everyone hopes to get more for less! For example, a personal computer with a new, faster chip may really be better but cost less, and a new antiwrinkle cream may work better but cost less if you've discovered a new formula. As long as you have — and can communicate to the customer — a plausible argument, you can undercut your competitors' prices at the same time that you claim superior benefits. But make sure you back up the claim, or the customer may assume that your lower price means your product is inferior. (Or maybe you'd be better off introducing the innovation at a high price initially, reaping high profits, and reducing the price gradually after establishing its reputation.)

If you're in a highly competitive market, you should exercise competitive pricing. Decide which competing products customers may view as closest to yours and then make your price sufficiently higher or lower to differentiate your product. How much difference is enough difference depends on the size of customers' indifference zone (see the earlier section "Step 3: Evaluate customers' price preferences" to find out about the indifference zone).

Designing Special Offers

Special offers are temporary inducements to make customers buy on the basis of price. Regardless of the form special offers appear in (often a coupon or a direct response ad on the web), they give consumers or intermediaries a way to get the product for less — at least while the offer lasts. When you design a special offer, such as a temporary discount or a redeemable coupon, make the offer as large — but only just as large — as needed to attract attention and stimulate increased purchases. A discount of 1 percent may not be enough to motivate customers, a 5 percent discount may attract a fair amount of action, and a 20 percent student discount may produce dramatic results. Similarly, a 25-cent coupon is too small for most people to bother with, but a coupon worth a dollar or more often generates action in the grocery store. For larger purchases than groceries, bigger inducements may be needed.

People aren't always very rational about price, so think about how the offer feels, not just what the math is. The following sections cover some types of special offers you can try as well as how to use them, how to determine their cost, and when to end them.

Creating coupons and other discounts

You can offer coupons, refunds, *premiums* (gifts), free extra products, free trial-sized samples, sweepstakes and other event-oriented premium plans, and any other special offer you can think up — just check with your lawyers to make sure the promotion is legal. (Legal constraints do exist. You can't mislead consumers about what they get. And a sweepstakes or contest within the United States has to be open to all, not tied to product purchase. See the "Staying Out of Trouble with the Law" section, later in this chapter, for more on marketing's legal no-nos.)

A large majority of all special offers takes the form of *coupons,* certificates entitling the holder to a reduced price. Additionally, roughly 89 percent of coupons are distributed in *Free Standing Inserts* (FSIs) — those colorful mini-newspapers that drop out of the main newspaper when you try to read it. So, for retail promotions, FSIs are likely to be part of your program, but plenty of alternatives exist, including in-store options, on-packaging options, and in-ad offers (which can be redeemed at a web landing page; see Chapters 10 and 13 for web and direct-response promotion details).

The next sections explain how to design special offers — whether coupon or not — for maximum effectiveness.

Pick your medium

The design of your coupon depends on the medium you want to use to reach your target audience. The *medium* is the communication channel; it can be a newspaper, magazine, fax, mailing, or printable e-mail or website coupon. In today's world, you're no longer limited to printed, clip-out offers on paper. A small, blinking display ad on high-traffic websites and search engines (such as Facebook and Google, respectively) or an e-mail to your house list can be just as effective — if not more so — than the traditional newspaper coupon.

When picking your medium, select a vehicle that you're confident reaches a large number of your potential buyers. The biggest variable is what percentage of the audience is in your target market, so look closely at readership or usage statistics to decide which medium is most efficient. For example, if you want to target an offer at young adults who are buying auto insurance for the first time, avoid newspapers because very few young adults read newspapers. A Facebook ad may be more optimal because many Facebook users are prospective customers.

Shift toward the web

The most effective ways to reach prospective shoppers are still emerging but you can try them now: scannable codes or web links to promotions near point of purchase (using handheld devices like phones to read them), and ads with direct-response special offers that pop up when someone is actually using shopping-oriented key terms to search the web from their computer or tablet. Electronic coupons are a small slice of the pie but a growing one, and it's a no-brainer that they'll displace more conventional methods in the next few years.

Although newspapers used to be the most common way to distribute a coupon to customers, in today's evolving technological world, the Internet has made getting coupons to the masses way easier and a lot more effective. When a customer does a key-term search on an Internet search engine, you can have your offer pop up on her screen. She can then click on a special landing page to find more information about the offer (see Chapter 10 for tips on web marketing).

You can also use direct mailings and e-mails to pitch an offer; these options usually work best for a fairly big discount or a special bundled offer, because you need to have something newsworthy to write about. If you're holding an event (such as a clearance sale), try using additional mediums (think transit and billboard ads, vehicle advertising, local television, and web radio) to spread the word and turn out a crowd.

Craft the look and feel

To get a good feel for the options and approaches to coupons, collect a bunch of recent coupons from your own and other industries. And don't forget to do key-term searches online, like your customers might, to see what special offers pop up on the web. This collection of recent coupons and special offers gives you the current benchmark for your industry.

Your offer needs to look appealing in the context of recent marketing activity by your competitors. If they're offering significant discounts, don't waste your time on a chintzy coupon that knocks off only 3 percent of the list price, because customers won't waste their time on you.

Appeal to intermediaries

If you're promoting to *the trade,* marketers' name for intermediaries such as wholesalers and retailers, then you can offer things like free-goods deals, buy-back allowances, display and advertising allowances, and help with their advertising costs (called *cooperative,* or *co-op, advertising*).

Any offer that helps the intermediary run her business more profitably is going to help you move product, so don't be afraid to get creative in how you craft your special offers to the trade.

Figuring out how much to offer

How much of a deal should you offer customers in a coupon or other special offer? The answer depends on how much attention you want. Most offers fail to motivate the vast majority of customers, so keep in mind that the typical special offer in your industry probably isn't particularly effective. A good ad campaign probably reaches more customers.

You can greatly increase the reach of your special offer simply by making the offer more generous (of course, the higher the price sensitivity of your customers, the more notice you generate). In consumer nondurables, whether toothpaste or canned soup, the classic research shows that you have to offer at least 50 cents off of your list price to attract much attention. All but the most dedicated coupon clippers ignore the smaller offers — less than 10 percent of consumers surveyed find these small offers attractive. But when offers rise above the 50-cent level, those coupons are a lot more attractive, appealing to up to 80 percent of customers! Within this larger percentage of interested consumers, you can find many brand-loyal, core customers — both yours and your competitors. *Note:* These core customers are far more attractive than the knee-jerk coupon clippers who flock to smaller offers.

I think (and I disagree with many marketers on this point) that you do better to use fewer, bigger offers than to run endless two-bit coupons. Too much noise exists already, so why add to the clutter of messages when you can focus your efforts into fewer, more effective programs? Also, you can now leverage a more major offer (like a monthly get-one-free offer or a contest) through your website, promoted on Twitter and Facebook, as a way to capture customer contact information for your database.

Forecasting redemption rates

Designing your offer isn't the hardest part. The biggest trick is guessing the *redemption rate* (or percentage of people who use the coupon). You raise the stakes when you use big offers, which makes them riskier to forecast (good luck trying to forecast these rates). Test an offer on a small scale first and gather some real data about how it works. Then use the info in this section to help make your guesstimate a bit more accurate.

On average in North America, customers redeem a little more than 3 percent of coupons (and the average coupon offers around 50 cents off the list price). You can use these statistics as a good starting point for your estimate, but the range is wide — some offers are so appealing, and so easy to use, that customers redeem 20 percent of those coupons. For others, the redemption rate can be close to zero.

A point-of-purchase and very easy-to-redeem offer will have far higher redemption rates than an offer that's remote from the point of purchase. For example, an offer placed in a web banner ad or in an FSI may redeem at a rate of 2 percent, but when the same offer is made available electronically at the register, it may redeem at 12 percent.

To forecast whether your coupon will have a high or low redemption rate, compare your offer to others. Are you offering something more generous or easy to redeem than you have in the past? Than your competitors do? If so, you can expect significantly higher-than-average redemption rates — maybe twice as high or higher. Test on a small scale, especially if the offer is generous. For example, on the web, test for one hour to limit exposure. At the end of your test, see what the redemption rate is and adjust the program if needed to avoid spending too much.

If you've ever used coupons before, your company should have rich information about response rates. Just be sure that you examine past offers carefully to pick ones that truly match the current offer before assuming the same response rate can be repeated. And if you're switching your medium — for example, from newspapers or fliers to the web — then do a test first, because the redemption rate may be very different when you start dabbling with different mediums.

Mathematical formulas for estimating the effect of a discount or coupon offer are out there, but they're complex and difficult to use, plus they tend to be more theoretical than practical. The best way to find out what effect an offer has is to test it on a small scale. Start with a modest offer. If it produces the bump-up in sales you want, then keep using it. If not, modify it (by making it more generous or by placing it somewhere more convenient to point of purchase) and see whether the modified version works better.

After you find an offer that produces added sales, check that it's profitable. If sales only go up a little but lots of existing customers make their regular purchases at a discount, then you won't make a profit from the offer. What you want is lots of new customers who buy because of the offer and then become regular users. If you don't get these new customers the first time, try a different medium that reaches new prospects better.

Many coupons don't shift the price very far beyond the indifference zone (see the earlier section "Step 3: Evaluate customers' price preferences") — that's why they generally attract those fringe customers who buy on price but don't attract the core customers of other brands. That's also why redemption rates are only a few percent, on average. However, if your coupon does shift the price well beyond the indifference zone, you're likely to see a much higher redemption rate than usual.

Predicting the cost of special offers

After you think about the redemption rate that I cover in the previous section, you need to determine what the cost of your special offer will be. For example, say you believe that 4 percent of customers will redeem a coupon offering a 10 percent discount on your product. To estimate the cost of your coupon program, you must first decide whether this 4 percent of customers accounts for just 4 percent of your product's sales over the period in which the coupon applies. Probably not. Customers may stock up to take advantage of the special offer, so you must estimate how much more than usual they'll buy.

If you think customers will buy twice as much as usual (that's a pretty high figure, but it makes for a simple illustration), just double the average purchase size. Four percent of customers, buying twice what they usually do in a month (if that's the term of the offer), can produce how much in sales? Now apply the discount rate to that sales figure to find out how much the special offer may cost you. Can you afford it? Is the promotion worth the money? That's for you to decide, and it's a true judgment call — the math can't tell you what to do.

Some marketers have their cake and eat it, too, when it comes to special offers. They use self-liquidating premiums, which don't cost them any money at all in the long run. A *premium* is any product that you give away to customers or sell at a discount as a reward for doing business with you. A *self-liquidating premium* is a gift that customers end up paying for — at least, they cover your costs on that product. Say you run a contest in which some of the customers who open your packaging are instant winners, able to send away for a special premium by enclosing their winning ticket plus $4.95. If your *direct costs* (the wholesale price plus any out-of-pocket costs for handling) for the premium are $4.95, you don't have to pay out of pocket for what the customer may see as a fun and valuable benefit.

Keeping special offers special

A price cut is easy to do, but it's hard to undo. A special offer allows you to temporarily discount your product's or service's price while still maintaining the list price at its old level. When the offer ends, the list price is the same — you haven't permanently given anything away.

Here are some cases in which maintaining your list price can be important:

- ✔ When your reason for wanting to cut the price is a short-term one, like wanting to counter a competitor's special offer or respond to a new product introduction

- ✔ When you want to experiment with the price (to find out about customer price sensitivity) without committing to a permanent price cut until you see the data

- ✔ When you want to stimulate consumers to try your product or service, and you believe that after they try it, they may like it well enough to buy it again at full price

- ✔ When your list price needs to stay high to signal quality *(prestige pricing)* or be consistent with other prices in your product line *(price lining strategy)*

- ✔ When your competitors are all offering special lower prices and you think you have no choice because consumers have come to expect special offers

Sometimes competitors make such heavy use of special offers that consumers begin to expect them all the time and wait for an offer before they buy. These competitors have effectively lowered their prices, because consumers are no longer willing to buy at list price and assume they won't ever have to.

When competitors get too focused on making and matching each other's special offers, they flood their customers with price-based promotions. Discounts and other freebies begin to outweigh brand-building marketing messages, focusing consumer attention on price rather than brand and benefit considerations. Special promotions can and do increase customer sensitivity to price. They attract *price switchers,* people who aren't loyal to any brand but just shop on the basis of price. Frequent special offers encourage people to become price switchers, thus reducing the size of the core customer base and increasing the number of fringe customers. Special offers are clearly useful, but they have the potential to erode brand equity, reduce customer loyalty, and cut your profits. Be careful not to lose your footing on this slippery slope!

Staying Out of Trouble with the Law

When dealing with special offers, you want to make sure you stay on the right side of the law. Check with an expert, monitor acceptable (and unacceptable) practices in your industry, and be aware that pricing and promotion decisions have legal implications.

Staying ahead of U.S. regulations

Although I suggest that you check with your attorney before making any final decision concerning special offers, this short list includes some of the more common and serious illegal pricing practices, as indicated by the federal laws of the United States. Allow me to reiterate — make sure you *never* engage in any of the following:

- **Price fixing:** Don't agree to (or even talk about) prices with other companies. The exception is a company you sell to — but note that you can't force any company to resell your product at a specific price.

- **Price fixing in disguise:** Shady marketers have tried a lot of ideas, none of which work. If your competitors want you to require the same amount of down payment, start your negotiations from the same list prices as theirs, use a standardized contract for extending credit, or form a joint venture to distribute all of your products (at the same price), recognize these seemingly friendly suggestions for what they are — forms of price fixing. Just say no. And in the future, refuse even to take phone calls from competitors who talk about price fixing.

✔ **Price fixing by purchasers:** If retailers you sell to are joining together to dictate the wholesale prices they want you to give them, that may also be price fixing. Have a lawyer review any such plans.

✔ **Exchanging price information:** You can't talk to your competitors about prices. Ever. Okay? If it comes to light that anyone in your company gives out information about pricing and receives some in return, you're in big trouble, even if you don't feel you acted on that information. Take this warning seriously. (By the way, *price signaling* — announcing a planned price increase — is sometimes seen as an unfair exchange of price information, because competitors may use such announcements to signal to others that everyone should make a price increase.)

✔ **Bid rigging:** If you're bidding for a contract, the preceding point applies. Don't share any information with anyone. Don't compare notes with another bidder. Don't agree to make an identical bid. Don't *split* by agreeing not to bid on one job if the competitor doesn't bid on another. Don't mess with the bidding process in any manner, or you'll be guilty of *bid rigging*.

✔ **Parallel pricing:** In some cases, the U.S. government can charge you with price fixing, even if you didn't talk to competitors, just because you have similar price structures. After all, the result may be the same — to boost prices unfairly. In other cases, the law considers similar prices as natural. To be safe, avoid mirroring competitors' prices exactly.

✔ **Price squeezes, predatory pricing, limit pricing, and dumping:** To the average marketer, these four illegal acts are effectively the same (although they're tested under different U.S. regulations). They all involve using prices to push a competitor out of business or to push or keep a competitor out of a particular market. Following are brief explanations of each act:

- The classic *squeeze* involves setting wholesale prices too high for small-sized orders. It drives the independent or small retailer out of business, giving unfair advantage to the big chain buyers that can qualify for a volume discount.

- At the retail level, *predatory pricing* involves setting prices so low that local competitors can't keep up. Predatory pricing is also used by chains and multinationals to drive locals out of business. If you're pricing at or below cost, you're probably engaging in predatory pricing.

- Similarly, if your prices are so aggressive that they lock other competitors out of a market (even if you price above cost), then you're probably guilty of *limit pricing*.

- A variant of limit pricing is *dumping,* in which you try to buy your way into a new market by dumping a lot of product into that market at artificially low prices. Don't ever do this.

Because so many pricing techniques are illegal, some people throw up their hands in despair. They say, "What can I do?" Well, trying to influence prices in certain ways is okay. You *can* offer volume discounts to encourage larger purchases, as long as those discounts don't force anybody out of the market. And although you, as a marketer, can't force retailers to charge a certain price for your product, you *can* encourage them to by advertising the suggested retail price and listing it as such on your product.

Additionally, you can always offer an effective price cut to consumers through a consumer coupon or other special offer (as explained earlier in this chapter). Retailers usually agree to honor such offers (check with an ad agency, the retailer, or a lawyer to find out how to form such contracts). However, if you offer a discount to your retailers, you can't force them to pass that discount on to your customers. They may just put the money in the bank and continue to charge customers full price. Test such offers to see how your intermediaries respond before assuming the offer will reach all the way to the end consumer.

Ultimately, know that you really do have a lot of influence on the price of your product. Just be careful to steer clear of illegal pricing actions. Consult a competent lawyer to safely avoid anything that might be illegal.

Watching out for tighter rules elsewhere

Pricing is regulated to varying degrees in different countries, so check local regulations when operating outside of the United States. Many European nations regulate coupons and special free offers more tightly than the United States does. There's a famous case of a German car wash that offered free washes to regular customers until the offer was shut down by the authorities. So check your local practices and restrictions before rolling out any program!

Chapter 16

Distributing Your Product Where Your Customers Are

───

In This Chapter

▶ Building your business with strong distribution strategies

▶ Finding distributors and retailers

▶ Considering the best marketing channel structure and maximizing retail sales

▶ Thinking about point-of-purchase incentives and displays

───

*T*he companies with the widest distribution are often the most successful because that distribution system gives them access to so many potential customers. Often the easiest way to grow your sales and profits is to improve your distribution systems. Adding retailers (or distributors if you're a B2B marketer) and increasing your accessibility on the web are two good ways to expand distribution. If you sell to other businesses, then you can expand your network of salespeople or work with a large distribution company to increase the reach of your distribution system.

In this chapter, I share ways of reaching prospects both in the real world and on the web to increase your potential customer base. Distribution can help make your offerings more visible and accessible, such as by cuing up your product in a customer's search on Amazon or making sure your product can be found and evaluated on the shelves of stores. For business-to-business marketers, distribution is also important and may mean getting in front of purchasing managers at conventions and in industry and trade showrooms or events as well as in online directories. As with all the other elements of marketing, innovations are changing distribution, and this chapter helps you consider web options, 3D modeling, and augmented reality along with more conventional options.

Taking a Strategic Approach

You need to decide how broadly to distribute your product (or service). To do so, it helps to have a firm grasp of the myriad distribution choices available to you. After you understand the different options, you can select the strategy that's right for your organization. Following are some of the main distribution strategies and advice as to when and why you may want to implement them:

- ✓ **Selective distribution strategy:** This strategy focuses on a small number of outlets and often creates a sense of scarcity, allowing for higher pricing and prestige branding. An old saying among entrepreneurs advises to "Stay small and keep it all." Does this strategy fit your marketing model and brand? Will it bring you enough business, or do you need more volume?

- ✓ **Exclusive distribution strategy:** This strategy is the extreme version of a selective strategy, in which you sell through one or a few specialized distributors only. You may make your product available through a boutique store in a major city or through a web or eBay store. If you have a unique product or service, why not limit the distribution and make customers come to you? This strategy gives you low costs and lets you support a relatively high price, so it can be highly profitable — but only if your product is special enough to make customers want to go looking for it.

- ✓ **Intensive distribution strategy:** This strategy (the opposite of selective distribution) aims to flood the market by making your product widely available in as many outlets as possible. If you offer a retail product to consumers, intensive distribution probably means getting onto the roster of accepted vendors for one or more of the giant retail chains. They're the key to high retail volume in the United States today, but they require you to use their software and systems so they can pull inventory from your warehouse as needed. Ramping up to the scale needed to do business with a giant chain is costly if you're a small business, so you may want to start with a selective distribution strategy and gain some experience and success before approaching the largest retail chains in your market.

- ✓ **80/20 strategy:** This strategy applies to distributors. You get 80 percent or more of your sales from just 20 percent of your distributors. Giving those hardworking top distributors plenty of attention, excellent service, and excellent trade deals (see Chapter 15) is a good strategy. You want to develop a strong personal relationship with them because if they know you, they're more likely to get in touch with helpful news or ask for your assistance with a problem. To do so, invest in wining and dining them and spending authentic time with them. After you give your top distributors plenty of attention, focus on a few of the low-producing ones and see whether you can move them into the high-producing category. If you can get 30 percent of your weaker distributors to sell at high volume, you can boost sales by an average of 50 percent, which is a good return for your investment in strengthening your distributor network.

You also have to decide whether you want to develop *parallel distribution channels,* also sometimes called *competitive channels.* Traditionally, a manufacturer would never sell direct to consumers if it also sold through wholesalers and retailers, so as to avoid competing with its own distributors who may get mad and stop selling its products. But parallel channels are increasingly common and accepted. For example, Apple sells through retail distributors, through its own Apple stores, through retail computer web stores, and through its own website.

Parallel distribution channels often lead to issues and tensions between company-direct and partner sales, but if you make an effort to communicate frequently and negotiate in good faith, such problems can almost always be worked out.

Here are more ways to get the most out of your distribution program:

- ✔ **Expand your distribution network.** If you can add distributors or get more out of the ones you have, you may be able to make your product available to more people and increase your sales. Also consider boosting availability on the web (see Chapter 10) and using more direct-response marketing (see Chapter 13) and events (such as trade shows; see Chapter 12), which bypass distributors and reach out directly to customers.

- ✔ **Move more inventory, more quickly.** Increasing the availability of products in your distribution channel can also help boost sales and profits. Can you find ways to get more inventory out there? Can you speed the movement of products out to customers so they feel they can more easily find your product when they need it? Either strategy can have a dramatic impact on sales by allowing more customers to find what they want more easily when and where they want it.

- ✔ **Increase your visibility.** Another way you can use distribution strategies to boost sales is to increase the visibility of your product or service within its current distribution channel by making sure it's better displayed or better communicated. Many retail chain stores provide better shelving (such as end-cap displays or eye-level shelving with a sign) if you offer them special promotional discounts or cooperative advertising fees, so see whether you can take advantage of one of their programs.

- ✔ **Target larger or more desirable customers.** Perhaps you can find a way to shift your distribution slightly so as to give you access to more lucrative customers. A consultant I know who helps small businesses with their hiring and employment issues is beginning to visit the human resources directors of large businesses in her area to explore what she can do for them. One contract with a big firm may be as valuable to her as 10 or 20 smaller clients, so this new effort to reach out to the largest companies in her area may grow her business significantly.

Getting close to your customer on eBay

To distribute on eBay, you must first get your auction or fixed-price listing noticed. The goal is to make sure it pops up near the top when prospective customers do a search on eBay. The problem is that thousands of other listings also compete for a prime spot on the first page or two of the search results. These tips can help you place your listing where people can see it:

✔ **Provide a detailed, descriptive title.** Describe exactly what you're selling *in detail* (for example, "Women's Fatboy cowboy boots size U.S. 7 new camouflage"). You get 55 characters, so take advantage of them (the preceding example is 54 characters). Feel free to repeat the category name in the title if that's appropriate to describing what you're selling.

✔ **Fill in all the Item Specifics fields.** Be very detailed and complete as you fill in the Item Specifics for your listing. Any left-out categories (such as Condition) may hurt you in the competition for a high place in search results.

✔ **List your product in two categories if customers may not know which one to search in.** This way, you're visible no matter which category they choose for their search. But note that you have to pay double the insertion fee when listing in two categories, plus you may want to pay some upgrade fees for both listings (such as the added cost of a bold-type title). Don't bother with a double listing if it's obvious that your product belongs in one category.

✔ **Offer free shipping.** eBay prefers listings with free shipping and gives them preference in its rank ordering of search results. eBay encourages free shipping because it requires you to build your shipping costs into the item price, which eBay takes a commission on. Make sure you do your math right and set a starting or reserve auction price, or a *fixed price,* that's higher than the product cost you need to cover plus normal ground shipping.

✔ **Avoid keyword spamming.** *Keyword spamming* is when you slip a popular keyword into your item description that doesn't really belong there. For example, saying "If you love Ralph Lauren's designs, you'll love these bath towels" is against eBay policy and may get your listing, and you, kicked off if the towels aren't actually Ralph Lauren towels.

✔ **Become a PowerSeller.** High-volume sellers with a 98 percent-plus feedback rating get promoted to PowerSeller status, which makes their listings more prominent. List lots of products, even if you have to pad your listings with things you sell at or near cost, to achieve a high sales volume. And, obviously, be sure to consistently provide excellent (meaning fast, reliable, accurate, friendly) service and honest ads and avoid inaccurate descriptions (be honest about any problems or signs of wear) so you'll earn perfect feedback. Remind buyers that you need good feedback if you've done a good job and give them good feedback as sellers.

✔ **Consider opening an eBay store.** That way, you can cross-promote so shoppers who view one of your listings also see relevant additional listings.

Note that eBay isn't a free service for sellers. You have to pay to list items, and you also have to pay a sales commission. In general, assume that you'll spend about 10 percent of sales on eBay fees and commissions, so build this expense into your pricing. Also, recognize that this is a modest cost for the extensive distribution eBay offers.

Tracking Down Ideal Distributors

Distributors want items that are easy to sell because customers want to buy them. It's that simple. So the first step in getting customers on your side is to make sure your product is appealing. (See Chapter 14 for help making your brand stand out.) After you're confident you have something worth selling, ask yourself which distributors can sell it most successfully. Who's willing and able to distribute for you? Are wholesalers or other intermediaries going to be helpful? If so, who are they and how many of them can you locate? Phone companies traditionally publish business-to-business telephone directories by region for most of the United States (call the business office of your local phone company to order them); these directories often reference the category of intermediary you're looking for in their Yellow Pages sections. Or cruise the web to track down possible distributors more quickly.

Here are some additional suggestions for locating your dream distributors:

- ✔ **Reach out to a trade association or trade show specializing in distributors in your industry.** For example, the International Foodservice Distributors Association (www.ifdaonline.org) puts on an annual conference for food distributors. A couple of days at an event like that, and you can locate dozens of possible distributors for your products.

- ✔ **Attend major conventions in your industry.** Hop on a plane, bring product samples and literature, put on comfortable shoes, and walk around the convention hall until you find the right distributors.

- ✔ **Contact the American Wholesale Marketers Association.** The AWMA publishes a member directory and stages a number of conferences and expos. Find out more about the AWMA by calling 703-208-3358 or by visiting www.awmanet.org.

- ✔ **Consult any directory of associations for extensive listings.** Such directories are available in the reference sections of most libraries. You can also go to the American Society of Association Executives' Gateway to Associations, a web database found at www.asaecenter.org/directories/associationsearch.cfm.

Want to find the retailers that may help you sell? The good news is they're easier to find than wholesalers for the simple reason that they're in the business of being easy to find. You can find listings for retail stores in the Yellow Pages phone directories in any U.S. metropolitan areas you're interested in. These stores also have their own trade associations, such as the International Council of Shopping Centers (www.icsc.org; 646-728-3800). ICSC's U.S. headquarters is in New York City, but it also has offices in London, Mexico, Singapore, and Beijing.

Understanding Channel Structure

Efficiency is the driving principle behind distribution channel design. (*Channel* refers to the pathways you create to get your product out there and into customers' hands.) Traditionally, channels have evolved to minimize the number of transactions because the fewer the transactions, the more efficient the channel.

As Figure 16-1 shows, a channel in which 4 producers and 4 customers do business directly has 16 (4 × 4) possible transactions because each producer has to make four separate transactions to get its product to all four consumers. In reality, the numbers get much higher when you have markets with dozens or hundreds of producers and thousands or millions of customers.

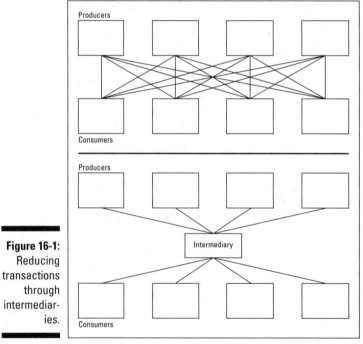

Figure 16-1: Reducing transactions through intermediaries.

© John Wiley & Sons, Inc.

You lower the number of transactions greatly when you introduce an *intermediary* (someone who handles the business transactions for you) because now you only have to do simple addition rather than multiplication. In the example shown in Figure 16-1, you need only 8 (4 + 4) transactions to connect all 4 customers with all 4 producers through the intermediary. Each producer or customer has to deal with only the intermediary, who links him to all the producers or customers he may want to do business with.

Although intermediaries add their markup to the price, they often reduce the overall costs of distribution because of their effect on the number of transactions. Adding a level of intermediaries to a channel reduces the total number of transactions that all producers and customers need to do business with each other.

This example is simplistic, but you can see how the logic applies to more complex and larger distribution channels. Introduce a lot of customers and producers, link them through multiple intermediaries (perhaps adding a second or third layer of intermediaries), and you have a typical *indirect marketing channel* (one involving intermediaries, as opposed to a *direct marketing channel* where you handle customers). Odds are you have some channels like this one in your industry.

Many channels are simpler and shorter than they used to be because handling numerous transactions is easier than it used to be. For example, Wal-Mart sources directly from manufacturers in many cases, relying on them to provide just-in-time deliveries into inventory in response to electronic messages. In the past, a retailer may have gone through a wholesaler who did business with manufacturers.

The trend is toward simpler, more direct channels, and you need to be prepared to handle a large number of customer transactions to be in step with this trend. A good general rule for you as a marketer is to use only as many intermediaries and layers of intermediaries as seems absolutely necessary to reach your customers. Try to keep it simple and add more parties only if you can't do it well yourself.

In deciding what kind of distribution channels will work for your product, I suggest you draw up a list of tasks you want distributors to do. For example, you may want distributors to find you more customers than you can find on your own. Decide what you want them to do and then seek distributors who say they want to do those things for you. That way, you're more likely to get a good match. Here's a starting list of functions you may want your intermediaries to perform; you may also have others:

✔ Finding more customers for your product than you can on your own

✔ Researching customer attitudes and desires

✔ Buying and selling

✔ Breaking down bulk shipments for resale

✔ Setting prices

- ✔ Managing point-of-purchase promotions (which I cover in the section "Stimulating Sales at the Point of Purchase," later in the chapter)
- ✔ Advertising at the local level (*pull advertising,* which is designed to bring people to a store or other business)
- ✔ Transporting products
- ✔ Inventorying products
- ✔ Financing purchases
- ✔ *Qualifying* sales leads (separating poor-quality leads from serious customers)
- ✔ Providing customer service and support
- ✔ Sharing the risks of doing business
- ✔ Combining your products with others to offer appropriate assortments

Reviewing Retail Strategies and Tactics

If you decide to improve sales at a retail store and you bring in a specialized retail consultant, you may soon be drawing *planograms* of your shelves (diagrams showing how to lay out and display a store's merchandise) and counting *SKUs* (stock-keeping units — a unique inventory code for each item you stock). You may also examine the statistics on sales volume from end-of-aisle displays (higher sales) versus middle of the aisle (lower sales), and from eye-level displays (higher sales) versus bottom or top of the shelf (lower sales). Great. Go for it. However, I have to warn you that although a technical approach has its place, you can't use this method to create a retail success story. The following sections show you why traffic flow is so important and how to capitalize on that traffic with the right merchandising strategies, store atmosphere, and pricing.

The real winners in retail are the result of creative thinking and good site selection — in that order. The two big-picture issues that determine whether your store has low or high performance are a creative, appealing store concept and a spot that has the right sort of traffic (and a lot of it).

Looking for heavy traffic

Traffic is a flow of target customers near enough to the store for its external displays and local advertising to draw them in. You want a great deal of traffic, whether it's foot traffic on a sidewalk, automobile traffic on a road or highway, or virtual traffic at a website. Retailers need to have people walking, driving, or surfing into their stores (see Chapter 10 for more on web marketing). Customers don't come into a store or onto a website in big numbers unless you have plenty of people to draw from, so you need to figure out where high traffic is and find a way to get some of it into your store.

An old joke about retailing goes like this: "The retail business has three secrets of success — location, location, and location." Not very funny, really, unless you've ever tried to market a store in a poor location. Then you laugh pretty hard over the joke, but with a certain hysteria. Pick a location carefully, making sure you have an excess of the right sort of traffic nearby. Think of designing a retail store like digging a pond. You wouldn't dig a pond unless running water was nearby to fill it. Yet people dig their retail ponds in deserts or up steep hills, far from the nearest flow of traffic, all the time.

You also wouldn't dig a huge reservoir beside a small stream. You must suit your store to the amount and kind of traffic in its area — or else move to find more appropriate traffic. If you're in a small town, don't open a highly specialized store that appeals to only a few percent of shoppers, because you won't have enough to keep you in business. A restaurant is a good option for a small town because just about everyone likes to eat out from time to time. If, however, you're determined to open a specialized store, such as a store for rock collectors or a boutique specializing in trendy clothing for pregnant women, then look for a high-traffic location in a major mall or in the shopping district of a mid-sized or large city.

You can optimize your business in any particular location by making sure your store has enough appeal to draw a healthy share of the shopping traffic in the area. The ultimate trick is to make your store and its merchandise so appealing to sell that people go out of their way to visit the store. This attraction power is termed *pull* or *draw,* and few retail concepts are so unique that they can draw traffic from beyond their immediate area. But some do.

For example, a jewelry store in my town has such a good selection of merchandise that it draws far more traffic than the surrounding stores. And its owner carefully stimulates this traffic through a direct-mail program and by giving the store a unique and highly visible appearance — the store is in a huge, ornate, yellow Victorian house with lots of ground-floor windows displaying interesting gifts. The store's strategy focuses on the one thing that old joke about retailing leaves out: the store concept. The *concept* is a creative mix of merchandising strategy and atmosphere (see the following sections for more on these) that you can use to give your store higher-than-average drawing power. An exciting, well-executed concept makes shopping an enjoyable event and can boost traffic and sales tenfold.

Tapping into web traffic with Amazon

Just like a busy sidewalk, a busy web address can draw shoppers to your door. Etsy and eBay deliver customer bases that you can draw from if you sell on their sites, and Amazon is by far the largest retailer — well, more like a giant virtual mall, because so many marketers now sell on the Amazon site, and/or dovetail into its customer base for their own web store checkout.

If you retail any products, consider becoming an Amazon seller. Start by setting up an Amazon Payments account, also called a Marketplace Business Account. With it, Amazon will process your sales at a fee of 2.9 to 1.9 percent, depending on volume, plus $0.30 on each sale; fees vary slightly lower if you're a nonprofit. By registering for this service (which is a lot like a traditional credit card merchant account but with a lower fee structure), you can easily process any sale on the web, either on the Amazon site or through your own shopping cart. Shopping cart providers, such as CoreCommerce (www.corecommerce.com), AspDotNetStorefront (www.aspdotnetstorefront.com), and 3dcart (www.3dcart.com), offer integration into Amazon's order processing and banking. Your customers will see a Pay with Amazon yellow button to click as they process their order. And if they're already Amazon customers, their details (such as preferred shipping addresses) pop up, simplifying their checkout.

To fully take advantage of Amazon's customer base, you may also want to become an Amazon seller (use your favorite search engine to look for "seller central at Amazon.com," or go to services.amazon.com, click on Solutions, and then select Selling on Amazon for the registration forms). Click on the Sell as an Individual button if you're a sole proprietor just launching a new product line; otherwise, select Sell as a Professional for the best all-around marketing options, which cost about $40 per month as the price of entry (plus about 2 to 3 percent checkout fees on orders). For your monthly cost, you can add your products to the Amazon catalog, use the fulfillment services of Amazon, and run special promotions and gift coupons for your products (with some exceptions, most notably books, videos, and music, where your list price is the only pricing variable you can play with). It's hard to get accurate data on the size of the Amazon customer base, but there must be at least 200 million active customers, which is an awfully good reason to include your products in the Amazon catalog.

Also consider advertising on Amazon (search for "Amazon product ads" to find the latest fees or to sign up). A product search on Amazon.com produces both catalog items and sponsored links advertising off-site web stores (which can be enabled to sell to Amazon customers), so you can troll for those millions of Amazon customers in multiple ways by listing in the Amazon catalog plus advertising products and special offers from your own web store.

Developing merchandising strategies

Merchandising is the set of activities used to sell products at retail. Whether you retail services or goods, you need to think about your merchandising strategy. You do have one, whether you know it or not — and if you don't know it, your strategy is based on conventions in your industry and needs a kick in the seat of the pants to make it more distinctive. *Merchandising strategy,* the selection and assortment of products offered, is an important source of competitive advantage or disadvantage for retailers.

I suggest a creative approach to merchandising. The majority of success stories in retail come about because of innovations in merchandising. So you should be thinking of new merchandising options daily — and trying out the most promising ones as often as you can afford to. The next few sections describe some existing strategies that may give you ideas for your business. Perhaps no one has tried them in your industry or region, or perhaps they suggest novel variations to you.

General merchandise retailing

The *general merchandise retailing strategy* works because it brings together a wide and deep assortment of products, thus allowing customers to easily find what they want — regardless of what the product may be. Department stores and variety stores fall into this category. *Hypermarkets,* the European expansions of the grocery store that include some department store product lines, are another example of the general merchandise strategy. In the United States, Wal-Mart is a leader because it offers more variety (and often better prices) than nearby competitors. Warehouse stores, such as Home Depot and Staples, give you additional examples of general merchandise retailing. And as this varied list of examples suggests, you can implement this strategy in many ways.

Limited-line retailing

The *limited-line retailing strategy* emphasizes depth over variety. For example, a bakery can offer more and better varieties of baked goods than a general food store because a bakery sells only baked goods. Limited-line retailing is especially common in professional and personal services. Most accounting firms just do accounting. Most chiropractic offices just offer chiropractic services. Most law firms just practice law. For some reason, I've seen little innovation in the marketing of services.

Try to combine several complementary services into a less-limited line than your competitors. If you can expand your line without sacrificing your quality or depth of offerings, you can give customers greater convenience — and that convenience should make you a winner.

After all, the limited-line strategy only makes sense to customers if they gain something in quality or selection in exchange for the lack of convenience. Regrettably, many limited-line retailers fail to make good on this implied promise — and they're easily run over when a business introduces a less-limited line nearby. What makes, say, the local stationery or shoe store's selection better than what a Staples or Wal-Mart offers in a more convenient setting? If you're a small businessperson, you should make sure you have plenty of good answers to that question! Know what makes your merchandise selection, concept, or location different and better than that of your monster competitors — then make sure your potential customers know it, too.

Scrambled merchandising

Consumers have preconceived notions about what product lines and categories belong together. Looking for fresh produce in a grocery store makes sense these days because dry goods and fresh produce have been combined by so many retailers. But 50 years ago, the idea would've seemed radical because specialized limited-line retailers used to sell fresh produce. When grocery stores combined these two categories, they were using a *scrambled merchandising strategy,* in which the merchant uses unconventional combinations of product lines. Today, the meat department, bakery, deli section, seafood department, and many other sections combine naturally in a grocery store. And many stores are adding other products and services, such as coffee bars, banks, bookshops, dry cleaners, shoe repair, hair salons, photographers, flower shops, post offices, and so on. In the same way, gas stations combine with fast food restaurants and convenience stores to offer pit stops for both car and driver. These scrambled merchandising concepts are now widely accepted, so see whether you can create a combination of your own that appeals to consumers in your area.

Creating atmosphere

A store's *atmosphere* is the image that it projects based on how you decorate and design it. Atmosphere is an intangible — you can't easily measure or define it, but you can feel it. And when the atmosphere feels comforting, exciting, or enticing, this feeling draws people into the store and enhances their shopping experiences. So you need to pay close attention to atmosphere.

Atmospherics are important because consumers increasingly seek more from retail shopping than just finding specific products. In consumer societies, shopping is an important activity in its own right. Surveys suggest that less than a quarter of shoppers in malls went there in search of a specific item. Consumers often use shopping to alleviate boredom and loneliness, avoid dealing with chores or problems in their lives, seek fulfillment of their fantasies, or simply to entertain themselves. If that's what motivates many shoppers, you need to take such motivations into consideration when you design your store.

Sophisticated retailers hire architects and designers to create the right atmosphere and then spend far too much on fancy lighting, new carpets, and racks to implement their plans. Sometimes this approach works, but sometimes it doesn't. And at any point in time, most of the professional designers agree about what stores should look and feel like, which means your store looks like everyone else's.

I think you should develop the concept for your store yourself. If you think a virtual tropical forest gives the right atmosphere, hire some crazy artists and designers to turn your store into a tropical forest. Or maybe you have some steam-punk friends and you really like old-fashioned steam engines. Great. Make that the theme of your children's toy store or men's clothing boutique. Run model train tracks around the store, put up huge posters of oncoming steam engines, and incorporate the occasional train whistle into your background music. Some people will love it; others will think you're nuts. But nobody will ever forget your store.

Perhaps you can honestly and simply provide some entertainment for your customers. Just as a humorous ad entertains people and attracts their attention long enough to communicate a message, a store can entertain for long enough to expose shoppers to its merchandise. For example, some Barnes & Noble bookstores create comfortable, enclosed children's book sections with places to play and read (or be read to) so families with young children can linger and enjoy the experience. When consumers can shop online from the comfort of home, it's important to make your store a special place worth going to.

Positioning your store on price

Retail stores generally have a distinct place in the range of possible price and quality combinations. Some stores are obviously upscale boutiques, specializing in the finest merchandise for the highest prices. Others are middle class in their positioning, and still others offer the worst junk from liquidators but sell it for so little that almost anybody can afford it. In this way, retailing still maintains the old distinctions of social class, even though those class distinctions are less visible in other aspects of modern U.S. and European society.

As a retailer, this distinction means that customers get confused about who you are unless you let them know where you stand on the class scale. And that means *you* have to know where you stand, so ask yourself whether your store has an upper-class, upper-middle-class, middle-class, or lower-middle-class pedigree. Do you see your customers as white collar or blue collar? And so on.

After you make a decision about how to place your store, you're ready to decide what price strategy to pursue. In general, the higher-class the store's image, the higher the prices that store can charge. But the real secret to success is to price just a step below your image. That way, customers feel like they're buying first-class products for second-class prices.

Stimulating Sales at Point of Purchase

The *point of purchase* (POP) is the place where customer meets product. It may be in the aisles of a store or even on a catalog page or computer screen, but wherever this encounter takes place, the principles of POP advertising apply. Table 16-1 shows you just how important point of purchase is; it gives you an idea of how much (or how little) shoppers' purchases are influenced by their predetermined plans. The statistics are from Point of Purchase Advertising International; its members are professionals working on POP displays and advertising, so the organization does a fair amount of research on shopping patterns and how to affect those patterns at points of purchase.

Table 16-1	Nature of Consumers' Purchase Decisions	
	Supermarkets Percent of Purchases	**Mass Merchandise Stores Percent of Purchases**
Unplanned	60%	53%
Substitute	4%	3%
Generally planned	6%	18%
Specifically planned	30%	26%

Customers plan some purchases outside of the store; 30 percent of supermarket purchases, and 26 percent of mass merchandise purchases fall into this category. In these cases, customers make a rational decision about what stores to go to in order to buy what they want. Because they have a clear idea of what they want to purchase, their purchases aren't highly subject to marketing influence. Even so, the right merchandise selection, location, atmosphere, and price strategy can help get customers to choose your store for their planned purchases rather than a competing store. And the right store layout and POP displays help customers find what they want quickly and easily. So even with so-called "specifically planned purchases," you do have an influence over what happens.

You can sway purchasing decisions your way and boost sales by designing appealing *displays* that consumers can pick your products from. Freestanding floor displays have the biggest effect, but retailers don't often use them because they take up too much floor space. Rack, shelf, and counter-based signs and displays aren't quite as powerful, but stores use these kinds of displays more often than free-standing displays.

Add QR codes to displays, signage, and other point of purchase communications if you want to give customers ways to link directly to a promo or an informational web landing page. Or, to really make the signage pop, have the QR code or a scannable app code (supplied by a 3D app maker) produce an augmented reality display on the shopper's phone or tablet. See the nearby sidebar on augmented reality for more.

Retailers are likely to use any really exciting and unusual display if they think it boosts store traffic and sales or boosts the sale of the products it promotes. Exciting displays add to the store's atmosphere or entertainment value, and store managers like that addition. Creativity drives the success of POP displays. A good display should

- **Attract attention:** Make your displays novel, entertaining, or puzzling to draw people to them.

- **Build involvement:** Give people something to think about or do to involve them in the display.

- **Sell the product:** Make sure the display tells viewers what's so great about the product. It must communicate the *positioning* (you better hope you have one!). Simply putting the product on display isn't enough. You have to sell the product, too, or else the retailer doesn't see the point. Retailers can put products on display themselves — they want a marketer's help in selling those products.

As you work on a POP design, check with some of your retailers to see whether they like the concept. Between 50 and 60 percent of marketers' POPs never reach the sales floor. If you're a product marketer who's trying to get a POP display into retail stores, you face an uphill battle. The stats say that your display or sign needs to be twice as good as the average, or the retailer simply tosses it into the nearest dumpster.

If you're selling through a web store of your own or on eBay (see the nearby sidebar for some eBay selling tips), don't think POP doesn't apply to you. You should consider options like more and better photographs, a streaming video demonstration of the product, the use of bold or prominent titles and captions, and special offers with time limits.

Wherever your product is for sale — whether in a store, at a business or professional trade show, or on the web — you need to present and promote it at that point of purchase if you want to stimulate a good response from prospective customers. Use in-store displays to boost retail sales and use extra photos, bold listings, and linked banner ads to boost sales of certain products on your website.

A closer look at augmented reality

Augmented reality is the overlay of digital imagery, often 3D, on some underlying context, usually what you see in front of you. So a customer encounters a sign saying, "What does this watch look like on you?" holds out his arm, and sees the watch on his wrist. All without a retail employee opening a case and handing over a real (and possibly quite expensive) sample. Or maybe it's in a B2B setting, where a sales rep uses a table to photograph a factory floor and then shows a 3D simulation in which new equipment is placed in context.

Firms such as Layar (www.layar.com), SnapShop (www.snapshop.com), Popcode (www.popcode.com), and Augment (www.augmentedev.com) are potential sources of 3D pop-up images and information that marketers can use to enrich the shopping experience. Generally, what you do is set up an account with an augmented reality supplier, upload 3D images, exploded views, within-the-package sequential 3Ds, videos, or other content associated with specific scannable symbols for your products, and then let shoppers know that they can download a free app that will give them an interactive and interesting experience at point of purchase (or elsewhere — for example, why not a 3D model or video leaping off a page of your brochure, catalog, or subway poster?).

Chapter 17

Succeeding in Sales and Service

. . . .

In This Chapter

▶ Designing your sales program

▶ Evaluating sales talent

▶ Managing the sales and service process

▶ Organizing and compensating sales staff

▶ Practicing great service and recovering unhappy customers

. . . .

Do you need to be doing personal sales and service that involves interacting with people directly as part of your marketing? The answer is always yes. Whether you have a formal sales role or not, selling should be a natural, everyday part of business life — something you do whether you're interacting with clients, ringing sales at a register, meeting other professionals, or taking a phone call. Also, sales should always be followed by good service. It's hard to win new customers, so don't throw them away the first time they run into a problem or have a concern.

Knowing When to Emphasize Personal Selling

How do you know whether you need *personal selling* — that is, selling face to face — as part of your marketing process? To find out whether your business should rely on sales, take the following sales-needs quiz.

Are personal sales and service the key to your marketing program?

❏ Yes ❏ No Our typical customer makes many small purchases and/or at least a few very large ones in a year.

❏ Yes ❏ No Our typical customer usually needs help figuring out what to buy and/or how to use the product.

❏ Yes ❏ No Our typical customer's business is highly complex and imposes unique requirements on our products/services.

❏ Yes ❏ No Our products/services are an important part of the customer's overall business process.

❏ Yes ❏ No Our typical customer is accustomed to working with salespeople and expects personal attention and assistance.

❏ Yes ❏ No Our competitors make regular sales calls on our customers and/or prospects.

❏ Yes ❏ No We have to provide customized service to retain a customer.

© John Wiley & Sons, Inc.

If you gave three or more "yes" answers, then you need to consider making personal sales an important part of your marketing plan and budget, along with good follow-up service. Although you certainly also want to use many other marketing methods, think of the rest of your marketing efforts as support for the personal sales process.

If personal selling is going to be the key to your success or failure, you need to give careful thought to how you hire, manage, organize, support, and motivate salespeople. Their performance determines whether your marketing succeeds or fails. You also need to decide whether you'll personally play a key role in selling. Do you have the time to make sales calls and follow through on them? And do you have the inclination and talent to be a top salesperson? To find out, read the next section.

Taking Stock of Your Sales Skills

If you're reasonably talented at selling, the more contact you have with customers and prospects, the better. If, however, you aren't skilled at selling, then it may be a waste of your time — and your customers' time — to have you play this role. You'd do better to hire a salesperson or use sales representatives in your place.

Embracing the virtual salesperson

Even if you have a low or moderate need for face-to-face selling — because you run a web-based business, for example — you may still find that adding a little human touch can help. In fact, the use of virtual salespeople is on the rise. *Virtual salespeople* are actually a library of video and audio clips recorded by paid actors. The actors spend time in a studio recording standard responses, and their clips live on the provider's website and stream to the end user.

You can add natural-looking human responses to your website by scripting and videoing the response library with the help of vendors such as the following:

- ✔ My Virtual Salesperson (www.myvirtual salesperson.com)

- ✔ Virtualtech (www.virtualtech.com/ WebsiteVideoSpokesperson.php)

- ✔ VirtualPerson (www.virtual-person.com)

- ✔ model2web (www.model2web.com)

As shopping migrates to smaller screens, such as smartphones, these virtual salespeople will, I suspect, become more common. After all, it's nice to be able to talk to someone face to face. And the cost is not beyond reach. As you draft a script, estimate about $1.50 per word to put a talking model on a web page based on your script.

The following questionnaire is a simple test of your sales ability. Take five minutes to answer the questions and then another couple minutes to score them. At the end, you find some useful feedback about your overall sales ability right now and your potential sales ability — areas you need to focus on if you want to improve your score in the future.

Employers, take note. I didn't design this test to screen candidates for hiring (and therefore candidates may find it possible to "fake" good results). Tests like this one don't guarantee someone's success — your management and the rest of your marketing program affect a salesperson's performance as much as her sales ability does. Also, ability alone doesn't go very far without appropriate training and technique. That said, anyone who ranks low on the qualities this test measures is unlikely to be a star salesperson.

Measuring Your Sales Ability

Check any statements that describe you well. If a statement doesn't fit you, leave it blank.

❏   1. I feel good about myself much of the time.

❏   2. I usually say the right thing at the right time.

❏   3. People seek out my company.

❏   4. I don't get discouraged, even if I fail repeatedly.

❏   5. I'm an excellent listener.

❏   6. I can read people's moods and body language with ease.

❏   7. I project warmth and enthusiasm when I first meet people.

❏   8. I'm good at sensing and bringing out the real reasons behind a negative answer.

❏   9. I can see many ways to define a problem and understand its causes.

❏ 10. I'm skilled at drawing out other people's concerns and problems.

❏ 11. I know enough about business to help others solve their problems with ease.

❏ 12. I'm so trustworthy and helpful that I quickly persuade people to work with me in true collaborations.

❏ 13. I manage my time so well that I'm able to get to everything that's important in a workday.

❏ 14. I focus on the big-picture goals that matter most to me and my company instead of always reacting to the latest crisis or chore.

❏ 15. I can balance the need for finding new customers with the demands of maintaining and strengthening all existing customer relationships.

❏ 16. I keep looking for and finding ways to be more effective and efficient.

❏ 17. I find that a sense of accomplishment is even more rewarding than money.

❏ 18. My internal standards and expectations are higher than any imposed on me by others.

❏ 19. I don't care how long it takes to succeed at a task — I know I can succeed in the end.

❏ 20. I feel I deserve the respect and admiration of my customers and associates.

Scoring:

A. Positive personality?

Total number of checks on Statements 1 through 4:

Fewer than three checks means you need improvement on personal attitude, emotional resiliency, and self-confidence.

B. Interpersonal skills?

Total number of checks on Statements 5 through 8:

Fewer than three checks means you need improvement on communication and listening skills, including your ability to control your own nonverbal communications and read others' body language.

C. Solution-finding skills?

Total number of checks on Statements 9 through 12:

Fewer than three checks means you need improvement on problem-finding, creative problem-solving, and collaborative negotiating skills.

D. Self-management skills?

Total number of checks on Statements 13 through 16:

Fewer than three checks means you need improvement on organization, strategy, and focus skills.

E. Self-motivation?

Total number of checks on Statements 17 through 20:

Fewer than three checks means you need to build your personal motivation and figure out how to find rewards in the pleasures of doing a job well and accomplishing a goal.

F. Overall level of sales ability?

Total number of checks, all statements (1 through 20):

Check out Table 17-1 to determine what your total score means.

Table 17-1	Figuring Out What Your Score Means
Total Number of Checks	*Score*
0–5	Guaranteed to fail. Sorry, but you should let somebody else do the selling!
6–9	Low sales ability. Not likely to succeed.

(continued)

Table 17-1 *(continued)*

Total Number of Checks	Score
10–12	Low sales ability. May become moderately capable with practice and study.
13–15	Moderate sales ability. Capable of improvement.
16–18	High sales ability. Will become expert with practice.
19–20	Superstar potential!

If you have a total of 13 or more checks, you have enough ability to be out there on the road making sales calls right now. However, this score doesn't mean you're perfect. If you checked fewer than 19 or 20 boxes, you should work on your weak areas — and when you do, your sales success rate should go up. (Be aware that rating yourself on such tests can be difficult and inaccurate. What do you think your customers would rate you on each item? Finding out may be useful!)

Technique can and often does trump natural ability. The salesperson who starts with high-quality prospects and then uses the right strategy at the right time doesn't have as tough a sales task as the salesperson who starts with less. You can close a sale far more easily when you start with good-quality leads (see the later section "Generating sales leads" for some help finding such leads).

Making the Sale

To manage sales effectively, divide sales into multiple steps and focus on one step at a time as you prepare a sales plan or look for ways to improve your sales effectiveness. As with any complex process, a weak link always exists. Try to find the step in your sales process that you perform most poorly right now and work to improve it.

Figure 17-1 displays the sales and service process as a flowchart. Note that the chart doesn't flow automatically from beginning to end. You may be forced to cycle back to an earlier stage if things go wrong. But ideally, you never lose prospects or customers forever — they just recycle into sales leads, and you can mount a new effort to win them over.

Figure 17-1 integrates the sales and service processes. Why? Because that's real-world selling. You can't stop when you close a sale and write the order. Your competitors certainly don't stop trying to win that client or account. So you need to think of a completed sale as the beginning of a relationship-building process. More sales calls, further presentations, and efforts to find new ways to serve the customer can help you retain and grow the account. The next sections delve into facets of this flowchart in more depth and help you seal the deal.

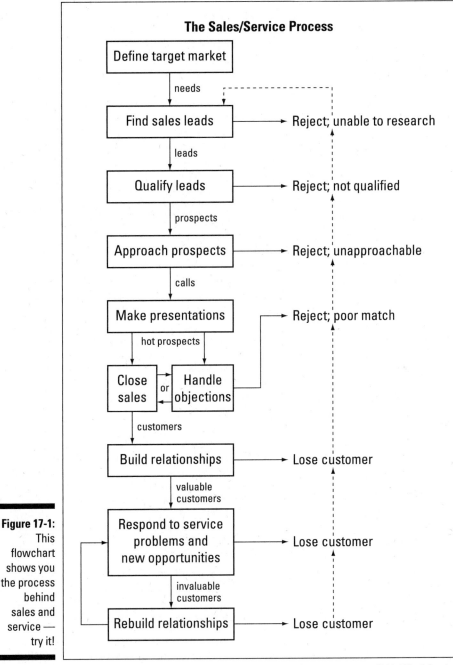

The Sales/Service Process

Define target market

needs

Find sales leads → Reject; unable to research

leads

Qualify leads → Reject; not qualified

prospects

Approach prospects → Reject; unapproachable

calls

Make presentations → Reject; poor match

hot prospects

Close sales — or — Handle objections

customers

Build relationships → Lose customer

valuable customers

Respond to service problems and new opportunities → Lose customer

invaluable customers

Rebuild relationships → Lose customer

Figure 17-1:
This flowchart shows you the process behind sales and service — try it!

Generating sales leads

The most common weakness in sales processes is lead generation — the first and most important step. Pay close attention to how you find leads and see whether you can improve the quantity and, especially, the quality of your leads. *Qualifying* a lead means gathering enough information about someone (or some business) to make sure she's appropriate. By that I mean the prospective customer fits the profile of a good customer. What is this profile? You need to decide, based on criteria such as wealth, age, and interests (for a consumer sale), or size, industry, timing, and location (for a business sale).

TIP

Many websites are still relatively passive. They showcase content but don't actively recruit qualified leads. See if you can add more interactivity to your website by creating (more) ways for people to sign in, sign up for deals, log in to see demo and how-to videos, and so forth. (These are called *calls to action*, and are very important sources of leads and sales.) Also, reach out with social media to find groups whose interests prequalify them as prospective customers, and use incentives as well as expert content to draw them to your site so they can sign in. People whose interests closely match your offerings are often eager to sign up and become leads. What people don't like is being pushed toward lead-capture when they aren't very interested.

WARNING!

Don't throw unqualified or underqualified leads into your sales and service process. Make sure you feed your sales process with a constant flow of quality sales leads. Know what your customer profile is and seek out qualified prospects with questions or screening criteria that allow you to sift through and eliminate poor-quality prospects quickly.

Sales leads can come from any of the other marketing activities I describe in this book. In fact, I recommend you try using as many alternatives as possible so you can find out which ones work best for you. Your website may produce the best leads (see Chapter 10), or joining a professional group or association may help you network and meet potential clients. A direct-mail campaign may produce leads, or you may find good sales leads by using direct-response advertising (Chapter 13 covers both). Then you can consider telemarketing (also in Chapter 13), trade shows and event sponsorship (see Chapter 12), and so on. You get the idea.

Here's a simple way to begin to develop a lead generation method, if you don't do anything right now and need to wade in and test the water:

1. **Select a magazine, website, or newspaper that your potential customers are likely to read.**

2. **Find the smallest, cheapest display ad in that publication or on that website and buy ad space for the shortest possible time.**

   Aim for just one insertion, if you can.

3. **Write a short, simple description of what you do or sell, keeping it clear and factual.**

   Include a clear, simple photo, if you have a relevant one (you can show the product if you're in a product business), or use your name and logo to illustrate the ad.

4. **End the ad with the following sentence: "Please contact us to find out more about our offerings by calling 800-xxx-yyyy or by using the inquiry form on our website at www.mywebsite.com."**

These four steps produce a very basic direct-response ad designed to generate sales leads. It may or may not work very well — you always have to experiment to get your lead-producing formulas down — but it certainly gives you a start. (If you already use some good lead-generation techniques, why not test something simple in a new medium? You should always be experimenting in marketing; otherwise, you may not improve.) If you get no response, try a variation and see what happens. Keep experimenting until you find a way to reliably generate inquiries from an inexpensive ad or from a key-term search on Google (see Chapter 10 for how to bid on searches and get your listing to appear).

Purchasing lists for lead generation

To cast a wider net for leads, buy names from list brokers. Mailing, e-mail, and call lists are widely available. You may find purchased names useful in your quest for leads, but don't make the mistake of thinking that they're leads in and of themselves. Nobody can sell you leads; you have to make them for yourself.

Design a web-based promotion with event-oriented excitement and outreach into the Twitter community with a hashtag linked to the promo signup, if you want to produce leads the modern way. Or (equally valid) write a phone script, letter, or e-mail describing your offer and what you do, and make sure you clearly and persuasively describe your brand's special qualities — whatever you're especially good at and want to be known for — along with a specific, action-oriented sales offer. Send your message out to the purchased list and see how many responses you get.

To increase your response rate, try including a special short-term offer and a prepaid postcard or fax form for recipients' replies. Or try following up on a letter or e-mail with a phone call to the recipient. You may have to make multiple contacts to sort out the real leads from the rest of the list (see the next section).

After you get some responses and capture their names and other information, you can call them leads. You own these leads and have the opportunity to follow up on them and see how many actually turn into customers. Good luck!

Conducting multistep lead generation

A *multistep lead-generation process* is one that draws possible leads from a plentiful source and then uses additional steps to identify the most promising ones and cull out the rest. Lynden International, a multi-modal freight forwarder based in Seattle, Washington, used a multistep system to generate qualified B2B sales leads for its 60 salespeople. The close ratio for sales calls improved by 70 percent after the company instituted this system. Here's how it works:

1. **Start by pulling the names of potential prospects from *Dun & Bradstreet's MarketPlace.***

   This database of U.S. companies groups companies by *SIC code* (a U.S. government designation based on product type), location, and size (as indicated by annual sales) so you can target companies by industry and city and eliminate any that seem too small. Head to www.dnb.com and click on the Sales & Marketing tab at the top of the page to find Marketing Lists. Here, you can get reports on firms of interest to you for a small fee. These reports include contact information, the name of at least one top executive, and some financial information (such as annual sales) to help you decide whether a company makes a good prospect. Anyone doing business-to-business sales finds this resource invaluable for lead generation.

2. **Call the names yourself or use a telemarketing firm (or hire a temp telemarketer) to call each of these companies.**

   You make this first call to find the appropriate decision maker and ask her some basic informational or qualifying questions to see whether she uses or may have a need for what you sell.

3. **Analyze the responses you get to identify prospects who should be interested in the kind of services or products you provide.**

   These leads, qualified by the telemarketing, now just need salespeople who can use them to set up personal meetings with the decision makers.

Don't forget to support your salesforce with ongoing web lead generation, too. If you're a consumer products marketer, venture into the social media (such as Facebook and Twitter) to steer potential leads to your website for capture. If you do B2B marketing, a LinkedIn profile may be a better outreach (because professionals in your industry are also on LinkedIn), and you can include a live link to your website on your LinkedIn profile.

Many companies give telemarketers a *survey script* for the calls they make to qualify leads. People answer a survey more often than they talk to a salesperson. But this practice is deceptive. As a card-carrying member of the American

Marketing Association, I happen to recall that its code of ethics prohibits selling or fundraising under the guise of conducting research. Why? I can give you a couple reasons:

- ✔ The practice abuses the respondent's trust. (And deception in sales can run afoul of *fraud laws* — so it may be illegal as well as unethical.)

- ✔ Deceptive prospecting irritates respondents, and if it's widely done, people stop participating in legitimate market research. That consequence, which is beginning to happen, poses a big problem for marketers.

You can also use a web page or professional blog to reach out for prospects and generate visits and inquiries that you can turn into sales leads. See Chapter 10 for more ideas on how to use the web to supply your salespeople with better leads. Another idea is to ask your current customers to supply you with referrals and to thank them or even reward them with gifts or discounts for the referral. Current customers can often find you good-quality leads through their personal networks.

Developing great sales presentations and consultations

At the sales presentation, the salesperson must convince the prospect to become a customer, which can be a challenge. Only a truly great sales presentation can persuade prospects to become customers at a high rate of success.

What makes a sales presentation great? Success. Any presentation that works, that gets customers to say "yes" quickly and often, is an exceptional presentation. Be prepared to think creatively and experiment until you come up with a presentation that works well for you and your customers.

Giving emotionally intelligent sales presentations

A sales presentation that's smart and thoughtful should cover both basic fact needs and basic feelings needs. Your presentation needs to inform while also making the prospect comfortable. Avoid sounding desperate for the sale, because doing so makes prospects uneasy. A calmly optimistic bearing is best. Present yourself well, avoid appearing messy or smelling strongly (whether of sweat or perfume), and behave in a friendly but respectful manner at all times. Avoid too much touching; give the prospect plenty of personal space. Your presence should be calming and reassuring, not stressful or anxiety producing.

Acting like a consultant rather than a salesperson

If the prospect is uncertain about what she needs, the right approach to the sales presentation is to be consultative. Start by asking thoughtful questions to figure out what the customer needs and then propose a somewhat customized solution, not just a generic purchase. Avoid rapid-fire questions. A consultative approach is good in cases where you sell complex services or products with many technical options and details.

Consultative selling may not be right for you if you can't see any obvious ways to sell customized services along with your product. If you just want to deliver an excellent product and let the customer worry about what to do with it, then the last thing you want your salespeople to do is pretend they're consultants.

Whether you use a simple, scripted approach or a sophisticated, consultative approach depends on what you sell and what the customer wants. Be sure to tailor your sales style to accommodate your customers' needs, purchase preferences, and habits.

Hitting your main points

I generally advise against a fully scripted sales presentation. Using a script makes you look like an amateur who has had to memorize her lines because she can't be trusted to speak for herself. However, I strongly recommend that you make a bullet list of three to five main selling points and memorize this list so you can be sure to cover your main points during your sales call. Your list of main points should include the main features and benefits of the product. If you anticipate that the prospect will want to compare your offering to the competition, then include two to three reasons why yours is superior.

Showing, not telling

Showing is usually better than telling. Bring the product with you if at all possible. If you can't, show a demo video. Also, prepare and bring professional printed sales materials, such as a catalog, spec sheet, brochure, or e-brochure (see Chapters 6 and 7). Or consider a short (15 slides or less) PowerPoint slide presentation that you can animate on your laptop or on a digital projector. Sometimes the prospect wants a structured, formal presentation, especially when you're making a business-to-business sales call. Be prepared. Have your slides at the ready and make sure you've rehearsed your presentation in advance.

Video is increasingly cheap and easy to make, thanks to the digital editing software available for free on many computers (especially Macs), so consider creating one or a series of very short, highly informative video demos that can be shown on calls and also posted on YouTube and your website for a virtual sales presentation.

Even if you have a good slide show or video, don't force unwilling or obviously bored prospects to sit through your formal presentation. Instead, engage them in conversation by asking questions that probe for insights into their motives and concerns. Then take a consultative sales approach.

Processing orders accurately and promptly

Take care of the order you receive before going on to your next sales call. If your customer says yes, make sure you collect all the information needed to get the order processed. Then follow up to see that everything is delivered promptly and properly. You'd be amazed at how often a new customer places an order and then cancels it in disgust because of some problem that arises.

Responding to problems

The most faithful customers are the ones who've had a problem that you managed to solve in a fair and generous manner, which means you have to anticipate problems. Inevitably something will go wrong that will upset, disappoint, or even anger your customer. That's why the sales process has to include a *service recovery* step. Make sure the customer knows to call her salesperson when a problem occurs. If you think you can use even more help in the customer service arena, read the later section "Retaining Customers through Great Service."

How well does the salesperson respond to a problem? If she finds herself overscheduled with sales calls, she can't take the time to solve problems. Therefore, budget, say, 1 in 20 sales calls as *service recovery time* to prepare for this contingency. (Over time, you should be able to drive down the need for recoveries; perhaps you need to budget only 1 in 50 calls next year if you make a point of trying to eliminate the most common root causes of these problems.) And keep in mind that the salesperson needs some resources, in addition to time, to solve customer problems and rebuild relationships. Give her some spending authority so she can turn the customer's anger into satisfaction (or, if you're a small business, budget some funds for yourself to use on service recovery).

Organizing Your Sales Force

Who does what, when, and where? Such organizational questions plague many sales or marketing managers, and those questions can make a big difference to sales force productivity. Should your salespeople work out of local, regional, or national offices? Should you base them in offices where staff members provide daily support and their boss can supervise their activities closely? Or should you set them free to operate on the road, maximizing the number of calls they can make and communicating with the company through high-tech laptop computers rather than through regional offices? Or — if you have a small business — should you do all the selling, or does bringing in a salesperson on commission make sense? These decisions depend on your situation, but I can help you decide by giving you an idea of the several options available and by sharing some of the conventional wisdom that helps you assess your particular situation.

Determining how many salespeople you need

If you have an existing sales force, you can examine the performance of each territory to decide whether more salespeople can help or whether you can do with less. Are some territories rich in prospects that salespeople just don't get to? Then consider splitting those territories. Also consider splitting — or adding a second person to create — a sales team if you're experiencing high customer turnover in a territory. Turnover probably indicates a lack of service and follow-up visits. Alternatively, if you see some territories that have little sales potential, you may be able to merge those territories with other territories. (And if you own a small business, you should consider adding commissioned salespeople if you can't cover all prospects adequately because of time or travel constraints.)

You can also use another, more systematic approach — which you really need when you have to design a sales force from scratch. Study your market to decide how many sales calls you want to make over a year-long period. The process isn't very complicated, and I explain it in detail in the sidebar "How many salespeople does it take to sell a light bulb?"

Hiring your own or using reps

You have to decide whether to hire salespeople yourself or subcontract. Most industries have good sales companies that take on the job of hiring and managing salespeople for you. Called *sales representatives* (or just *reps*), they usually work for a straight commission of between 10 and 20 percent, depending on the industry and how much room you have in your pricing structure for their commission. Also, in areas where you need more work done — customer support through consultative selling and customized service — reps earn, and deserve, a higher commission.

If you have a small company or a short product line, I recommend using sales reps. They're the best option whenever you have *scale problems* that make justifying the cost of hiring your own dedicated salespeople somewhat difficult. Scale problems arise when you have a too-short product line, which means that salespeople don't have very much to sell to customers. Each sales call produces small orders that don't cover the cost of the call. Reps usually handle many companies' product lines so that they have more products to show prospects when they call.

How many salespeople does it take to sell a light bulb?

Follow these steps to determine the number of salespeople you need:

1. **Count how many potential customers you have in your entire market.**

2. **Decide what proportion or how many of those customers you want to call on.**

3. **Decide how many calls you want to make over the next year for each customer, on average (for example, 2 per month or 24 per year).**

4. **Multiply the answer to Step 2 by the answer to Step 3.**

   Doing so gives you the total sales calls you need for the entire year.

5. **Decide how many calls one person can reasonably make in a day.**

   The answer depends on the nature of the call and the travel time between customers.

6. **Multiply the daily figure from Step 5 by the number of working days in your company's calendar.**

7. **Divide the total number of calls needed per year (from Step 4) by the number of calls one salesperson can make per year (from Step 6).**

   Doing so gives you the number of salespeople needed to make all of those calls.

For example, 10,000 sales calls needed next year, divided by 1,000 calls per salesperson per year, means you need a sales force of ten people to execute your plan. If you have only five on staff, you'd better hire five more or bring on some sales reps to help your staff. If you can't, scale back your sales goals by half. You won't ever sell that light bulb to 10,000 customers with only five salespeople.

If you have a long enough product line to justify hiring and managing your own dedicated salespeople, by all means do. You have much more control and better feedback from the market this way, and a dedicated sales force generally outsells a sales rep by between two and ten times as much. Why? The dedicated salesperson is focused and dependent on your products. Often, the rep doesn't care what she sells, as long as the client buys something. Consequently, reps tend to make the easy sales, which may not be yours. The following sections help you figure out how to locate quality sales reps and keep them under your control.

Finding good sales reps

How do you find sales reps? Word-of-mouth referrals or meeting at a trade show or industry conference are great ways to find out who's reputable, presents well, and available. Or, even simpler, ask the buyers of products such as the one you sell for names of reps who currently call on them.

A growing number of hub websites offer access to sales reps and manufacturer's reps as well as freelance salespeople who work under short-term contracts. These sites provide leads, not final answers, so make sure you do your screening carefully, and if you do hire someone, do it on a trial basis (seeing is believing!). Here are some of the options on the web today:

- Goodcall (www.goodcall.io), which claims to have "everything you need to run an outsourced sales team"
- Time to Hire (www.timetohire.com), which helps you locate sales reps
- Guru (www.guru.com), which cues up sales reps' ads or posts your project description for them to respond to
- RepHunter (www.rephunter.net), which specializes in manufacturers reps and independent reps
- SalesAgentHUB (www.salesagenthub.com), where you can register as a company in need of reps
- GreatRep (www.greatrep.com), where you can search the rep database, view postings of Lines Wanted, or post under Reps Wanted

Managing your reps — with an iron glove!

After you have reps lined up for each territory, your work has only just begun. You must — absolutely must — monitor their sales efforts on a regular basis. Which rep firms sell the best (and worst)? Usually, 10 or 15 percent of the reps make almost all of your sales. If you notice such a pattern developing, you can quickly put the others on notice. And if they don't heat up in a hurry, you can replace them. Also make sure your reps know and stick to your brand story — the ways you want your brand presented and talked about. Give them some training and a cheat sheet to keep them on the same brand page as you.

Compensating Your Sales Force

You face one of the toughest and most important management decisions in marketing when you have to figure out how to compensate salespeople. Compensation has a significant impact on the sales staff's motivation and performance, and salespeople's performance has a big effect on sales. The issue becomes difficult because compensation's effect on motivation isn't always obvious.

If you want to recruit special salespeople, you may need to offer them a special compensation plan. You want to do something sufficiently different from the norm in your industry to make your job openings really stand out. For example, if you want to make sure your salespeople take a highly consultative, service-oriented approach, with long-term support and relationship building, make your compensation salary-based. If you give them sales incentives, consider bonuses linked to long-term customer retention or to building sales with existing customers. Your compensation plan thereby stands out from your competitors and sends a clear signal about the kind of sales behavior you expect. Similarly, if you want the hottest, most self-motivated salespeople, offer more commission than the competition.

The details of what you must offer in base salary and in commissions vary so much from industry to industry and region to region that you need to research comparable positions to establish a base before you design your compensation plan. Search for sales openings in similar businesses to your own, as if you were looking for a job yourself. Most job listings include a detailed description of the compensation plan. Build a table of at least a half dozen comparable job postings, including columns for base pay, commission rates and caps, and perks (such as a company car or health benefits). Then craft your own position's compensation so as to make it competitive enough to attract good candidates.

Whatever you pay them, salespeople and reps do best when they have high *task clarity,* defined as clear links from their sales efforts to positive results. Make sure they have the products, leads, knowledge, and support (sales follow-up) to be successful. You'll find that success is the greatest motivator, and your sales force enjoys the process of selling for you!

Retaining Customers through Great Service

Sales and service go hand in hand. When your business relies on personal selling — like in many business-to-business markets and a variety of consumer markets as well — you can bet that you also need great customer service. Why? Although personal selling produces new customers, personal service keeps them. If you don't know how to keep new customers, you shouldn't waste your time seeking them — you'll just lose 'em anyway. The following sections show you simple methods for keeping customers happy.

Measuring the quality of customer service

Do you know your *customer turnover rate* (the percent of customers who leave each year; also called a *churn rate*)? If your turnover goes over 5 percent in most industries, you probably have a customer service problem, and you need to build retention to lower that percentage. Find out by comparing customer lists from two consecutive years — or by asking your salespeople (if you have any) to gather the data if you can't do so easily from your central customer database or billing records.

Sometimes companies define a lost customer as one whose business has fallen by more than half, which gives you a more conservative measure than one based only on customers who've stopped ordering entirely. To figure your rate of customer turnover, follow these steps:

1. **Compare last year's and this year's customer lists to find out how many customers you lost during the year.**

   Ignore new customers for this calculation.

2. **Count the total number of customers on the list from the previous year.**

   That gives you your *base,* or where you started.

3. **Divide the number of lost customers (from Step 1) by the total number of customers (from Step 2) to get your turnover rate.**

For example, if you started the year with 1,500 customers and lost 250, your turnover rate is 250 ÷ 1,500, or nearly 17 percent. If you find yourself in that situation, you fail my 5 percent test and need to focus on improving your customer service.

Profiting from good manners

Good manners and aggressive sales don't usually go hand in hand, but they should. Don't assume you have to be pushy and overly assertive to maximize sales. In fact, the opposite is true: Polite sales and service personnel do far better in most cases. Emphasize being polite to prospects and customers, and keep your ear tuned to how your employees and salespeople are treating your customers. Set a good example and hold people accountable for their manners.

Here are a few tips for making a positive, polite impression with customers:

- ✔ **Avoid saying no.** Try to find a way to say yes, even if it has to be a qualified yes. When you say no to customers, you reduce their enthusiasm for doing business with you. Saying "yes, and . . ." sets you out on a more positive verbal path than "no" or even "yes, but. . . ."

- ✔ **Listen more than you talk.** Be attentive and take an interest in what the customer has to say.

- ✔ **Get to know your customers bit by bit.** Don't ask pushy, personal questions, but do ask appropriate questions and make note of the answers so you remember next time you talk to them.

- ✔ **If you aren't available, prep someone else to handle calls and e-mails from your customers.** Make sure they're always in good hands.

✔ **Warn impolite and rude employees three times (documenting the warnings in their files), and if they haven't shaped up by then, fire them.** The sooner you get rid of impolite employees, the fewer customers you'll lose.

✔ **Thank customers for their business.** A personal thank you, a note, or a small but tasteful gift lets customers know you appreciate them placing their business, and their trust, in you.

Offering virtual service and a helpful knowledge base

Perhaps you've already used service-knowledge bases in dealing with questions about your credit card or mortgage. You'll also find them on the front lines of service for electronics and communications giants, whose customer base number is in the millions. Some companies are already handling more than half of customer service inquiries through helpful FAQs and searchable databases of questions and answers. The best of these systems are actually quite sophisticated, using self-tracking mechanisms such as the following:

✔ **Tracking key search terms and adding or elevating relevant content:** You can use the (evolving) patterns of customer searches to make the knowledge base behind your customer service portal ever more intelligent so that your percentage of successful answers goes up and up.

✔ **Correlating top search inquiries to ratings of satisfaction:** By gathering (automated online) satisfaction-with-experience ratings, you can identify the wins and the problem areas and know what needs rewriting in your service portal.

✔ **Making it fairly easy to bail by asking for a chat room or telephone contact with a real person:** Sometimes customers don't get what they need from the service web page experience. It's okay to ask them to work a little to find their answers, but somewhere short of angry dissatisfaction, you should allow them to give up and ask for a real service representative. Angry customers turned away by annoying web pages aren't likely to be good for business.

If you have in-house capacity to build sophisticated interactive websites driven by knowledge bases that evolve with customer inquiries as well as updating to reflect new products and services or special promotions, then go for it! These are not common capabilities, even in fairly large organizations, so I presume you'll be shopping for help.

Many consultants and designers create web pages, but most of them don't do the fancy interactive service sites I'm talking about. Screen for current client lists that include the building and maintenance of service portals that seem to really work. The web is getting so specialized that the only certain guarantee a vendor can give you is comparable work. Even the president of the United

States has trouble hiring the right web programmers to build complex, service-oriented websites (witness the debacle of the Affordable Care Act enrollment rollout in 2013!), so take this task seriously and make sure you have proposals from vendors who've already proven they can do exactly what you need.

Practicing service recovery

Service recovery starts with recognizing when service isn't going well. What makes your customer unhappy? Which customers are stressed or frustrated? Talking and thinking about these questions can lead to a list of the five top warning signs of an unhappy customer. I'm not going to write your list for you because every company has a different one. Whatever your top warning signs, educate your employees to recognize them and to leap into action whenever they see one of them.

Service recovery requires empathy and polite sensitivity. You should make the starting point just paying polite attention to someone. In fact, sometimes that can be enough to turn the customer around. To win the customer back by solving her problem, you have to start with her unhappy feelings. Use your emotional intelligence to empathize with her. Let her vent or complain and don't argue with her (the unhappy customer is always right). After she has calmed down a bit and is ready to listen to you and look to you for help, you can ask factual questions and give her information in return.

Every service recovery starts with working on the (hurt) feelings of the disgruntled customer, not on the facts. That important insight can save a lot of customer relationships and help you build a reputation as a great company to buy from.

Using content to court customers

Throughout this book, I encourage you to keep your marketing message clear and simple, with plenty of calls to action. However, occasionally, I also encourage you to provide valuable information to your customers. So which is it: sell, sell, sell or inform, inform, inform? As it turns out, both approaches have merit.

Content marketing is the generous provision of really useful and interesting content for your prospective and current customers. On a website, it may involve the offering of a monthly e-zine with in-depth how-to articles. John Deere's magazine, *The Furrow,* delivered by mail for many years, is now posted as an electronic magazine (you can scroll through the pages by going to www.deere.com and typing "The Furrow" in the search box). If customers come to rely on your content, they'll come to rely on you, making it natural for them to step forward and make a purchase when the need arises. So information can actually make the sale for you, without the need for a salesperson or a hard sell of any kind! Consulting firms sometimes release in-depth reports or white papers to the media to take advantage of this phenomenon.

Part VI
The Part of Tens

 Check out www.dummies.com/extras/marketing for helpful tips to get you thinking like a guerilla marketer as well as free advice on surviving sales downturns.

In this part . . .

- ✔ Keep your marketing program out of the red by avoiding the most common errors and mistakes.

- ✔ Boost your sales by using web-based techniques that minimize cost and offer quick feedback and budgetary flexibility.

Chapter 18

Ten Common Marketing Mistakes (And How to Avoid Them)

In This Chapter

▶ Understanding that marketing to everyone and relying on discounts hurts profits

▶ Recognizing the importance of treating all customers (even angry ones) with respect

*P*erhaps nothing's worse than reinventing the wheel — especially if you invent a square one. This chapter presents ten all-too-common marketing mistakes so you know how to avoid them and keep your sales and marketing efforts on track.

Buying into Too-Good-to-Be-True Website Claims

Every day marketers are barraged with tempting offers for too-good-to-be-real web results. Hundreds of web marketing agencies or businesses claim to be able to boost web page traffic dramatically or to create instant popularity on social media sites. Buyer beware! Most of these claims are ludicrous. And often they verge toward the deceptive and unethical, if not being outright cases of fraud.

Nobody can script a few lines of code to make your website pop up to the top of search engine listings, ahead of sites with more visitors or more relevant content. Real web visibility has to be earned by building up a website's content and commerce bit by bit via attractive offers (calls to action) and/ or useful or interesting content (content marketing), until it naturally belongs near the top of the search engine listings. Then keep it there with regular promos or updates to content (with tweeted pointers).

Scamming, Social Media Style

Social media followers shouldn't be bought. Notice I said *shouldn't*. I wish I could say *can't*, but in truth, many opportunists are out there, selling followers for your blog or tweets. They'll even quote you a price per hundred Facebook followers. It's fiction, of course. Either they have a program that's trying to trick the social media site by clicking automatically, or, where that fails, they've hired a building full of people in some low-labor-cost country to sit and click on as followers using shallow, just-created identities. The idea is to try to scam the system by creating the impression that you're a lot more popular than you really are. If that seems appealing to you, think for a moment about how much product you'll sell to the sweat shop workers who are lining up to be your sham followers. A million false followers on Facebook won't translate into near as many sales as a thousand genuine ones.

Always make your social media interactions genuine. Keep your customers satisfied, and they'll likely help you drum up social media buzz that's earned rather than purchased.

Selling to the Wrong People

Most people are the wrong people — meaning they probably don't want to buy your product, or even if they do, the timing is wrong. Case in point: My office keeps getting free subscriptions to *CFO Magazine,* even though we don't have a chief financial officer. After a decade of wasted magazines, they seem no closer to realizing I'm not in the target market. When you market on the web, you can easily sort by many variables, including search patterns, purchase patterns, and even interests and tastes, and then eliminate the obvious mismatches. Also, you can and should track who does *not* respond to repeated offers. By pulling out mismatches, you get rid of lost-cause prospects and avoid wasting your money on them. And, as a happy side effect, you also reduce the distracting waste of poorly aimed promotions, which is becoming a major social problem.

Competing on Price

Many marketers devote half or more of their budgets to price-oriented promotions, perhaps because a manager says something like, "Sales seem to be off this month. Why don't we cut prices and see whether that helps?" Sure, discounts and price cuts have their role, especially if you need to stimulate first-time trial, but you should never use cheap pricing unless you're pretty darn certain that the market currently overprices your product and you can afford to sell it for less.

Most of the time, a price-oriented promotion produces quick increases in sales, but the increases are unsustainable, just the result of bargain shoppers. Repeated price promotions can erode brand value and create fickle customers who abandon you for the competitors' promotions.

Sometimes customers are highly price sensitive, competitors undercut you, and you have no choice but to slash your prices, too. But in general, you don't want to compete on price. Making a profit (and staying in business) is far easier when you compete on the elements that make you different and better from the competition. Be the friendliest local supplier, the best organic option, the best performing, the best tasting, the most durable, the most advanced . . . anything but the cheapest!

Forgetting to Edit

If your letter, e-mail, website, print ad, sign, or billboard has a typo in it, people remember that goof and forget the rest. I often see business cards and signs outside of businesses or on vehicles that have obvious typos. Talk about making a bad first impression! Edit carefully and get someone else to look over your shoulder to make sure nothing slips by. Your brand's reputation will thank you.

Consider hiring an expert to clean up all your communications, including everything you post on the web. Shorter, clearer, sharper means more effective and, often, less embarrassing.

Not Emphasizing the Brand

Quick, think of a TV ad that greatly amused you. Now, what brand was it for? Having trouble remembering? Me too. Most people do, likely because about half of the really amusing and memorable TV ads out there fail to brand the brand name into consumers' minds. The end result is that viewers get distracted by the amusing story or imagery and don't recall what the ad was for.

A good general rule is to hit the brand name both visually and in type about twice as often as you think you need to. Go back and add more references to the brand in your marketing communications (TV ad, catalog, website, mailing — you name it). Make the logo larger. Repeat the brand name more often. Make a silly joke involving the brand name or put it in a jingle. Whatever else your ad accomplishes, make sure it drills the brand name into everyone's head!

Okay, I admit, some of the ubiquitous Geico television ads, especially those with the gecko, are memorably amusing and actually do highlight the Geico brand effectively. They're the exception to my humor-doesn't-sell rule. How do they do it? First, the gecko works as a consultant for Geico, helping design ads to sell insurance, so the humor is tied directly to the product. Second, the brand name stars, appearing in the sound track and visually multiple times in each commercial. Even the reptilian star was chosen for his humorous affinity with the brand: Geico, gecko, get it? But unless you can weave your jokes in and out of the core identity of the brand as deftly as the best of the Geico commercials do, just offer a straight ad that focuses on the core message and burns the sound and sight of the brand name into the audience as quickly and efficiently as possible.

Here's a demonstration of how effective playing it straight can be. Fill in the blank in this sentence: "Like a good neighbor, _____ is there." Yes, State Farm's old jingle has become part of the culture and so memorable that it defines the brand. When State Farm's marketers decided to try their hand at humor, they went back to this jingle with the humorous idea that if you sing it, your State Farm agent (or whatever else you want) will suddenly appear.

Offering What You Can't Deliver

Telling customers you'll give them something that you really can't is bad business and bad publicity. Perhaps you recall what happened in 2013 when the U.S. government rolled out the flagship website for the new healthcare insurance marketplace (www.healthcare.gov). That's right. It didn't work. Oops. Political pundits and the media had a field day talking about how stupid the rollout was, and President Obama's popularity reached record lows as a consequence.

You may or may not have regulatory limits on what you can do and sell, but you certainly have many practical limits. Don't advertise a new service or product until you're *sure* that it works, you can deliver it promptly, and you can scale up with demand. If you're in a service business, avoid getting sucked into the temptation of bidding on work that you don't have enough expertise to do well. Wandering from your core always hurts the bottom line in the long run, whereas success usually comes from having a sharp focus on that core.

Treating Customers Impersonally

Every customer is a person who likes to be treated as such. Yet sometimes businesses send out generic bills or mailings that have misspellings of customers' names, and occasionally whoever answers the phone doesn't know that the caller is an old customer. You can make these casual mistakes often without even noticing.

Put yourself in the customer's shoes and take a hard look at all of your customer interactions. Are they as personal as they should be? If not, invest in better list-checking, a central database of customers, training in how to pronounce customer names, and whatever else it takes to allow your business to treat all customers like important individuals. For example, I go into The Loose Goose, a local sandwich shop, to buy lunch every week or two. The kid at the register may or may not remember me, so I always offer my name with my to-go order. However, the owners, a couple who both work in the business, always make a point of greeting me warmly by name if they see me waiting for my order. Their personal touch makes a difference. Yours can, too — whether you see customers in person, talk to them by phone, or interact with them on social media (where canned responses stick out like sore thumbs).

Blaming the Customer

It's easy to think that an irate customer must be crazy, but what if his reaction is actually quite reasonable given the treatment he received? A while back, my company received a past-due notice on a bill from a cleaning and maintenance company we'd used many months ago. My bookkeeper was puzzled because she thought she remembered paying the bill when it first came in. After reviewing her records, she called the company and provided the check number, date, and amount of our payment and asked the contractor to correct its records. The manager on the other end of the phone then chewed her out for "sending a misleading check" and "not making it completely clear which account it applied to" (even though she'd returned the invoice with the check). So instead of apologizing for the confusion, this contractor blamed us for the error. He may have felt better after venting on the phone, but he lost our business forever. Don't make the same mistake with your customers!

Avoiding Upset Customers

Avoiding someone who's irritated with you is a natural reaction — but don't give in to it. Customers can get unpleasant or abusive if they feel they've been treated poorly, even if you don't think they have been. Treat an unhappy customer as your top marketing priority, and don't stop working on him until he's happy again. If you win him back, he's especially loyal and brings you new business. If you let him walk away mad, he becomes an antimarketer, actively trying to drive others away from your business.

Chapter 19

Ten Tips for Boosting Web Sales

Good web marketing is still quite rare, despite the flood of sales over the web. My hunch is that the costs are low enough to allow marketers to get away with C or B work. But why stop there? Wasting time and money by blasting ads at poorly defined audiences is plumb stupid and annoying to those who don't care about the product. In fact, it's not even marketing, if you define marketing as helping to bring about a sale. In this chapter, I help you target web messages effectively with ten tactics for boosting orders on your web store.

Take Well-Lit Product Photos

Seeing is believing, right? So make sure your website offers good views of what you have to sell. Your photos should clearly show your products — and make sure your products are well lit in your photos. Bright, diffused light is the key to clear, high-resolution photos (or videos) that don't have a grainy look, whitewashed spots, or dark areas. To capture the best lighting possible, use studio-quality lighting sources (which are brighter than ordinary lighting) and diffuse the light with a photo screen or white umbrella.

If you can't afford professional photography, you can simulate studio lighting by hanging a thin piece of white cotton a few feet in front of two powerful halogen work lights positioned at a 45-degree angle to the product.

Choose the Right Backdrop

An effective backdrop for your product shot is second only to quality lighting. The goal is to make your product stand out, so stick to neutral or clean backdrops that allow the product to pop. To create a neutral backdrop, hang a white or off-white cotton or linen cloth (without any wrinkles!) behind the product. Taupe may work better than white for subtle colors or for products displayed on a human model. Black can be effective for contrast, especially when the product is very light in color (such as a white dress or a string of pearls). Whatever you do, avoid bright red or bold textures, which typically draw the eye's focus away from the product.

Also give some thought to the color of your web page because it will be the backdrop for your product photos. A modest contrast that doesn't call too much attention is best. For example, a pale blue background for your web page sets off a white background in a product photo.

Include Info for Comparative Shoppers

Most web shops don't offer enough information about their products. Any details you can provide about your product (think technical info, measurements, performance specifications, compatibility guide, and so on) are helpful to shoppers and can give them the confidence to buy.

Consider including a table to summarize the main features or benefits of your product for at-a-glance viewing. And if you can honestly show that your product beats the competition, include columns for the competition, too. If your web store gets big enough to make scanning all the offerings at once a chore, add a feature to your site that makes shopping recommendations based on customers' search and purchase histories. Personalized recommendations often increase the size and frequency of web orders because they present products shoppers may find appealing.

Comparative shoppers may want to check both your website and a shopping engine service, which cues up the best prices on products from multiple sources. To make sure you're visible and competitive on shopping engines like Google Shopping (www.google.com/shopping), PriceGrabber (www.pricegrabber.com), and Become (www.become.com), either contact each site directly and follow its instructions or work with a web ad agency skilled in this area. Services such as Channel Intelligence claim to be able to keep your products visible and updated in shopping engines, too.

Add Streaming Video

Streaming video can boost sales by giving shoppers even more information and confidence about your product. Show the product in use, walk viewers through a 20-second review of the product's greatest features, and include short clips of happy customers giving honest testimonials. But don't force everyone to watch the video; some shoppers may value speed and simplicity of purchase and be chased away by a video that stands between them and the order form.

Provide Prompt E-Mail Support

Buying is a process, and e-mails can keep the buyer company and help her stay oriented throughout that process. Make sure you integrate plenty of informative, helpful, and prompt e-mail contact into your customers' web shopping experiences. Every time someone fills in a form, requests information, participates in a promotion, or makes even the smallest purchase, she should immediately receive a confirmation e-mail. If you do business on a small scale, you can write these e-mails yourself, but usually the frequency is too great, so an *auto-responder* (a software application that sends prescripted responses) is necessary.

Supply a "Contact Me Now" Option

Some people don't feel confident enough about the product, or about the seller, to make an online purchase. For shoppers who need a more personal touch, include a Contact Me Now button that produces a simple contact form for the customer to enter her name, address, phone number, and e-mail address and type up a short note with her question or request and how she prefers to be contacted. By offering this feature, you won't lose people who are unsure of what to purchase on your website or who don't think they see exactly what they need. Or if you have retail stores that carry your products (or offices that deliver your services), provide a Store Locator function.

Design a Clean, Uncluttered Site

Cramming too much into your opening page can turn off potential customers. Make your web store's home page simple enough to take in at a glance. Take your most important content and cue it up front and center, putting other content behind tabs or clickable buttons in a side column.

Most product lines follow the 80/20 rule, where roughly 80 percent of sales come from 20 percent of the products or services, so showcase the top sellers on the home page and let shoppers navigate deeper for the less-frequently bought items.

Offer Straightforward Site Navigation

Don't let your website navigation get too complicated; a prospective customer should always be able to move around your web store or site easily. Avoid dead ends and long, winding pathways. Keep the links logical and don't give the site too many layers. Also, make sure the shopping cart icon is visible on every page, because purchasing something should be quick and easy every time. Test your web store over and over to identify any quirks, confusions, and complexities that need to be removed.

 I prefer a shopping cart in a pop-up window so that shopping in the store can continue uninterrupted. Update the cart as customers add to it. If your shopping cart program doesn't do this or feels awkward and outdated, look for another.

Build an Appealing, Trustworthy Brand

 Branding is just as important on the web as it is in the real world, so make sure your logo and name are presented in a clean, professional, and appealing manner on the top of each and every page of your site. Also, use colors and typestyles that complement your logo and remind shoppers in a subtle way that they're still under your brand umbrella.

Put Your Web Address Everywhere

Use your other marketing communications to promote your website. Every e-mail that your firm sends should have an attractive, clickable logo, linking to your site as well as your address and phone number(s) for follow-up. Add QR codes on your signage and packaging (see Chapter 8). A special offer with a landing on your home page with the details of the offer is a great way to draw people to your web shopping environment. A Facebook page, a WordPress blog, or other social media adventures can help build an image and following for an appealing web brand and should always have links to your site. Also put your web address on everything you print, including business cards, envelopes, brochures, bills, packaging, and letters. Make it easy for people to find you!

Index

About the Author

Alex Hiam helps organizations (including nonprofits and government agencies) think through their branding and marketing strategies and their leadership development programs. He has served on the boards of directors of a variety of organizations and also as an instructor in the Isenberg School of Management at UMass Amherst.

Alex earned his BA from Harvard and his MBA in marketing and strategic planning from the Haas School at U.C. Berkeley. He has led creative retreats for top consumer and industrial firms to facilitate innovative thinking about strategic plans, branding, naming, and product ideas. He also writes novels and believes that all good writing (including advertising) is, at heart, good storytelling.

Alex is the coauthor of the bestseller *The Portable MBA in Marketing* (Wiley) as well as numerous other books and training programs. His most recent book is *Business Innovation For Dummies*.

Publisher's Acknowledgments

Acquisitions Editor: Stacy Kennedy

Project Editor: Jennifer Tebbe

Copy Editor: Jennette ElNaggar

Technical Editor: Scott Werner

Project Coordinator: Rebekah Brownson

Cover Image: ©iStockphoto.com/c_vincent

Apple & Mac

iPad For Dummies,
6th Edition
978-1-118-72306-7

iPhone For Dummies,
7th Edition
978-1-118-69083-3

Macs All-in-One
For Dummies, 4th Edition
978-1-118-82210-4

OS X Mavericks
For Dummies
978-1-118-69188-5

Blogging & Social Media

Facebook For Dummies,
5th Edition
978-1-118-63312-0

Social Media Engagement
For Dummies
978-1-118-53019-1

WordPress For Dummies,
6th Edition
978-1-118-79161-5

Business

Stock Investing
For Dummies, 4th Edition
978-1-118-37678-2

Investing For Dummies,
6th Edition
978-0-470-90545-6

Personal Finance
For Dummies, 7th Edition
978-1-118-11785-9

QuickBooks 2014
For Dummies
978-1-118-72005-9

Small Business Marketing
Kit For Dummies,
3rd Edition
978-1-118-31183-7

Careers

Job Interviews
For Dummies, 4th Edition
978-1-118-11290-8

Job Searching with Social
Media For Dummies,
2nd Edition
978-1-118-67856-5

Personal Branding
For Dummies
978-1-118-11792-7

Resumes For Dummies,
6th Edition
978-0-470-87361-8

Starting an Etsy Business
For Dummies, 2nd Edition
978-1-118-59024-9

Diet & Nutrition

Belly Fat Diet For Dummies
978-1-118-34585-6

Mediterranean Diet
For Dummies
978-1-118-71525-3

Nutrition For Dummies,
5th Edition
978-0-470-93231-5

Digital Photography

Digital SLR Photography
All-in-One For Dummies,
2nd Edition
978-1-118-59082-9

Digital SLR Video &
Filmmaking For Dummies
978-1-118-36598-4

Photoshop Elements 12
For Dummies
978-1-118-72714-0

Gardening

Herb Gardening
For Dummies, 2nd Edition
978-0-470-61778-6

Gardening with Free-Range
Chickens For Dummies
978-1-118-54754-0

Health

Boosting Your Immunity
For Dummies
978-1-118-40200-9

Diabetes For Dummies,
4th Edition
978-1-118-29447-5

Living Paleo For Dummies
978-1-118-29405-5

Big Data

Big Data For Dummies
978-1-118-50422-2

Data Visualization
For Dummies
978-1-118-50289-1

Hadoop For Dummies
978-1-118-60755-8

Language &
Foreign Language

500 Spanish Verbs
For Dummies
978-1-118-02382-2

English Grammar
For Dummies, 2nd Edition
978-0-470-54664-2

French All-in-One
For Dummies
978-1-118-22815-9

German Essentials
For Dummies
978-1-118-18422-6

Italian For Dummies,
2nd Edition
978-1-118-00465-4

Available in print and e-book formats.

Available wherever books are sold. **For more information or to order direct visit www.dummies.com**

Math & Science

Algebra I For Dummies,
2nd Edition
978-0-470-55964-2

Anatomy and Physiology
For Dummies, 2nd Edition
978-0-470-92326-9

Astronomy For Dummies,
3rd Edition
978-1-118-37697-3

Biology For Dummies,
2nd Edition
978-0-470-59875-7

Chemistry For Dummies,
2nd Edition
978-1-118-00730-3

1001 Algebra II Practice
Problems For Dummies
978-1-118-44662-1

Microsoft Office

Excel 2013 For Dummies
978-1-118-51012-4

Office 2013 All-in-One
For Dummies
978-1-118-51636-2

PowerPoint 2013
For Dummies
978-1-118-50253-2

Word 2013 For Dummies
978-1-118-49123-2

Music

Blues Harmonica
For Dummies
978-1-118-25269-7

Guitar For Dummies,
3rd Edition
978-1-118-11554-1

iPod & iTunes
For Dummies, 10th Edition
978-1-118-50864-0

Programming

Beginning Programming
with C For Dummies
978-1-118-73763-7

Excel VBA Programming
For Dummies, 3rd Edition
978-1-118-49037-2

Java For Dummies,
6th Edition
978-1-118-40780-6

Religion & Inspiration

The Bible For Dummies
978-0-7645-5296-0

Buddhism For Dummies,
2nd Edition
978-1-118-02379-2

Catholicism For Dummies,
2nd Edition
978-1-118-07778-8

Self-Help & Relationships

Beating Sugar Addiction
For Dummies
978-1-118-54645-1

Meditation For Dummies,
3rd Edition
978-1-118-29144-3

Seniors

Laptops For Seniors
For Dummies, 3rd Edition
978-1-118-71105-7

Computers For Seniors
For Dummies, 3rd Edition
978-1-118-11553-4

iPad For Seniors
For Dummies, 6th Edition
978-1-118-72826-0

Social Security
For Dummies
978-1-118-20573-0

Smartphones & Tablets

Android Phones
For Dummies, 2nd Edition
978-1-118-72030-1

Nexus Tablets
For Dummies
978-1-118-77243-0

Samsung Galaxy S 4
For Dummies
978-1-118-64222-1

Samsung Galaxy Tabs
For Dummies
978-1-118-77294-2

Test Prep

ACT For Dummies,
5th Edition
978-1-118-01259-8

ASVAB For Dummies,
3rd Edition
978-0-470-63760-9

GRE For Dummies,
7th Edition
978-0-470-88921-3

Officer Candidate Tests
For Dummies
978-0-470-59876-4

Physician's Assistant Exam
For Dummies
978-1-118-11556-5

Series 7 Exam For Dummies
978-0-470-09932-2

Windows 8

Windows 8.1 All-in-One
For Dummies
978-1-118-82087-2

Windows 8.1 For Dummies
978-1-118-82121-3

Windows 8.1 For Dummies,
Book + DVD Bundle
978-1-118-82107-7

e **Available in print and e-book formats.**

Available wherever books are sold. **For more information or to order direct visit www.dummies.com**